PLATO ON THE LIMITS OF HUMAN LIFE

STUDIES IN CONTINENTAL THOUGHT

John Sallis, *Editor*

Consulting Editors

Robert Bernasconi
Rudolph Bernet
John D. Caputo
David Carr
Edward S. Casey
Hubert Dreyfus
Don Ihde
David Farrell Krell
Lenore Langsdorf
Alphonso Lingis
William L. McBride

J. N. Mohanty
Mary Rawlinson
Tom Rockmore
Calvin O. Schrag
†Reiner Schürmann
Charles E. Scott
Thomas Sheehan
Robert Sokolowski
Bruce W. Wilshire
David Wood

PLATO ON THE LIMITS OF HUMAN LIFE

Sara Brill

Indiana University Press

Bloomington and Indianapolis

This book is a publication of

Indiana University Press
601 North Morton Street
Bloomington, Indiana 47404-3797 USA

iupress.indiana.edu

Telephone orders   800-842-6796
Fax orders   812-855-7931

© 2013 by Sara Brill

All rights reserved

No part of this book may be reproduced or utilized in any form or by any means, electronic or mechanical, including photocopying and recording, or by any information storage and retrieval system, without permission in writing from the publisher. The Association of American University Presses' Resolution on Permissions constitutes the only exception to this prohibition.

∞ The paper used in this publication meets the minimum requirements of the American National Standard for Information Sciences—Permanence of Paper for Printed Library Materials, ANSI Z39.48–1992.

Manufactured in the United States of America

Library of Congress Cataloging-in-Publication Data

Brill, Sara.
   Plato on the limits of human life / Sara Brill.
   pages cm — (Studies in Continental thought)
   Includes bibliographical references and index.
   ISBN 978-0-253-00882-4 (cloth : alk. paper) — ISBN 978-0-253-00887-9 (pbk. : alk. paper) — ISBN 978-0-253-00891-6 (ebook) 1. Plato. 2. Soul. I. Title.
  B398.S7B75 2013
  128'.1092—dc23

2013000401

1 2 3 4 5 18 17 16 15 14 13

To Ryan, who calls it as he sees it

"The soul doesn't die," he said. "She becomes a stranger."

—Andrey Platonov

Contents

Acknowledgments	*ix*
Introduction	*1*
Part I. *Phaedo*	*15*
1 Socratic Prothumia	*19*
2 The Body-like Soul	*37*
3 Psychic Geography	*64*
Part II. *Republic*	*83*
4 City and Soul	*93*
5 Psychic Fragmentation	*106*
6 Philosophy in the City	*123*
7 Politics and Immortality	*138*
Part III. *Laws*	*165*
8 Psychology for Legislators	*171*
9 Psychology for the Legislated	*179*
10 Psychic Excess	*192*
Notes	*209*
Works Cited	*249*
Index	*257*

Acknowledgments

I AM INDEBTED TO my parents, Pam and Bob, and brother Rob, for creating an environment in which eccentricities are warmly accepted, supported, and treated as sources of amusement. I would also like to acknowledge my wonderful colleagues in Fairfield University's Philosophy Department for providing a welcoming and friendly environment in which to work; I am grateful to the university for granting me a pretenure leave in 2006–7, during which time I drafted several chapters of this book. Dee Mortensen at Indiana University Press has been a model of professionalism and expertise and a delight to work with.

I have had the great fortune of studying with several scholars who understand the act of thinking to be an expression of joy—Charles Solomon, Larry Kimmel, Judith Norman, and especially John Sallis—and I am profoundly grateful to those friends and colleagues whose conversation and companionship have shaped these ideas in more ways than I can say. I would like to acknowledge in particular Ryan Drake, whose humor and acumen make all things better, as well as Jocelyn Boryczka, Jill Gordon, Chris Long, Marina McCoy, and Hasana Sharp.

The ideas for this book have been vetted in a number of professional conferences and speaking engagements, and I would like to thank the philosophy faculty and students at Boston College, Colby College, Trinity College, University of Kentucky, and Baylor University, as well as the members of the Ancient Philosophy Society, whose annual conferences create a rich environment for the sharing of ideas and an intellectual home. It has been my great honor to receive the benefit of the time and attention of a number of people who have read and commented upon portions of this manuscript and given invaluable feedback. In addition to those already mentioned, I would like to thank Claudia Baracchi, Emanuela Bianchi, Walter Brogan, Sarah Glenn, Francisco Gonzalez, Benjamin Grazzini, Gary Gurtler, Drew Hyland, Brooke Holmes, Sean Kirkland, Robert Metcalf, Mitchell Miller, Holly Moore, Mark Munn, Michael Naas, Kalliopi Nikolopoulou, Gregory Recco, Eric Sanday, Michael Shaw, Anne-Marie Schulz, Christina Tarnopolsky, Lew Trewlany-Cassity, and Adriel Trott.

Portions of a few of the chapters in this book first appeared as journal articles, and I thank these journals for permission to reprint this scholarship: an early version of chapter 3's arguments about the myth in the *Phaedo* first appeared in "The Geography of Finitude: Myth and Earth in Plato's *Phaedo*," *International Philosophical Quarterly* 49, no. 1 (2009): 5–23; the "Immortality" section of chapter 7 first appeared in "Alive and Sleepless: The Politics of Immortality in *Republic* X," *Polis* 24, no. 2 (2007):

231–61; and portions of chapters 9 and 10 first appeared in "Psychology and Legislation in Plato's *Laws*," *Proceedings of the Boston Area Colloquium in Ancient Philosophy* 26 (2010): 211–42. Research for portions of part 2 (on the *Republic*) was undertaken while enjoying the hospitality of the Albert Ludwigs Universität in Freiburg, Germany, made possible by a Fulbright grant and the sponsorship of Dr. Günter Figal.

Introduction

NEAR THE END of *Alcibiades I*, Socrates proposes an image for attaining the knowledge of soul that he and Alcibiades have agreed is necessary for self-knowledge. Just as the eye, in attempting to see itself, must look at itself in another eye (133a) and at the image of its seeing reflected therein, so too, the soul, if it is to know itself, "must surely look at a soul, and especially at that region of it in which occurs the virtue of a soul—wisdom, and at any other part of a soul which resembles this" (133b).[1] The uncanny image of a self-seeing eye, gazing at its reflection in the pupil opposite it, and thus gazing at the topos in which its virtue, sight, occurs (133b), is meant to set in more concrete form the means by which a soul could come to know itself. If Socrates's comparison is to be maintained, soul must be able to understand itself in an "other," thereby catching glimpses of its wisdom. Whether this "other" of the soul is the soul of another, whose workings are grasped in the actions, passions, and thoughts of which it is the source, or the soul sufficiently alienated from itself in order to encounter itself,[2] it nevertheless stands that the task of self-knowledge requires the soul to become an object for itself. Exactly how it is to do so remains undetermined in this dialogue, but we are presented with a compelling portrait of soul attempting to see itself in its portrayal of Socrates's seduction of Alcibiades, a seduction which, for all its talk of eyes, takes place in words, that medium through which (as Socrates himself points out) their souls have been interacting (130d).[3]

This image of self-knowledge contains two strains of thought whose persistence in the investigations of soul undertaken throughout Plato's dialogues proves useful for anyone wanting to measure the philosophical status of psychology in Plato's work:

first, self-knowledge hinges upon soul's capacity to be estranged from itself; second, soul's access to itself is mediated by logos, whether that be the logos that emerges between souls or the silent logos with oneself that is, elsewhere in the dialogues, indicative of thought (*Theaet.* 190a; *Soph.* 263d–e). Insofar as self-knowledge requires a logos of the psuchē,[4] psuchē-logy is inextricably tied to the philosophic project Socrates bequeathed to his followers and Plato took up and interpreted.

This is certainly borne out by the frequency and prominence of Plato's discussions of soul throughout the dialogues. It is equally the case, however, that Plato's thoughts on the best way to go about conducting this psuchē-logy remain deeply mysterious. The subtlety Plato exhibits in describing psychological phenomena is haunted by the conspicuous absence of any direct or simple account of how such descriptions come about. Indeed, how to gain knowledge of soul, that is, to see soul in another, is as much a question for Plato as what soul is. When, in the *Gorgias,* Socrates observes that only when the soul is stripped of its adornment (that is, separated from the body) and judged by a soul also separated from its body, will the judge be able to contemplate the soul of each person with his own soul (523e), he offers a particularly succinct formulation of a leitmotif of the Platonic corpus. Throughout the dialogues, unmediated access to the soul is denied to human beings; soul is treated as naming the very enigma by which humans are constituted. To inquire into soul is thus to encounter the limits of human knowledge.

This is all to say that any study of Plato's accounts of soul will have to grapple with the strangeness of the two terms by which it is comprised—ψυχή and λόγος—and with the inadequacy of the word "psychology" to describe them, given its contemporary connotations of systematicity and comprehensiveness.[5] The coherence of Plato's investigations of soul is the subject of much debate.[6] Indeed, perhaps the strongest critic of his psychological investigations is Plato himself, who emphasizes throughout the dialogues the difficulty of giving a λόγος of ψυχή and the tentative and qualified nature of his own accounts.[7] While lengthy and serious considerations of what soul is, what it does, and what is done to it appear throughout the dialogues, these investigations rarely occur without some qualification as to their precision.[8] This is particularly true of Plato's most elaborate descriptions of soul.[9]

Thus, the student of Plato's "psychology," like the student of his "metaphysics" or his "ethics," is faced with a topic that held his sustained interest but about which we possess no single authoritative text or unqualified account. This is not to say that it is never asked what soul *is*, only that the exploration of this question is deflected and refracted, extended over multiple texts, and never conclusively formulated. The coherence of Plato's many accounts of soul can be properly investigated only by a careful consideration of the full range of Plato's discussions of soul.

This is a daunting task, as these discussions are variable, wide-ranging, and ruminative. The accounts of soul offered throughout the dialogues describe an entity whose kinship to eternal, changeless beings occurs alongside its capacity to undergo radical and ceaseless transformation, an entity which thus exceeds both the scale of a single human life and the forms of measure that make human happiness possible. To attend to soul, then, is to turn one's attention to an entity whose deathlessness is attested to by both its virtuous and its many vicious conditions.[10] Under the vexed idiom of immortality, Plato explores the manner in which soul's ability to support myriad conditions engenders a number of powerful impediments to human flourishing, impediments whose description and critique require one to locate this flourishing within both the polis and the cosmos.[11]

Psuchē emerges from these accounts as having a double valence, as stretching out toward both Being and body, such that neither a metaphysics of forms nor a materialist account of body is suitable for giving an adequate philosophic account of the varieties of psychic conditions. A robust account of soul, then, requires one to cultivate a double gaze, to examine becoming as well as Being. Plato is particularly persistent in emphasizing soul's capacity to endure its own fragmentation, an emphasis evident in the accounts of the psychic sources of cognition,[12] cruelty,[13] motion,[14] and life[15] in a number of dialogues. Indeed, throughout these descriptions, soul emerges as a uniquely plastic entity: *plastic* because it is subject to a wide variety of transformations with respect to its condition—it can be unified or divided, simple or multiform and complex—and *unique* because of its exemplary capacity to sustain itself as an entity through radical forms of fragmentation. How an entity could be capable of both profound complexity and of achieving a degree of selfsameness akin to the most intelligible entities provides the interrogative horizon within which Plato's psychology unfolds.

This book undertakes an investigation of Plato's psychology by treating psychic plasticity as a central problem with which Plato grapples in three dialogues long noted for the prominence of their discussion of soul and for the richness and variety of narratives they employ to do so: *Phaedo*, *Republic*, and *Laws*. I argue that, when viewed in their context, Plato's psychological investigations are particularly revelatory of his conception of the character of philosophic thought, both because philosophy for Plato requires a particular condition and action of soul and because the study of soul itself is conducted only with the most nimble forms of thought and account. Possessed of soul but yet denied direct access to it, the all-too-human psychologist is in need of images capable of disclosing something about soul and of a heightened critical capacity to avoid mistaking those images for soul itself. For Plato an adequate philosophical psychology requires both an exploration of psychic conditions for which a sufficiently subtle vocabulary is wanting, and the development of a critical eye by means of which the images used to forge this vocabulary can be evaluated.

Plato responds to the various phenomena in which he discerns evidence of psychic plasticity by attempting to offer as subtle and dense an account of the varieties of psychic condition and the mechanism of the soul's transformations as he can assemble. Because a standard vocabulary for describing these phenomena was not ready to hand, Plato's accounts have an experimental quality; he is literally forging a manner of describing soul. Moreover, because the conditions of soul are not limited to the souls of individuals, but bear upon the character of the city and the cosmos itself, the subject matter of this investigation is vast, and requires conceptual vocabularies culled from a variety of sources. Plato thus produce a dense network of images, metaphors, concepts, experiences, and myths gleaned from a variety of sources (medical, sophistic, poetic), all the while inscribing these within a self-critical frame.[16]

Moreover, the manifold discursive registers Plato employs in investigating soul present the means to develop the conceptual tools and vocabularies needed not only to study soul, but also to critique the presuppositions about soul that impede such investigation. Indeed, any assessment of Plato's use of images in light of his critique of the image must take into account his efforts to render evident the limits of his images, to make their potentially distorting character explicit. What is distinctive about Plato's rich image-making faculty, I submit, is that his very critique of images occurs by way of the frictive interaction between images; that is, he constructs his images in such a way as to make their limits visible and to invite their critique, a critique which itself often proceeds by way of images. The result is a critical iconography of remarkable subtlety and depth.

In its study of Plato's development and use of this iconography for his investigations of soul, this book argues for three interrelated theses, which I rehearse in some detail below.

Psychology and Politics

First, I argue that at decisive junctures in his exploration of psychic plasticity, Plato is compelled to take a sharply political turn and focus on the demands that soul's malleability places upon the city as the arena wherein human flourishing is won or lost. This turn toward the polis is necessary for several reasons. For one, certain conditions of soul (emerging in the life of the human it animates) can only be seen within the context of the city; in order to give an account of these conditions, it is thus necessary to view the soul *in* the city.[17] Indeed, it is in the city that we glimpse the full range of meanings Plato's use of psuchē conveys: as life force, as source of motion, as moral agent, as source of cognition.[18] How, if at all, these senses cohere with one another is a serious question for Plato. However, if we take the tension between, for example, the senses of psuchē as life force and as the source of rationality as irreconcilable in advance, we are likely to overlook the manner in which Plato's presentation of the tension between competing impulses that emerges in human political life grapples precisely with the question of whether this tension is intransigent.[19] In fact, Plato goes out of his way to assert that the political life of the human is precisely the site wherein biological and cognitive concerns are inextricably *intertwined*, and to interrogate moments when this perplexing intertwinement erupts into the field of human experience.[20]

But a turn to the city in an investigation of soul is also necessary because of Plato's conception of what the city itself is, a conception shaped by his comparisons of the city to a living being, animated not only by the actions and passions of its citizens, but also by the actions and passions enshrined within its laws, its institutions, its form of education, the tales it supports, etc. This is not the same thing as saying that the polis *has* a psuchē.[21] As we will see, however, Plato treats the laws, institutions, and customs of a city that frame the way of life of its citizens as themselves expressions of psuchē.[22] In housing and memorializing psychic traces in its laws, myths, institutions, customs, etc., the city itself emerges as a psychological phenomenon. A comprehensive study of soul must then attend to the city's own manifestations of psuchē.

The interaction between these two features tells us something about why humans need a city, that is, what the work of the city is, and in so doing reveals with particular clarity the intersection between Plato's psychology and politics. Plato's psychological explorations not only develop a means to account for and evaluate kinds of psychic conditions, but also mark out the role of the city in producing and sustaining these conditions. The soul's capacity, to borrow from the *Republic*, to bear all good and all evil (621c), the endurance of soul through its many forms of fragmentation, the particular limitlessness of soul described as its immortality (all ways of explicating soul's plasticity) suggest that soul's plasticity can, from the perspective of the individual human being, give rise to excesses that threaten human flourishing. In the face of the potentially disastrous effects of these excesses for human life, Plato treats the city as possessing a mandate to impose limits upon human action in the form of law and, for reasons I will offer presently, myth. I argue that, because these limits compensate for individual psychic structures and impulses that impede the creation of salutary political institutions, enhance the ability to sustain those institutions, and generate new institutions, they serve a prosthetic function. That is, on the basis of its semantic association with replacement, augmentation, and generation, with filling in, enhancing, and innovating, and because it is reducible neither to the natural nor to the artificial, yet is answerable to the living, the idiom of prosthesis is uniquely suited to describe the relationship between soul and city in Plato's thought.[23]

To be sure, Plato also explores the limits of human political life. In a number of dialogues he suggests that, for one who is capable of grasping time as a whole, the "human things" mean little that is of worth.[24] He also composes several elaborate afterlife myths that present these limits by describing the cosmic context in which the individual strivings of the human soul unfold. These assertions of the insignificance of human affairs are often interpreted as Plato's affirmation of a transpolitical or extrapolitical telos of human life.[25] However, it is important to keep in mind that a glimpse of these limits is immanent to the account of the human life they appear to transcend, that is, it is attained only by a careful analysis of the human soul, one which attends to those moments when human experience points beyond itself, a "beyond" that includes the city as well as the cosmos. They thus serve a critical and corrective role, one embedded within a concern for human political life. Indeed, Plato is careful to emphasize the salutary political effects of this awareness of limit on one's approach to the city. The description of the indifference of philosopher rulers to human matters in the *Republic*, for instance, occurs in order to assert that such a ruler would be above the petty jealousies and squabbling for power that mark the customary vying for rule (500b–c). The compulsion to rule that this dialogue places upon philosophers enshrines this perspective on the human things in the best city. Thus, I am most interested in Plato's treatment of extrapolitical aspirations as conditions for the existence of the best human city, and thus as forming a part of human flourishing within the city itself. While the aspiration may be for something beyond the city, the city's ability to foster this aspiration is itself a feature of the city's excellence. This book investigates how the desire to be beyond the city is itself a political gesture. Such an investigation requires consideration of just what "beyond" is figured in Plato's afterlife myths, which brings us to my second thesis.

Psychology and Eschatology

I also argue that it is in the context of Plato's reflection on the need the human being has for the city that we should read his eschatological myths, as these myths provide the means to gain some purchase on human life as such, as it unfolds in some time and place, among a community of others. All too often the afterlife myths are treated in a manner whose hermeneutic viability is called into question by the very dialogic nature of Plato's work itself; that is, they are treated as statements of belief rather than as forms of investigation. With a few notable exceptions,[26] the general scholarly tendency has been to treat these myths as regrettable digressions from philosophic argumentation.[27] To be sure, the exposition of these myths tends toward longer speeches and away from the rapid back-and-forth between characters, but as a critical appropriation of traditional material, their dialogic character is found precisely in the manner in which Plato engages with this tradition.[28] It is in the details of this critical appropriation that we can locate the myths' philosophic work. This is a complex task, and for all of the current scholarly debate surrounding Plato's use of myth,[29] its philosophical import,[30] and the analyses of particular myths,[31] David Sedley's recent observation rings true: "It remains the case that Plato's myths, for all the interest they have attracted, are far too rarely used in the interpretation of the dialogues to which they belong."[32]

If we discern the influence of myth broadly to include not only those passages explicitly called a muthos, but also the use of mythic imagery, we find the dialogues so permeated by mythic content as to place scholarly consternation about the philosophical significance of myth for Plato's thought already at some remove from Plato's work. Frequently, Plato's myths provide a change of scale by means of which human life, action, and character can be located within a much broader context. As such, they serve the goal of attaining some purchase on one's life as a whole, especially as that life is lived in some definite place and with particular others. Because many of these muthoi purport to describe in detail the consequences of the reciprocal relation between action and character, they make especially vivid the differences between kinds of character, the actions they commit, and the effects of those actions (including the forms of community to which these actions give rise). This is to say, the myths dramatize the very kinds of lives described in the dialogues, for example, body-loving and wisdom-loving (*Phaedo*); just and unjust (*Republic*); pleasure-seeking, thought-seeking, and mixed (*Philebus*); gentle and courageous (*Statesman*); gluttonous, petty, cowardly, philosophic, justice-loving, etc. (*Phaedrus*); subject to weakness, restraint, and toil, or free from these things (*Statesman*).³³ These myths thus contribute to the overarching philosophic aims of the dialogues in which they occur by opening, continuing, and, at times, critiquing inquiry. In short, Plato's myths are both companions to and supplements of his arguments.³⁴

When we treat Plato's afterlife tales as forms of investigation,³⁵ we see they are particularly well suited to offer a means to observe one's life. Their concern with τά ἔσχατα is a concern with the limits of things; as such, they draw in sharp outline what something is by identifying what it is not. More specifically, they mark out what human life is by demarcating it from its others, as Andrea Nightingale has so effectively demonstrated.³⁶ Thus, what is ἔσχατος also marks out what is οἰκειότατος, what is most one's own. Understood in this sense, the myth of Er, for instance, is a culmination of the "eschatological" trajectory of the entire dialogue.

By presenting the extraindividual and extrahuman context in which one's life unfolds, the eschatological myths allow the dialogue's participants some purchase on their lives as a whole and invite them to consider its happiness and unhappiness in light of this augmented conception (especially as these are tied to one's deeds and dependent upon a public arena of action). The spectacle of the life of the soul over "all time" presents, as unfolding in the future life of the soul, the effects of one's actions on the human community. It furthers the practice of seeing the soul in another by making one's actions and passions its object and considering their effects on oneself, on others, and on the community as such. When in the *Phaedo* Socrates turns to relate a tale about the "true" earth, for instance, he offers not only a valorization of the philosophic life but also a nascent phenomenology of violence, one which emphasizes the political significance of forgiveness and explores the impediments to it.

Indeed, I argue, these myths offer a manner of conceiving of not only one's life, but also the city itself. As we shall see, they provide a this-worldly meditation on the uncanny endurance of vicious deeds and envision the forms of human community that make their expiation possible. Moreover, they open for reflection the array of attitudes toward death that human beings possess and consider whether believing in an immortal soul produces salutary effects on one's life.³⁷ This is to say, the afterlife myths have a prosthetic function: they correct a shortsightedness with respect to the effect of one's deeds and the character of one's life, they augment one's awareness of the political and cosmic contexts in which one's life unfolds, and they aim to generate a particular orientation toward one's mortality.

By means of the eschatological myths, Plato's psychology thus includes an exploration into the "biological" status of belief in an immortal soul as well as into the ontological status of soul. This exploration is tied to his orientation toward the polis, insofar as he maintains that there is a burden upon human community to create and enforce laws that resonate with certain beliefs about the soul.[38] Thus, Plato's account of the ways in which human communities foster or inhibit human flourishing is deeply connected to his psychological investigations.

Finally, in taking up traditional afterlife myths, Plato is afforded the opportunity to critically assess not only the inherited images and assumptions about their lives that shape his dialogues' interlocutor's approach to the soul, but also his own psychological efforts. We will note, in fact, a marked and persistent self-critical gesture inscribed within Plato's eschatological myths, whereby the makers of the myths are themselves put into question. In following Plato's appropriation of mythic language and images for the purposes of investigating the soul, we will also need to consider his reflection on how an account of the afterlife that is answerable to the demands of living well stands with respect to an account of the soul answerable to the demands of what Plato conceives to be the truth. This brings us to this book's third thesis.

Psychology and Philosophy

Finally, I argue that for Plato an investigation of soul recoils upon philosophy itself. On the one hand, Plato emphasizes that one only wins the right to pose the question of what the soul is by critically engaging with one's own assumptions, not only about soul but also about one's own life, and suggests that philosophers are uniquely able to do this. On the other hand, there is a persistent assertion throughout the dialogues that certain beliefs about the soul are necessary if one is to lead the kind of life described as wisdom-loving, beliefs which cannot be insisted upon precisely because of the complexities and obscurities that attend the study of soul.[39] An investigation of soul would then involve an inquiry into those beliefs that make a philosophic life possible, beliefs whose status vis-à-vis the truth has yet to be established. While Plato's Socrates may claim (as he does in the *Phaedo*, for instance) that the philosopher, in her passionate pursuit of what is, has an exemplary condition of soul (e.g., 82e–83c, 84a–b), whether this condition comes about by studying soul, any more than by studying Being or the Good, remains an open question.[40] We cannot assume in advance that a systematic study of ψυχή is part of a philosophical education; neither can we assume that the philosophical status of the study of the soul is self-evident in Plato's work.[41] In short, insofar as philosophy requires the cultivation and maintenance of particular conditions of soul, a study of soul is a study of the very conditions in which philosophy arises. Undertaking this curiously reflexive study, in which the studier herself is at stake, is not without its risks. Philosophy thus has an ambivalent relationship to psychology; it is an investigation that threatens its very practice with instability.

City and Soul in the *Phaedo*, *Republic*, and *Laws*

By my argument, the range of discursive registers, narrative styles, and tropes that Plato develops in his investigations of soul are necessary in order to make the soul an object to itself; they serve the psychological estrangement necessary for self-knowledge. It is this task that connects the analyses of experience, argumentative demonstrations, rich imagistic language, and appropriation of myth that are all employed by Plato in his psychological investigations. The intermingling of styles and tropes outlined in the previous sections troubles any effort to extract a demonstrative argument from out of the broader narrative and dialogic context, and warns that one dismisses parts of an account as window dressing, as "merely" rhetoric, only at the risk of serious misunderstanding. The sizeable body of work on the literary dimensions of the dialogues indicates that such a focus results in an impoverished understanding of Plato's thought.[42] The philosophic challenge is to see how these discursive forms hang together in the pursuit of the issue in question. If we fail to pay attention to the full range of Plato's narrative, we risk hypostatizing some elements of his investigation while overlooking his critical appropriation of culturally embedded images and concepts and the uses to which he puts them. With respect to Plato's psychology in particular, we risk failing to mark the subtlety of his exploration of corrupt conditions of soul and the political environments that foster them and thus missing the political implications of much of his psychological investigations.

My arguments hinge upon demonstrating the interplay between argumentative demonstration, appeals to experience, elaborate imagery, and eschatological myth, and to the place of a dialogue's investigations of soul within its broader animating questions. Of the dialogues that include detailed afterlife myths, the *Phaedo*, *Republic*, and *Laws* form a natural group on the basis of the length and location of their afterlife myths.[43] All three exhibit well the variety of forms of discourse Plato employs in speaking about the soul and the rigor of his critical appropriation of them. All three also include a self-conscious consideration of how they are to conduct their investigations, one which concedes the necessity of image making (*Phdo.* 99d–100a; *Rep.* 435c–d, 504b, 506d–e; *Nom.* 897d–e).

Nevertheless, this is certainly not an exhaustive list of dialogues with prominent explorations of soul. Comprehensive claims about Plato's psychology as such would have to take into account the *Timaeus* and the *Philebus* as well as passages from the *Charmides*, *Crito*, *Gorgias*, *Phaedrus*, *Theaetetus*, and others; my own claims are limited to the investigations of soul in these three dialogues, and I refer in the notes to places of overlap or divergence with other dialogues. Beyond my acceptance of Aristotle's description of the *Laws* as having been composed late in Plato's life, my arguments do not rest on strong claims about the order of composition of the dialogues.[44] I do make comparative claims based upon my perception of a similar constellation of questions to which these dialogues are responding, but these are not progressive claims. Nor do I make any claims about the unity or lack thereof of the Platonic corpus.

The psychological investigations of the *Phaedo*, *Republic*, and *Laws* emerge out of conversations with three different sets of interlocutors engaged in three different inquiries: friends of Socrates (a few of whom are also students of Philolaus) who exhort him to defend his cheerfulness in the face of his imminent demise, and whose response to this defense motivates an extended discussion of whether soul is immortal (*Phaedo*); young aristocratic men friendly toward Socrates but also influenced by a dominant cultural discourse about what is valuable and eager to consider the kind of life they will lead in the city (*Republic*); and, last, aging Dorian gentlemen—whose lack of experience with philosophical argumentation is emphasized throughout the dialogue—contemplating the foundation of a colony in Crete with the assistance of a stranger from Athens (*Laws*).

In order to give the defense of his confidence in the face of death with which the *Phaedo* opens, Socrates offers a description of the human soul as stretched in two directions, yearning, on the one hand, for the eternal changeless Being to which it is akin, and infused, on the other hand, by a love for the body in which it is entangled. This bivalent soul provides the basis for two forms of life, wisdom-loving and body-loving, which Socrates sketches in some detail. Socrates defends the life of the philosopher on the grounds that the attempt to isolate the soul from the body that this life undertakes gives expression (and satisfaction) to the impulses of the soul that are most its own. His defense is greatly aided by his use of the religious language of pollution and purification, language which he will try, throughout the dialogue, to translate into the idiom of philosophy, but whose bodily commitments trouble this effort.

The care with which Plato depicts Socrates's spirited defense of the philosophic life, as well as his concern for his friends' grief and worry about the possible dispersion of their philosophic community, opens a tension between the life of the "true" philosopher Socrates has described and Socrates himself. Chapter 1 investigates the conception of soul implicit in Socrates's infamous account of the life of the "true-born" philosopher as spent practicing for death, drawing out the terms on which this conception rests, and charts the tension between Plato's depiction of Socrates and Socrates's depiction of the philosopher. This tension reverberates throughout the four logoi about immortality that follow Socrates's defense of himself, logoi which deepen the division between the love of wisdom and the love of the body he described therein at the same time that they attempt to turn Socrates's friends' grief about his passing to a concern for their souls.

As we will see in chapter 2, the result of these logoi, however, is not absolute conviction but a crisis of both thought and account about the nature of living being—a crisis brought about by the very terms by means of which soul's striving toward Being and capacity for becoming body-like are identified and described—and an exhortation to continue investigating. I argue in chapter 3 that the myth Socrates tells toward the end of the dialogue responds to this crisis not by rejecting these terms but by intensifying them in order to render in the most vivid shades the forms of life that are available to humans and the kinds of community they entail. The myth's eschatological geography frames its own telling within a critical perspective on the condition of its tellers, opens to reflection the effects of violence, and envisions those forms of human community necessary for its expiation. In this, it performs a prosthetic function.

In the *Republic*, we see a shift in the dominant terms by means of which its investigation of soul is undertaken from the language of pollution and purification to that of medicine.[45] But, as in the *Phaedo*, the terms by which the soul is investigated are critiqued and have their limits revealed, and the opening concern for the sake of which these terms were introduced (in this case with choosing the life that is best) is reiterated and intensified in a concluding myth. The task Glaucon and Adeimantus set out for Socrates—that he offer an account of the most just and unjust lives for the sake of judging between them—requires him to mark out the conditions and forms of the transformation of a complex soul. He does so by means of an elaborate strategy of philosophical portraiture, one which not only compares soul to city but also attends carefully to the transformations of soul wrought within the city, and culminates in the portraits of the philosopher and the tyrant as images of extreme psychological unity and fragmentation respectively. Chapter 4 charts the inception of the city/soul analogy and the oscillation between mimēsis and poiēsis that functions as the internalizing and externalizing mechanisms by means of which city and soul interpenetrate. This portraiture gives rise to an elaborate image of the complex soul that enables the judgment of which life is best.

Chapter 5 marks out the discussion of the parts of the soul, the analogy between health/disease and virtue/vice that this discussion sets up, and the account of desire upon which both of these rest, an account which also sets the stage for the distinction between the lovers of wisdom and the lovers of sights. This account, in turn, sets up the distinction between the philosopher and the tyrant. Chapter 6 explores this distinction, arguing that these two figures provide images of the most extreme form of psychic unity and fragmentation that the human life is capable of expressing, highlighting the interdependence between philosophy and the city this portraiture suggests and the challenge to the language of health and sickness that is implicit in the portrait of the tyrant.

Socrates's accounts of philosopher and tyrant give rise to an elaborate image of the complex soul, an entity whose limitlessness includes, from the perspective of the human life, excesses which threaten this life with deep instability and which require limits. I argue at the start of chapter 7 that this conception of psychic excess informs the much-maligned discussion of immortality in book 10. The city itself emerges from this discussion as a psychological entity, housing and sustaining those traces of psuchē that are capable of limiting the excesses to which human life is prone.

The depth of Socrates's investigation of the complex soul, however, has also offered glimpses of psychological phenomena that cannot be accounted for on the basis of complexity; that is, the investigation of the human soul points beyond itself, and gestures toward a psychological investigation of a different sort. However, as with the *Phaedo*, Socrates's critical perspective on his and his interlocutors' view of the soul is immanent to the perspective that is being critiqued. Throughout the dialogue, the medical vocabulary that Socrates employs enables not only the description and evaluation of conditions of soul but also of the perspective from which Socrates and his interlocutors could best judge these conditions and determine what is best, a perspective that combines immersion and distance in a mindful engagement, and that requires a capacity for self-critique. That is, in the *Republic* the medical trope enables its own critique. I argue in the end of chapter 7 that the myth of Er does not turn then to offer an alternate investigation of soul, but to further sharpen their understanding of human life, by marking out the choices by means of which one's life is given a particular character and shape, considering what effect philosophy can have on this choosing, and highlighting the extent to which one's knowledge of the nature of the soul is dependent upon others.

The *Laws* is decisively shaped by *both* a theological context, in which the grounding of the dialogue's legislative project in divine nous includes a radical reconfiguration of traditional theology, *and* a medical framework by means of which it justifies the specific legislative best practice of appending therapeutic preludes to the formulation of laws. I argue in chapter 8 that the intimacy of the *Laws'* legislation is taken to be warranted by its particular conception of the law as the "external" expression of the capacity for calculation that is "internal" to each individual human soul. At its best, law is an expression of a force that infuses both individuals and cities, and that eventually is identified as mind. The laws the Athenian and his interlocutors create for Magnesia, with their appended preludes, are intended to encapsulate and enshrine within both the city and the character of its citizens, the conception of soul that informed their creation. An investigation of these laws is thus an investigation of the psychology at work in them. Chapter 9 offers just such an analysis, taking the laws against temple robbing, homicide, and impiety as particularly vivid examples of the conception of soul informing the dialogue's approach to legislation. The vision of soul these laws and their preludes promote is of a prodigious force responsible for all motion. Chapter 10 focuses on the lengthy account of soul in the preludes to the impious, preludes which claim that when soul operates with mind it produces the orderly motion of the cosmos, reflections of which can be seen in those human laws capable of drawing out and sustaining the excellences to which human life, both singularly and collectively, can attain. Mind thereby grants to soul those motions most indicative of what soul is, even as soul is capable of operating without mind. Thus, I argue, the relationship between soul and mind in the *Laws* is paradigmatic of the prosthetic function of myth and law that is at work in the *Republic* and *Phaedo*. In the *Laws*, the account of this relationship culminates in a vision of human political life that asserts the fragility of human happiness, the contingency of the particular character of its political life, and the need of a critical eye trained upon this life and the institutions to which it gives rise. I end this chapter with an analysis of the image of politics as painting which the *Laws* offers, an image which also permits a few concluding comments about the study of soul undertaken in all three dialogues we have studied.

I would like to conclude by marking out what I take to be at stake in the theses posed above. Plato's descriptions of psychic plasticity make of soul an entity which defies easy assessment of its ontological status and destabilizes the distinctions that reside at the heart of Platonic metaphysics as it is traditionally conceived. This account sits uneasily with the standard conception of the complementary relationship between Plato's psychology and his metaphysics. While, in the more than sixty years since Francis Cornford declared the "doctrine of forms" and the "immortality of soul" to be the twin pillars of Platonism,[46] a vast body of scholarship has been produced that is critical of the doctrinal status of the former, the same cannot be said of the latter. Specifically, little critical inquiry has been devoted to the pervasive assumption of symmetry between the eternality of forms and the deathlessness of soul, even as scholars have long pointed out that what Plato means by immortality is far from clear, a fact that Plato himself takes pains to demonstrate.[47] The influence of Plato's investigations of soul, especially his assertion of soul's immortality, on contemporary evaluations of his metaphysics endures; the assumed complementarity between Plato's metaphysics and his psychology in which this influence lies is maintained both by students of his metaphysics and by those actively engaged in critiquing it.

However, any assessment of the relationship between Plato's psychology and his metaphysics would be well served by noting Friedrich Solmsen's diagnosis of the Christianizing of Platonism; namely, that it was precisely Plato's conception of psuchē that early Christian thinkers overlooked, turning for their conception of divinity not to the demiurgic world soul that mediates between Being and becoming but instead to Plato's assertion of a Good that is beyond Being.[48] If Solmsen is correct in identifying Western onto-theology as emerging from an appropriation of Plato's thought that fails to take the full measure of his psychological explorations, that is, if this onto-theology can be only uneasily attributed to Plato, a study of these explorations is likely to yield challenges to the very philosophical system Plato is claimed to have founded. Thus, an investigation of Plato's descriptions of psychic plasticity, one which focuses upon their political dimension, demonstrates the need for a reassessment of the relationship between Platonic psychology and metaphysics.

The merits of studying Plato's psychology extend beyond the realm of Plato scholarship, however. Inquiry into psuchē comprises for Plato a study of the sources of life and thought. More than this, it is a study of that by means of which we can be said to be courageous or cowardly, just or unjust, moderate or licentious, wise or ignorant. This is to say, to study psuchē is to inquire into the human capacity not only for thought but also for violence. Insofar as an investigation of thinking participates in that reflexive gesture inscribed within the human being's capacity to put herself into question, an inquiry into psuchē seeks to discern that which ties thinking to living, and thus to discern the scene of thought, its time and place, the transformations and motions (both violent and gentle) in which it takes part.

PART I

Phaedo

From a zoological perspective, the *Phaedo* contains a bestiary to be reckoned with. References to swans and swallows, bees and bulls, ants, frogs, and dogs, to name just a few, appear throughout its pages. This profusion of living beings is matched in the *Phaedo* by a profusion of kinds of accounts. During the course of the dialogue we encounter the musikē of poetry and song, the quasi-clinical utterances of incantation and charm, the language of mathematical Pythagoreanism, the eschatological beliefs associated with Orphic poetry, and the threat of eristic. Amid this proliferation of logos, we also encounter four logoi about the immortality of the soul whose flaws as demonstrations have been noted by scholars spanning both decades and schools of thought,[1] and a myth whose discursive excesses have led to an inverse paucity of discussion in contemporary *Phaedo* commentary.[2]

It is within the milieu of these flowering forms of zōon and logos that the *Phaedo*'s investigation of soul takes place. Indeed, it is the very profusion of zōon and logos that opens up a crucial dimension of the *Phaedo* as a whole, namely, its overarching concern with the relationship between modes of discourse about death and that entity so powerfully and, for contemporary readers, enigmatically associated with life, soul. Thus, in order to determine what contributions the *Phaedo* makes to Plato's investigation of soul, we will need to sort out how this investigation is both inspired and determined by the overarching interconnection between zōon and logos that the dialogue posits.

The question that motivates an investigation of soul in the *Phaedo*, however, is not what the soul is, but whether it is immortal. An inquiry into the soul's immortality is an inquiry into the manner in which human life is circumscribed by limits in which the soul is somehow implicated but to which the soul itself may not be subject. To assert that the soul is deathless is to attribute to the soul a certain limitlessness that is not exemplified by human life and that finds only uneasy expression in it. Thus, the *Phaedo*'s exploration of the soul involves an investigation of how the soul's limitlessness affects human life. This focus on the human soul should be noted even if, as the dialogue strongly suggests, understanding the human soul requires understanding living being as such and the cosmos as a whole.

Most immediately, the dramatic context of the dialogue draws into sharp relief the extent to which giving an account of one's life requires one to acknowledge the opinions about one's soul that have influenced one's actions. For the life that is most immediately at stake in the dialogue is the life of a particular human being, Socrates, and it is Socrates's confidence in the face of his imminent demise that ultimately inspires the specific focus in the dialogue on the question of whether or not the soul is immortal. When compelled to defend this confidence to his friends, Socrates provides an account of a course of life, which he describes as philosophic and espouses as best, whose assumptions about the endurance of the soul beyond death prove sufficiently dubious to his interlocutors as to provoke them to ask for further demonstration of the soul's deathlessness. In the conversation that ensues, Socrates engages in a series of accounts, on the one hand, which he characterizes as attempts to soothe his interlocutors' fear of death (77c–78b), and, on the other, an elaborate myth, which Socrates hopes will illustrate the need to care for one's soul (107c–d).

Thus, Plato's depiction of a music-practicing Socrates who cheerfully greets his death situates the investigation of soul undertaken by Socrates and his interlocutors within a consideration of the influence one's opinions about death and the soul have on one's life. Indeed, one of the dialogue's most compelling features is its demonstration that the fear of death, with all of its power to influence one's actions, implies certain assumptions about the nature of the soul. Socrates's expressly therapeutic efforts to contend with this fear require both the articulation and critical assessment of the assumptions about the soul that inspire it. Plato presents Socrates's discussion of immortality as motivated, in part, by the wish to replace his interlocutors' sadness about his death with the desire to care for their own souls.

Because Socrates's therapeutic endeavors are expressly identified as a persuasion about the nature of the soul,[3] the *Phaedo* possesses an irreducibly rhetorical dimension, a dimension that deploys the persuasive power of a number of discursive registers from a variety of sources. At the same time, Socrates's own careful qualification of many of his claims demonstrates the necessity of a critical engagement with the beliefs about the soul available to Socrates and his interlocutors. The *Phaedo* thus includes a reflection upon both what is required in order to investigate the soul and why such an investigation is philosophically significant. Indeed, depicting Socrates's conversation with his friends on the day of his death allows Plato to (*a*) critically assess several influential beliefs and theories about the nature of the soul and reflect upon the experiences they attempt to account for; (*b*) explore the importance of the investigation of soul for philosophy; and (*c*) illustrate the need for a reflective comportment toward death that neither asserts unwarranted optimism about one's knowledge of the soul, nor paralyzes inquiry into what the soul is.

The possibility of such paralysis is illustrated (and risked) throughout the dialogue in a series of passages which emphasize the mortality of logos itself.[4] The connection between the dialogue's logoi about living and dying on the one hand, and its allusions to the life and death of logos on the other, suggests an intimacy between zōon and logos that receives perhaps its fullest articulation in the dialogue in Socrates's account of his own life (95e–102a). This mutual implication of zōon and logos is, as we will observe, intimately related to the dialogue's investigation of soul.

The next three chapters will argue that one of the *Phaedo*'s most significant contributions to Platonic psychology is its demonstration of the soul's plasticity and the challenges that this malleability poses to a philosophical investigation of soul. Reducible to neither changeless permanence nor uninterrupted transformation, the soul presents to Socrates and his interlocutors an entity subject to myriad changes in condition whose very capacity to undergo such changes marks it as unique. Once this plasticity has been illustrated, the task taken up by a good portion of the dialogue is to develop as complex and subtle a means of delimiting the various conditions of soul as possible. This is to say that the dialogue's emphasis on the soul's malleability determines its exploration of soul as an exploration of the various conditions of soul. It is this task that the variety of kinds of living beings and forms of logoi serve.

This interplay between the substance of the dialogue and its structure challenges any strict hierarchical distinction between the *Phaedo*'s dramatic and argumentative elements. Indeed, the necessity of the variety of living beings and discursive registers to the dialogue's psychological inquiry remains concealed if one does not take into account the intertwining of structure and function that unites the dialogue as a whole. More specifically, the mutual implication of zōon and logos outlined above, and its importance for the dialogue's investigation of soul, is obscured if one focuses on the four logoi about the immortality of the soul in isolation from the full range of utterance presented in the dialogue. However, with few exceptions, the centrality of the demonstrative logoi has been assumed throughout contemporary *Phaedo* commentary. The reasons for this are complex and best addressed in the course of examining the passages themselves. At this juncture I will simply note one effect of this focus, namely, the broadly dubious reception of the myth of the earth that follows upon these logoi. Such a response is not, I believe, sufficiently attentive to the dialogue's permeation by myth throughout, from the early allusion to Theseus to the later description of the true earth.[5] In fact, the four logoi are themselves infused with mythic imagery, from their start in the ancient saying that souls reside in Hades (70c) to their use of Homeric and Pythagorean imagery in what has come to be called the Affinity Argument (78b–84b). In the *Phaedo*, muthos and logos function in such a manner as to be neither reducible to one another nor understood in isolation from one another.[6]

In what follows, I take this interdependence between logos and muthos to be intended by Plato and to be necessitated by the dialogue's particular investigation of soul; thus, the relationship between muthos and logos in the *Phaedo* cannot be understood in isolation from their collective contribution to the dialogue's psychological inquiry, nor can the dialogue's contribution to psychology be adequately discerned without taking into account Plato's deployment of muthos and logos. I will argue that both the four logoi about the immortality of the soul and the muthos about the true earth serve the dialogue's overarching and persistent effort to develop as subtle and precise an account of the varieties of soul's conditions as possible. Further, each does so by critically engaging with and appropriating a number of culturally embedded conceptions of soul espoused by Socrates in his defense of his confidence in the face of death and by his interlocutors in their engagement with this defense.[7] While the four logoi about the soul's immortality involve a critical engagement with mathematical, religious, and poetic conceptions of the soul, they ultimately fail to be fully persuasive because they rely upon an incomplete conception of the relationship between body and soul, a conception that denies them meaningful reference to the lives and deaths of embodied beings. The myth of the true earth provides, I will show, a necessary complement to these logoi by offering a critical engagement with the very perspective from which Socrates and his interlocutors assess these conceptions—thereby providing a dimension of self-critique that is called for by the four logoi—and by locating the question of the relationship between soul and body within the context of living and dying.

The following three chapters will attempt to make good on these claims by focusing upon three sections of the *Phaedo*: Socrates's defense, which encapsulates the main themes that will be subject to scrutiny throughout the rest of the dialogue (chapter 1); the four demonstrative logoi, including the interludes between demonstrations (chapter 2); and the concluding myth (chapter 3). Because the dialogue's psychological insights hinge upon the reciprocity between its structure and substance, I make every effort to remain sensitive to the complex texture of the dialogue by grounding my discussion of these sections within the context of the dialogue as a whole. Bearing in mind the choices Plato makes in framing the entire discussion, I take quite seriously Socrates's critical assessment of the demonstrative logoi (the arguments), his insistence on their limitations (that they are neither comprehensive nor complete), and on the need continually to investigate their claims, as well as his persistent refusal to insist upon the veracity of the myth that he tells toward the dialogue's end. Doing so requires a denial of the doctrinal character of any of the discussions in the dialogue. To attribute such a status to them is to treat a question as though it were an answer, thereby committing what is for Plato a fatal philosophical error. Instead, we need to scrupulously observe that Plato has his Socrates utter claims about which he is ultimately uncertain, and we must begin by asking what philosophical end is served by staging the elaboration and critical assessment of these claims.

1 Socratic Prothumia

Socrates's defense of the calmness with which he confronts his death unfolds within a theological framework with which he has a vital, if also uneasy, relationship. Indeed, he is granted the opportunity of giving this defense because of a delay in his execution due to a religious observation: the citywide observance of a vow to Apollo, involving a ritual mission to Delos in memory of Theseus, prohibits the civic pollution that accompanies executions. Further, Socrates's attempts to give both an account of himself and of the "true" philosopher are shaped by the need to determine both of these entities' stances toward the theology he outlines very early on in the dialogue. With respect to the dialogue's psychology, this theological framework provides a number of the dominant conceptual and linguistic tools through which soul is investigated; consequently it will be necessary to outline this framework in detail. At the same time, Plato's depiction of the uneasiness Socrates feels about certain elements of this theology provides an important orientation toward this framework that neither rejects it nor uncritically appropriates it.[1] Instead, the *Phaedo* illustrates that for Plato it is incumbent upon the investigator of the soul to make apparent the conceptual and linguistic apparatus through which soul is interrogated. Insofar as theology provides one such lens, this theology must be made explicit and subject to scrutiny, and this is precisely what Plato has Socrates do.

Socrates is drawn into a defense of his confidence in the face of death by the charge that it is irrational not to flee from death, a charge to which Socrates has opened himself by his advice to the sophist and poet Evenus to follow him to death as quickly as possible, advice qualified only by Socrates's concession to the injustice of suicide. Socrates is in the position of giving advice to Evenus because of his peculiar response to the possibility of impiety: having been haunted his entire life by a dream commanding him to practice music, and having interpreted this dream as encouragement to continue philosophy, Socrates decides as the end of his life approaches to take up demotic music as well, in order to "test" (ἀποπειρώμενος) the meaning of the dream and, in Socrates's words, "to acquit myself of any impiety (ἀφοσιούμενος)" (60e).[2] Socrates's hesitation, his uncertainty about the appropriateness of his interpretation and thus about the piety of his life, not only punctuates the liminal context of this conversation (the time of death is a time in which everything is drawn into question) but opens the questions of whether and to what extent a philosophic life can be circumscribed within pious service to the gods.[3] Thus, what Socrates and his interlocutors have to say about philosophy in this dialogue is motivated by, and bound to, a question about the relationship between the philosopher and the divine. This question is posed throughout Socrates's defense, and can be heard in Socrates's playful expectation that Evenus will follow his advice insofar as Evenus, too, is a philosopher (61c).[4]

The law (61b) prohibiting suicide to which Socrates gestures in qualifying his advice to Evenus is one that Socrates assumes Simmias and Cebes have heard from their Pythagorean teacher Philolaus.[5] Socrates's invocation of Philolaus imparts instructive information about his interlocutors, and thus about the shape that the ensuing conversation is to take. Philolaus is widely attributed with developing the mathematical branch of Pythagoreanism.[6] However we determine the historical circumstances of the fracture of Pythagoreanism into acousmati and mathematici, and however much we attribute to Plato the development of mathematical theories that would come to be called Pythagorean, it is safe to say that Plato found in the Pythagoreanism of his day resources for positing and exploring a unity between a cosmology determined by number and a series of practices determined by a conception of soul's immortality and transmigration.[7] In fact, throughout the dialogue Plato plays with the possibility that a cosmology based upon a rational principle also makes demands upon human action and thus entails a certain kind of life. This can be seen in the interest Socrates has in convincing his two mathematically inclined interlocutors that they are part of an intellectual tradition that also involves serious commitments about the nature of the soul and the afterlife, commitments about which they appear to be unaware. Some anticipation of this interest can perhaps be read in Socrates's characterization of his own knowledge of such matters as from hearsay (ἐξ ἀκοῆς [61d]).

Socrates is willing to share this hearsay with his friends,[8] and his stated reason for doing so is noteworthy for the dual critical and speculative tasks it assigns to the conversation that follows. "For perhaps," he states, "it's especially fitting for somebody who's about to emigrate to that place to examine and also to tell stories [διασκοπεῖν τε καὶ μυθολογεῖν] about the emigration There—what sort of thing we think it is. For what else would one do in the time before the setting sun?" (61d–e). The particular tradition that receives elaboration and scrutiny here pertains to the manner in which the relationship between gods and humans bears upon pious human action. Socrates tells his companions both what he finds difficult to understand—the account in the Mysteries that "we humans are in a sort of garrison and one is bound not to release oneself from it nor to run off" (62b)[9]—and what he finds well put—"The gods care for us, and we humans are one of the gods' possessions [τὸ θεοὺς εἶαι ἡμῶν τοὺς ἐπιμελουμένους καὶ ἡμᾶς τοὺς ἀνθρώπους ἐν τῶν κτημάτων τοῖς θεοῖς εἶναι]." Socrates concludes this account of the tradition surrounding the law prohibiting suicide with a question: "Or doesn't it seem this way to you?" (62b). The component of this tradition that receives Socrates's approval—that humans are the property of gods who care for them—places servitude at the heart of human life and determines a pious life as a life of service to benevolent owners. This conception of piety thins the line between humans and other possible possessions of the gods (and prepares the way for the comparison that Socrates will draw at 85a between himself and the swans as coservants of Apollo). At the same time, because the gods care for humans, the service humans render to the gods, Socrates suggests, is necessary for human flourishing.[10] Their conclusion is that removing oneself from the service of the gods would be worthy of punishment (τιμωρίαν) (62c).

Plato's presentation of a music-practicing Socrates who, like the swans also in Apollo's service, has just composed an ode to the god is certainly in keeping with this notion of human piety, but the incredulousness with which Evenus receives word of this practice (60d) provokes the reader to question just how easily Socrates's life fits in with such a model of dutiful service to the gods. As Cebes is quick to note, this conception of human life seems to conflict with Socrates's earlier suggestion that philosophers should be willing and even eager for death. Cebes knows just where to press his friend on this point, using this objection to draw out what he thinks (and assumes Socrates thinks) are the qualities that a philosophical person should possess:

> For its not reasonable for the most thoughtful men [τοὺς φρονιμωτάτους] not to make a fuss when they leave behind this position of service [θεραπείας], in which the very best overseers there are, the gods, watch over them. For at least the thoughtful man does not, I suppose, imagine that he'll take better care of himself once he's become free. But a mindless [ἀνόητος] human being would perhaps imagine that one must flee from one's master. He wouldn't reason [οὐκ ἂν λογίζοιτο] that one must not flee from one's master—at least a good one—but all the more remain with him, and hence he'd flee irrationally [ἀλογίστως]. But the mindful man [ὁ δὲ νοῦν ἔχων] would, I suppose, always desire to be with somebody better than himself. (62d–e)

Socrates defends himself against the charge of irrationality and mindlessness by asserting that if he did not believe that he would find himself in the company of entirely good gods after his death, he would be neither so hopeful nor so cheerful about his approaching demise (63b–c). As the defense progresses, this theological framework is transformed into a philosophical one. The gods with whom Socrates hopes to keep company after death become the truth and Being with which philosophers are in love, and which are graspable only upon attainment of a thoughtfulness which is had only in the separation of soul from body. The connection between truth, Being, and the divine that is suggested by this defense's initial claims about the gods invites us to investigate further the ease with which the philosophical can be subsumed within this theological framework. The remainder of this chapter offers some preliminary considerations about the tenor of Socrates's defense followed by a detailed analysis of it and concludes with a few observations about its import for the rest of the dialogue and for the accounts of the soul contained therein.

Preliminary Considerations

In his elaboration of his defense against the charge of mindlessness, Socrates describes the eagerness (προθυμία) with which those whom he describes alternately as the trueborn philosopher (66b) and those who philosophize rightly (67e) practice for death, training to gather their souls to themselves and avoid comportment with the body in order to commune with and strive for (ὀρέγηται) that which is (63b–70b). In this defense, Socrates makes the notorious assertion that the very activity the philosopher most pursues—the separation of soul from body for the sake of fostering the soul's thoughtful grasp of Being—is also characteristic of death; the philosopher's love of wisdom is, therefore, also a love of death, and philosophy is the practice for death. It would be irrational, Socrates concludes, for one who has devoted his life to philosophy to then fear and mourn the culmination of his efforts.

Socrates's subtle polyvocity, the ease with which he slides between a number of discursive registers, warns against reading this defense as a simple expression of what Socrates takes to be true of himself (as does Socrates's own emphasis on the preliminary character of the opinion that comprises his defense [63c]). Plato's Socrates is not a model of isolation or separation from his fellow citizens and from his city.[11] There are several distancing moves that Plato makes in the *Phaedo* which need to be taken into account in turning to Socrates's defense.

First, it is important to note that Socrates is outlining precisely a manner of living, a manner of taking up the conjunction of body and soul that constitutes living being. The specific manner of life Socrates will describe, namely, the life that attempts to *separate* soul from body as far as possible, must be read within the general context of Socrates's account of how best to take up the *coincidence* of soul and body in life. Thus, this defense has less the character of an account of the ontological status of soul and body (indeed, as we shall see, the nature of both soul and body are left undetermined, which helps to account for why Socrates will be required to elaborate upon and explain further certain elements of this defense) than an account of how to accomplish embodied existence in such a manner as to attain whatever thoughtfulness is available to human beings.

Moreover, that one can *have* a manner of life—that is, that one can *take up* one's life as something about which to have a deliberate and thoughtful orientation by means of which one determines one's actions—implies the possibility of a certain coherence and intelligibility to one's life. This in turn provides another layer to the intertwining of zōon and logos that we are charting in the dialogue. More specifically, the dialogue's presentation of these possibilities with respect to human life helps to account for Plato's interest in Pythagoreanism.[12]

Second, Socrates's frequent reference to the προθυμία, the eagerness, required for this practice of separating soul from body (see in particular 64a, 67d, and 69d) also calls into question the nature of the separation between soul and body for which Socrates appears to be advocating. Προθυμία means "readiness," "willingness," "eagerness," and "zeal." Its verbal form, προθυμέομαι, means "to be ready, willing, eager, zealous."[13] Προθυμία is very nearly nonsensical without reference to something with thumos, and thumos itself is severed from a number of the meanings it embraces if one thinks of it without thinking of an embodied being that possesses it.[14]

A playful tension thus hangs around Socrates's exhortations to "put one's heart into" separating soul from body. In emphasizing the eagerness with which true-born philosophers attempt to separate soul from body, Socrates appeals to a comportment toward such separation that could only be achieved on the basis of a certain community or communion between soul and body. Plato indicates that this προθυμία is shared beyond the limits of the conversation in Socrates's cell when he has Echecrates exhort Phaedo to "put his heart into" recounting Socrates's final hours (58d). Indeed, προθυμία has a uniquely infectious and communicable character to which Socrates appeals at critical junctures throughout the dialogue. Socrates's suggestion that προθυμία is a condition necessary for the practice for death signals that the uncritical distinction between soul and body employed throughout this defense will receive more careful treatment later on.

Finally, Socrates's description of this way of life as indicative of one who has gotten in touch with philosophy in the right way (64a),[15] one who philosophizes truly (64e) and rightly (67e), and one who is a true-born philosopher (66b), suggests that he is presenting it in order to correct a misconception about philosophy and to juxtapose it with other manners of life that only pretend to be philosophical. The moniker of the true-born philosopher here is particularly troubling. While a number of dialogues explore the qualities and conditions that are necessary for the practice of philosophy, they also are careful to elucidate the kind of city and mode of education and nurture that is necessary in order for philosophic natures to develop into philosophers. Socrates's emphasis in this very defense on the investigations that the philosopher undertakes implies the need for such political and civic structures (even if they do not explicitly elucidate them) as does the reliance in the defense at a crucial juncture on what it is lawful to say and believe. At the very least, even in the *Phaedo*, the investigation of Being that comes to be the distinctive hallmark of the philosopher is a function of the practice of one's life, a fact which strongly suggests that birth is not sufficient to make the philosopher. To look a bit further ahead, while the *Phaedo* is noticeable for its absence of commentary upon the city, this does not mean that political concerns are absent from it.

The corrective character of Socrates's defense provokes one to ask what other forms of life are implied in it. We have already observed Socrates's engagement with the Pythagorean way of life, and the schism within it as represented by Simmias and Cebes; this engagement will continue throughout the dialogue. However, the invocation of Evenus also calls to mind the life and standing of the sophists and teachers of rhetoric; very presently Socrates will gesture to the lives of the "investigators of nature," the phusiologoi, both as represented by Anaxagoras and, for a brief time, himself. But also and perhaps most importantly, we are to read the defense as distinguishing most sharply the life of the lover of wisdom from that of the lovers of honor, money, and the body, whom we will meet presently.

This corrective tenor also helps to set the stage for the discussion between Socrates and Simmias about what constitutes a philosophical person. Their conclusions on these matters have the tone of a statement of creed. However, the extent to which Socrates, Simmias, and Cebes agree with one another (that is, the borders of their intellectual kinship and friendship) will be tested throughout the conversation that ensues, to all of their pleasure. In the end, the final comments that Socrates will make about their claims, far from characterizing them as a definitive account that could be held as doctrine, all emphasize the need to continue investigating them. This is all to say that even withstanding this tone, a stated agreement is that with which the conversation about the soul's immortality begins; it is not where it ends.

The concern with a mode of life, the invocation of prothumia, and the corrective tone of Socrates's defense, along with other distancing gestures Plato makes throughout this defense, serve to call into question whether Socrates's characterization of the true philosopher is true of Socrates himself. Socrates's explicit description of himself at the end of this defense opens more questions than it answers: "Now I too, as one of them, have left nothing undone in my life that was in my power, but have put my heart [προυθυμήθην] into becoming one of them in every way. But whether I've put my heart into it rightly [ὀρθῶς προυθυμήθην] and whether we've accomplished anything, we shall know for sure, as it seems to me, only when we've gone There—I in just a little while, if god is willing" (69d). Socrates's equivocation between being one who philosophizes rightly and the more qualified description of himself as having attempted to become one who philosophizes rightly, as well as the uncertainty of knowing if he has done so until he is already dead, and finally his invocation of the prothumia necessary in doing so, remind us of the curious nature of this attempted separation, which seems to require the cooperation of the very things one is attempting to separate. The meaning of this practice, even as it has been described in the defense, requires much further elaboration. The Socrates of the *Phaedo*, who cares for the condition of his friends regarding the practice of philosophy, is not an immediately obvious choice for the paradigm of the true-born philosopher, and Plato has his Socrates go to great lengths to indicate that this is the case. Such distancing gestures should make one wary of reading Socrates's defense as a thinly veiled espousal of a series of metaphysical principles.[16] This is not to say that such principles are not implied by the speech but rather that it is necessary, in exploring the metaphysical implications of Socrates's defense, to remain sensitive to the contingent, preliminary, and interrogative character of their articulation. Plato goes out of his way to indicate that this defense is an introduction and that further investigation, and perhaps revision, is to follow. These distancing gestures call attention to the heuristic/didactic register of the *Phaedo*, which illustrates Socrates's care for his interlocutors and distances him from a robust ascetic practice.[17] It will remain to be seen whether Socrates's life is a life spent separating soul from body; Plato's characterization of Socrates in the subsequent conversation continues to put this into question and to explore Socrates's character vis-à-vis the true-born philosopher. Socrates's character, like the soul, the body, and the relationship between them, stands in need of and receives further discussion. The next few pages explore in greater detail Socrates's defense, beginning with his preliminary discussion of death (64a–65d), then turning to the refinement of the portrait of the philosopher (66a–67d) and finally to the return to the characterization of philosophy as a practice for death (67e–69e).

Socrates's Defense

64a–65d

Socrates's defense to his friends of the confidence with which he meets his death begins with the following lines:

> "Others are apt to be unaware that those who happen to have gotten in touch with philosophy in the right way [ὅσοι τυγχάνουσιν ὀρθῶς ἁπτόμενοι φιλοσοφίας] devote [ἐπιτηδεύουσιν] themselves to nothing else but dying and being dead [ἀποθνῄσκειν τε καὶ τεθνάναι]. Now if this is true, surely it would be absurd (ἄτοπον) if they put their heart into [προθυμεῖσθαι] nothing but this all their life, and then, when it comes, they make a fuss about the very thing to which they had long given both their hearts and their devotion [ὃ πάλαι προεθυμοῦντό τε καὶ ἐπετήδευον]." (64a)

Simmias greets this characterization with amusement, noting that the philosopher's pursuit of death is exactly what the many remark about him. Socrates dismisses the many on the grounds that they are unaware "in what way those who truly are philosophers are ripe for death and in what way they are worthy of death and of what sort of death [αὐτούς ᾗ τε θανατῶσι καὶ ᾗ ἄξιοί εἰσιν θανάτου καὶ οἵου θανάτου οἱ ὡς ἀληθῶς φιλόσοφοι]" (64b). The two then turn to give this claim about the philosopher's devotion to death their attention in order to avoid the ignorance of which the many are guilty.

Since exploring how the philosopher is devoted to death requires some common conception of death, they first begin by agreeing upon what death is. That much of the rest of the dialogue is spent in giving further attention to the terms of this agreement recommends full citation: "And is [death] anything but the freeing of the soul from the body [τὴν τῆς ψυχῆς ἀπὸ τοῦ σώματοος ἀπαλλαγήν]? And is this what it means to have died: for the body to have become separate [χωρὶς], once it's freed from the soul and is itself all by itself [αὐτὸ καθ' αὑτό], and for the soul to be separate [χωρὶς], once she's freed from the body and is herself all by herself [αὐτὴν καθ' αὑτήν]? Death couldn't be anything other than this—could it?" (64c).[18] Every term of this description[19] upon which they agree is somewhat mysterious, as is indicated by the series of interrogatives with which Socrates articulates this conception of death. This is especially the case with the two entities whose separation constitutes death: soul and body. At this early stage of the dialogue, however, the distinction between soul and body upon which this preliminary conception of death relies garners not even a second thought from Simmias, Cebes, or any of the other interlocutors. That the soul's distinction from the body—in what way it is distinct, how it is distinct, and why it is distinct, if it can even be said to be distinct—must be drawn into question, interrogated, and given an account of becomes clear as the conversation proceeds, but it is not immediately at stake for any of the interlocutors. In fact, it also becomes clear that Simmias and Cebes have not looked closely into their presuppositions about this distinction. At this juncture in the discussion, however, all that can be said is that whatever death is, its characterization as a separation is tied up with a presupposition about a difference between soul and body.

Having arrived at a preliminary agreement about what death is, they turn to the second major term of the contentious claim that the philosopher is devoted to death by determining whether they share the same opinions about what it means to be a philosophic man (φιλοσόφου ἀνδρὸς) (64d). This sharing of opinions about what constitutes the philosophic person marks an important moment in their conversation. Ostensibly, it is their belief that Socrates is such a person that draws Simmias and Cebes to him, as well as their conviction that they too share some interest in these qualities. Thus, this series of agreements about who the philosopher is draws out the unexpressed foundation of the friendship between Simmias, Cebes, and Socrates and exposes this foundation to scrutiny. They agree that such a person is not serious about the pleasures that accompany food, drink, and sex. They agree that, in general, the "true philosopher" (ἀληθῶς φιλόσοφος) (64e), holds in dishonor any other "servicings of the body" (τὰς περὶ τὸ σῶμα θεραπείας) save for the small amount of concern it is necessary to have about such things (64d). They agree that such a person's business (πραγματεία) is not with the body but rather is turned toward the soul as much as possible (64e). This focus on the servicing and care of the body distinguishes the philosopher from others and anticipates the portrait to come of the lover of the body.

At the same time, this focus on the philosopher's stance toward the pleasures, servicings, and cares of the body draws attention away from inquiry into the body as such. The business of the body, the attainment of food and drink and fine cloaks and other forms of ornamentation and sex, all suggest that devotion to the body is devotion to acquisition. In other words, the discussion of the care of the body suggests that a devotion to soul involves either a reorientation of one's primary activity (a move away from acquisition), or an acquisition of things whose attainment would have a radical effect on one's character, or both. This discussion of what the philosopher takes seriously as the focus of his business and devotion punctuates the fact that a way of life is being described here and this description will thus engage the person as a whole. Insofar as this way of life is a devotional practice, the philosopher's desires and attentions must be addressed and directed.

Socrates and Simmias continue their portrait of the philosopher by noting his exemplarity in "releasing the soul from communion with the body as much as possible" [ἀπολύων ὅτι μάλιστα τὴν ψυχὴν ἀπὸ τῆς τοῦ σώματος κοινωνίας] (65a). This release of the soul from communion with the body is the first elaboration of what activities the philosopher's devotion to death involves. That this release implies a condition of previous communion or kinship between soul and body is noteworthy.[20] Why the philosopher would be particularly interested in this release is made clear in the lines that follow: the body is an impediment to the attainment of thoughtfulness (τὴν τῆς φρονήσεως κτῆσιν) because our physical senses are neither precise nor clear (μὴ ἀκριβεῖς εἰσιν μηδὲ σαφεῖς) (65b). They continue with the following exchange:

"So when does the soul get in touch with the truth [Πότε οὖν, ᾖ δ' ὅς, ἡ ψυχὴ τῆς ἀληθείας ἅπτεται]? For when she attempts to look at something along with the body, it's clear that then she's deceived by it."

"What you say is true."

"Then isn't it in her act of reasoning [ἐν τῷ λογίζεσθαι], if anywhere, that something of the things that are becomes clear to her [κατάδηλον αὐτῇ γίγνεταί τι τῶν ὄντων]?"

"Yes."

"And I suppose the soul reasons most beautifully [κάλλιστα] when bidding farewell to the body, she comes to be herself all by herself as much as possible and when, doing everything she can to avoid communing with or even being in touch with the body, she strives for what is [ὅτι μάλιστα αὐτὴ καθ' αὑτὴν γίγνεται ἐῶσα χαίρειν τὸ σῶμα, καὶ καθ' ὅσον δύναται μὴ κοινωνοῦσα αὐτῷ μηδ' ἁπτομένη ὀρέγηται τοῦ ὄντος]." (65b–c)

There are several important characteristics of soul asserted in these lines. For one, this description of soul as attempting to be itself by itself (terms infamous in the history of metaphysics) focuses the conversation on the ontological status of soul.[21] That soul is capable of becoming is significant in its own right, as it explicitly claims that the soul is subject to transformation and change. That soul can come to be itself suggests that soul's very being involves activity and change which therefore implies that soul could fail to become alone by itself, could somehow fail to flourish. The conception of soul's attempt to be by itself specifies the transformations to which soul is subject as oscillation between coalescence and diffusion; in so doing, it privileges coalescence as the condition necessary for soul's flourishing. Moreover, Socrates's suggestion that this attempt of the soul to be itself is subject to the dictates of the possible implies a certain limit to soul's capacity to coalesce (to become itself). Yet, the further implication is that this limit is a function not of soul itself, but of soul's condition when it is conjoined to body.

The description of the soul's reasoning as its "striving" (ὀρέγηται) after Being assigns a conjoined epistemological/desiderative task to the soul. The extensional character of this striving is both disclosive and troubling. In what manner does the soul strive and thereby extend itself out toward Being? This striving suggests some kinship between soul and Being such that soul could extend itself toward Being, a suggestion furthered by the requirement that the soul's striving toward Being requires the soul to be itself.

Socrates's wondering about how the soul gets in touch with truth resonates with this extensional, striving activity. Yet it does so in a perplexing manner. Indeed, Socrates's reference to "getting in touch" with the truth is extremely odd, especially as it occurs along with a denial of the efficacy of the body for apprehending truth. In what way could it be meaningful to say soul gets in touch with truth? What does touching mean here? What could soul be such that it could touch? And what could truth be such that it could be touched? When we look to what the correlate of getting in touch with the truth is in the passage on the soul's reasoning, namely that beings become clear to the soul, we are no less in need of considering a condition with strong bodily concomitants. The move from haptic to visual references only punctuates the underlying issue; namely, that soul's withdrawal from body yields an access to truth and Being that is described by appeal to bodily actions and conditions. In fact, Socrates continues to attribute an entire sensorium to soul, describing it as looking, as listening, as touching, as being nourished and sated. Thus, for all of his assertions of the priority of soul over body, Socrates does not avoid using the body as a descriptive device for characterizing soul. The tension between his apparent denigration of the body and his descriptive use of it will be brought to the fore in the third logos on immortality, as we will see in the next chapter.

Socrates's reference to touch in this context evokes a dense network of concepts pertaining to the transmission or communication of certain conditions by contact. This language of touch is intimately bound up with the notion of the soul's defilement by contact with the body and need for purification, a notion Socrates will deploy both presently (65e–66a) and throughout the third logos for immortality. In fact, defilement or pollution and their opposite, purification, enter meaningfully into the discursive universe of this investigation of soul by means of this notion of the soul's 'touching,' as well as its capacity to be transformed by that with which it comes into contact. While Socrates calls eyes and ears the clearest and most precise of senses (65b), he implicitly privileges touch for its capacity to connect and implicate.[22]

By invoking the language of pollution and purification, Socrates is able to describe and account for soul's various transformations. Touch opens a circuit or inaugurates a passage by means of which the soul is transformed; to touch or grasp truth is to have truth communicated to one. For this reason there is something not entirely adequate about conceiving of touch in terms of immediacy of contact. Rather than providing direct access, touch institutes a passage or communication between two or more entities. That the contact inaugurated by touch has this communicative or expressive character is perhaps most clearly evinced in early Greek religious conceptions of the polluting effects of contact. Robert Parker's succinct formulation is helpful here: pollution is "a vehicle through which social disruption is expressed."[23]

That such contact cannot be reduced to direct physical contact[24] furthers the point that the entire trope of touch, used in this way (to bring into play pollution and purification), complicates the relationship between soul and body rather than asserts either a kinship or divergence between them. In other words, the contact inaugurated by Socrates's references to touch and to the pollution and purification that this conception of touch conveys cannot be thought of without some conception of the body, nor is it reducible to the body. Touch, in the religious context Socrates invokes here, problematizes the distinction between soul and body.

The importance of this characterization of soul's transformations for the dialogue can hardly be overemphasized. For one, this language of touch characterizes the soul's relationship with truth and with body as circumscribed by notions of proximity and distance, by spatial notions. Moreover, the spatiality at stake here is regional: it is defined by community and relationship. The soul's capacity to be alone by itself is presented as a capacity to remove itself from such proximity, a presentation that is predicated upon the haptic model of the soul's transformation. This suggests that even the infamous metaphysical language of being alone by oneself is tied to the language of touch: isolation becomes possible only when contact is possible too. Thus, conceptions of the soul's touching or grasping the truth enforce the conception of the soul's placement, that to which it is proximate and that from which it is distant. The language of defilement and purification, as well as that of isolation, coalescence, and diffusion, provide ways of describing the soul's transformations as a function of its residence and its ability to move between regions. The entire framing of the discussion of death as a migration (as a movement to another place) at work from the very beginning of the dialogue is tied to a notion of soul that includes its capacity to touch and to reside in proximity to or distance from the body. This notion of soul itself is, in turn, also ineluctably tied to body by the overarching question of how to best accomplish their coincidence.

In using this broadly religious language as a means of figuring soul's various transformations, Socrates also gains a means to describe the soul's capacity to establish or institute contexts on the basis of the actions it enables. The appeal to a conception of pollution and purification through contact allows Socrates to exploit a conception of action as exceeding the agent and as instituting a context in which multiple parties are implicated and affected[25] and to apply it to investigation, specifically to the investigation of Being. Thus, it allows a presentation of ontology as exceeding the efforts of any individual ontologist, and as instituting a community of inquiry, a network, in which all members are implicated in the pursuit of Being. The relevance of this institutionalizing operation for the particular context, that is, Socrates's imminent demise and his friends' fears that philosophy will die with him, is clear.

In summary, when Socrates applies the concept of pollution to the soul and considers the soul either polluted or purified on the basis of how it conducts its investigations, we see him making the trope of pollution and purity his own, using it as a means to consider the effects of a given inquiry on that which inquires. He makes investigation a vehicle of access to the sacred. But he also thereby grants a certain epistemological function to the activities of purification, furthering the characterization of purification as a kind of pursuit of Being. It is not possible at this juncture to simply describe all of this language as metaphorical. Rather, Plato explores what this language discloses about soul and uses it to gain a stronger purchase on the unique malleability of soul. But I would most like to emphasize at this point that the language of purification and pollution is deeply complicit in and perhaps even motivated by a much larger conception of the soul as somehow spatial and capable of touch. Moreover, this notion of the soul's regionality, its transformation on the basis of that which it touches, connects the language of pollution and purification with the language of isolation and being alone by itself. That this touching implies, and may be no more than, a certain communication and kinship of soul and truth or soul and Being is suggested in the discussion that follows.

This kinship has significant implications for the practice of philosophy, as Socrates's immediate reiteration of the philosopher's exemplarity asserts: "Then here too, doesn't the soul of the philosopher especially hold the body in dishonor and flee it and seek to become a soul herself all by herself?" (65d). Because the philosopher is most likely to do that which is most indicative of soul, and is thus most likely to foster soul, the philosopher has a privileged relationship with soul. This is the case, as Socrates and Simmias will eventually agree, because the philosopher is the most ardent pursuer of Being; the philosopher's pursuit of Being predisposes the philosopher to be most interested in doing the things that most foster soul's coalescence. This, in turn, is the case because the soul has some kinship with Being. The characterization of philosophy as ontology and the symphony or kinship between soul and Being become the specific focus of the next leg of the conversation. The portrait of philosophy as the pursuit of Being, as ontology, that Socrates and Simmias are about to embellish is predicated upon the soul's capacity to strive toward Being. And this, in turn, makes the philosophic life that life in which soul flourishes.

66a–67d

In order to refine their portrait of the philosopher, another series of agreements are needed, which also further the intellectual community between Socrates and his interlocutors. Socrates and Simmias agree that there is something as the Just itself and the Beautiful itself and the Good itself as well as Bigness itself, Health itself, and Strength itself, and that these things are not grasped by the body but must instead be grasped by thought if they are to be grasped at all. The investigator of Being does this most purely (καθαρώτατα, 65e) when, "using unadulaterated [εἰλικρινεῖ] thought itself all by itself, he attempts to hunt down each of the beings that's unadulterated [εἰλικρινὲς] and itself by itself" (66a).[26] This is perhaps the first passage that specifies the kinship between soul and being as operating on the basis of a shared character of both thought and being—both are able to be unadulaterated.

Socrates then turns to give the opinion that it would be necessary for "the trueborn philosophers" (66b) to have, and thus turns to speak in the voice of such a philosopher for an extended passage, one that begins by asserting, "as long as we have the body accompanying the argument in our investigation, and our soul is smushed together [συμπεφυρμένη] with this sort of evil, we'll never, ever sufficiently attain what we desire. And this, we affirm is the truth" (66b). This is the case, Socrates continues, because the body deprives people of leisure, comes down with diseases, unsettles the person with all sorts of erotic strivings, and generally renders thoughtfulness impossible. Socrates continues: "After all, nothing other than the body and its desires produce wars and factions and battles; for all wars come about for the sake of getting money, and we're compelled to get money for the sake of the body to whose service we're enslaved" (66c–d).[27] Bellicose, acquisitive, aggressive, and enslaved, the lover of the body is doomed to the path of life marked out by distraction and diffusion. Granted the body's impediment to the attainment of thoughtfulness, it appears that either the attainment of thoughtfulness is impossible or it is only possible for those who have met their end.

Socrates concludes this opinion with some consideration of what should be done in the meantime between birth and death that might bring about the attainment of thoughtfulness:

> "And in the time we're alive [καὶ ἐν ᾧ ἂν ζῶμεν] here's how we'll come closest, it seems [ὡς ἔοικεν], to knowing [εἰδέναι]: if as much as possible we in no way consort with the body or commune with it—unless its an absolute necessity—or fill ourselves up with its nature [μηδέ ἀναπιμπλώμεθα τῆς τούτου φύσεως], but purify ourselves from it until the god himself shall release us. And when, in this way, we are pure and free of the thoughtlessness [ἀφροσύνης] of the body, we shall, as is likely [ὡς τὸ εἰκός], be in the company of things that are pure as well and, through

our own selves, shall recognize everything unadulterated [καὶ γνωσόμεθα δι' ἡμῶν αὐτῶν πᾶν τὸ εἰλικρινές]—and this, no doubt, is the True. For it isn't at all lawful that the not-pure should touch the pure [μὴ καθαρῷ γὰρ καθαροῦ ἐφάπτεσθαι μὴ οὐ θεμιτὸν ᾖ]." (67a–b)

By invoking the ancient rule of "like to like," this portrait of the philosophic life draws the various references to touch more explicitly into contact with conceptions of pollution and the communication of impurity that comes from contact with what is impure, which is precisely how we are to think of the effect of communion with the body on the soul. Parker's assessment of this gesture is instructive: "Plato is half playfully presenting abnormal doctrine in a familiar guise. The truism 'Religious law forbids the impure to touch the pure' is applied to the necessary conditions for contemplation of unadulterated reality."[28] Invoking this law, then, returns Socrates to the theological background with which his defense began.

Socrates and Simmias then agree that the philosopher does indeed practice for that separation of soul and body that is purification (67c) but also death (67d), and thus that it would be laughable to fear the approach of that for which one has been longing (67d). In bringing together the philosopher's attempt at separating soul and body with purification, Socrates also appears to meld philosophical and religious concerns, drawing out two valences of purification: one, the condition of thoughtfulness desired by the philosopher; and two, the condition of soul desired for the happy fate in Hades that it guarantees. This dual valence opens the possibility of simply maintaining two parallel discourses about purification: a demotic account represented by the various mythic and religious traditions about the afterlife, and a philosophic account that presents purification as a this-worldly intellectual endeavor capable of freeing one from the fear of death. However, as becomes clear, Plato does not follow two parallel discourses; rather, he actively interrogates the relationship between these two conceptions of purification in the course of the dialogue. The question of where philosophy stands with respect to theology persists as a living question throughout the dialogue and structures, in very important ways, not only the coming demonstrative logoi but also the myth that follows them.

67e–69e

Having made explicit the philosopher's identification of purification with death, Socrates turns in the final leg of his defense to characterize the philosopher as one who, in pursuing being and thoughtfulness by means of practicing the separation of soul from body, overcomes the fear of death: "those who philosophize rightly," states Socrates, "make dying their care, and of human beings to them least of all is being dead terrifying" (67e). Socrates's subsequent account of the philosopher's triumph over the fear of death emphasizes the desire proper to the philosopher. In dying, philosophers have hope that they will "get what they've been in love with throughout life [διὰ βίου ἤρων]—and they were in love with thoughtfulness [ἤρων δὲ φρονήσεως]—and to be free of the company of that with which they have been at odds" (68a). Socrates continues, invoking Hades (returning again to the theological backdrop that frames the defense): "many people have been willing to pursue their human loves to Hades when they've died—their boyfriends, wives and sons—led by the hope that they'll see and be together There with those they desired. Then will the man who's genuinely in love with thoughtfulness [φρονήσεως δὲ ἄρα τις τῷ ὄντι ἐρῶν] and who's taken a firm hold of this same hope that nowhere else but in Hades will he encounter it in a manner worth speaking of, make a fuss about dying and not be pleased to go There? We must suppose this is so, my comrade, whenever somebody's a genuine philosopher" (68a–b). So thorough is the philosopher's excision of the fear of death that the display of this fear is a sufficient sign (τεκμήριον) that a person is "not a lover of wisdom but a lover of the body [οὐκ ἄρ' ἦν φιλόσοφος, ἀλλά τις φιλοσώματος]" (68c).

In conquering the fear of death through his love for thoughtfulness, the philosopher emerges as the most truly courageous, moderate, and virtuous of human beings (68c–69a), while virtue itself emerges as a form of purification (69a–d), or rather, given the terms upon which they earlier agreed (67c–d), a process of dying. The connection that Socrates establishes between thoughtfulness and virtue expands the terms that can be used to describe conditions of soul to include not only various degrees of thoughtfulness but also such conditions as courage and cowardice, moderation and greed. At the same time, these terms are also grounded in the intelligibility of Being and one's access to this intelligibility, which Socrates asserted in his earlier discussion of thoughtfulness. Socrates then invokes Hades again, to give praise to those who have instituted their mystic rites insofar as they have recognized that those who come to Hades unpurified suffer while those who come to Hades purified dwell with the gods (69c–d). Identifying the celebrants of mysteries as those who have philosophized rightly (οἱ πεφιλοσοφηκότες ὀρθῶς) (69d), thereby connecting the theological backdrop with the practice of philosophy, and asserting his kinship with them, Socrates concludes his defense: "So then, Simmias and Cebes, that's my defense of why its reasonable for me to leave you and the masters I've got here without taking it hard or making a fuss: because I believe that There too, no less than here, I shall meet up with good masters and good comrades as well. If I've been at all more persuasive to you in my defense than I was to the Athenian judges, it would be well" (69d–e).

Conclusions

Socrates's defense of his confidence in the face of death proceeds by way of outlining a kind of life that finds death attractive. Along the way, he presents a series of beliefs about the soul and its afterlife, beliefs that will be analyzed, refined, and defended in the conversation that follows. Before moving on to this further discussion, let us summarize the main assertions about the nature of soul in this defense. First, Socrates asserts that the soul is that by means of which humans grasp being and attain thoughtfulness. Second, the soul's alignment with thought is juxtaposed with its capacity to care for body, given that the soul's communion or investigation with the body actually impedes the soul's attainment of thoughtfulness. Thus, the soul's alignment with both thought and care of the body reveals it to be an extremely malleable entity, subject to a variety of conditions. Further, since some of these conditions are more amenable to soul than others, some of these conditions enable soul to be more soul-like (to flourish as soul) than others, an instant hierarchy is introduced between those conditions that foster soul as such and those that compromise soul's capacities.

Third, in this defense the transformations of soul are conceived as a function of the soul's proximity to and distance from bodies, on the one hand, and those beings that are alone and by themselves, on the other. This is to say that the primary means for figuring soul's plasticity in this passage is through the soul's complex and mysterious capacity for contact. The regional spatiality that this capacity opens up ties together the language of pollution and purification with that of isolation and coalescence. Insofar as virtue is purification (as Socrates submits for consideration), then virtue too is a function of proximity and distance. Virtue names a condition of residence, a regionality, a way of speaking about soul's condition by thinking about what it resides next to and away from, or even where it resides. When Socrates then connects virtue and thoughtfulness, he furthers the sense that the soul's thoughtfulness is a function of that with which it is in contact. Both virtue and thoughtfulness are, among other things, ways of describing and ordering soul's condition. Moreover, they are ways of doing so that have some connection with soul's regionality, which suggests that one way of describing soul's conditions is to describe the various residences of soul. An explication of soul, then, will involve an explication of place. This way of figuring the soul's malleability sets the stage for the cosmological considerations that come with the subsequent demonstrative logoi as well as the psychic geography that is outlined in the concluding myth.

Socrates and his interlocutors also assert a number of things about the soul of the philosopher. Because the philosopher desires thoughtfulness and a grasp of being more than any other human, and because the soul is most itself when in pursuit of thoughtfulness and Being, the philosopher is most able to foster his soul, and the philosophers' desires are most amenable to the soul's flourishing. Thus, the philosopher has a privileged position with respect to the soul. Moreover, we learn that in his pursuit of thoughtfulness over the course of his life, in his efforts to isolate soul from body in order to grasp Being, a certain eager and zealous comportment is required of the philosopher. The philosophic life is not possible, then, without singular forms of passion and eagerness.

This defense also contains a number of implications about the relationship between philosophy and psychology. Because the pursuit of Being is best done by soul, ontology cannot be done well in the absence of a certain condition of soul. The defense goes even further to suggest that, because there is a sympathy between soul and Being, the soul that is most itself can learn Being from itself (67a–b), thereby elevating a certain kind of knowledge of soul to the status of knowledge of Being and blurring the boundary between psychology and ontology. But the question then seems to be whether ontology must include psychology, whether study of Being must include study of soul? To phrase the question in a slightly different way: Is *study* of soul necessary to ontology, or is it simply the cultivation of a certain condition of soul which could be transmitted by things other than study (cultivation of certain habits, of a certain way of life)? If the latter, then soul would have to be studied to the extent that the condition least likely to disturb investigation of Being or most likely to yield grasp of Being is discovered. Once this knowledge is arrived upon, however, it is possible that one could simply work to bring about this condition of soul without studying soul itself. Is such a condition of soul capable of being imparted to one (perhaps through ascetic practice, for instance) without one having to study soul itself? This is a living question in the *Phaedo,* with its complicated presentation of Socrates's relationship with friends and people who consider themselves his followers.

Finally, we learn something about Plato's orientation toward the soul. Insofar as Socrates's defense suggests a powerful relationship between the manner of one's life and the condition of one's soul, it reveals the reciprocity of action and character as an essential feature of human life. Plato presents Socrates as concerned for human life and the communities it produces, at least to the extent that these communities are necessary for a philosophic way of life; this is a political as well as a philosophical concern. We can discern an outline of this concern in the association between soul and residence in place highlighted above. The political dimension is also evident in the care that Plato takes to illustrate the influence that people's opinions and beliefs about the soul and about death have on the way in which they live their lives. Moreover, Plato's stance on several particularly powerful sources of these opinions is quite revealing. Socrates does not simply reject his interlocutors, nor does Plato simply reject the religious and scientific perspectives to which they give voice. Content neither to do away with a mythological tradition nor to simply accept it, he submits it to investigation. This investigation also prohibits Plato from maintaining two parallel but separate discourses (demotic and philosophic). With respect to Plato's psychology, this stance suggests that inquiry into the soul requires a critical engagement with one's preexisting opinions, beliefs, and cultural traditions about the soul. Since these opinions are closely and intimately held, critically assessing them is a delicate task, one which requires dealing effectively with the pathē it provokes. What is needed, and what this critical assessment paves the way for, is not direct access to soul, but a self-aware and self-critical lens, a philosophical mythology.

From the beginning of the defense, Socrates is clear that its terms are not things upon which he can insist: this defense opens conversation; it does not conclude it. While the specific line of inquiry will be introduced by Cebes and will follow his request to elaborate upon the endurance of the soul beyond death, both body and the nature of the relationship between body and soul remain underdetermined and mysterious, in need of further exploration. In order to engage in this further exploration, Socrates will find it necessary to shift their perspective from human life to the cosmos as a whole and from human death to the beginnings and ends of all living things.

2 The Body-like Soul

SOCRATES'S AND HIS interlocutors' extended investigation of the soul's immortality begins as a more thorough telling, a διαμυθολόγος (70b), of an opinion about death that Socrates playfully presented as his apologia of his confidence in the face of death (63b). That it is the defense's conception of the soul that is particularly problematic is suggested by Cebes, who objects that the soul's endurance beyond death is in need of further discussion (70a–b). Socrates's eager agreement to offer a more thorough story inaugurates the first of four logoi about immortality (70b).

This first logos inherits a definition of death which Socrates, as we have observed, gives in his initial defense with a noteworthy nonchalance: death is the separation of soul and body (64c). Throughout the discussions of soul's immortality, Socrates draws out and reframes a number of assumptions about the nature of this separation. However, the *Phaedo*'s depiction of Socrates speaking with friends who are at once eager to philosophize and grieving the looming loss of their friend opens an investigation not only of assumptions about what death is, but also of how to properly comport oneself toward mortality, whether one's own or that of others. That is, the conversation about immortality is directed not only at death but also at grief, and at marking out what should be grieved and how. This dimension is perhaps made most explicit during the interlude on misology (88e–91c), but it is at work early on in the dialogue as well in, for instance, the care Plato takes to describe the curious blend of affect had by Socrates's interlocutors (58e–59a). With the first logos, Socrates begins to contend with his interlocutors' assumptions about death and their attitudes toward grief by trying to wrest death away from an association with utter destruction.

Genesis

The first logos on the immortality of the soul begins with a logos about beginnings:

> "And let's investigate it in some such way as this: Either the souls of human beings who've met their end are in Hades or they're not. Now there's a certain ancient account [παλαιὸς μὲν οὖν ἐστι τις λόγος], one that we hold in memory [μεμνήμεθα], that souls are There having arrived from here, and that they arrive here again [πάλιν] and come to be from the dead. And if this is so, and the living come to be again [πάλιν] out of those who've died, could anything else be the case but that our souls are There? If they weren't somewhere [οὐ γὰρ ἂν που], they couldn't come to be again [πάλιν]; and it'd be sufficient proof that this is so, if it should in fact become clear that the living come to be nowhere else but from the dead. But if this isn't so, we'd need another account." (70c–d)

The service that this mythopoetic tradition offers to an investigation of soul's immortality is that of grounding this immortality in the nature of genesis, of coming to be. In doing so, it makes three assumptions about soul. First, that soul is such as to reside somewhere. As we have noted, some sense of soul's "residence" is operative from early on in Socrates's defense. However, second, in this statement the spatial character of soul is bound up with a recursive temporal structure granted to genesis, namely the time of return.[1] Indeed, according to Socrates's version of this tradition, the character of return, of palingenesis, implies the spatial character of the soul, with its residence in some abode. Third, Socrates exploits the ancient association between the soul and life in such a manner as to elide the soul's coming to be "here" with the genesis of living beings. If birth, as Socrates and Cebes will eventually agree, is a returning to life (τὸ ἀναβιώσκεσθαι) (71e–72a) and death a returning to Hades, then both living and dying take on the recursive spatiotemporal model of returning to some place.[2] Socrates will note, granted these agreements, "I suppose it seemed to be sufficient proof that it's necessary for the souls of the dead to be somewhere [εἶναι που], whence [ὅθεν] they come to be again" (72a). Thus, the genesis of living being is figured as a change in residence of the soul; as soul moves from "Hades" to "here," living beings come to be. Dying, in turn, names the coming to be of the dead from the living, although what genesis means when applied to the dead is extremely obscure and invites further consideration, which it will receive. Conspicuously absent from this traditional account of becoming is any reference to body and to that generation of living beings wrought by erotic engagement. Nor is any explicit association between body and death made in this conversation. This silence with respect to the body in generative and degenerative activity becomes even more pronounced as the conversation continues; for now it is sufficient to note that the equation of birth and death with movements of the soul is given here with a marked tentativeness (71e–72a).

Socrates's version of the ancient account suggests that if his interlocutors want to understand the immortality of soul, they must adjust their scale beyond that of a single life to the field of becoming as such. Thus, one effect of Socrates's deployment of this mythopoetic tradition is its deflection of attention away from the demise of Socrates and toward the nature of genesis itself. States Socrates: "Now if you want to understand this more easily, don't look only to human beings but also to all animals and plants. And in sum, let's take a look at all things that have a becoming—whether they all, as contraries, come to be from anywhere else but from their contraries, at least those that happen to have some such contrary" (70d–e). By locating living and dying within the broader phenomena of genesis, Socrates shifts the context of their investigation of soul's immortality from human life to all life. According to these terms, a thorough psychology must include cosmology. Moreover, the language of contrariety that Socrates employs here invokes the thematic research interest of a variety of phusiologoi and medical writers (the treatment of diseases by contraries being one contentious model for medical treatment), for whom the interaction between contraries accounted for a wide range of phenomena.[3]

Granted these considerations, this first logos begins to take on a curious structure. Starting with an ancient mythopoetic tradition, Socrates elaborates upon it using conceptual tools that were also influential in the broader intellectual milieu. Thus, this first discussion of soul's immortality involves a very fluid motion from mythopoetic to phusiologic discourse. This is a particularly appropriate tack to take with Pythagorean interlocutors. Socrates appears to be conjoining religious and what we could call scientific perspectives on phusis, as though to remind his Pythagorean friends that they are part of an intellectual tradition that at least at some point in its history asserted a common account of the two, for all of their seeming antagonism.[4]

At the same time, as this passage at 70d–e indicates, the ability of the specific mechanism of becoming that Socrates identifies, contrariety, to extend to all generated things is not something that Socrates asserts without qualification. As will quickly become clear in the course of the conversation, the benefit of connecting genesis with the transformation of one contrary into another is the curious stability of identity that is granted by contrariety: whatever can be said about one thing, it must be said that it cannot be the same as its contrary. Thus, contrariety opens up a stable negotiation between same and different. This stability also grants a certain order of transformation, that between contraries, and thus asserts not only an identity that endures through transformation but also assigns a certain stability to transformation itself.

Socrates further elaborates the logic of transformation that he attributes to contraries by giving a series of examples of contraries matched by their transformation into one another: bigger and smaller (70e–71a, whose duo becomings are growing and decaying, 71b), weaker and stronger (71a), worse and better (71a), just and unjust (71a), being asleep and being awake (71c–d). Throughout this discussion, Socrates presents to his interlocutors the ceaseless transformation from contrary to contrary as one movement proper to genesis (that this motion is also an essential constituent of phusis itself is suggested at 71e). Eventually, he applies this logic to the specific contraries of being alive and being dead (71d), concluding that they must agree that soul is immortal (71d–e).

Contrariety thus inaugurates a dynamic of transformation that is taken to be revelatory of the immortality of the soul because it identifies a certain persistence of soul. The example that precedes their discussion of living and dying—namely being asleep and being awake and their accompanying becomings of falling asleep and waking up—is instructive for the character of persistence that it extends to soul. In this example, it is the living being who is asleep and awake, or falling asleep and waking up; the living being is that which persists as a being in order for these various transformations to take place. The suggestion is that the soul's endurance is like the living being who abides, even as these contrary "conditions" or events happen to it. Insofar as Socrates and his interlocutors accept the mythopoetic attribution of life and death to movements of soul, soul is that entity whose persistence through radical changes in its condition is evinced by the very phenomena of living and dying themselves.

Not only do living and dying attest to the endurance of soul, but the sheer existence of a variety of things whose generation and decay can be observed attests to this endurance (insofar as contrariety speaks not only to the stability of living things but to all generated things having a contrary). Thus, Socrates is able to use the very experience of a world populated by variant entities as evidence of the immortality of soul. As Socrates states: "Then look at it this way, Cebes, and you'll see we did no injustice when we so agreed, as it seems to me. For if things that come to be didn't always make a return, each to its corresponding other, just as if they were going in a circle, but if instead becoming were a kind of straight line that proceeded only from one end to the directly opposite end and didn't bend back again toward its other or make any bend at all—do you know that all things would end up being in the same shape and would be affected in the same way and would stop coming to be?" (72a–b).

Judging from his response (72d), Cebes is quite persuaded by this evidence. But of course there is a series of problems here. In ascribing both living and dying to movements of soul, Socrates never explicitly addresses whether soul itself has a contrary.[5] Given assumptions about the difference between soul and body offered earlier in the dialogue, we might wonder if the suggestion is that body is the contrary of soul, but Socrates does not state this here; indeed, for very good reason. If soul and body were contraries, then not only would soul have to come to be from body and body from soul, but also, the conjunction of soul and body that has been treated as synonymous with living being would be impossible, and the phenomenon of life itself would be denied. That such a possibility has been broached by other thinkers is something to which Socrates explicitly calls their attention, but in a decidedly critical tone (72c). Nevertheless, that something of this sort is risked here can be inferred from the complete lack of consideration given to the body and to the generative capacities that attend to erotic engagement.⁶

Moreover, not only is a denial of life risked in this discussion; death too is collapsed into a moment of ceaseless circular motion. Until Socrates and his interlocutors arrive at a means to account for the difference between being big, being strong, being better, being awake, and being alive, they have no means of distinguishing between the various becomings that govern their transformation into being small, being weak, being worse, being asleep, and being dead. More specifically, we might wonder where to locate the linear character of human life within this realm of ceaseless cyclical motion. Given the terms of this first discussion, this linearity is brought into communion with the cyclical motion of nature by the soul itself. But of course, what the difference between human linearity and natural circularity means requires sorting out; correspondingly, while the attribution of the cyclical journey of the soul from life to death to life again aligns human experience with the movement of nature by means of the soul, what this alignment really means for the person also needs to be clarified.

There is nonetheless something deeply seductive in what Socrates is doing here, especially for his companions, who are already mourning the coming loss of their friend. If death is simply a transformation involving only genesis and no loss or deprivation, then what have they to mourn and what has anyone to fear about death? However, as cloying as such thoughts may be, they prove, to Socrates's pleasure (78b), dissatisfying to at least two of his interlocutors.

By way of summary: in this first logos, the immortality of soul is taken to be demonstrated by the nature of genesis itself, or at least by the dynamic of genesis elucidated by the logic of contrariety. According to this logic, all coming to be is a function of the transformation between contraries. This logic grants stability both to the unique identity of each contrary and to the motion between them such that generation emerges as occurring within a perpetual cyclical play between contraries. Soul exhibits in an exemplary manner this stability through transformation by means of its capacity to undergo radical changes of condition (conjoining with body/separating from body, residing in a body/residing in Hades) and yet somehow to still be. Of course, this logic depends upon at least three features of the discussion that require further investigation, namely, the intertwining of soul's residence in place with the return assumed to be characteristic of genesis, the consequent characterization of life and death as functions of movement of soul, and the absence of any consideration of body and of erotic engagement in genesis. It is precisely to these difficulties that Socrates and his interlocutors turn in their second logos.

Anamnēsis

While the discussion of contraries exploits the cultural association between soul and life, this second logos exploits the association (also operative in Socrates's initial defense) between soul and thought; it does so by arguing that the phenomenon of learning, conceived famously as recollection, attests to the soul's kinship with Being. The heart of this argument consists in a description of recollection whose sheer ubiquity, Socrates hopes, will assure its persuasive power.

Socrates begins this account of recollection by characterizing it as part of a dual recognition: "Whenever somebody who's either seen or heard something—or has grasped it by some other sense—not only recognizes that thing but also takes note of another, the knowledge of which isn't the same but different, don't we justly say that he recollects that of which he grasped the notion?" (73c–d). Recollection, then, is dependent upon that meaningful relatedness between things that obtains when one thing can refer to another. That this reference is also dependent upon a certain distinction between things means that an exploration of reference will also involve an exploration of difference. Socrates emphasizes the difference between the two entities that are at stake here, as though the stability of difference that was won in the account of contrariety from the first logos is taken for granted here and extended not only to entities but to the knowledge of them. With such a stability assumed, Socrates and his interlocutors can inquire into the way in which different things are related to one another in order to produce recollection. Thus, what will come to be of primary importance in their conversation is the ability to demonstrate and analyze the conditions under which things come to be related to one another; because such relatedness also hinges upon difference, the conversation will also explore a variety of ways of differing. In the ensuing discussion, Socrates offers a series of examples of ways in which things are related to one another, a series whose progression we will follow in some detail.

The first kind of relation Socrates gives examples of marks a significant moment in the dialogue. That is, it finally broaches that mode of generation absent from consideration in the first logos: the erotic. Having gained Simmias's agreement that knowledge of a human being and of a lyre are different, Socrates observes: "Don't you know, then, that lovers, when they see a lyre or cloak or anything else that their boyfriend was in the habit of using, are affected in this way: They recognize [ἔγνωσάν] the lyre and they grasp in thought [καὶ ἐν τῇ διανοίᾳ ἔλαβον] the form of the boy whose lyre it was? And that's recollection. Just so, somebody who's seen Simmias often recollects Cebes. And there'd be a thousand such cases" (73d). Socrates's extension from the relation of beloved to lover to the relationship between Simmias and Cebes expands the relational principle at work in recollection from erotic engagements to more broadly philial engagements.[7] In both cases, however, we are dealing with human relationships and with the interconnectedness between people and things that is at play in human communities. The lyre provides an instance of recollection because the lyre is associated with the beloved; the lyre stands in for the beloved in that form of metonymy that so frequently accompanies erotic relations. The friendship between Simmias and Cebes that would make the presence of one an instance for calling the other to mind is treated in its strong similarity to the interconnectedness produced by eros, and is useful also because it exploits the difference between two people in order to illustrate the kind of difference that is operative here. In both cases one entity brings to mind another, different, entity and the context of their relation is the network of human community wherein friendships and erotic relationships are forged and dissolved.

The second set of examples of relatedness that enables recollection is one that complicates matters by adding a second conception of difference into the fray. Socrates asks: "Is it possible for somebody who's seen a sketched horse or a sketched lyre to recollect a human being, and who's seen Simmias sketched to recognize Cebes?" (73e). Certainly, the beloved is different from the sketch of his lyre just as Cebes is different from a sketch of Simmias; these examples add to the conversation the invocation of a difference not simply between independent objects (a lyre and a human being or Simmias and Cebes), but between an image and that of which it is an image (the lyre and a sketch of the lyre, for instance). The replacement in this series of examples of one entity by an image of that entity does not impede the resulting recollection: one thing is still called to mind by another thing different from it (the human being is still called to mind by the sketch of the lyre), although now this difference has taken on an added layer of meaning. That is, another model of difference has been placed before us, namely the difference that obtains between image and original. That Plato elsewhere treats this difference as of a significantly distinct order than the difference of independence, namely, as a difference in which there is some dependence involved (the image may enjoy a great deal of independence from its original, but its original is still somehow its source) should not distract from the fact that, in this passage, this difference is not something to which Socrates draws his interlocutors' attention; as it is presented here, recollection is indifferent to this shift in kind of difference.

While the second example maintains parallel modes of difference (the difference of independence and the difference of dependence), the third example focuses solely on the difference between image and original: "Then isn't it possible for somebody who's seen Simmias sketched to recollect Simmias himself?" (73e). Thus, the difference between persons gives way to a difference between image and original. This series of examples provides a progression from relation on the basis of erotic and philial engagement to relation on the basis of a kind of ontological dependence. While the need for this progression is not immediately obvious, the subsequent course of the conversation suggests that it is the final example that is most disclosive of soul's immortality: yet if the point was to arrive at it, why does Socrates bother with the examples that precede it?

Ostensibly, the purpose of the progression of examples that we have been outlining is to arrive at the agreement that recollection occurs regardless of whether the two entities at stake are similar or dissimilar, a fact to which Socrates calls attention on more than one occasion (73e, 74 c–d).[8] Socrates goes so far as to collapse the difference between similarity and dissimilarity (or at least strongly emphasizes that both are species of difference) by pointing out that the recognition that something is similar also requires one to acknowledge that in being similar (rather than the same) the thing falls short of that to which it is similar (74a). An acknowledgment of similarity is also an acknowledgment of difference; recollection can be said to occur regardless of the kind of relationship (similar or dissimilar) existing between the two entities.

However, more than recollection's indifference to similarity and dissimilarity is illustrated here. This progression also presents eros as one of the principles of interconnection upon which recollection depends. Socrates thus calls attention to the manner in which human community influences human understanding, and in so doing illustrates the erotic and philial underpinnings of humans' capacity for knowledge. Moreover, the progression of examples suggests a kinship between erotic connectivity and ontological connectivity that requires elaboration. Is there not an important difference between the connections asserted by eros and those asserted by the model of image/original? After all, the lyre is not a likeness of the beloved. In what sense, if at all, can the interconnection between things that are produced by human community be akin to the relationship between image and original? As we shall see, Socrates attempts to strengthen the suggested connection between these two kinds of relations by asserting a proto-erotic principle of striving at work in all things; it is the experience of striving that will be introduced as evidence of soul's immortality. Nevertheless, we should maintain some concern as to how seamlessly these two forms of relatedness can mesh.

Having outlined the general structure of recollection, Socrates turns to offer an example of it, one which he takes to be indicative of the soul's immortality. He begins by determining the distinct entities whose relationship will enable the recollection: "We claim [φαμέν], I suppose, that there's some 'equal.' I don't mean stick equal to stick or stone to stone or anything else like that, but something other [ἕτερόν τι], beyond [παρὰ] all these things—the Equal Itself. Shall we claim that this is something, or nothing at all?" (74a).[9] Once the difference between equal sticks and the Equal Itself has been asserted, they can turn to outlining an interaction between the two that is implied by our knowledge of both of them: "And we grasped the knowledge of [the Equal] from—where? Isn't it from the things we were talking about just now: We've seen sticks or stones or some other things that are equal, and from these we've noticed the Equal Itself, although it's other [ἕτερον] than these? Or doesn't it appear [φαίνεται] to you to be other?" (74b). Once Socrates and Simmias have guaranteed the alterity of the Equal (74c), they agree that when equal sticks call to mind the Equal Itself, recollection has indeed occurred (74d). The specific relation between equal sticks and the Equal Itself is such that equal sticks appear not only to be equals but to also be different from, and more importantly, to fall short of the Equal Itself. This particular experience of recollection, in which there is an acknowledgment that one thing somehow falls short of the thing it calls to mind, attests to the preexistence of soul because soul must have had some grasp in advance of the thing of which the original entity falls short.

However, before Socrates makes this move, he first grounds this conclusion in experience. Socrates asks: "Do we undergo some such thing as this concerning equals among sticks and the other equals we were talking about just now: Do they appear to us to be equals in just the same way as the Equal Itself, the Equal that is? Or do they fall somewhat short of being the sort of thing the Equal is—or not at all?" (74d). Once Simmias agrees that they do indeed fall short, Socrates maintains the inquiry on the level of experience, asking whether they can agree that whenever someone who has seen something notes, "What I'm now seeing wants [βούλεται] to be of the same sort as something else among the things that are; yet it falls short and isn't able to be that sort of thing but is inferior" (74d–e). They must agree that this person has seen beforehand that of which the initial entity falls short. Socrates is then very careful to ascertain the ubiquity of this experience with his interlocutors, asking, "Have we too undergone some such thing with respect to equals and the Equal Itself, or not?" (74e). Socrates thus illustrates that a certain commonality of experience conjoins him and his interlocutors, and it is their analysis of this experience, which they have agreed is shared, that produces the following further agreement: "Then it's necessary that we saw the Equal before that time when we first saw equals and noted: 'All these things are striving (ὀρέγεται) to be like the Equal [εἶναι οἷον τὸ ἴσον] but fall short of it'" (74e–75a).

Socrates's account of this particular species of recognition accomplishes at least three things. First, it grounds the "necessary" admission of some kind of grasp of Being in their experience by presenting this grasp as the only way of explaining an experience that they all agree to having. Second, it creates of Socrates and his interlocutors a community bound together by shared experience. Third, in characterizing this experience as one thing's striving to be something else (the alterity of which had been assured by their previous conversation), Socrates attributes to "things" an activity—a striving—that must be compared with the erotic engagement to which Socrates gestured at the start of the conversation. The verb ὀρέγω means principally "to reach, stretch, stretch out." In its middle and passive forms, it means "to stretch oneself out," and thus "to reach at or to a thing, to grasp at," from which it gains the more metaphorical sense of "to reach after, grasp at, yearn for."[10] The noun formed from this verb, ὄρεξις, is later used frequently by Aristotle to indicate desire and appetite. To attribute the verb ὀρέγω to two sticks is to attribute to them an extensional character, and to suggest that their relationship to that toward which they strive is fundamentally akin to the yearning and longing exhibited by a lover. In each instance an entity has stretched itself out to something that is different from it but yet somehow also gives meaning to it.

Moreover, in this account of the sticks' striving, Socrates develops the prioritization of contact and touch that we observed in his initial defense as a vehicle of transformation. The strangeness of this discussion is stressed when Socrates goes on to describe the sticks as "putting their hearts into [προθυμεῖται] being the sort of thing the Equal is but are inferior to it" (75b). Here Socrates attributes προθυμία, that very stance of eagerness which characterizes the appropriate way to take up a philosophic life, to sticks.[11] This attribution furthers the suggestion that there is in fact a deep kinship between human erotic engagement and the ontological status of all things. This notion of striving thus mediates between the erotic engagement that began the series of examples of recollection and the relationship between image and original that ended the series of examples. We noted previously a potential tension between these two modes of connection (the erotic and the image/original) that demanded some skepticism about whether the order put into place by eros would necessarily attest to or be an expression of the order whereby one thing acts as an image of the other. The attribution of a principle of striving to all things serves to connect these two forms of connection; striving mediates between erotic attachment and ontological attachment. The ground for asserting a similarity between the relation of lyre to beloved and of two sticks to the equal (or of their precursor in the series of examples, namely the sketch of Simmias and Simmias himself) is provided by the interposition of this principle of striving, whereby human erotic engagement emerges as one expression of a much broader phenomenon.[12]

Socrates takes care to refine their understanding of the interaction between the senses and the notion of the Equal Itself which must be operative in order to have this experience that is common to himself and his interlocutors. It is from nowhere but the senses that we attain the "notion" that the sticks they perceive both strive after and fall short of the Equal Itself (75a). Some grasp of the Equal Itself must thus have been had prior to the operation of the senses; this grasp is necessary, claims Socrates, "if we were ever to refer There the equals that came from our senses and to think that all such things are putting their heart into being the sort of thing the Equal is but are inferior to it" (75b). Socrates and Simmias spend some time discussing when this knowledge is attained and lost, and finally come to the agreement that it is attained prior to birth and lost at birth, such that whatever learning occurs in the course of one's life is precisely a retrieval or recollection of what one's soul grasped previously. Socrates then summarizes all that they have agreed upon about the particular species of recollection they have been analyzing in a passage that merits full citation:

> "If what we're forever babbling about is—some Beautiful as well as some Good [καλόν τε τι καὶ ἀγαθὸν] and all such Being—and if we refer [ἀναφέρομεν] to this Being everything that comes from the senses, since we've discovered that it was present before and was ours, and if we liken [ἀπεικάζομεν] the things of sense to that Being, then just as surely as these beings are, so also our soul is, even before we were born. And if they are not, then wouldn't this account we've given be beside the point? Is this our situation, and is there an equal necessity that these things be and that our souls were even before we were born, and if the former are not the latter were not?" (76d–e)

There are two things we need to note about this remarkable passage. First, the treatment the senses receive is significant: Socrates claims they are "referred" to being. The verb ἀναφέρω can mean both "a bringing or carrying up" and "a bringing or carrying back"; it signifies both an elevating and recovering, both an ascent and a homecoming.[13] In this passage, Socrates suggests that in the experience he and his interlocutors have been analyzing, the senses are both elevated and restored. In turn, Socrates's addition that the "things of the senses" are *likened* to being installs a poetic and fabricating action, an image making, in the heart of this experience.

Second, this passage returns to a consideration of the kinship between soul and Being. In the defense, this kinship was determined by the deployment of the ancient law "like to like." In this second logos, the preexistence of soul is tied to Being because nothing else, Socrates asserts, can explain the experience of noting that things strive toward something to which they are bound but which is other than them. In fact, this striving appears to offer an elaboration or reformulation and potential refinement of the "like to like" law asserted in the defense, such that because humans strive, as revealed in their erotic engagements with one another, they are capable of recognizing the striving of things. The striving of things, in turn, attests to the permanent and unchanging structure of Being. But we have also noted that recollection, or those instances of it that are predicated upon erotic attachments, implies an order and structure to human life, and we have wondered how this order stands with respect to the cosmic principle of striving. To reiterate the question: Is there any sense in which it can be said that the lyre is striving to be the beloved? It is with the introduction of the Good in this passage that Socrates tacitly broaches a response to this question. Insofar as both the beloved and the lyre are discussed in the light of an eros that imbues them with value, both are involved in an idealizing gesture. The lover's love of the beloved is bound up with lover's conception of what is good and worthy. The lyre is imbued with a certain meaning on the basis of its "participation" in a larger network formed by desire and human community. Can it be said that the beloved grants the lyre its meaning, just as the Equal Itself grants meaning to the sticks? If so, all would then be bound up in a striving toward the Good; human community would then be negotiated on the basis of this striving, as is the striving of all things. The gap we highlighted earlier between erotic and cosmic striving would be subsumed under the larger umbrella of the Good.

There are, however, remaining problems that plague this image of cosmic striving toward the Good, not the least of which is the contingency and fickleness of human erotic attachment. The attraction to a beloved seems fundamentally different than the striving of two sticks to be equal. Moreover, there is nothing as of yet that has suggested that an inquiry into human striving after the Good would necessarily overlap with an investigation of the good human community. At this juncture, all that we can say is that Plato seems keenly interested in including within the *Phaedo*'s exploration of soul's immortality a consideration of the possibility of accord between human institutions and the larger cosmic order of which such institutions are an uneasy part. This interest is displayed throughout the first two logoi. In the second logos it is attested to by the three dimensions of human community that Socrates illustrates: the erotic dimension alluded to in the first examples of interconnection between entities; the imagistic relationship that concludes the series of examples of relations that produce recollection; and finally, and perhaps most important, the relationship of common experience and opinion on which Socrates relies throughout the central portions of this discussion.

What, then, do we learn about the soul from this second logos and the phenomenon of recollection that it analyzes? First, soul's connection with thoughtfulness is again emphasized and elaborated upon by the connection between learning and recollection. Recollection provides an attestation to soul's plasticity, that is, it describes a transformation, but one which has the character of a return, a revolution, and a recovery rather than a voyaging out, a progression, or a discovery. Second, soul's capacity to recollect is also tied to the striving and extensional structure of the cosmos and the expression of this structure in human life through erotic and philial engagements. Insofar as this is the case, the study of soul also needs to involve the study of those erotic and philial engagements. The structure of human communities is thereby affirmed as a relevant object of study for psychology. We are beginning to see the intertwining of psychology and politics in addition to that between psychology and ontology which we noted earlier and which is also at work in the second logos. Third, the capacity to recognize that some one thing is striving to be something else demonstrates an experiential basis for asserting a kinship between soul and Being.

Finally, the logos's focus on the connection between things that eros can produce resonates with larger considerations about the order of things. The kind of order that is outlined here, proximity and distance to the loved object, sets up the determination of things on the basis of their nearness to one "determining" object and relationship, which seems to anticipate the logic of participation. However, Socrates's express indifference about the specific degrees of proximity and distance or the specific degrees of similarity and dissimilarity suggests that this particular logic is not the focus of the conversation. Socrates chooses instead to emphasize that recollection is predicated upon a certain interconnectedness of things. It is the principle or principles of connection that are at stake here, which further suggests the relevance of political considerations to a study of the soul.

Affinity

Throughout the discussion of recollection in the second logos we are invited to compare the fate of things to the fate of ideas, precisely because recollection involves a certain activity of comparing which we experience whenever we note that something has failed at that which it is striving to be. However, for Simmias, while such an experience suggests that being born is not coextensive with the coming to be of the soul, there is nothing in this account guaranteeing that death is not utter destruction: "For what keeps [the soul] from being born and being put together from somewhere or other and *being* before she arrives in a human body, and then, once she's arrived and is freed from the body, from reaching her end and being destroyed [τότε καὶ αὐτὴν τελευτᾶν καὶ διαφθείρεσθαι]?" (77b). Socrates initially attempts to respond to this objection by tying the phenomenon of recollection and the realm of changeless eternal being to the realm of becoming and its operation of ceaseless circular motion (77c–e).

Eventually he abandons this course and adopts a third logos about the immortality of the soul, but not before Plato includes an interlude that reminds his readers of the very community, with its curious dynamic, in which this entire conversation is taking place. This reminder emphasizes the second logos's identification of human community as a source of connection capable of giving rise to recollection. In objecting to the thoroughness of the second logos, Cebes and Simmias playfully admit to a certain childish fear, namely that the soul is blown away and scattered at death. Cebes goes on to ask Socrates to persuade the child within all of those present that death is not to be feared. Socrates's response—that they should "sing him incantations each day until you sing away his fears" (77e)—offers an apparent elision of persuasion about the soul with a mystical and therapeutic act and prompts Cebes to ask where they will find such a singer, since Socrates is abandoning them (78a). Socrates's response to Cebes presents the possibility of a community that refigures military conquest and colonization as intellectual odyssey, recruitment, and introspection: "There's a lot of Greece. I suppose there are good men in it—and there are many races of foreigners too. You must ransack them all in search of such a singer, sparing neither money nor toil, since there isn't anything more necessary on which you might spend your money. And you must search for him in company with one another, too, for perhaps you wouldn't easily find anyone more able to do this than yourselves" (78a). This episode reminds the reader that Socrates is dealing with the specific set of opinions, thoughts, and fears that his interlocutors bring to the table, and that Plato presents his responses as shaped by a desire to speak to these specificities. The engagement with his interlocutors is an engagement with one version of human community, and, as the conversation continues, where the philosopher fits into this community will become an increasingly important focus.

Socrates begins the third logos with an investigation of the kind of thing that undergoes "scattering." According to Socrates, "scattering" is a fate undergone by things have been composed (συντεθέντι, 78c), as such things are subject to change and alteration. What is noncomposite does not suffer change, alteration, or "scattering." The fear that the soul is scattered at death relies upon a construction of death as the decomposition or dissolution of a composite entity. Socrates then attempts, infamously, to systematically distinguish between what is composite and what is noncomposite along the lines of what is visible and what is invisible, and thereby to assert the body's affinity with what is visible (79a–b) and the soul's affinity with what is invisible, on the basis of its capacity for reckoning (λογισμῷ) (79a). Thus, in order to contend with Simmias's and Cebes's suggestion that the soul disperses and scatters (διαφυσᾷ καὶ διασκεδάννυσιν) (77d–e) when separated from the body, Socrates must turn to deal explicitly with the distinction between soul and body that has until now driven their discussion of death without itself being examined. As the conversation continues, soul and body are distinguished along the following lines: soul is most akin to what is divine, deathless, intelligible, single-formed, indissoluble and always keeps to the selfsame condition. Body is most akin to what is human, death-bound, many-formed, unintelligible, dissoluble, and never keeps to the selfsame condition (80b).[14] Given the distinction between body and soul along these lines, Socrates concludes, "Well then, since this is how things stand, isn't body apt to be dissolved [διαλύεσθαι] quickly and soul in turn apt to be altogether indissoluble [ἀδιαλύτῳ], or something close to this?" (80b).

This is an enormously fruitful and problematic passage and there is much that has been and should continue to be said about it. I would like to focus upon the effect that this construction of death as dissolution has for any logos about the soul. If death is an activity whose paradigmatic agent is the body, and soul is distinct from body in the way that visible is distinct from invisible, then the vocabulary that is best suited to account for the soul is not a vocabulary of what is bodily and mortal,[15] but a vocabulary of what is eternal and formal. Were the distinction between soul and body to be all that Socrates gives an account of in this third logos, we would be left with the assertion that the soul is best understood by and through a logos of forms.[16]

However, and this is of utmost importance, this is *not* all that Socrates offers in the third logos. In addition to *distinguishing* between soul and body, Socrates's third logos gives an account of the *exchange* between the two. In fact, when Socrates turns to describe the various means of investigation that are available to the soul (79c-d), he reveals the inadequacy of the logos of forms to provide an account of the soul. Soul and body are not so different as to be incapable of affecting one another.[17] While the soul's capacity to grasp what is eternal and changeless aligns soul with what is divine and deathless, the soul's capacity to investigate by means of the senses aligns soul with what is bodily and mortal. Moreover, the soul must exert some effort in order not to be affected by the body. If the soul fails to exert this effort and instead throws its concern into the body, the soul itself will cease to be as distinct from the body as it could be. The soul itself will become body-like (σωματοειδής) (81c). Thus, the distinction between body and soul is not a distinction that is given to the two in completeness; rather, it is a distinction that requires some degree of action and whose fullest expression requires effort. The soul's ability to learn, to be educated and nurtured, asserts both its potential simplicity and its frequent complexity. What we gather from Socrates's account of the soul's relationship to the body is a further refinement of the sense of the soul's plasticity; this plasticity begs comparison with the body and will stand in irreducible tension with assertions of the soul's deathlessness until the variety of conditions of the soul are handled at length.[18] Consequently, Socrates and his interlocutors are in need of a means to distinguish between conditions of soul with some degree of sophistication.[19]

The soul's capacity to become body-like leads to a proliferation of psychic conditions and presents to the would-be psychologist the task of discerning and describing them. In elucidating the varieties of psychic states, Socrates begins with the distinction between philosophic souls and bodily souls (invoking the lover of learning and the true philosopher introduced in Socrates's defense) by illustrating their difference as a divergence of their fates. According to Socrates, while all soul is most akin to what is invisible and deathless and to all of the attributes agreed upon earlier in the conversation, it is only the philosopher's soul that has had this kinship fully realized. The exemplarity of the philosophic soul is illustrated in the third logos by an account of the fate that this soul can expect once it is separated from the body. This fate is first introduced as a journey to a region that corresponds to the soul, a region that Socrates describes as noble, pure, and unseen (80d), as that of the true Hades (the good and thoughtful god [80d]), and as divine, deathless, and thoughtful (81a). The journey of the philosophic soul, because it is pure, is unproblematic; this soul resides in its corresponding region, happy and in the company of gods (81a). In fact, Socrates will go on to tell us, it is the soul of the lover of learning that is allowed to enter into the class of the gods; it is not lawful for any other soul to do so (82c).[20]

Those unfortunate souls who attempt to go off to their appropriate region without the purification attained by the philosopher—those souls that Socrates collectively refers to as souls that have cared for, loved, and intermingled with the body beyond what was necessary—have a significantly more difficult time. For one, they do not accomplish separation from body with ease. According to Socrates, such a soul is released from body

> "defiled and impure [μεμιασμένη καὶ ἀκάθαρτος], because she was always having intercourse with the body and servicing it and loving it and being bewitched by it [ἅτε τῷ σώματι ἀεὶ συνοῦσα καὶ τοῦτο θεραπεύουσα καὶ ἐρῶσα καὶ γοητευμένη] and its desires and pleasures to the point that nothing else seemed true to her but what's body-like [τὸ σωματοειδές] (which one can touch and see and drink and eat and use for the pleasures of love-making), and because she was in the habit of hating and trembling at and fleeing what's shadowy to the eyes and unseen but is intelligible and seized on by philosophy [τὸ δὲ τοῖς ὄμμασι σκοτῶδες καὶ ἀιδές, νοητὸν δὲ καὶ φιλοσοφίᾳ αἱρετόν]." (81b)

These souls are "pervaded [διειλημμένην] by the body-like [ὑπὸ τοῦ σωματοειδοῦς], which the company and intercourse [ἡ ὁμιλία τε καὶ συνουσία] with the body have made grow together [ἐνεποίησε σύμφυτον] with her because the soul was always with the body and gave it lots of care" (81c). The body-like by which this soul has been filled is described as "oppressive and heavy and earthy and visible" (81d). Both because of their love for the body and because this love has made them more like the body, such souls are unwilling to leave their bodies behind for fear of the region to which they are traveling, opting instead to remain by their graves, mournful and fearful, made visible by their communion with the visible. Such a soul "is made heavy and dragged back [καὶ ἕλκεται πάλιν] into the visible region through terror of the Unseen and of Hades and, as they say [ὥσπερ λέγεται], circulates among the memorials and tombs, around which certain shadowy apparitions of souls have been seen, ghostly images produced by the sort of souls that weren't released in purity but participate in the Visible [ἀλλὰ τοῦ ὁρατοῦ μετέχουσαι]—which is why they too are visible" (81c–d). The dense texture of this description provides crucial detail for enriching the reader's conception of the complex relationship between soul and body that is at work in this dialogue. Socrates casts this relationship in a strongly erotic light—the soul is personified as a lover of the body, serving it, having intercourse with it, being enchanted by it. The sexual language that Socrates employs here elaborates upon the powerful effects on soul's conditions wrought by the tenor of its relation to body, a relation in which the soul is deeply implicated. This implicating function is also at work in the care that the soul gives the body. Care, like erotic love, is a relationship of intimacy, a relationship in which both entities are transformed by their contact with one another. Thus, the soul's erotic and nurturing relationship to body elaborates upon the context of exchange and communication that was first broached in the defense as the soul's capacity for touch. This relationship also further illustrates the mechanism by means of which soul is polluted in its dealings with body. The effects of the soul's intimacy with body, the vehicles or symptoms of its pollution, are many: in loving the body, the soul is enchanted by the body's pleasures and pains—which deceive soul about what constitutes the true—habituates itself to a fear of what is unseen, grows together with the body, and is even made visible by its participation with the visible. The rendering visible of souls into ghost-like shades that haunt graveyards and circulate around the graves, mournful and fearful, is a particularly gripping image of this soul's degraded condition, one that will eventually be figured in the soul's taking on a new body. Socrates's emphasis on the manner in which one's erotic and nurturing investments render one more like that in which one is invested provides an elaboration of the "like to like" law deployed in the defense.

However, soul's capacity to become like body implies certain things about body as well, and while these implications are not drawn out explicitly by Socrates, they can be read in the very language that Socrates employs in order to speak of a soul made body-like. The word translated variously as bodily or body-like, σωματοειδής, is formed by using εἶδος as a suffix; this is a grammatical structure that was found, prior to Aristotle, mainly in medical texts in which it was used to indicate that the shape or character of an organ was x-like.[21] The comparing and classifying function of this formation is clearly appropriate to the third logos insofar as this is a logos about affinity and kinship. However, this construction also confers a certain degree of selfsameness and coherence to the body that is at odds with the complaints against the body lodged in Socrates's defense.[22] What this construction suggests is a kind of order to body that makes communication between it and soul possible. Bodies themselves have a certain intelligibility, earthy and shadowy though it may be. Indeed, this construction asserts that the bodily is not simply subsumed within the visible; it thereby posits the bodily as a third category between the visible and the intelligible. Thus, the apparent elision between body and the visible that Socrates makes in this logos is rendered problematic by the very language he must deploy in accounting for the body-like soul. This is perhaps why Socrates and his interlocutors characterize their speech at this juncture in the conversation as "likely," as of the order of the eikos, the image (81d). This image making imparts a certain formal, eidetic character to that of which it is an image. Thus, the bodily emerges as a kind of poetic conceit, an image making, but one whose necessity for accounting for certain psychic phenomena requires the psychologist to wrestle with its metaphysical implications for the status of the body. As we shall see, Plato calls attention to these implications as the conversation ensues.

Socrates is careful to fill out this sketch of the body-loving, body-like soul with an assessment that centers upon the actions which correspond to it:

> "And it's not at all likely that these are the souls of the good—they're the souls of the inferior, souls compelled to wander [πλανᾶσθαι] around such places paying the penalty for their former way of life, which was bad [δίκην τίνουσαι τῆς προτέρας τροφῆς κακῆς οὔσης]. And they wander about [πλανῶνται] until, through the desire for the body-like that stalks them [ἕως ἂν τῇ τοῦ συνεπακολουθοῦντος τοῦ σωματοειδοῦς ἐπιθυμίᾳ], they're again entangled in a body [ἐνδεθῶσιν εἰς σῶμα]. And as is likely [ὥσπερ εἰκός], they're entangled in whatever sort of characters they happen to have made their care in life [εἰς τοιαῦτα ἤθη ὁποῖ' ἄττ' ἂν καὶ μεμελετηκυῖαι τύχωσιν ἐν τῷ βίῳ]." (81d–e)

Socrates's emphasis on action, as well as his invocation of punishment for a way of life, call attention to the mutually determining relationship between action and condition of soul. Moreover, his assessment of the inferiority of these souls illustrates the manner in which the particular plasticity of soul grants a certain limitlessness to it.[23] Because the soul admits of inferior and corrupt conditions, but is not utterly destroyed by them, the soul presents the possibility of unending corruption. This passage thus also reminds readers that the account of the body-like soul is in part given in order to illustrate the need to care for one's soul. The fate of such souls involves not only a difficult death and wandering in search of their proper abode but also an eventual reentanglement in bodies. Thus, the suffering of the bodily soul is expressed by the manner of its separation from body, by the region in which it resides for a time, and by the body it comes to animate. Region and living being serve as means of characterizing the condition of these souls;[24] they correspond to soul, as Socrates emphasizes, and are appropriate to them.

The examples that Socrates gives of the correspondence between condition of soul and kind of body again stress the sorts of cares and the kinds of actions in which the person was engaged while living. Gluttons become donkeys, tyrants become wolves and falcons, orderly people without the benefit of philosophy become bees and ants, and perhaps even moderate humans again (81e–82b). Alternatively, "those who care for their own souls but don't live to serve the body, bid farewell to all these people and don't make the same journey as they do, since these others don't know where they're going [ὡς οὐκ εἰδόσιν ὅπῃ ἔρχονται]" (82d).[25]

Socrates describes in some detail how a love for the body accomplishes these transformations of soul and how philosophy can liberate one from them, returning to the language of coalescence and diffusion he employed in his defense. It is the lovers of learning who recognize that philosophy takes over a soul that is "utterly bound within the body and glued to it [ἀτεχνῶς διαδεδεμένην ἐν τῷ σώματι καὶ προσκεκολλημένην], and she's compelled to investigate the things that are through it as through a cage rather than herself through herself, and she wallows in every sort of ignorance [καὶ ἐν πάσῃ ἀμαθίᾳ κυλινδουμένην]" (82e). This passage marks a return of the conception that knowledge of Being can be accomplished through knowledge of soul if one possesses the coalesced soul of the lover of learning, while such knowledge is impossible to attain through the senses, although how such a soul could become an object for itself remains at this juncture undetermined.[26] Socrates also reserves a vital rhetorical activity for philosophy: the lovers of learning recognize that philosophy operates by gently persuading the soul to retreat from investigating by means of the senses and by attempting to release the soul.[27] Moreover, "philosophy exhorts [παρακελευομένη] her to gather and collect herself into herself and to trust in nothing but herself and what she perceives herself all by herself of what's itself all by itself among the things that are, and to regard nothing else as true that she investigates through anything that's different from herself and differs under differing conditions" (83a–b). Thus, the senses are incapable of giving a stable account of being because the senses themselves are radically unstable; variant and varying, they are not suited to grasp what is selfsame and invariant.

The deceptive character of the senses accounts for one of the dangers that the body poses to the soul. Another danger, which Socrates describes as the greatest evil (83c), is a function of an effect of pleasure and pain: "every human being's soul is compelled, at the very moment she's violently pleased or pained at something, to regard what above all brought about her suffering as both most manifest and most true [τοῦτο ἐναργέστατόν τε εἶναι καὶ ἀληθέστατον]—although this isn't the case" (83c).[28] It is, in fact, the experience of violent pleasure or pain that most binds soul to body (83d). Socrates elaborates on the mechanism of this binding:

> "Because each pleasure and pain—as if it had a nail [ὥσπερ ἧλον]—nails [προσηλοῖ] the soul to the body, pins [προσπερονᾷ] her and makes her body-like [καὶ ποιεῖ σωματοειδῆ], so she opines to be true exactly whatever things the body says are true. For as a result of her having similar opinions with the body and delighting in the same things, I imagine that the soul is compelled to become similar in ways and similar in nurture [ἐκ γὰρ τοῦ ὁμοδοξεῖν τῷ σώματι καὶ τοῖς αὐτοῖς χαίρειν ἀναγκάζεται οἶμαι ὁμότροπός τε καὶ ὁμότροφος γίγνεσθαι] so as never to arrive in Hades pure; instead, she always leaves full of [ἀναπλέα] the body, so that she tends to fall [πίπτειν] quickly again into another body and takes root [ἐμφύεσθαι] there as if she had been sown [ὥσπερ σπειρομένη]. And as a result of this, she has no share of intercourse with the divine and pure and single-formed." (83d–e)

Thus, while the senses deceive because they are variant, pleasure and pain deceive on a more fundamental level; they skew and disfigure the soul's capacity to determine what is true, evident, and valuable. Pleasure and pain deceive soul about Being, thereby damaging soul's ontological investigation by impeding its capacity to recognize what is truest and most manifest. Moreover, they complete the soul's becoming body-like by manipulating soul into holding body-like evaluations of things. Pleasure and pain make the soul hold the same opinions as the body and delight in the same things as the body; they habituate the soul to the body such that soul becomes similar in temperament and in nurture. The personification of both soul and body is particularly striking in this passage; throughout the discussion one gets the sense that Socrates is talking about two different human beings, one of whom is being made to be like the other through the particular structure of their community together, rather than two entities that make up the single living being.[29] How else could it be said, within the confines of this dialogue, that body evaluates and opines? This personification serves to underscore the point that what is really at stake throughout this discussion is two courses or manners of life, body-loving and wisdom-loving.

At the same time, Socrates's sliding between technical and agricultural metaphors, the ease with which he moves from images of carpentry to images of farming, furthers the sense of the body-like soul's absolute estrangement, on both human and natural levels, from itself. The body-loving soul is a conflicted soul. Finally, we should note the sliding between soul's journey in Hades and soul's eventual reembodiment, as if these were two approaches to, two tropes of, the same phenomenon.

Socrates concludes the third logos with a final juxtaposition of the philosopher's soul with the bodily soul, a juxtaposition which returns to the theme of soul's residence. A philosophic man's soul

> "wouldn't think that philosophy should release her and that, once released, she should of herself give herself over to pleasures and pains and tie herself down again [πάλιν αὖ ἐγκαταδεῖν] to the body and engage in the unfinishable task of a Penelope unweaving the web she's woven. No, instead his soul provides a calm sea untroubled by these things, follows reasoning and always abides in it [ἑπομένη τῷ λογισμῷ καὶ ἀεὶ ἐν τούτῳ οὖσα], and beholds the true and the divine and the not-to-be-opined and is nurtured by what she sees. That's how she thinks she must live [ζῆν] while she's alive [ἕως ἂν ζῇ] and how, when she meets her end, she'll arrive at what's akin to her and of her sort and be freed from human evils [εἰς τὸ ξυγγενὲς καὶ εἰς τὸ τοιοῦτον ἀφικομένη ἀπηλλάχθαι τῶν ἀνθρωπίνων κακῶν]. And because her nurture [τροφῆς] has been of this sort, and since she has devoted herself to these things, there's no danger at all of her being terrified, Simmias and Cebes, that at the moment of her getting free of the body, she'll go off scattered and, all aflutter, be blown away by the winds and no longer be anywhere at all." (84a-b)

Socrates's emphasis on the soul's nurture reminds us that the soul is in need of some process, some transformation, if it is to be itself. Socrates's description of the soul as following and being in reason suggests that the perfection of soul's condition does not exempt it from residence, but rather makes for a dwelling that most secures its flourishing. On this front, note too the depiction of soul's "end" as an arrival at what is akin to her. Finally, the soul is freed from danger not because of the nature of the soul but because of the kind of nurture and devotion it possesses, the kind of "life" this soul has lived. Thus Socrates returns to the issue of how to lead one's life and connects manner of life with soul's purification.

The possibility of exchange between soul and body adds a dimension of complexity to the soul that problematizes the associations that Socrates and his interlocutors have employed thus far in speaking about the soul. In fact, the enigma of the body-like soul so challenges their capacity to conceive of soul as to cause a crisis of reference and to necessitate the flurry of images in this account, images mined from multiple cultural sources. This crisis of reference circulates around a growing aporia about living being and the bodily. Because a soul can become body-like, certain souls can be more or less adequately accounted for by the same vocabulary that is used to describe bodily conditions. At the same time, the soul's capacity to grasp what is eternal and changeless, as evinced by the phenomenon of recollection, defies simple and uncritical reduction to the bodily. Consequently, no matter how precise or subtle their vocabulary of the body is, Socrates and his interlocutors are still in need of a vocabulary for conditions of the soul that are not reducible to those of the body. Thus, while some souls can be meaningfully referred to as hungry or thirsty even after they have been separated from the body, the agreement Socrates and his interlocutors make about the capacities of soul forces them to acknowledge the limit of the adequacy of words like "hungry" and "thirsty" in describing the soul. They must concede that hunger and thirst will always carry a certain metaphorical haze to them when applied to the soul. Thus, neither a bodily vocabulary nor a vocabulary of forms is sufficient to account for the variety of conditions to which a soul is subject. A study of soul is marked out here as requiring its own vocabulary, one which is capable of drawing subtle distinctions between psychic conditions. Specifically, the tension between the soul's capacity to recollect forms and its complexity, especially as expressed by the variety of its corrupt forms, gives rise to a need for an account of viciousness.

Socrates vividly illustrates the varieties of the soul's corrupt conditions by a number of traditional stories about the fates a soul can suffer as and after it dies.[30] As we have observed, Socrates's account of the possibilities of exchange between soul and body is infused with the language of myth. Here he speaks of souls infected with the heavy and earthy (γεῶδες) body (81c-d) and thus incapable of having a genuine death (80d-e). Unable to overcome their fear of the invisible, such souls are stalked instead by a heavy and brooding love for the bodily (τοῦ σωματοειδοῦς ἐπιθυμίᾳ) (81d-e). Uneasy, unquiet, eventually rendered visible by this love for what is visible and by their fear for what is invisible, these souls can be seen haunting the memorials for the dead (81c-d). So alienated are they from Hades that eventually they find their way into bodies again, bodies corresponding to their various loves (82a-b). Socrates's commitment to demonstrate to his companions the importance of care for the soul finds a persuasive ally in this combination of Homeric and Pythagorean traditions. By means of this fusion of mythic images, the variety of living things affords Socrates a way of accounting for a variety of conditions of soul. This proliferation of animals offers a taxonomy of souls, and serves an ethical ordering demanded by the acknowledgment of exchange between body and soul.

Thus, Socrates uses animality in the context of transmigration as one means of providing a vocabulary for virtue and viciousness. However, how this language measures up to the demand to give an account of the soul that is reducible neither to the bodily nor to the formal needs to be determined. At this juncture in the dialogue, "living being" is even less clearly accounted for than the bodily or the eidetic; consequently, its capacity to provide an alternate description of the soul has yet to be demonstrated. Without a robust account of living being that includes a clear indication of the status of the living body with respect to the bodily, this "ethical zoology" is particularly difficult to distinguish from a bodily vocabulary. The study of the soul, Socrates seems to be saying, must thus include a study of the full range of living beings. Because in the *Phaedo* the primary ethical distinction between virtue and vice is founded upon the nature of the soul's relation to the body, the mapping of virtue and vice onto varieties of living things only underscores the need for an account of the living body. In the absence of such an account, the alignment between mortality and the bodily that was forged early on in the third logos remains deeply ambiguous and the status of the application of bodily vocabularies to the soul as figurative or metaphorical in character remains uncertain.[31]

What should not escape notice is that Socrates's use of mythic images highlights this ambiguity and absence, rather than covers them over. Socrates deploys the themes of residence in Hades and transmigration to illustrate the exchange between body and soul. While these themes aid the suggestion that one must care for one's soul, they nonetheless interfere with a neat distinction between body and soul that would indicate easily the deathlessness of the soul on the basis of its difference from the body. Thus, in the third logos there emerges a tension between the mythic language Socrates uses to describe the exchange between body and soul and the associations used to demonstrate the deathlessness of the soul. This tension calls for an account of living being that remains unanswered in the third logos and echoes into the fourth. By the end of the third logos, much of what we learn is aporetic. The soul's capacity to become body-like, along with its associations both with life and thought, requires a robust consideration of the status of the body-like and with how living beings (embodied and ensouled) stand with respect to it. This is to say, an account of the soul requires an account of life for which sufficient terms have not yet been found. Nor have sufficient means for accounting for soul's conditions been arrived at, although we see Plato's attempt to appropriate existing vocabularies and traditions (transmigration and various fates/places in Hades) in order to do so. Thus, while the concern for how to live one's life that is displayed in the defense is transposed onto the afterlife and becomes a concern with the fate of the soul after one's death, the fundamental question about the nature of living being remains. By the end of the third logos it is clear that Socrates and his interlocutors need to return to a consideration of an association explored in the first logos, namely that between soul and life.

By way of summary, many of the themes introduced in Socrates's defense receive further elaboration in the third logos. The soul's plasticity is detailed in the juxtaposition of soul's kinship with being, on the one hand, and its kinship with, or capacity to become like, the body, on the other hand. These dual kinships are schematized into two main conditions of soul, philosophic and body-like. Doing so allows Socrates to translate the tension presented in the defense between philosophers and lovers of the body into a tension between two conditions of soul. We also gain a clearer sense for the manner in which the body impedes the soul's attainment of thoughtfulness: by deceiving the soul about what constitutes being, truth and clarity (83c).

As Socrates elaborates upon the conditions and fates of philosophic and body-like souls, it becomes clear that the possibility of a bodily soul introduces myriad conditions of soul. Indeed, a release from transformation, and thus from variance, is one of the things philosophic souls win.[32] Two registers emerge for describing this plethora of conditions: living being and place. The fates of these souls, their entering into a specific kind of body, and their going to specific places prior to their embodiment, provide a visible index of the condition of soul. Living beings are animate illustrations of conditions of soul; places are geographic illustrations of conditions of soul. This rhetorical strategy illuminates the relationship between place, action, manner of life, and condition of soul. We see this relationship highlighted, for instance, in Socrates's emphases that souls are entangled in the characters they happen to have made their care (81e) and that souls go to places that correspond to them (80d).

By reintroducing the trope of punishment (which is elided with purification) into the conversation, this strategy also provides a persuasive illustration of the need to care for the soul. The body-like soul poses one of the most fundamental aporiai attendant upon an investigation of soul; namely, its dual immortality and complexity, which, because all of the various conditions of soul this complexity entails, implies the soul's corruptibility. This dual nature of soul resolves certain epistemological and ethical conundrums, but produces a metaphysical perplexity. The disconcerting examples of the endurance of injustice, the uncanny capacity of unjust action to remain efficacious in the world well beyond the life of the "agent" of such action, are reminders of this enigma by which, judging from the frequency and centrality of such examples in the dialogues, Plato was deeply impressed. Neither limited nor without corruption, soul presents the enigma of deathless specificity, immortal situatedness, eternal regionality.

Plato's engagement with this aporia at this juncture in the *Phaedo*, namely, through his investigation of the enigma of the body-like soul, opens up the aporia in a manner that sharply illustrates its profound significance for human life: such an entity exposes human life to the possibility of a corruption without internal limit. To look a bit further ahead, one result of this investigation is an illustration of the relationship between place, action, and condition of soul in such a manner that emphasizes both the need human flourishing has for community as well as the dangers and impediments to human flourishing that certain forms of human community can offer. One effect of the way that Plato takes up the enigma of the body-like soul (that is, his use of a variety of mythic tropes) is the illustration of the need humans have of this community, and thus the vital significance an investigation of political life has for human flourishing. Such a focus poses the questions of what kinds of human community foster the flourishing of soul and vice versa. It also broaches the role of law, myth, and punishment as limits to the limitless corruption that soul introduces into human political life. Indeed, the very persuasiveness that the myths about the fates to which souls are subject have with respect to exhorting people to care for their souls calls attention to the efficacy and strength of such tales, the power they have to manipulate human action. At the same time, the crisis of terms that is so sharply illustrated by this third logos not only discloses something of the impediments to psychology, as Plato has conceived it, but also reveals the tentative nature of these speeches. It is not without significance that in the next leg of the conversation it is to the vulnerability of speech that Socrates turns.

Interlude

After Socrates has delivered his third logos about the soul's immortality there is silence for a time, as many of his companions bask in the glow of the persuasive power of this account. But soon, Simmias and Cebes are overheard whispering, and when they are finally coaxed into sharing their conversation, each delivers an objection to this third logos. The effect of these objections is sufficiently powerful as to merit emphasis, which Plato accomplished by duplicating the effect on Socrates's interlocutors in Phaedo's listener Echecrates. As Phaedo tells it, he and his companions were struck with worry that either they themselves, who had been so compelled by Socrates's third logos, were poor judges of argument, or that, more frightening still, "these matters themselves might even be beyond trust" (88c). And as Echecrates tells Phaedo, he himself was wondering, "What argument will we trust from now on?" (88d). Socrates begins to address this crisis of trust by reorienting their approach to the logoi that produced it. Gathering Phaedo's hair in his hands, and noting the custom of cutting one's hair at the death of a loved one, he exhorts Phaedo to consider only the demise of the logos as worthy of such a gesture. Socrates himself would be willing to share in this custom, "if our argument meets its end [τελευτήσῃ] and we can't bring it back to life [ἀναβιώσασθαι]" (89b). In order to do so, they must guard against the danger of misology. Socrates's subsequent comparison of misology to misanthropy—both occur as a response to the betrayal of trust, but misology is worse than misanthropy—suggests that the quality of one's life and the lives of those around one depends upon comporting oneself toward logos in a certain way. The danger of misology consists in arriving at the conclusion that there is no such thing as a logos worthy of one's trust. This is the case not only for logos, but for all things, such that nothing is sufficiently stable to merit one's trust and all things are as much their opposite as themselves. The person drawing this conclusion would be enormously disadvantaged if it were the case that there were a logos that merits one's trust and if there were things that truly were themselves. In order to avoid being robbed of this possibility, Socrates states that they must avoid the hatred of arguments at all costs. When they encounter an impasse that calls into question the trust they have placed in a logos, they should, rather than deciding that the logos itself is unsound, "admit that we're not yet sound but must act like men and put our hearts into being sound [καὶ προθυμητέον ὑγιῶς ἔχειν]" (90e–91a). What is required in order to avoid the dangers of misology is an acknowledgment of one's limits and, most importantly, the adoption of a spirited comportment, a zeal, toward correcting one's confusion. The resuscitation of logos, the avoidance of that event about which it would be most appropriate to mourn, comes about by means of adopting a spirited stance toward one's confusion. One must venture the possibility that one does not know what death is. Thus, the life of the logos is contingent upon the soundness or health of those who would take logos up, just as previously the condition of the interlocutors had been contingent upon the status of the logos. Logos and person are mutually implicated and bound to one another in this conversation. Both are at stake in one another. A concern for the logos is not distinct from a concern for the condition of oneself and one's friends.[33] Thus, to allow the logos to pass away, in both the immediate sense of the logos concerning the immortality of the soul and the more radical sense of a disavowal of logos as such, is to ignore one's own unhealthy condition. It is with this discussion in mind that Socrates eventually turns to offer a fourth account of the immortality of the soul.

Causality

This fourth logos evolves out of Simmias's and Cebes's objections to the third. Rather than work through the fine points of each objection, I will simply note here that both supply an alternate conception of the relation between soul and body to those suggested in the third logos. More specifically, both present an alternative image of a body-like soul that Socrates will reject. Accordingly, Socrates's replies to Simmias and Cebes will focus upon the relationship between soul and body that each objection supplies. Much of the fourth logos involves showing that each objection either denies or fails to account for some quality or condition of soul that the objector would want to maintain.

With respect to Simmias's assertion that the soul is a harmony of bodily elements, Socrates demonstrates that conceiving of the soul as a tuning or harmony fails to account for two qualities that Simmias would want to attribute to the soul: that it can be disposed to be contrary to the body in which it finds itself and that there are differences between souls as regards their virtue (93a–c). Thus, in replying to Simmias's objection, Socrates points once again to the need for as sophisticated a vocabulary concerning virtue and vice as possible. This need is made even more pressing in his reply to Cebes.

In order to respond to Cebes's concern that the soul, while more noble and more enduring than the body, is not sufficiently distinct from the body as to escape the dissolution that is synonymous with bodily demise, Socrates takes a famously circumspect route. It is in the course of his response to this concern that Socrates feels compelled to offer an extended account of his own intellectual history, wherein he describes how he came to philosophy and to that movement he takes to be definitive of his thought: taking refuge in logos (95e–102a). Throughout his account of his own intellectual history, Socrates emphasizes the loss of certain ways of speaking, a loss that accompanies philosophical reflection. For instance, upon closer consideration of his own understanding of causes, he loses the ability to speak of cause as a function of material elements and the processes they undergo (96c–97a). In fact, he loses the ability to speak of causes at all for a time (97b), until he regains some of that capacity in his hypothesis of form and participation (100b–d). And even here, as he regains a certain surety of speech, it is a poverty-stricken vocabulary to which he is returned, a fact upon which he explicitly remarks and remedies later on in his discussion with Cebes (100c–d, 105b–c).

With respect to Socrates's hypothesis of participation, what Socrates gains in certainty, he loses in phenomenal resonance—what his words gain in surety, they lose in sophistication. However, Socrates himself is dissatisfied with this trade-off and seeks some means to regain the variety and sophistication of vocabulary he had once possessed (he seeks to regain the phenomenal world).[34] Moreover, this dissatisfaction is not simply a function of some kind of idiosyncrasy, philosophical or otherwise, on the part of Socrates. This dissatisfaction is born from an acknowledgment that the main object of inquiry here, the soul and its relation to death, cannot be sufficiently accounted for by the vocabulary of forms and ideas. The paucity of terms available to Socrates when he keeps most simply to his hypothesis of participation is inadequate to the task, as he himself demonstrates when he embraces a more sophisticated means of speaking about those things that bring contraries to bear (105b–c). Thus, some way of regaining a rich and complex vocabulary, one that at the same time does not violate his initial hypothesis, must be found. His means of doing so is to refine his understanding of the relationship between contraries and things, an act that will require the introduction of a mediator between forms and things: shape (μορφή).

Socrates takes up this task in the following manner. Socrates and Cebes agree that in addition to contraries like Bigness and Smallness, Hot and Cold, there also exist things that have contraries (103b), or that always bring the contrary to bear when they occur. These things are named by means of the contraries that come to be in them (103b–c).[35] For instance, some thing is called hot when the contrary of the Hot comes to be in it. As the contrary will never come to be its contrary (the idea of the Hot will never come to be the idea of the Cold [103c]), so will the thing in which the contrary comes to be never be able to come to be the other contrary (the hot thing cannot become cold and still be itself). The hot thing will perish rather than admit into itself the contrary of that contrary which has given it its name.[36] It is in such a manner that the hot thing brings the contrary of the Hot to bear. As Socrates suggests, were we to wish to refine our vocabulary a bit, we might come up with a name for this hot thing, perhaps, "fire," and know that with this name we are naming a coming to be of a contrary in a thing.

In fact, given the relationship between contraries and things that Socrates is developing, he and Cebes are in great need to come up with some means of referring to things in a manner that characterizes the thing as a coming to be of a contrary without creating the possibility of confusing the thing with the contrary. Such names offer Socrates a more sophisticated and complex vocabulary than his initial hypothesis had allowed him. It is with the "rediscovery" of such names that Socrates begins to regain a rich and varied world.

Accordingly, we see the significance of these names emphasized as the conversation continues, where Socrates brings to bear all that they have agreed about things and names to the question of the soul. We can see this emphasis, for instance, in the care with which Socrates instructs Cebes on speaking about these things:

> "Then go back and speak to me from the beginning. And don't answer me with the terms I use to pose the question but by imitating me as follows. I now give an answer beyond the first one I spoke of—that safe one—since I see another safety coming out of what we're saying right now. If you should ask me what comes to be in the body by which the body will be hot, I won't give that safe and unlearned [ἀμαθῆ] answer and say that it's Hotness; instead I'll give the fancier [κομψοτέραν] one coming out of what we were discussing just now and say that it's fire. Nor when you ask what comes to be in a body by which the body will be sick, will I say that it's sickness but rather that its fever. Nor when you ask what comes to be in a number by which the number will be odd, will I say that it's Oddness but rather that it's the unit, and so on for other things." (105b–c)

Socrates's instruction of Cebes's speech is obtrusive, and underscores the sense in which Cebes is learning a language, developing a way of speaking, cultivating a lexicon whose significance he has only just begun to grasp. Second, Socrates himself notes the refined quality of this vocabulary. We cannot, of course, hear this description without some sense of irony attached to it, but I take it to be part of Socrates's point that these refined names are in fact needed, provided that one understands what is being said by them and what the need for their generation is: "fire," "fever," and "unit" all specify the coming to be, the genesis, of contraries in things. All three specify a kind of relationship that secures for us an intelligible world.

Finally, as Socrates will immediately turn to illustrate to, and with, Cebes, "soul" is just such a word that, like "fire" or "fever," indicates the genesis of a contrary. More specifically, soul names the coming to be of life in the body. As the contrary of life is death, the soul, by being the emissary of life, cannot admit death (105d).³⁷ Because the soul cannot admit death, the soul must be undying or deathless (ἀθάνατος). Via this investigation of contraries, we now have our final construction of death: death is the contrary of life.

However, this account of death as the contrary to life and of the soul as that which always brings life to bear on that which comes to possess soul leaves something unsaid, namely, how we are to conceive of body within this framework? On the one hand, we are not permitted to think of body as simply the contrary to soul, for the same reason that we do not think of two as the contrary to three. Moreover, insofar as the soul can be made to become body-like, and still be a soul, soul and body cannot be contrary to one another. So, perhaps body, while not acting as the contrary to soul, is such as to have a contrary in it—death—that is precisely the contrary to the idea that the soul somehow possesses. The body's alignment with death is certainly asserted in the third logos. However, were body to be that which brings death to bear on what possesses it, then soul could not possess body nor body soul, for the same reason that fire cannot possess ice and ice cannot possess fire. But this would be to deny the possibility of an entity capable of possessing both body and soul, which is to say this would be to deny the possibility of living being. We are returned, then, to the same problem we encountered in the third logos, namely the need for an account of living being that addresses how the living body stands with respect to the bodily. In the absence of such an account, Socrates's alignment of soul with life and body with death threatens his capacity to speak of living beings.³⁸

3 Psychic Geography

When Socrates concludes the four logoi about immortality with the observation that it is to the care of the soul that they must turn, "not only for this time in which we call 'being alive' goes on, but for time as a whole" (107c), it would seem as though he simply passes over the need to give an account of "being alive." Socrates does not go on to offer a logos of living being in the same manner in which he has discussed the immortality of the soul. And yet, if his subsequent account is indeed of time as a whole, it is the place in which such time unfolds that is given the greatest attention. The myth about the earth that Socrates offers provides an image of the scene of duration, an image of what we might call "doing time," in which the site of the "doing" is the subject of description. Socrates returns to the mythic context in which the four logoi began by first offering a preliminary description of the soul's journey to Hades (107c–108c), followed by an extended myth of the earth (108d–114c) in which he describes the whole earth (108d–109b) and its various regions (109b–113c), and concluding with an account of the experiences of the souls of the dead under and upon its surface (113d–114c). Thus, Socrates follows the fourth logos about soul's immortality—a logos whose failure to provide an adequate account of living being we have charted in some detail—by recounting a description of the earth in which death is presented as the soul's migration to a region on the earth appropriate to it. Justice is enacted by the soul's dwelling therein.

Certainly, the myth resumes the valorization of the philosophic life begun early on in the dialogue with Socrates's defense of his cheerfulness in the face of his imminent demise. Socrates does indeed conclude the myth by observing that its conception of the afterlife urges confidence in the face of death for those who have led a certain kind of life (114d–e). However, the account of the fate of philosophic souls hardly exhausts the descriptive possibilities opened up by this passage, nor does it explain the length and detail with which Socrates speculates about the afterlife. Moreover, given the questions raised in chapter 1 surrounding Socrates's resemblance to the true-born philosopher (a figure who seems to fare so well in this image of the afterlife), there is reason to wonder why we should impute to this myth any motive other than the one Socrates himself gives, namely that it is good to chant such stories to oneself in confronting one's death.[1]

There is a touch of fantasy to this tale, and the myth's therapeutic function is bound up with its fantastical character. In the hours before his death, Socrates allows himself in private conversation with his friends to dwell on a topic he permitted himself only brief mention in his public defense (*Apo.* 29a–b and 39e–41e), namely, what might await one beyond death. However, the fantastical character of this passage is not by itself grounds for ignoring it or refusing it scrutiny. Fantasy lends itself to analysis, and this is a very particular vision. Moreover, Socrates's conclusion, namely that care for the soul should be one's concern in the course of one's life (114d–e), emphasizes the this-worldly effects of belief in an immortal soul: such a belief involves a particular stance toward one's mortality and toward the manner of life one attempts to lead.

Socrates's this-worldly orientation is apparent throughout this story, wherein souls accompanied by only their nurture and education (107d) submit themselves to a justice that is enacted by the manner and duration of their dwelling upon an earth outfitted with regions appropriate to them. Indeed, the myth's emphasis on place sharpens the focus on the manner and conditions in which human lives are lived in community with one another. While the duration of soul's residence in these places is mentioned, it is less the temporality of finitude that Socrates explores in this passage than its geography.[2] Given the tenor of much of the dialogue, this assurance of theodicy by means of the regions and features of the earth is remarkable. The sense in which souls dwell remains deeply mysterious if one focuses upon soul as akin to what is purely intelligible and eternal. Nor has the place of such dwelling, the earth, been treated as an innocuous entity in the *Phaedo*. In the third logos, Socrates aligned the earthy with the bodily, and presented both as negative characteristics a soul could come to have but to which it could not be reduced (81c–d).[3] In the myth that Socrates produces, what had represented the characteristic heaviness of the body is now outfitted with a variety of regions to which particular kinds of souls belong and in which they are at home.

I will argue over the following pages that the myth's emphasis on place is decisive for considering its role in the dialogue. That is, Socrates produces here a sustained meditation on the relationship between human action embedded within a particular environment, condition of soul, and quality of life. Part cosmology, part anthropology, Socrates's myth of the earth describes a human universe resplendent with a variety of communities and a variety of means for expiating actions. It is an account of divine justice, but also a nascent phenomenology of violence, grounded in a description of human dwelling as the site in which justice is enacted, violent deeds are expiated, and souls are perpetually reabsorbed and digested or quarantined. It provides a vision of human life that takes seriously the burden of describing the effects of action on the condition of one's soul and the quality of one's life. As such, it provides a response to the impoverished account of living being with which Socrates and his interlocutors were left by their logoi about immortality. There are three features of Socrates's discussion of the afterlife that recommend this reading: the critical and self-reflective tenor of the passage, its description of a selfsameness engendered by variety and multiplicity, and its particular model for the expiation of unjust deeds. Below I describe each of these features in detail before turning to illustrate their development in the passage itself.

The myth of the earth is introduced with a retelling of what is said about the soul's fate in Hades, a retelling whose emphasis on the variety of souls results in a critique of Aeschylus's character Telephus, who claimed the journey to Hades was simple (108a).[4] Instead, states Socrates, taking as evidence "the rites and lawful ceremonies practiced here" (108a), the ways to Hades are many.[5] As the story unfolds, the variety of paths available to souls provides one way in which differences between souls can be described and illustrates both their need for a guide and the wretchedness of those souls who, on account of their viciousness, are bereft of guidance (108a). The critical tenor of Socrates's retelling is maintained throughout this initial exchange, which culminates in Socrates drawing into question not only what has been said about the soul's journey in Hades but what has been said about the earth itself: "And many and wondrous are the earth's regions, and earth itself is neither of the sort nor the size it's held to be in the opinion of those who usually speak about earth, as I've been persuaded by somebody" (108c). Insofar as he is now disagreeing with "those who usually speak about the earth," he extends his critical eye from poets to any number of other intellectuals; his reticence to name names may in part be explained by this extension. In any event, Socrates's corrective engagement with poetic and early philosophic traditions about the soul's journey to Hades and about the size and constitution of the earth underscores that critical engagement which he has maintained throughout the four logoi. It also indicates that the realm of myth is not a placid telling of accepted doctrine but an agonistic battle for authority.[6] Thus, Socrates's return to myth is not a move from dialectical engagement to uncontested territory.

Moreover, Socrates's myth of the earth is not merely one version of an account of earth that would vie with others; nor is it simply a myth about the earth at all. It is a description of the very perspective from which he and his interlocutors have been speaking about the earth, the soul and body, and the fates that await them. The myth of the true earth offers, among other things, a commentary on perspective itself. The myth creates an image of the earth that incorporates, in a decisively critical manner, the mythmakers themselves: Socrates and his interlocutors are likened to residents of the earth's hollows who mistake their dwelling for the surface of the earth (109c–d). Thus, this myth includes a self-description which serves as an acknowledgment of blurred vision and as a provocation to correct this vision.[7] Specifically, according to Socrates, he and his interlocutors have been operating with an impoverished view and understanding: they are guilty of mistaking their own experience for how things really are. Socrates's repeated assertions that he would not insist upon the truth of the tale he is telling must be read in light of the depiction he has given of his own fragmentary perspective (108d, 114d).

Were we tempted to wonder how Socrates has gained this purchase on his own perspective, this viewing of his own place, we would have to recall that Socrates is using a vocabulary that has already been made available to him by a long tradition of myths which he himself has reattained after having lost it. The variety and plasticity of traditional mythic stories provides Socrates with the very means of critiquing this tradition, and, moreover, allows Socrates to make an image of himself. Plato thus utilizes the language of myth to critique not only other myths but to critique the mythmakers themselves. The *Phaedo*'s play with a number of afterlife themes results, as we will find, in a self-critiquing myth, a dialectical mythology.

The description of the earth that is produced from this appropriation of poetic language is striking in its fecund and self-possessed complexity. In fact, the true earth that Socrates describes teems with the variant and the plural, and it is this emphasis on multiplicity that forms a second essential feature of this passage. This character connects Socrates's myth of the true earth with his recognition of the need to arrive at a discourse that can account for the plurality or variety of souls, and suggests that this myth will further flesh out their need for just such a vocabulary. Socrates explicitly links the variety of souls to the varied character of the true earth, such that the topography of the earth mirrors the taxonomy of souls. Thus, the geography serves the purpose of providing Socrates with a more sophisticated means of speaking about the vices at the same time that it ventures an image of the earth in which all souls are at home,[8] and where some souls are purified by the very activities of the earth itself.[9] Purification emerges not as a flight from physical processes, but as accomplished precisely by physical processes.

Indeed, the particular model for purification that Socrates develops in this myth mingles the language of purification with that of punishment but also with a bodily, medical vocabulary, and suggests that the focus of this myth is on the expiation of unjust deeds. This concern with expiation, with having done with violent and/or unjust action, and the particular model for such expiation Socrates proposes, is a third essential feature of this passage. Socrates's description of the pendulous motion by means of which the rivers that encircle and run beneath the earth flow suggests he is moving from one culturally salient mode of expression (the Pythagorean trope of transmigration) to another (a generally physicalist account of motion). The processes to which souls are subject in this myth, their being rushed about, their being frozen and burned, are physical processes, which is to say, they are things that bodies undergo. Socrates's figuration of the soul as a kind of body for the purposes of illustrating the conditions a soul can possess, and the variety of kind of souls, is the same general figuration afforded by the variety of animals in the theme of transmigration.[10] That Socrates has explicitly questioned the merits of material explanation does not prohibit him from mining such accounts for figurative resources any more than his criticism of sense perception prohibits him from asserting the role of the senses in recollection (76a). This state of affairs suggests that we cannot take his denigration of the bodily at face value. Plato does not deny himself the descriptive and heuristic possibilities that this language offers to some conception of expiation (the digestion and reabsorption of souls, for instance), and it is to outlining these possibilities that we now turn.

The Journey to Hades

Socrates begins the myth with an initial account of what happens to the souls of the dead, an account which he presents as both a recapitulation of an ancient story and a correction to Aeschylus's Telephus. According to Socrates, all souls are led by the daimon that was assigned to them in life to a region where the dead, who have been collected together and submitted themselves to justice, begin their journey. Because there is a variety of paths or ways to take, a guide is necessary for each soul to transport that soul "There" (presumably to Hades and to the specific region of Hades that corresponds to each), where the soul encounters and undergoes what it must, "for the needed time" (107e). Once this period of time has elapsed, another guide returns the soul "here," and does so "over the course of many—and long—circuits of time" (108b).[11]

Socrates is quite clear from the start of this account what it is designed to illustrate: because the soul is deathless and because death is therefore not "freedom from time as a whole" (which would be a comfort to "bad men" [107c]), there is the greatest need to care for the soul and to seek the only refuge and safety available, namely that attained by becoming as good and thoughtful as possible. Such conditions of soul can provide a refuge because soul goes into Hades, "with nothing else except her nurture and education [τῆς παιδείας τε καὶ τροφῆς]" (107d).[12] Indeed, one's nurture and education will help determine the kind of journey one undergoes. The soul that is both "orderly and thoughtful" follows along and isn't ignorant of what has happened to it, namely, that it has been separated from body. The body-loving and body-like soul remains for a long time fluttering around the body, and only goes off to make the journey to Hades resistant and suffering, led away by its daimon.[13] Of the souls that have arrived at the staging ground for their journey to Hades, those who are impure and have done impure things are shunned by the other souls, who want neither to journey with nor guide them. Such a soul "wanders around all by herself, lost in a state of total perplexity, until certain periods of time have passed, and, once they're over, she's carried under pain of necessity to the dwelling that is fitting for her" (108c).[14]

This preliminary account of the soul's journey to Hades operates by way of a logic of containment that connects deed with agent, a logic opened with the observation that the roads to Hades are many. This is the case because different souls have different fates allotted to them on the basis of the condition in which they "enter" Hades, that is, the condition they are in at the time of death. Thus, a detail of landscape provides the means for indicating differences of psychic condition. Accompanied by their nurture and education, souls are submitted to a fate that belongs to them alone. Led by guides that have been assigned to them, to a path that is their own (later we learn that this includes traveling on a vehicle reserved for them [113d]), they embark on a journey that will take them to their place of residence for a fixed amount of time. In containing the expiation of the deed to the treatment undergone by the soul of the agent, Socrates's tale strives to avoid the context that is the setting of many a tragedy, namely, the visitation of unexpiated wrongs and their effects upon generation after generation of the agent of the deed. Socrates's tale seeks to eliminate the possibility of unexpiated deeds by maintaining the connection between deed and agent, and accomplishes this by presenting death as a landscape and expiation as a function of residence. However, that souls are accompanied by their nurture and education is a sign that action alone is not the sole determinant of condition of soul. The effects of other people and institutions are also worn on the psuchē, so to speak, and the accompaniment of nurture and education gestures toward the effects on the soul of extraindividual institutions, familial dynamics, and community. In these accompaniments, the polis looms large.

The logic of containment is complemented by a system of distinctions by means of which souls are distinguished on the basis of their purity and impurity and allotted fates according to these conditions. The distinction between pure (orderly and thoughtful) souls and impure (filled with desire for the body) souls eventually mutates into a more complex set of distinctions with at least four types: middling souls; corrupt but curable souls; corrupt and incurable souls; and just or holy souls. However, this complex typology is collapsed at the conclusion of the passage back into two kinds: body-loving and learning-loving (114e). Finally, the differing fates of pure and impure souls are bound up with the differences between those souls' knowledge of their own condition: orderly and thoughtful souls are aware that they are separated from the body, and submit themselves to their fates without resistance. Body-loving souls are ignorant of themselves and their status, resist departure from the realm of the living, and haunt the resting place of the body. It is as though these souls themselves enact the attitude of people who have failed to properly comport themselves toward their own mortality, failed to acknowledge themselves as subject to death. In its account of their ignorance about themselves, this description resonates with that of the lives of those who have body-loving souls. They are unable to grasp being, unable to understand what is really the case. Such souls are only carried off to their fate by force and with difficulty (βίᾳ καὶ μόγις) (108b). When such souls finally arrive in Hades, if they have committed unjust and violent deeds, they are isolated, bereft of companions or guides; filled with perplexity (ἀπορίᾳ) they wander (πλανᾶται) until carried to their proper region, "under pain of necessity [ὑπ' ἀνάγκης]" (108c). Their ignorance about themselves subjects them to violent compulsion and necessity; their commission of unjust deeds to isolation and wandering. Alternately, the pure and sensible soul journeys with and is led by gods, and also dwells in a region that is fitting for it (108c). After this description of the conditions of souls' journeys, Socrates offers a description of the earth and its regions.

The Earth

Socrates carries out the themes of variety and plurality in the description of the true earth as a whole and its regions: the hollows, the surface, and the underworld. In his discussion of the true earth as a whole, we learn that this earth is free from compulsion (ἀνάγκης), possessing sufficient equanimity (ἰσόρροπον) as to be capable of holding its place in a self-similar condition (ὁμοίου) without external force (108e–109a). We learn also that the true earth is very big, and that "all over the Earth, there are many hollows with all manners of looks and sizes" (109b). It is in one such hollow that Socrates locates himself and his interlocutors. Were one to attain the bird's-eye view of the whole of the earth, what one finds is that the earth's selfsameness is not simple, but rather consists in an enduring identity that holds variety to itself:

> "the earth itself, if one should catch sight of it from above, looks just like those twelve-piece leather balls—dappled, divided up into colors of which the colors here seem like samples painters use. But up there the whole earth is made of such colors, indeed of colors still more splendid and pure than the ones here. For in one part it's purple,[15] in another it has the look of gold [χρυσοειδῆ], and all the part that's white is whiter [λευκοτέραν] than chalk or snow—and in just the same way it's composed of other colors, indeed of colors still greater in number and more beautiful than all those we've seen." (110c)

Saturated in color, this ultrareal earth is also an ultravivid, ultravisible earth, the vision of which involves not a transcendence of what is visible to those residing in its hollows, but an intensification of what can be seen there. This intensification is especially at work in his description of colors: the purple is literally sea-wrought purple, the gold is paradigmatic gold (of the eidos of gold), the white is whiter than chalk or snow. Socrates's emphasis on the variety and purity of colors possessed by the true earth is conspicuous. Throughout the myth, color emerges as a primary example of the harmony of purity and plurality that is evinced by the earth itself, and suggests a relation between variety and selfsameness other than that of opposition.[16] Far from denying the validity of variety, Socrates's imagery creates a singular earth that is apparent precisely in and as a multiplicity of colors: "For even these very hollows of the Earth, being filled with water and air, themselves provide a certain form of color as they glisten within the dappling of other colors, so that a single form of Earth, continuous and dappled, makes its appearance [ὥστε ἕν τι αὐτῆς εἶδος συνεχὲς ποικίλον φαντάζεσθαι]"

(110c–d). Plato's point here bears emphasis: earth is not a whole in spite of its many various regions, but because of them. It is on the basis of its many parts that it has the particular look, the particular unity he has described. How we are to take this ultrareal and ultravivid earth was a puzzle to some of the dialogue's earliest commentators—for Damascius, for example, the earth here described is reducible neither to phusis nor eidos, neither to nature nor form.[17] Rather than resolve this irreducibility, Plato goes to great lengths to make plain both the benefits and the limits of the linguistic and conceptual tools available to him. While eventually the placid surface of the earth will be juxtaposed to its seething underworld, Plato goes out of his way to emphasize that surface and interior are parts of a single unity, one which could not have the look that it does without its various parts. The incongruence of this imagery with the juxtaposition asserted earlier in the dialogue between pure, selfsame forms and variant, tainting beings is striking. In fact, Plato draws our attention to this incongruence in his description of the hollows, extending Socrates's emphasis on variety and multiplicity not only to colors but also to life and living things themselves.

The Hollows

Socrates's initial description of the earth's hollows highlights their number and variety: "For everywhere, all over the Earth, there are many hollows with all manner of looks and sizes, into which the water and the mist and the air have flowed together" (109b). The mingling and flowing of elements punctuate the fluid and volatile environment of the hollows, one in which a variety of living things make their home. Indeed, we find a flurry of references to living things within this myth. We have reference to ants and frogs, to trees and flowers and fruits, to fish and winged things. Socrates continues this listing by providing a triad of gems—carnelians, jaspers, emeralds (110c–e). In short, we are invited to delight in the variety and brilliance of things.

Nor is this myth without multiform reference to those things that are lacking in brilliance, things like rot, brine, disease, deformities, monstrous mud and muck, caverns, and sand (110e). The flowering of discourse here, the wild exuberance of terms, whether for the beautiful or for the ugly, also invites us to delight in discourse itself, to immerse ourselves in a tale that is teeming with life and living.

Socrates's delight in storytelling, in giving likenesses of the earth, extends even to his account of his and his interlocutors' position within this earth, and here the character of the story as a likeness is underscored by the limited purchase that Socrates attributes to himself and his friends:

> "Now we are unaware that we dwell in its hollows,[18] and we think we dwell on top of the Earth. It's just as if somebody who dwells in the midst of the bottom of the deep should think he dwells on top of the sea, and, because he sees the sun and the other stars through the water, should consider the sea to be the heaven, and since he'd never yet gotten to the surface of the sea because of his slowness and weakness, should neither have seen by emerging and leaping out of the sea into our region

here how much purer and more beautiful it happens to be than the region where his people dwell, nor should have heard from another who has seen it. Now that's how we too have been affected." (109c–d)

This image of their place and perspective is complex. Not only does Socrates employ the image[19] of a hollow in the earth populated by him, his interlocutors, and many like them, he also creates an image of the very perspective on place that this position affords: Living as they do in their hollow (one image), they mistake their hollow for the whole earth just as one who lives under the sea (another image) might mistake the bottom of the sea for the surface.[20]

This second image, and the aquatic environment it figures, draws a distinction between the earth "here" (in the hollow that Socrates and his interlocutors occupy) and the surface of the earth: "for this earth and the rocks and the whole region here are damaged and corroded, just as things in the sea are by brine" (110a). But the very nature of this second image implies that the difference between "hollow" and "surface" is a difference between two regions of the same entity, and not two utterly separate entities devoid of exchange. The perspective of one who occupies a hollow, like the perspective of one who lives under the sea, is not utterly erroneous, suggests Socrates; rather, it is flawed only because it is fragmentary. It is a perspective that does not yet take its own position into consideration. What would be gained by altering their perspective is not a new earth but a firmer grasp, a fuller and richer dwelling upon the very earth on which they already find themselves. Such a change in perspective (at 109e Socrates likens it to a fish flopping out of water) yields a fertile earth populated by a variety of forms and living beings.

While it may be the case that Socrates cannot adopt this perspective without having undergone some transformation with respect to his understanding of the world of sense perception and the realm of the visible, the critical purchase he attains never transcends the language that this world affords him; it only invests this language with a certain self-critical awareness. Consequently, a tension emerges between Socrates's claim that they cannot compare the beauty of the surface of the earth with the earth "here" and his subsequent comparisons of these two regions. This is, however, a fecund tension that he justifies by an appeal to the merits of mythmaking itself: "for if it's a beautiful thing to tell a story [μῦθον λέγειν], then, Simmias, it's also worth hearing what those things happen to be like that are on that Earth beneath Heaven" (110a–b). Socrates's denigration of the earth "here" cannot be read in isolation from the context of his celebration of the beauty of speaking about the spectacle that this earth manifests in its plurality.

The Surface

Socrates's description of the surface of the earth continues the account of the ultrareal, ultravivid earth as a whole. His imagery of the happy and blessed fate of those pure souls who dwell upon the earth's surface is not that of the transcendence of life but of the *intensification* of life: their "lives" are richer, fuller, better lives. Their communion with the gods is more complete, their grasp of Being more perfect, their relation to nature more harmonious, their relations with one another more sustaining. What cannot be overlooked in this account is precisely the community it outlines; these souls are not isolated, they are not alone by themselves. They dwell on an earth, under the heavens, with the gods and with one another, and all of these things are apparent to them with a greater brilliance and saturation than to any others. And it is in this discussion of the intensification of living that accompanies the fate of blessed and holy souls that Socrates invokes twice the condition of flourishing, eudaimonia. Reveling in the sight of the earth, they are made happy by it and by their interactions upon it:

> "But the Earth Itself has been adorned by all these things—and moreover by gold and silver and again by other such things. For by nature they appear right out in the open, being great in multitude and big and all over the Earth, so that the Earth is quite a sight for happy sightseers [εὐδαιμόνων θεατῶν]. And there are many different animals upon it, and also human beings, some dwelling inland and others around the air—just as we dwell around the sea—and still others who dwell on islands around which the air flows and which are near the mainland. And, in a word, the very thing water and the sea are to us with respect to our needs, the air is to those up there; and what the air is to us, the ether is to them. And the blending of the seasons is such that those people there are without disease and live a much greater span of time than people here; and in sight and hearing and thoughtfulness and in all such things, they stand apart from us in respect of purity by the very same interval by which air stands apart from water and ether from air. And in particular, they have both groves and temples for gods in which gods are really dwellers; and their utterances and prophecies and perceptions of the gods and all such forms of intercourse with gods come about for them face to face; and the sun and moon and stars are seen by them such as they really happen to be; and the rest of their happiness [εὐδαιμονίαν] follows in the train of these things." (110e–111c)

The blessed do not cease being human, nor is their view and experience of the earth of some radically different world (requiring a new set of terms) but a perfected version of this world. Again, Plato does not eschew visibility, but rather presents an image of its intensification; neither does he eschew that vocabulary this world supplies to him, but uses it to create an image of flourishing.

The Underworld

While the description of the whole earth emphasizes a plurality of color and life, the description of the various regions under the earth locates us within a world of teeming forces and flows, of pulsions, of pendulums, of breaths and winds, a world of manifold forces. The variety of flows—flows of water, of mud, of air and of fire—interact with force by coiling, by descending and ascending, by seething, by erupting, by rushing. The motions of the underworld animate the earth. Prior to this account of the underworld, the primary movements described in this passage are those of ascent and descent; this vertical movement is complicated by the circular movement that governs the underworld, as well as by the pullings and pushing, the surgings and swayings and swingings that are at work under the earth's surface. These motions are a function of water and air circulating through underground passageways that connect the hollows to one another. Socrates's description of these motions carries further the general tendency toward multiplicity and hyperbole exhibited in this tale, while also offering a causal account of the varieties of motion to which it is subject:

> "under the earth there are monstrous [ἀμήχανα] amounts of ever-flowing [ἀεν-άων]²¹ rivers and of waters hot and cold, and lots of fire and great rivers of fire, and many rivers of liquid mud, both purer and muckier [καθαρωτέρου καὶ βορβορ-ωδεστέρου], just like those rivers of mud that flow ahead of the lava in Sicily and like the lava-stream itself. By them each of these regions is replenished [πληροῦσθαι] as the circulation [περιρροὴ] happens [τύχῃ] to reach each one in turn. And it moves all these things to and fro, as though there were some sort of swing [αἰώραν] present within the earth." (111d–e)

The underworld is a realm of mingling and mixing, where water, earth, air, and fire blend with one another and with the hot and the cold, pure and impure. Socrates's invocation of tuchē and his description of the movement as a sort of swing or oscillation serves as a signal that a certain kind of causality is at work here, one which Socrates describes in greater detail: "one of the gaps of the earth happens to be greatest in other respects and is also bored right through the whole earth [ἕν τι τῶν χασμάτων τῆς γῆς ἄλλως τε μέγιστον τυγχάνει ὂν καὶ διαμπερὲς τετρημένον δι᾽ ὅλης τῆς γῆς]" (111e–112a). This gap is what the poets, Homer included, have called Tartarus. All rivers flow into this gap and out of it again, "and each of them becomes like whatever sort of earth it flows through" (112a). Socrates continues: "The cause of all the streams' flowing out from here and flowing into there is that this liquid has no bottom or base [ὅτι πυθμένα οὐκ ἔχει οὐδὲ βάσιν τὸ ὑγρὸν τοῦτο]. So it swings and surges to and fro, and the air and breath of the wind around it do the same, for they follow along with the liquid both when it rushes on the far side of the earth and to this side" (112b).

Socrates's invocation of tuchē, of chance, twice in his description of the motions of the underworld resonates with his attribution of the cause of this motion to a baseless, groundless flowing, and it is precisely this lack of base or foundation that gives to the liquid its swaying motion. Thus, the motion of water, earth, and air under the earth is errant and pendulous, subject to chance and without foundation.²² Surely this identification of the cause of the swinging motion under the earth is as distant as can be from the balance and equipoise, the selfsameness, of the earth when viewed from above and as a whole. Nevertheless, this very earth encases the foundationless, baseless liquid and is traversed by the very flowings it makes possible. Nor is even this motion without some homoiousis—the rivers become like the earth through which they flow—and predictability: when water recedes in one area, it flows into the opposite area. Thus, Socrates's account of the motions under the earth includes a kinesiology that invokes *both* chance and selfsameness. The mingling of chance and necessity, the description of foundationless yet predictable motion, serves the imagery of an earth that is a complex whole, one capable of maintaining its equilibrium amid even the strongest of internal motions. Like the living body itself, and the bodily to which Socrates has had recourse throughout this dialogue, the earth's underworld is a mixture of constancy and inconstancy, errancy and repetition. Indeed, the very physical, bodily account of the underworld and its circulatory system is made more explicit, as Socrates continues his description of the movement of water, earth, and air under the earth: "just as when people breathe, the breath, as it flows, is always breathed out and breathed in, so also there the breath, as it swings along with the liquid, brings about certain dreadful and monstrous winds as it goes in and out" (112b).

Such an account invites one to compare the motions of the rivers that encircle and run beneath the earth with desire and its workings, which Socrates will describe in the *Republic* as like a stream whose current can be made to flow in a number of directions (485d).[23] And it is with this oblique reference to the pushings and pulling of desires that Socrates then turns to locate souls within this myth of the earth. In this general milieu of mingling and resemblance, four bodies of water are marked off from one another, at least two of which are distinct because they do not mingle with the others (113b–c), the rivers Pyriphlegethon and Cocytus. Once Socrates has described the earth and its various regions, he returns to the task with which he began his mythic geography, namely, locating the fate of the human soul in and on the earth.

Doing Time in Hades

When Socrates returns to the theme of the soul's journey in and through this earth, he offers the following general schema of what happens to souls in Hades. He reiterates that all souls, regardless of how they have lived their lives, are gathered together and submit themselves to justice. Those souls that led what Socrates describes as "middling lives" can expect the following journey: they travel on foot to Acheron, encountering rafts "reserved for them" by means of which they arrive at the Acherousian Lake, where "the souls of many who've met their end keep arriving, and after staying for certain allotted times—some longer, some shorter—are sent out again into the generation of the living" (113a). These souls dwell on the lake and, "purified [καθαιρόμενοι] by paying the penalty [διδόντες δίκας] for their unjust deeds" (113d–e), are eventually released, carrying off honors for their good deeds. This presentation of purification as a payment of penalty elides punishment with an alteration of psychic condition. Moreover, Socrates leaves his account of this payment somewhat underdetermined—it seems to consist simply in dwelling in a particular place for a particular period of time. Thus, purification is purchased by taking up residence in a certain environment.

Another category of souls, the incurables, so called because of the "magnitude of their misdeeds," are cast into Tartarus, "from which there is no exit" (113e–114a). Presumably, these souls are incurable because there is no payment possible to return their injustice, no value can be set that would allow for such payment. So excessive are their misdeeds that no calculus exists to calculate their payment, no currency to make such payment.

Those souls who have committed misdeeds that are curable, "although great"[24] (a designation presumably made to distinguish between these, the lesser injustices that some of the souls residing on the Acherousian Lake have committed, and the deeds that render their doer incurable) are "of necessity [ἀνάγκη]" rushed into Tartarus (114a). However, for these souls some mechanism of release has been devised. After residing in Tartarus for a year, they are discharged: the homicides to freezing Cocytus and the patricides and matricides to fiery Pyriphlegethon.[25] The path of these rivers is such that they grant for a brief period sufficient proximity to the Acherousian Lake as to allow the souls rushing along them to call out to the souls residing in the lake, supplicating and entreating those souls against which they have aggressed, with the hopes of persuading them and attaining reception into the lake. Those souls who are successful are granted entry into the community of the majority of souls.

The mechanics of redemption presented by this account are dubious. There seems to be no guarantee that the souls of those against whom one has aggressed will even be residing in the lake at the same time as the aggressing soul is rushing around in its respective river; this state of affairs suggests to many scholars a pessimistic attitude toward the possibilities for absolution.[26] I would like, however, to draw attention to the descriptive possibilities that this passage provides. I am particularly interested in two features of this discussion. First, the geography in this part of the myth provides a way of thinking about action and its effects on the whole. In drawing distinctions between kinds of vicious acts, the myth offers a way of considering carefully the effects of certain actions, and a way of describing those effects. By concretizing these effects into places and processes, one gets a sense for the effect of the action on an entire collective. This is to say, the myth provides resources for considering the effect of human action within the entire arena of human community. Second, I would like to explore the specific possibility for contending with certain unjust actions that this section of the myth presents through the possible reabsorption of fugitive souls.

With respect to its framing of the effects of human action, the earth's mythic geography offers a way of figuring liminal action, both that which is exemplary and that which is utterly degenerate. Pure and pious souls (the souls of the philosophers) are permitted to dwell on the surface of the earth in the company of gods. The suggestion here is that adopting the manner of life of the philosopher wins one a certain freedom from the circulation between various dwellings and processes that most other souls must undergo. Impure souls whose actions are incurable (that is, of a number and/or magnitude of injustice as to be incapable of compensating for their effects) are cast into Tartarus with no possibility of release. Thus, on the one hand, the extremity of these actions is emphasized; bereft of a means of correcting them, such souls are also exempt from the processes that offer a means of repayment. On the other hand, because even the worst injustices are neither without place nor without some description of them and their effects, the intelligibility of even these actions is assured. The allocation of incurable souls to Tartarus assures the quarantine, and thus the limitation of the effects, of even the most heinous deeds. There is no crime so great that it does not have some corresponding place, some means of describing its effects. Even the prohibition of reabsorption does not render impossible some illustration of the effect of the act: radical isolation. Throughout this discussion, the concern seems to be with restoring a certain kind of order by forcing those whose action disrupts this order to undergo certain processes. This section of the myth offers a categorization of actions (those that can be reabsorbed and those that cannot), a way of viewing their effect on the whole, and also a way of thinking about how to contend with some of those actions (reabsorption or quarantine).

A second feature of this geography is the mechanism that it provides for the digestion of vicious deeds through the reintegration of fugitive souls into the process which most souls undergo. Isolated by their misdeeds both in their journey to Hades[27] and once they have arrived, those who have committed great but curable misdeeds spend a year in Taratarus and then are rushed to either Cocytus or Pyriphlegethon (depending on the kind of misdeed), rivers which Socrates emphasizes do not mix with any others (113b and c). These souls are literally consumed by the earth and brought into its circulation by their placement in its rushing rivers. The digestion of these souls can go in one of two ways, it seems: either they circulate in perpetuity or they are received into the company of the majority of other souls. The possibility of reintegration is granted by another geographical feature: the brief proximity to the lake that each river affords them is the necessary means by which they gain access to the ears of their potential liberators. The geography depicts, and its curious structure enables, a digestion of (a having done with) misdeeds by means of a process whereby the doer is potentially permitted reentry into normalcy. Denied community with one another by the rushing to which they are subject, these souls focus instead on gaining reception to the Acherousian Lake, and their means for doing so is to supplicate, entreat, and persuade those against whom they have aggressed. It is only if they are successful in doing so that they are released from the rushing river and allowed entry into the lake, and thus eventually back into the circulation to which most souls are subject.

We might wonder about this rhetoric for the damned, in what it would consist, what kinds of arguments and claims might be made that would be effective, in what ways it might resemble courtroom rhetoric and in what ways diverge. Socrates's silence on this front makes these questions unanswerable, at least within the context of this passage.[28] However, what stands out here is the connection that this geography permits between aggressor and aggressed.[29] The passage gives an account of what is required for the expiation of certain deeds and of the condition of the agent of such deeds. It also suggests that redemption is made by gaining some access to the victim and attaining some rhetoric by means of which to persuade the victim to release and receive the agent. The "time" of the deed is the "time" in which this particular relationship stands. Expiation consists of forgiveness, or, to follow more closely the language of the text, expiation is the attainment of reception, winning the victim's willingness to extend hospitality to the offender. The contingency of expiation places the burden of its accomplishment upon securing a particular form of access and a particular kind of rhetoric.

We are now in a position to reintegrate this account of the various fates which human souls encounter on and in the earth with Socrates's account of the earth itself. The language of flow and the emphasis on multiplicity serve as a way of describing varieties of souls, as souls find themselves in particular regions (subject to particular modes of conveyance) by means of their various conditions with respect to virtue and vice. Because souls find themselves in places that correspond to them, which is itself determined by their actions, the emphasis on places appropriate to the soul is also an emphasis on the reciprocity between action and place. The description of what happens to corrupt souls entails a description of the environment that surrounds the corrupted soul. The isolation, confusion, and wandering of unjust souls at the start of their journey to Hades (108a–c), the drowning, freezing, and burning of murderous souls while in Hades, and the need of these souls to perpetually and perhaps fruitlessly seek forgiveness in order to be liberated from their circumstances (113e–114c), all provide resources for speaking about the conditions of souls in this life as much as in another. Thus, in this myth, a vocabulary of virtue and vice is wedded to a vocabulary of physical process and earthly multiplicity. What is accomplished in this myth is not only a vocabulary for variation, but also an intertwining of a means for referring to souls and a means for referring to earth. Earth and soul are connected in a single mythic vocabulary.

Dialectical Mythology

In chapter 2 of the first book of *De Anima*, Aristotle concludes his review of various theories about the soul with the observation that, of all the elements, only earth has never been judged a candidate for what the soul is.[30] Socrates's myth of the true earth may come as close as any source that we possess to connecting the soul with the earth.

It is certainly possible to understand this myth as representing the transcendent grasp of the whole afforded by a philosophical rejection of the sensory world. According to such a reading, "true earth" is a triumph of a metaphysics that posits only what is neither visible nor earthy as true. However, there are elements of the myth that advise against this reading. Having attained an awareness of his own immersion in the earth, Socrates does not transcend the terms available to him to describe the phenomenal world. Rather, he conjoins an investigation of soul with an account of the earth whose exuberant and excessive profusion of terms stands in stark contrast to the impoverished vocabulary that Socrates possesses early on in the fourth logos. The ethical demand to produce a taxonomy of souls is met with a topography of places, and the metaphysical demand to give an account of unity is met with the equanimity of the earth as a whole. As both ethical and metaphysical considerations were required in order to approach an investigation of the soul, so are unity and plurality required in an account of the earth in which the conditions of the soul are literally written onto the body of the earth. In a sense, Socrates has en-souled the earth. But he has also thereby en-earthed the soul.

At the same time, there are grounds to be wary of reading this myth as an attempted reconciliation with the earth. Doing so risks presenting the myth as a naturalization of ethics that brings with it the disturbing suggestion that the modification of psychical conditions is neither more nor less problematic than an alteration of landscape. Rather than limit ourselves to these two readings, however, a third possibility presents itself in the critique that this myth accomplishes. The connection between earth and soul that Socrates provides occurs only after he has been afforded a critical purchase on his own grasp of these things. Having arrived by the end of the fourth logos at an aporia about the nature of living and dying, the myth provides a critical lens through which Socrates and his interlocutors can view their own purchase on the soul. What is won in the myth is the identification of Socrates's and his interlocutors' own perspective; they are put in their place.

This place, the earth as Socrates's myth presents it, encompasses, on the one hand, a variety of processes, circuits, and locales, some more desirable than others, and, on the other, the possibility of freedom from process (as figured by the dwellings of the pure, on the surface of the earth and in even more fantastic dwellings). In so describing the earth, this myth provides Socrates and his interlocutors the resources for considering the effects of their actions on the community in which they reside in this life. In so doing, it implicitly locates the force of Socrates's claim to care for their souls in the effects that such care has for the city. Ultimately, the myth also presents the dream of limiting the effects of vicious deeds and doing so in a manner that is in accord with, and even a function of, the structure and operation of the whole earth. While, as Brann has noted,[31] no cities appear in Socrates's myth of the earth, the myth provides an image of human community that limits viciousness in accord with the cosmos. In so doing, it presents a provocation to arrive at such a human community and to establish a city that enables human flourishing.

Throughout the *Phaedo*, Socrates exhibits a certain philosophical humility before myth. Unwilling to simply accept poetic and religious accounts of the soul, neither is he willing to cast off the vocabulary that they supply for speaking about the mysterious and enigmatic workings of the soul. Socrates mines these cultural resources, searching for tools with which he can better grasp the soul, much as he exhorts his companions to look both outside the Greek-speaking world and among themselves for philosophical dialogue (78a). The specifically philosophical service that Socrates offers his interlocutors' engagement with these vocabularies is that of critique, which involves the recognition that these resources have proven neither final nor exhaustive. Rather than ending it, his myth of the earth resuscitates discourse about the nature of the soul.

Plato, in turn, leaves his readers with a text that is a provocation for interpretation, rather than a doctrine that forecloses investigation.

Conclusion

The *Phaedo*'s investigation of soul occurs in the context of examining how one should lead one's life, outlining the philosophic way of life and defending it as best. It is this set of interests that motivates the discussion of soul's immortality. However, throughout the dialogue Socrates himself stands at some distance from the very form of life which he identifies as philosophic, both in his eagerness to speak and his care for those with whom he is speaking. Moreover, as this discussion unfolds, we see that the defense of the philosophic life depends upon a particular conception of soul that includes not only its immortality but also its plasticity. Indeed, what has been seen as Socrates's overarching message, that one must care for one's soul, is argued for on the basis of the implications of psychic plasticity for human life. The exploration of the variety of psychic conditions throughout the four logoi and the myth leads to a reflection upon the effects of psychic malleability on human community and to an emphasis on the need to make those effects clear. Socrates's observation, at the start of the myth, that death does not mark freedom from time sets the stage for the myth's meditation upon the endurance of action and the reciprocal effects of deeds and condition of soul. This meditation could occur only within the arena of human community wherein the effects of action are made most vivid.

Socrates's defense sets up these themes by presenting the philosophic life as a way of accomplishing the communion of body and soul that frees soul up for thought. By employing the language of pollution and purification, he is able to characterize soul, on the one hand, as reaching out toward and being akin to Being (and as finding its coalescence in such striving), and on the other, as capable of diffusion, care for and permeation by the body. This trope's capacity to describe the excessive and enduring effects of vicious action recommend it for a project designed in part to illuminate the full range of effects on both individual and community of various conditions of soul and the actions that accord with them. The presentation of human community as a site in which the conditions and effects of soul can be analyzed as well as altered is echoed throughout the dialogue by Plato's careful portrayal of Socrates's relationship with his own interlocutors and, ultimately, with himself (through his self-analysis or self-portrait).

The defense's initial presentation of psychic plasticity as stretching out toward both Being and body is elaborated upon throughout the four logoi and the myth that follows them, wherein we find Plato mining a variety of vocabularies to arrive at the richest and subtlest account of the conditions of soul, their effects on human life, and their place within a larger cosmic structure. The logoi attempt to mark out a way of life (and thus a stance with respect to one's mortality) that takes into account: the structure of genesis as such (the emergence of things from their opposite); the erotic striving that characterizes not only human relationships but the cosmos itself; the affinity between soul and Being (and thus the alienation of the lover of the body and the flourishing of the lover of Being); and the stability of Being that is signified by the resistance of one contrary to another. The myth allows for a critique of the impoverished vision of living being that is at work in these logoi by providing a sense for the limited perspective of Socrates and his interlocutors themselves. Armed with this self-critical stance, Socrates's myth goes on to envision the forms of community and lives to which human action gives rise. It thus serves, no less than the logoi, the account of kinds of lives with which the dialogue begins.

Throughout these discussions, the philosophic life is treated as having a privileged position with respect to soul because of its particular stance toward psychic plasticity and as recommending a particular form of community to foster this stance. We also encounter, however, a series of questions (or even crises) about the relationship between the study of soul and philosophy: Are there beliefs about soul that must be maintained by the philosopher? Is Socrates more or less philosophic in his chanting of myths and his singing of songs and his exhortation to love the truth more than himself? Ultimately, is there a tension to be found between care of the soul and study of the soul? The crisis of the loss of logos, the aporia surrounding living being, the question of what the philosopher must believe (the question of the adequacy of Socrates's transformation of theology into philosophy) all suggest a certain philosophical ambivalence toward the study of the soul. That these are questions with which the *Phaedo* leaves us further suggests that this ambivalence is neither easy to solve nor bereft of fruitful provocation to thought, and it is with these questions in mind that we turn to the *Republic*.

I would like to conclude with a few brief comments looking forward to the next section's study of psychology in the *Republic*. While the relationship between an investigation of soul and an investigation of city was broached obliquely in the *Phaedo*, the relationship between the two is brought to the fore in the *Republic*. Rumblings of it are heard in Glaucon's and Adeimantus's requests of Socrates, but made explicit almost immediately thereafter in the analogy between city and soul that Socrates proposes will supply them with a means for investigating justice and injustice in the soul, and thus for investigating the perfectly just and unjust persons.

This is not to say that the concern with zōon and logos that proves so pervasive in the *Phaedo*, and so shapes its investigation of soul, are not of interest in the *Republic*. Rather, what we encounter is a difference of approach. It is the relationship between life and what is variously characterized as rule, management, and constitution that is most of interest in the *Republic*. It is to life as it is circumscribed by the polis that the *Republic* addresses itself. And, while in the *Phaedo* Socrates translates theology into philosophy, so in the *Republic* he will translate politics into philosophy. This shift in perspective does result in some important intersections with, and divergences from, the *Phaedo*, a few of which are outlined below.

While both the *Republic* and the *Phaedo* go to great lengths to describe the soul's plasicity, the *Republic* utilizes different language and concepts to do so. More specifically, we will see in the *Republic* a move away from the language of pollution and purity to characterize the conditions of soul and toward the language of health and sickness. Correspondingly, we see a move away from the *Phaedo*'s model of soul's transformation as a function of that with which it comes into contact or touches and a move toward a more complex model of reciprocal transformation between outside and inside represented by a spectrum of mimetic activity. Similarly, insofar as mimēsis is bound up with what the soul loves—people imitate what they find to be valuable, praiseworthy, and attractive—the *Republic*, like the *Phaedo*, takes desire quite seriously. However, whereas there seem to be only two loves or two directions in which desire can be turned that are of main interest in the *Phaedo*—love of the body or love of Being—in the *Republic* the soul's loves and desires are significantly more complex.

Moreover, there is noticeably less emphasis on the soul's immortality in the *Republic* than in the *Phaedo*. While the *Republic* is certainly not bereft of concerns about purification and pollution and some reference to an immortal soul, the focus has moved from the resources provided by the language of purity and impurity to the language provided by mimēsis and medicine. These shifts are not without some connection to the broadly religious language of the *Phaedo* and to the regionality it asserts, as we shall see. The difference between disease and health and pollution and purification is not always one of kind in ancient Greek culture, much to the chagrin of many of its medical writers.[32] A similar state of affairs stands with respect to the *Republic*'s use of the language of parts. The *Republic*, like the *Phaedo*, is deeply invested in describing conditions of soul. While in the *Phaedo* these various conditions are a function of that with which soul was in contact, the soul's general surroundings, in the *Republic* the primary means for characterizing conditions of soul is through the organization of parts of the soul. Any particular condition of soul is a function of the particular organization or regime of parts of the soul. Thus, in the next section we will explore how the language of parts compares with and diverges from the language of touch and contact (and all of the conceptions of pollution and purity that attend these). As a preliminary pass at doing so, we can note that the regional spatiality granted to soul in the *Phaedo* by characterizing it as like that with which it comes into contact has a certain resonance with the *Republic*'s treatment of mimēsis as "becoming like" and with its characterization of soul itself as possessing a regime or order. Insofar as the soul has a politeia, not only is its likeness to a city furthered, but also a kind of regional or environmental quality is maintained in Plato's conception of it. While the soul's politeia has significantly heavier political overtones, it only makes more explicit what was implied in the notion of the soul's various dwellings (as reciprocally determined by actions the soul enables).

PART II
Republic

IN THE TENTH book of the *Republic*, Socrates concludes the discussion of the immortality of the soul and introduces the myth of Er with a powerful, if also ambiguous, qualification. The study of soul that he and his interlocutors have conducted in order to judge what form of life is best has discerned the conditions of soul in its human life, but has, Socrates notes, failed to grasp soul in its true nature (612a). That is, the question of what the soul itself *is* is most fully formulated not in the beginning of the dialogue, with their discussion of the work that is proper to the soul (353d), nor in the middle of the dialogue, with their investigation of whether the soul has parts (435c–d), but near its end, and we cannot adequately assess the psychology of the *Republic* without taking this into account.

Socrates's qualification serves as a reminder that what is said of the soul in the *Republic* is said in the context of a contest to win the capacity to choose the best life and thereby to become good or bad (see 344d–e, 352d, 608b, 618b–c). Indeed, the first reference to psuchē in the dialogue arises in the context of concern for one's course of life, that is, in Cephalus's description of the fear that grips the souls of many of his friends, a fear of punishment in the afterlife for deeds that they committed in this life (330d–e).[1] In presenting the spectacle of the choosing of lives, the myth of Er envisions the task with which the entire dialogue has been concerned, albeit on a different register.[2] Indeed, it is in their acknowledgment that the effects of justice and injustice cannot be adequately seen and measured by focusing upon the course of a single life—that is, in their recognition that the individual human soul points beyond itself—that Socrates and his interlocutors come to win this critical understanding of their purchase on the soul. I thus take Socrates's qualification to tell us something crucial about Plato's approach to psychology, namely, that we must develop the ability to pose the question of what soul is from out of a critical engagement with our own assumptions about our lives and character. The investigation of soul that Plato offers in the *Republic* stages just such an engagement, and the insight that it offers us into his understanding of soul occurs not only by way of what is said about soul but also by the manner in which this articulation is submitted to critical investigation and transformation.

In doing so, Plato makes use of a remarkable, radical, and rich image-making faculty. Dominated by a landscape of peaks and valleys, ascents and descents, winding paths, dense thickets, caves, plains, and plateaus, the *Republic* offers its readers a rugged and varied terrain. Presented as taking the place of a spectacle, the conversation that comprises the *Republic* teems with its own spectacular visions. Ships, animals, fabulous and mythical creatures, sea gods, astronomical bodies, fingers, and sticks all join the geographic images in the service of elucidating what is elusive and obscure (even if only to do so as elusive and obscure). It is not inappropriate that Socrates describes himself in the *Republic* as greedy for images (487e–488a). Indeed, the dialogue's infamous critique of the image proceeds by way of a proliferation of images.[3]

This is to say that the *Republic* is in many ways a dialogue about vision and the terrains that afford it; it is deeply concerned with generating logoi that gain purchases, points of view, and privileged perspectives. The *Republic* also often attests to the difficulty of viewing, and it is especially in its capacity to image that logos is treated as a vehicle of motion and critique, as capable of displaying the limits of the view which one possesses and the landscape one surveys. Indeed, the infamous qualification of their understanding of the soul in book 10 referenced above is presented as a function of their particular and situated vision of the soul: "Now we were telling the truth about it as it looks at present. However, this is based only on the condition in which we saw it" (611c). Socrates will go on to describe the limitation of their purchase on the soul by offering an image: they, in their view of the soul, are like "those who catch sight of the sea Glaucus" (611d).

We thus find in the dialogue's long list of likenesses a series of images of vision and viewing themselves. Indeed, the *Republic* contains a variety of gazes. Not only do we find the possibility of the view of time as a whole (486a, 500b–c, 608c–d), and the contemplative theory of forms (517b, 532b–c), but also the sharp penetrating gaze needed to look into the soul of the tyrant (576d–577a), the panoptic gaze of the whole soul (579e), the scanning gaze of readers (368c–d), the sweeping gaze of children on horseback (467e), the searching gaze of hunters in pursuit of their prey (432b–c), the double gaze of philosophic rulers who look both to the forms and to what is called godlike in human beings (501b).[4] The choosing of a life, it would seem, requires all of these, as well as the ability to determine who could help one with this discernment (618b–c).

Throughout their attempts to judge which kind of life is best, Socrates and his interlocutors emphasize the *intimacy* with which their objects must be viewed. For instance, in order to judge the city under a tyranny they must "creep down into every corner" (576e), just as to judge the life of the tyrant they must "creep into a man's disposition" (577a).[5] This view culminates in the three psychic vistas found at the dialogue's end: the image of the soul necessary in order for the advocate of the unjust life to understand what he is really saying (book 9); the image of the view of the soul that they have had in the course of the dialogue (book 10's Glaucus image mentioned above); and the view of the terrain in which the souls of the dead find themselves, undergo punishment, select lives, and are reborn (book 10's myth of Er).[6]

Our study of the *Republic*'s investigations of soul focuses upon the visions of the soul made available to Socrates and his interlocutors throughout the dialogue, and the ways in which these viewings come about. We will also trace their attainment of awareness of the limits of their view of the soul, an attainment signified, as we have seen, by an image of a kind of viewing. In discussing soul, Socrates and his interlocutors must have their discernment trained to detect not only those intelligible beings toward which the soul strives, but also the many transformations of soul that foster or inhibit this striving. As Socrates observes, the human soul to which they have been attending "teems with ten thousand . . . oppositions arising at the same time" (603d). They are thus in need of nimble and sharp eyes; what they do not possess in advance they must develop to the best of their abilities in the course of their conversation.

This study of the *Republic* follows Plato's depiction of this development. While we take our start from the famous image of viewing that inaugurates the majority of their conversation, that of viewing the letters of the soul in the larger letters of the city in book 2, some discussion of the questions about soul opened in book 1 is necessary. I will begin there, and move on to sketch in broad outline the main features of the dialogue's approach to soul and the structure of the following four chapters.

In the first book of the *Republic*, Socrates and Thrasymachus attempt to identify the specific deeds and excellences of the soul. Socrates asks:

> "is there some work [ἔργον] of a soul that you couldn't ever accomplish with any other thing that is? For example, managing, ruling, and deliberating, and all such things [τὸ ἐπιμελεῖσθαι καὶ ἄρχειν καὶ βουλεύεσθαι καὶ τὰ τοιαῦτα πάντα]— could we justly attribute them to anything other than a soul and assert that they are peculiar to it?" "To nothing else." "And, further, what about living [Τί δ' αὖ τὸ ζῆν]? Shall we not say that it is the work of the soul?" "Most of all." (353d-e)

Socrates's attribution of both living and ruling to the soul has proven controversial. Robinson's assessment that in doing so Plato places biological and ethical demands on the soul that are ultimately incompatible is indicative of a broadly held concern about the psychology at work in several dialogues.[7]

However, whether the biological and ethical dimensions of human life are irreconcilable is open to question; the sphere of politics is precisely the site of their tense interaction. The attribution of multiple deeds to the soul produces at least two possibilities for consideration. First, it provokes one to wonder whether ruling, managing, deliberating, and living share some unifying elements that allow them to be the proper work of a single entity. In the *Republic*, Plato explores this possibility, treating the collision of ethical and biological concerns as less a contradiction than a fundamental dimension of political life. Because the dialogue delimits such life as lived within and by means of rule and regime, the conjunction of a set of executive capacities (managing, ruling, and deliberating) and living as the soul's activity connects an investigation of the soul with an investigation of the political phenomenon of the life of the citizen and provokes us to ask what the work of the city is.

The play between ruling and living receives a great deal of attention in the dialogue, which suggests that Plato is not only aware of the potential problems surrounding the attribution of both activities to the soul, but also that he attempts to address them in a manner appropriate to the scope of the dialogue. While Socrates's commitment to Glaucon and Adeimantus may not entail a detailed account of the status of the living body with respect to all of its biological and political dimensions, he does find it necessary to give an account of the correlation between the condition of the soul and the quality of one's life. Socrates's turn to examine regimes and souls in books 2, 4, 8 and 9 asserts that the condition of the human soul, like the quality of the human life, cannot be examined without investigating the city. Moreover, Plato refigures political phenomena themselves to refer not exclusively to the things of the patris, the fatherland, but to the activities of conglomerates of ruler and ruled (see especially 592a). For Plato, both city and body are such conglomerates, and both therefore emerge as good analogues to describe the complexities of psychic politics as well as the conditions under which this politics emerges.

Second, the conjunction of ruling and living that is the work of the soul suggests the possibility of a certain psychic excess. While Plato explores the relationship between ruling and living, he is also careful to document the emergence of anarchic psychological tendencies that make constant the threat of instability. In the absence of an account that would unify ruling and living into an single act, soul defies the economy of labor that will prove to be so crucial for the coming organization of the city (one person, one job) and for the conception of justice that such an organization recommends (minding one's own business). The business of the soul may very well be neither single nor simple. This excessive character, soul's capacity to step beyond itself, provides a crucial key to understanding the relationship between city, body, and soul by highlighting the role of desire in mediating between these three. In its extension and outward orientation as well as its irreducibility to need and its tendency toward subtlety, refinement, and intensification, desire is particularly revelatory of soul's plastic and transformative character.

As the dialogue unfolds, pleonexia—the tendency toward boundless acquisition—becomes a primary signifier of psychic excess. A subtle account of the becomings of soul in the context of the city must thus include an equally subtle account of desire and pleonexia. This, in turn, requires an analysis of the means by which city and soul affect one another; as we shall find, mimēsis and poiēsis emerge as particularly powerful vehicles of their interpenetration. Plato treats the play between mimēsis and poiēsis as a basic feature of human life, one which is of grave philosophical concern, if only because this play has significant implications for the practice of philosophy itself.[8]

The questions about soul opened in book 1, namely, whether there is some unifying feature of ruling and living and, if not, whether the soul is irreducibly excessive and complex, are taken up in book 2. The assumptions voiced in Glaucon's and Adeimantus's opening speeches, assumptions that viewing kinds of lives requires viewing conditions and becomings of soul, and that viewing these conditions and becomings requires viewing city, are the conceptual parameters within which the *Republic* unfolds. In order to orient our inquiry into the psychological investigations undertaken in the *Republic*, and thus to map out the course of study of the next four chapters, I sketch out below the inception and influence of these parameters as well as the forms of analysis to which they give rise.

Glaucon's restoration of Thrasymachus's argument that justice is the rule of the stronger at the start of book 2 marks a new approach to the question of the value of just and unjust lives, one which will require extensive discussion of the nature of the soul. There are several features of this new approach that prove decisive to the character and form of the dialogue's psychological investigations, and that will thus act as orienting points for our discussion of the *Republic*. First, the task that Glaucon and Adeimantus set for Socrates takes the form of a kind of philosophic portraiture. In investigating what justice and injustice are in order to defend the just life and to aid in the discernment of what kind of life is choice-worthy, Socrates is asked to present the lives of the most unjust and most just person side by side for comparison (360e). Eventually, in the later books of the dialogue, this results in the portraits of the philosopher and the tyrant, whose characters and fates inform the construction of the wisdom-loving, honor-loving, and money-loving lives that are presented to Glaucon and Adeimantus for judgment. In connecting these two tasks—investigating what justice and injustice are and developing images of forms of character for judgment—the dialogue already tacitly suggests that to know what justice *is* is also to know what form of life and character are choice-worthy. But more than this, the creation of images of forms of life serves the particular needs of Glaucon and Adeimantus. It does so by providing them with a relatively concrete presentation of the kind of character and life that actually result from justice and injustice, one which diverges sharply from the opinions they summarize at the start of book 2. Thus, the strategy of philosophic portraiture serves several interests; with it, Plato dramatizes the act of choosing one's life, and considers what role philosophy could have in such a choice. It is also worth pausing to note the uniqueness of the objects this portraiture attempts to bring to light, namely kinds of lives. Hovering between the particular life of the individual, which will end even if her soul does not, and the enduring fixity that Plato attributes to the form of justice itself, kind or type of life presents a combination of the fluid and the fixed. The just life, for instance, on the one hand comes into being and thus likely suffers also some form of passing away;[9] and on the other, attains a degree of self-sameness that makes it not only coherent, but also *iterable*, that is, the kind of thing that can be chosen again.

Second, Socrates's addition to the task Glaucon and Adeimantus set before him is that they observe the emergence, the coming-to-be, of just and unjust people (369a), a demand that cannot be met without a sophisticated conception of the interpenetration of city and individual soul. Thus, while the particular form in which this portraiture begins, the city/soul analogy, is treated as a necessary feature of their discussion because of the obscurity of the soul and their own "shortsightedness" (368c–d), an account of political environments in which certain forms of soul and life are fostered is likewise necessary.[10] It is not just that the democratic city provides an image of the democratic soul, for instance; it is also that the city as such is the arena in which forms of soul are forged and come to light. This is to say that in the *Republic* an account of the city is treated as necessary not only because city is an analogue to soul, but also because it is that medium in which people become just or unjust. Certain aspects of soul can only come to light when soul is viewed in the context of the city. Put another way, even if they did have eyes to read the letters of the soul, they could not do so without also understanding the city. An investigation of conditions of soul thus cannot proceed without an investigation of city. Indeed, city emerges as constructed by and housing psychic effects, as itself a psychological phenomenon.[11]

This peculiar and complex intertwining of city and soul is better understood in the context of the emergence of the city/soul analogy. What city and soul share, what provides the basis for their parallel accounts, is that both possess forms of 'character' (ἦθος) (435e, 545b) determined by and striving toward a similar constellation of excellences which are, indeed, described using the same names. Over the course of the dialogue, we will see suggestions of differences emerge between these excellences, but the basis of the analogy lies in the shared capacity of city and soul to be relevantly described as courageous, just, etc. As the dialogue unfolds, the object of analysis common to city and soul, character type, emerges as a function of the interaction between desire and a variety of other factors; the comparison between city and soul the dialogue develops identifies a causal framework, a dynamic, common to the two entities as that by means of which each can be said to possess a particular character type and course of development, and thus illuminates the psychopolitical complex that must be taken into account in order to discern, make claims about, and, ultimately, judge the most just and unjust lives. The character of the soul does not merely resemble that of the city, it is created within the city, by the desires and affects the city promotes and memorializes in its laws, rituals, and myths. The character of the city, in turn, is created by the souls that it houses, that produce its legislation, enact its rituals, tell its tales. Thus, the task of elucidating the character of city and soul is also a task of elucidating the effect of soul and city on one another. And this in turn requires a nuanced account of desire and of the causal mechanisms by means of which it operates in both city and soul.

This is obscured if we construe our understanding of Plato's psychology too narrowly. Jonathan Lear's diagnosis of the failure of contemporary scholarship to get a handle on Plato's general psychology, in that it keeps psuchē-analysis and polis-analysis separate, is instructive.[12] For all of the significance of the city/soul analogy, the relation between individual soul and city in the dialogue is more complex than that of analogy and cannot be reduced to it. In addition to the analogical relationship between city and soul, the *Republic* also posits and investigates a causal relationship between city and soul.[13] In the powerful effects of poetry and communal praise and blame on young souls, for instance, in the perverting effects of a corrupt city on the philosophic nature, in the enduring effects of city on soul presented in the myth of Er, we see this causal relation at work. The analysis of this relationship is particularly significant not only because it is motivated by a central animating question of the *Republic*, namely which kind of life is happiest, but also because it provides Plato the opportunity to investigate what role the philosopher is to have in the city, and to consider whether the philosopher can be reconciled to citizenship and to rule.[14] To be sure, this analysis could not provide the approach to these questions about happiness, philosophy and citizenship that it does without drawing upon the robust parallel analyses of civic politics and psychic politics provided by the analogy. We must recognize, however, that the result of such an analysis gives expression to the possibility of a radical refiguring of what politikē and what the things of the city mean, a possibility presented perhaps most clearly in book 9, wherein Socrates exhorts Glaucon to attend to the politeia and polis within his soul (591d–592b). Nevertheless, the nuance and subtlety of account by means of which Socrates arrives at this psychopolitical complex is a direct function of its having also analyzed each entity on its own. Thus, the service that the analogy offers to the dialogue is that of a perspective from which city and soul can be viewed as a whole.[15] As we shall see, this perspective includes both immersion and distance; it calls upon the intimacy unique to thought, as is asserted throughout the dialogue.

Finally, the particular path that Plato's Socrates takes to investigate and defend the just life—the creation of a city in speech—forges two simultaneous communities for analysis which I will describe here in some detail: the city in speech and the "city" of speakers. The drama of the city in speech begins with its founding (book 2), and then unfolds in the purgation of its decadent elements (books 2 and 3), the description of its organization and excellences (books 4 and 5),the account of its rulers (books 6 and 7) and the catalog of the various stages of its demise (books 8 and 9). The account of soul that emerges from this drama begins with an emphasis on the plasticity of the souls of the young, as it is their susceptibility to mimēsis and poiēsis which requires the purgation of the city (books 2–3), turns to the identification of the parts and excellences of the soul by means of analogy with the city (book 4), focuses upon the forms of unity and fragmentation to which souls are subject (with the philosopher and tyrant representing the two opposite poles between which most souls fluctuate, books 5–7), offers a description of the corrupt forms of soul (again in analogy with the corrupt forms of city, books 8-9) and culminates in an image of the complex soul capable of making clear the conditions of soul indicative of justice and injustice (book 9). Throughout the development of the city in speech, I will argue, the language of partition and its accompanying normative assessment of the various conditions of soul through the models of health and disease act as ways of gaining access to and articulating the complex plasticity of soul, and specifically to the transformations and becomings wrought by mimēsis and poiēsis. Put another way, the infamous language of partition and the analogy between vice and disease are tools used to develop as subtle an account as possible of the becomings to which soul is subject and to evaluate these becomings. That is all to say that the focus of much of the dialogue is precisely on the motion of the soul, its transformation and its becomings, its dynamics; the language of parts, like the language of depth, is an instrument of the psychodynamics attempted in the *Republic*.[16]

Insofar as the *Republic* undertakes not only an account of soul's plasticity but also a judgment about the value of its conditions, the tropes of health and sickness work hand in hand with the account of mimēsis and poiēsis. The language of parts of the soul and their order or regime supports the dialogue's characterization of health and sickness as the proper and improper ordering of rule between parts (a characterization that receives wide cultural support).[17] In turn, the circuit between mimēsis and poiēsis that the *Republic* describes illustrates how city and soul affect one another through a reciprocal process of internalization and externalization. This is to say that while the civically housed actions of mimēsis and poiēsis comprise one governing idiom through which the conditions of both city and soul are explicated in the *Republic*, health and sickness offer another. Medicine thus provides the dialogue with one of its most influential overarching perspectives. At the same time, the border between medical, legislative, and political activity is porous, both within the dialogue itself and in Athenian culture at large; this is an ambiguity upon which Plato capitalizes (as well as critiques, as we will see). In fact, medicine's influence is not only acknowledged and used by Plato in this dialogue to characterize conditions of soul and to serve his portrait of the philosopher in the city, but also to provide the conceptual tools by means of which Socrates and his interlocutors can judge the kinds of life that their conversation has illuminated. His use of the trope of medicine extends, then, beyond the city in speech to the "city" of speakers.

The drama of the city of speakers begins with Socrates's and his interlocutor's agreement to accept the role of founders of the city, an agreement expressed in the language of the assembly (369b). During the course of the formation, purgation, and organization of the city in speech, the members of the city of speakers will see their own assumptions about tyranny, human political life, and happiness drawn out, scrutinized, and—by the time they turn in book 9 to judge the just and unjust lives that have been presented to them—transformed. Throughout the dialogue, the vehicles of this transformation—the arguments and figures used to persuade Glaucon and Adeimantus to reject the opinions about justice and injustice that they voice at the start of book 2—are themselves presented for scrutiny and critique. This is particularly true of the trope that enables the very particular form of noetic immersion necessary for their analysis and judgment of forms of soul, that of medicine. As we will see, Plato builds this trope carefully throughout the course of the dialogue, developing a hybrid medical/juridical stance adopted by Socrates and his interlocutors that allows them to discern and diagnose the sicknesses of city and soul. Moreover, this stance valorizes self-analysis and culminates in its own critique, a critique necessitated by the very purchase on psuchē that it has enabled them to attain. Plato's use of the medical trope relies upon his construction of it as self-critiquing, as a trope capable of indicating its own limits, that is, as a trope that can and must eventually be overcome. This overcoming and its implications for their understanding of the nature of human life are drawn out in book 10.

In the course of the dialogue, Socrates, Glaucon, and Adeimantus will have their gazes sharpened and trained by a carefully constructed course of philosophical diagnostics. How this training compares to the training of philosophic natures described in book 7 requires careful consideration not only for what we learn about philosophy but also for what we learn about the capacities of soul. We must concede that in Socrates's and Glaucon's analysis of degenerate forms of regimes and souls, in their gaze into the depths of the tyrant soul and around the corners of the tyrant city (a gaze directed not at Being but at things that are subject to becoming) they are engaged in a task that is different from the contemplation of the form of the Good that is permitted the ideally educated philosopher in book 7. That is, what Socrates and Glaucon conclude about Being and what they conclude about the best life are reached through different, if also intimately related, activities of thought. Or, put differently, while the life that is emerging from this conversation as choice-worthy may be a life spent contemplating Being, the choosing of this life requires the careful discernment of a variety of forms of becoming.[18] The project with which much of the *Republic* is concerned, then, cannot be confused with the turn toward Being that the dialogue describes, just as Socrates himself cannot be confused with the philosophic nature that he describes in books 5 and 6, and educates in book 7. The *Republic*'s investigation of soul thus recoils upon its complex and multilayered investigation of philosophy itself.

In assessing what we learn about psuchē from the *Republic*, then, we must attend to the lessons gleaned from both of these dramas. That is, we must look not only to the description of psychic unity and fragmentation provided by the portraits of the philosopher and the tyrant respectively, for instance, but also to the depiction of the psychic transformation required in order to gain some understanding of the soul that is presented by the relationship between Socrates, Glaucon, and Adeimantus. What is more, we must look at the role of self-analysis and self-critique in this transformation.

Over the course of the next four chapters, I will argue that the *Republic*'s investigation of soul is an exercise in immanent critique. The critical perspective on their own understanding of soul that Socrates and his interlocutors attain by book 10 is made not only necessary but also *possible* by the terms of their prior account. Because Socrates's concern arises out of the failure of an account of the complex human soul to arrive at an understanding of the soul in its "true nature," we will attend to those moments in which their account of the complex soul points beyond itself, charting the emergence of these moments from out of the very arguments and images that will be judged, eventually, to be lacking. Doing so will allow us to discern the dialogue's handling of psychic plasticity (its attribution of a certain limitlessness to soul), the role of the polis granted this character of soul, and the place of both an investigation of soul and a love of wisdom within the city. We will begin with the task that Glaucon and Adeimantus set before Socrates and his strategy for dealing with this task, a strategy that forms, simultaneously, a city in speech and a community of its founders, a city of speakers. This strategy, as I will argue in chapter 4, allows them to discern the interpenetration of city and soul operative in the workings of mimēsis and poiēsis, a discernment whose eventual diagnostic character is foreshadowed by the strange construction of the cleverness of the doctor in book 3.

While Glaucon's and Adeimantus's requests presume already the complexity of soul with which Socrates will eventually take issue, that the soul they are describing is complex is made explicit in book 4's discussion of the "parts" of soul (a discussion undertaken with an acknowledgment of its limits), and in the employment of an analogy between health/disease and virtue/vice as a way of evaluating the differing conditions arising out of soul's complex structure. Chapter 5 argues that the analysis of desire, the identification of the parts of the soul and the training in desire productive of a unified city and soul that occur in books 4 and 5 indicate that one's character and quality of life hinge upon how one takes up one's desires. The distinction between lovers of wisdom and lovers of sights on the ground of their differing comportments toward their desires with which book 5 concludes sets the stage for the portraits of the philosopher and the tyrant drawn in books 6–9. Chapter 6 argues that the images of psychic unity and fragmentation these portraits offer draws upon the relationship between knowledge and desire intimated in book 4, while the judgment of these lives is rendered possible by the increasingly clinical comportment toward them that Socrates and Glaucon display throughout books 8 and 9. The power of this comportment, however, lies as much in its emphasis on self-critique as in its ability to cast certain conditions of soul as sick or healthy. In fact, the portrait of the tyrant they produce calls into question the adequacy of the analogy between health/disease and virtue/vice and requires that the full critical force of their philosophic diagnostics be brought to bear: Socrates and Glaucon must analyze their own conception of tyranny, their own poetic proclivities, and their own political commitments (or lack thereof). Book 10's presentation of the results of this analysis—their enhanced vision of the limitless nature of soul and its effects on human life, the role of the city in contending with these effects, and what is truly required in order to choose one's life well—is explored in chapter 7.

4 City and Soul

THE MAJORITY OF the conversation that comprises the *Republic* occurs because Socrates is trapped by his own piety: unable to hear justice slandered, he agrees to defend the just life by showing the effects of justice and injustice on the soul. Glaucon and Adeimantus offer a number of formulations of this task. Glaucon desires to hear what the powers of justice and injustice are when they are in the soul, alone and by themselves, stripped of their wages and consequences (358b). Adeimantus, observing that no one has adequately argued that injustice is the greatest evil a soul can possess and justice, correspondingly, the greatest good (366e), fills in his brother's argument. He calls attention to the effect on the soul of the customary opinion that justice is good but hard, namely, the development of the belief that happiness is best attained by gaining the reputation for justice while cultivating the unscrupulous advantage-gaining of the unjust (365a–366b). He twice asks Socrates not only to show that justice is stronger than injustice, but also what each does to the person who has them (367b, e).[1]

Adeimantus's focus on the capacity of people to seem to be what they are not (and thus on the capacity of the soul to mask its condition) in order to gain the reputation of conditions which they ultimately do not possess, intimates the connection between the dialogue's preoccupation with seeming, likeness, and image, on the one hand, and its investigations of soul on the other. At stake in the brothers' requests to produce an account of the perfectly just and the perfectly unjust person, in order to judge which of the two is happiest, is precisely the question of the relationship between condition of soul and quality of life.[2] How such portraiture is to be accomplished quickly becomes a topic of conversation. Socrates's initial response to this task is to call attention to the imagistic character of an account of justice and injustice that proceeds by way of creating portraits of perfectly just and unjust men: "My, my," I said, "my dear Glaucon, how vigorously you polish up each of the two men—just like a statue—for their judgment" (361d).[3]

In making their requests of Socrates, the brothers reveal themselves to be susceptible to assumptions about the unjust life, assumptions that have a profound impact on the iconography of justice and injustice that is to be produced in the subsequent conversation.[4] Both of their speeches treat the effects of virtue and vice as external to the people who possess them, imposed on them only by the social and political circumstances in which they find themselves. The unjust person is presented as unassailable and impervious to his possession of virtue and vice, indeed, as capable of flourishing in his possession of vice on the grounds of the assumption that the unjust person is more likely to achieve happiness than the just. Such a person is viewed as sufficiently untouched by the conditions that he brings about as to be able to bask in the riches and rewards that follow upon his injustice; implacable, unperturbed, and serene in his wealth and corruption.

It is with this vision of tyranny that Socrates must ultimately contend, and because Glaucon and Adeimantus also assume that justice and injustice are conditions of soul, and further that it is by having such conditions that one can be said to be just or unjust and to live a corresponding life, arguing against their vision of tyranny requires investigating the corruptions of soul. The brothers request an alternative conception of the relationship between the soul, virtue and vice, and quality of life, one which makes convincing the claim that it is good to be just. Their allusions to the divergence of appearance and reality, their identification of facades that make studying the soul difficult, dictate a depth psychology that would counteract a variety of impediments to viewing the soul, not the least of which are the very opinions about soul summarized above. It is in this context of the need to discern the nature of psychic corruption and flourishing that Socrates conducts an investigation whose limitations he will note on more than one occasion.

At the same time, the authority of the opinion about the happiness of the unjust, as the brothers have presented it, also requires the investigation of soul to reconfigure the relationship between people and the political environment in which they reside. In order to contest the assumption that the effects of virtue and vice are solely imposed from without, along with the antagonism between person and city that this presumes, Socrates will have to present an alternative conception of civic life. That this will require a critical engagement with certain assumptions about the relationship between polis and phusis is most clearly indicated by Glaucon, who restores Thrasymachus's argument that justice is the advantage of the stronger. His restoration presents the unjust desire to get the better of others as natural, and any curbing of this desire as conventional and, it is implied, unnatural (359c).

This chapter charts in some detail those features, emerging early on in the dialogue, that decisively shape its investigation of soul by orienting the discussion of justice and injustice toward the transformations to which souls are subject and the conditions of life they bring about. This turn begins with Glaucon and Adeimantus's assumption that a person is just or unjust on the basis of the condition of his soul; and it is sealed by Socrates's insistence that an account of just and unjust lives requires some grasp of the process by which these conditions come to be, that is, it requires a psychodynamics. By the end of book 3, Socrates and his interlocutors have specified the context in which psychic transformations can be observed, identified their primary mechanisms, and offered a preliminary formulation of the standard by which conditions of soul will be evaluated. The following four sections chart out this development, beginning with the demands Glaucon and Adeimantus make of Socrates, moving on to the foundation of the analogy between city and soul, then turning to their discussion of the transformative effects of mimēsis and poiēsis, and finally observing the emergence of health as the standard for judging soul's conditions. Throughout, I focus on the demands that these efforts place on all participants in the conversation.

Glaucon and Adeimantus

The task to which Socrates eventually assents is first introduced as a function of Glaucon's desire: "For I desire to hear what each [justice and injustice] is and what power it has all alone by itself when it is in the soul-dismissing its wages and its consequences" (358b). The implications of this request for our understanding of Glaucon's conception of soul are considerable. First, he elides condition of soul and condition of person. Second, in restoring Thrasymachus's argument, he assumes the same antagonism between phusis and nomos embedded therein. Justice emerges as a legal phenomenon that, as a mean between a desirable condition and an undesirable condition, is a symptom of weakness. Such a conception of nature presents the negative effects of injustice as purely external to the person committing unjust deeds; the unjust person is benefitted both materially and psychologically in the exercise of his power. This person is only harmed by his weakness and, should he get caught, by the laws that propose penalties for such actions. Thus, injustice, according to Glaucon's argument, is not a form of corruption; rather, it is an expression of strength, and a natural one at that. Third, and closely related to the second point, the position that Glaucon is outlining assumes a deeper equality between just and unjust person, namely, that both have the same kind of desires (this is made explicit in the ring of Gyges passage; see especially 360b–d). This is to say that the effects of neither justice nor injustice spill over to one's desires; whatever their power when in the soul, they are not, according to this opinion, sufficient to affect what one wants. If anything, injustice is a more honest expression of what one wants; the just person is treated as weaker because he is willing to give up some of what he wants in order to avoid the pain of suffering injustice.[5]

Finally, the comparison between the lives of the perfectly just and the perfectly unjust person for which Glaucon calls requires him to stipulate a condition—that each of these men "go unchanged till death" (361c)—which overlooks an essential feature of these characters: their development. To consider such figures under this condition of stasis is to do just this, to consider figures, and figures bereft of the transformations, changes, and becomings to which human beings are subject over time. It is to the static as well as the imagistic character of these two "men" that Socrates calls attention in his description of Glaucon's narrative as polishing up statues for judgment (361d). As the conversation continues, it becomes clear that one can understand neither the character nor the quality of life of either the just or the unjust person without taking into consideration their having become just or unjust, and thus one cannot fulfill Glaucon's request without observing the emergence of justice and injustice both over time and according to the influence of place. Whatever giving an account of the power of justice and injustice in the soul means, it must include an account of the various forms of becoming just and unjust, as well as the contexts in which these possibilities arise.[6] It is these *processes* of becoming that Glaucon overlooks when he presents for judgment two men who go unchanged to death.

Glaucon's oversight is partly corrected by his brother, whose description of the opinions of those who praise justice and blame injustice includes a careful consideration of the political environment in which such praise and blame is made, and, moreover, the effect they have on the souls of the young (365a). Adeimantus's speech thus marks out the specific economy of honor to which he has been exposed, as well as the political institutions and actors that support it. Fathers, poets, rhetoricians, and priests all are indicted as complicit in a message that pays lip service to justice, lauds injustice, and presents the gods as indifferent to human affairs, subject to bribes, or nonexistent (365d–e). The conclusion that the impressionable youth is likely to take from all of this, according to Adeimantus, is that seeming overpowers the truth, and that one must set about fortifying oneself with the reputation of justice, scaling it as though it were a wall, or, to switch metaphors, the young man will conclude: "as façade and exterior I must draw a shadow painting of virtue all around me, while behind it I must trail the wily and subtle fox of the most wise Archilochus" (365c). The metaphors of which Adeimantus avails himself, scaling and drawing, are instructive; they both suggest a dissembling that marks out territories, an interior and an exterior, and set the two sides in opposition to one another.

Having outlined this social and political terrain, Adeimantus concludes by identifying the lacuna in this system of praise and blame: "But as to what each itself does with its own power when it is in the soul of a man who possesses it and is not noticed by gods and men, no one has ever, in poetry or prose, adequately developed the argument that the one is the greatest of evils a soul can have in it and justice the greatest good" (366e). The request that Adeimantus builds off of his earlier observation echoes his elision between soul and person: "Now don't only show us by the argument that justice is stronger than injustice, but show what each in itself does to the man who has it that makes the one bad and the other good" (367b). And again, just a few lines later: "So don't only show us by the argument that justice is stronger than injustice, but show what each in itself does to the man who has it—whether it is noticed by gods and human beings or not—that makes the one good and the other bad" (367e).

Both brothers display a certain naivety with respect to politics in that both overlook the extent to which the person is a product of the city in which she finds herself: Glaucon by not recognizing all that is entailed in becoming just or unjust and the role of the city in these becomings, and both brothers by assuming that the effects of justice and injustice are always imposed from without. This is to say, each assumes a significantly less porous relationship between outside and inside than their ensuing conversation will illustrate. And while Adeimantus's question about the effects on the soul of contradictory claims about justice and injustice (365a) anticipates the work of mimēsis in facilitating this relationship, he initially assumes too rigid a distinction between surface and depth to comprehend the full significance of his question. Socrates's turn from the soul to the city as the unit of analysis draws out for the two brothers the limits of these assumptions. This turn allows them to observe the emergence of a variety of psychic phenomena from out of the interaction between souls. Because the city houses multiple souls and multiple psychic effects, it can provide a view of the soul for even the shortsighted.

Our analysis of the task Glaucon and Adeimantus set for Socrates has identified three main features of the psychology needed to give an account of just and unjust lives for the purposes of choosing between them. First, it must be a *depth* psychology; the ability to judge the lives of the just and unjust requires an intimate view of the tyrant soul. Second, it must be a *dynamic* psychology; it must mark out the environmental (natural as well as political) engines of soul's transformations. Third, it must be a *developmental* psychology; it must be able to offer an account of those transformations of soul that seem to be either maturing or regressive. As we will see, Socrates's strategy for taking up this multidimensional psychology begins with the creation of a context in which complex psychological transformations can be discerned (the formation of the city in speech), turns to identify the dynamic by means of which city and soul affect one another and then begins to develop a means of evaluating the various conditions of city and soul that emerge from their interaction.

The City in Speech

Socrates and his interlocutors construct their city in speech by means of five architectural elements which are to be understood on the basis of their relationship with one another: need (χρεία), deed/work (ἔργον), art (τέχνη), nature, (φύσις), and opportune time (καιρός) (369b–370c). Any city, observes Socrates, is founded on the basis of need. Moreover, as Socrates goes on to point out, the archē of the city as such is also what motivates him, Glaucon, and Adeimantus to create the city in speech: "Come, now," I said, "let's make a city in speech from the beginning [ἐξ ἀρχῆς]. Our need, as it seems, will make it [ποιήσει δὲ αὐτήν, ὡς ἔοικεν, ἡ ἡμετέρα χρεία]" (369c). Presumably, the need to which Socrates is referring is the need of shortsighted people to read large letters rather than small (368d). The duplication of need has the effect of founding two communities, the city in speech, whose citizens are bound together by mutual need, and, as we have noted above, the "city" of speakers, the community of those who, because of their poor eyesight, are in need of a larger arena in which to observe the emergence of justice and injustice. Their inability to directly observe conditions of soul results in a particular strategy (the creation of the city in speech) that also creates them as founders.

Need, as the basis of this founding, is introduced as a means of specifying the general organization of the city; need defines boundaries and groups based upon the particular demands of human beings (the need for food, the need for clothing, the need for shelter, etc.). However, the discussion quickly turns to illustrate the ease with which the needs that shape the limits and boundaries of civic organization mutate into desires which defy these very limits and boundaries. While Socrates holds out the possibility of a "city of utmost necessity [ἀναγκαιοτάτη πόλις]" (369d), a simple and healthy (ὑγιής) city, this is not a possibility that turns out to satisfy Glaucon, who demands that they examine a more complex, luxurious and, according to Socrates, feverish (φλεγμαίνουσαν) city (372e). Certainly we learn something about Glaucon from this discussion. However, given the discussion's forthcoming illustration of the instability of the distinction between need and desire, I am inclined to read this passage as Plato pointing to the impossibility of the simple city. Both the healthy city and the feverish city have relishes; the distinction between them is not between the absence and presence of relishes but the degree of their refinement (372c–e). As this feverish city develops, it is organized into parts or classes in connection to need; however, the possibility of its justice and injustice seems to be anchored in the labile play between need and desire, a play perhaps most vividly displayed in human acquisitiveness. The invocation of need opens up already a conceptual framework that requires one to consider the limited capacity of need to act precisely as a limit. Thus, the organizational work performed by need is also subject to the instability of its particular ordering.

The invocation of need makes necessary and draws together the work that must be performed to fulfill that need, the time of completion dictated by that work, and the technai that make the performance and cultivation of that work possible. The products of technē and the manner of their production are subject to a standard by means of which the success or failure of the performance can be determined.[7] The conjunction of ergon, kairos, and technē elaborates upon the organizational work of need, further inscribing and articulating the possibility of disorganization. Cities, that is to say, can simply fail to perform the works that are needed of them. Similarly, while the kairos of this work connects human community to a larger order, it also indicates another way in which these communities can fail with respect to the fulfillment of need—they can fail to heed and/or provide the proper time necessary for the performance of work.

Finally, phusis mediates between the needs that are the archē of the city and technē's capacity to fulfill those needs. States Socrates: "I myself also had the thought when you spoke, that, in the first place, each of us is naturally not quite like anyone else, but rather differs in his nature; different men are apt for the accomplishment of different jobs" (370a). Nature in this passage names a certain kind of aptitude or propensity for particular deeds. It emerges as that differentiating element corresponding to the particularities of needs and the deeds capable of fulfilling them. Human civic life is defined by the relationship between need and nature: as need presents the motivation for founding cities, nature offers a means of locating particular human beings within those cities.

The ordering, placing, and differentiating operation of nature also marks out a disordering and disfiguring of the city, namely, the allocation of work for which one is not suited.[8] Given the tacit anthropological assumption at work here, namely, that human nature itself "is minted in smaller coin" (395b) than would allow for the good performance of multiple jobs (an assumption stated but not explicitly argued for), we also have a model of personal disfigurement or disordering, namely, the performance of jobs for which one is not suited. Thus, when Socrates concludes his identification of these architectural features as follows: "on this basis each thing becomes more plentiful, finer, and easier, when one man, exempt from other tasks, does one thing according to nature and at the crucial moment" (370c), the implication is that the human being, like the task she is attempting, becomes more plentiful, finer, and easier by means of this distribution of labor.[9] Throughout the development of the city in speech, this intertwining of work, city, and human flourishing informs Plato's analysis of the means by which city and soul interconnect. The following section focuses upon two particularly prominent ways of characterizing this interconnection in the dialogue, mimēsis, and poiēsis.

Mimēsis and Poiēsis

Once Socrates has acceded to Glaucon's demand for refined luxury in the city in speech, the "founders" of this city find themselves in need of installing well-educated guardians in it. Initially, Socrates justifies the supervision of poetry that he claims is vital to this education on the grounds of the malleability of the young:

> "Don't you know that the beginning is the most important part of every work and that this is especially so with anything young and tender? For at that stage it's most plastic [μάλιστα γὰρ δὴ τότε πλάττεται], and each thing assimilates itself to the model whose stamp anyone wishes to give to it [καὶ ἐνδύεται τύπος ὃν ἄν τις βούληται ἐνσημήνασθαι ἑκάστῳ]." "Quite so." "Then shall we so easily let the children hear just any tales fashioned by just anyone and take into their souls [καὶ λαμβάνειν ἐν ταῖς ψυχαῖς] opinions for the most part opposite to those we'll suppose

they must have when they are grown up?" "In no event will we permit it." "First, as it seems, we must supervise the makers of tales; and if they make a fine tale, it must be approved, but if it's not, it must be rejected. We'll persuade nurses and mothers to tell approved tales to their children and to shape their souls with tales more than their bodies with hands [καὶ πλάττειν τὰς ψυχὰς αὐτῶν τοῖς μύθοις πολὺ μᾶλλον ἢ τὰ σώματα ταῖς χερσίν]. Most of those they now tell must be thrown out." (377a–c)

As their discussion of education develops, mimēsis emerges as one of the primary means by which the *Republic* traces psychic plasticity in the context of the city, that is, as it operates in the interaction between souls. As a means of indicating this interaction, their account of mimēsis acts as a complex instrument of psychological analysis, several features of which prove decisive for the rest of the dialogue. First, while the discussion in books 2 and 3 begins with the mimēsis performed by the young as a primary and unavoidable vehicle for their education, the discussion rather quickly moves to the mimetic artist. Elsewhere in the dialogue, mimēsis, as a form of likening oneself to something, will be extended well beyond children and artists and a narrow conception of education and artistic production. At its most general, mimēsis names a stance or posture of psychic receptivity.[10] Indeed, Plato charts a spectrum of mimetic behavior distinguished by the intimacy or intensity of receptivity, from the mimetic behavior of the young that produces "habit and nature on body and sound and speech" (395d), to the focused absorption of the mimetic artist in the characters he portrays,[11] to the sympathy of the audience, with its variant capacities for critical distance and judgment.

Second, the interactions between soul and cultural vehicle take several forms: between friends, between family members, between child and adult, between citizen and poet, citizen and lawgiver, and citizen and politician/ruler. Such interactions can also become quite abstract, as when the citizen or child is interacting not directly with another person but with the cultural, artistic, intellectual, and political artifacts available throughout the city. These artifacts bear the values and expertise of their makers, reflect the opinions and desires of their consumers, and enjoy a certain degree of independence from both. Tragedy is an excellent example of such an artifact insofar as it is shaped by three intertwined forces: (*a*) a broad mythic tradition, (*b*) the hand of the poet, and (*c*) the eyes and ears of the audience.

Indeed, Plato's conception of the interplay between mimēsis and poiēsis is complex. Broadly conceived, mimēsis and poiēsis are internalizing and externalizing activities, answering to desires and creating new desires. More narrowly, the poiēsis of the tragedian is treated as a kind of mimēsis (although, again, not the only kind; both mimēsis and poiēsis are extended well beyond the realm of artistic production). Moreover, insofar as mimēsis establishes a condition of soul, it too operates as a kind of making, a poiēsis. The difference between these conceptions is often simply analytic, and in all three cases the tragic poet is implicated as both artist and audience.[12] The complexity of the tragic poet's mimetic activities is another illustration of the manner in which this figure troubles the organizing principle of specialization in the city. As both audience and actor, both recipient and producer, the tragic poet defies reduction to a single activity. To the extent that any citizen of a city in which such poetry flourishes will also be both recipient and maker, the tragic poet reveals a deeper challenge to this principle within citizenship itself.[13]

The training in what is desirable and what is not that mimēsis offers both accounts for the intimacy of its influence and depends upon the plasticity of desire. To supervise poets and craftspeople is to take up and shape the training in desire in which they engage, and thus to take a direct hand in the creation of the character of citizens. Insofar as mimēsis is unavoidable (500c), so too is the political necessity of such supervision, at least for one who holds a vision of politics as the shaping of citizens. When the guardians imitate:

> "they must imitate what's appropriate to them from childhood: men who are courageous, moderate, holy, free, and everything of the sort; and what is slavish, or anything else shameful, they must neither do nor be clever at imitating, so they won't get a taste for the being from its imitation [ἵνα μὴ ἐκ τῆς μιμήσεως τοῦ εἶναι ἀπολαύσωσιν]. Or haven't you observed that imitations, if they are practiced continually from youth onwards, become established as habits and nature, in body and sounds and thought?" (395b–d)[14]

The supervision of poets and craftspeople is at least initially presented as the attempt to create an environment that encourages and fosters "virtuous" character, and the extension of this supervision is justified on the grounds of the capacity of artifacts to make manifest grace or gracelessness (400d–401a).[15] Only those artifacts that are graceful, well made, truth telling, and simple should be encouraged, and in the realm of poetry, only those stories that fit within the general parameters that they have been outlining will be permitted. As this description develops, the environmental trope is brought to the fore:

> "Must we, then, supervise only the poets and compel them to impress the image of the good disposition on their poems or not to make them among us? Or must we also supervise the other craftsmen and prevent them from impressing this bad disposition, a licentious, illiberal, and graceless one, either on images of animals or on houses or on anything else that their craft produces? And the incapable craftsman we mustn't permit to practice his craft among us, so that our guardians won't be reared on images of vice, as it were on bad grass, every day cropping and grazing on a great deal little by little from many places, and unawares put together some one big bad thing in their soul? Mustn't we, rather, look for those craftsmen whose good natural endowments make them able to track down the nature of what is fine and graceful, so that the young, dwelling as it were in a healthy place [ἵνα ὥσπερ ἐν ὑγιεινῷ τόπῳ], will be benefited by everything; and from that place something of the fine works will strike their vision or their hearing, like a breeze bringing health from good places [ὥσπερ αὔρα φέρουσα ἀπὸ χρηστῶν τόπων ὑγίειαν]; and beginning in childhood, it will, without their awareness, with the fair speech

lead them to likeness and friendship as well as accord [εἰς ὁμοιότητά τε καὶ φιλίαν καὶ συμφωνίαν τῷ καλῷ λόγῳ ἄγουσα]?" (401b–d)

A proper constellation of artworks and artifacts functions like a healthy dwelling place full of proper, nourishing grasses and beneficent breezes.[16] The use of eating and grazing as metaphors for psychic absorption and internalization occurs throughout the *Republic*. We will see it in the discussion of philosophic natures in book 6 that compares them to seeds in need of proper nourishment (491d), and also in the image of the soul in book 9, with its contemplation of which "parts" of soul should be fed (588e–589a). In many of these examples, the trope of ruling (which was extended to all technai in book 1) is connected with what does the feeding and starving, such that to feed and to starve are actions reserved for the ruler, whatever part that ruler may be, and feeding and starving become forms of rule. This play between agricultural and political metaphors was introduced in Thrasymachus's example of the shepherd to counter Socrates's claim that rulers rule for the sake of the ruled (343b). Feeding, watering, starving, pruning, cultivating seeds, or destroying them; all of these images tacitly connect politikē to both technē and phusis.

At the same time that supervision is expanded from poetry to other arts, the unique or "sovereign" character of education in music (of which poetry is a part) is asserted, precisely on the grounds of its intimacy with soul:[17]

> "So Glaucon," I said, "isn't this why the rearing in music is most sovereign [κυριωτάτη]? Because rhythm and harmony most of all insinuate themselves into the inmost part of the soul [τὸ ἐντὸς τῆς ψυχῆς] and most vigorously lay hold [ἅπτεται][18] of it in bringing grace with them; and they make a man graceful if he is correctly reared, if not, the opposite. Furthermore, it is sovereign because the man properly reared on rhythm and harmony would have the sharpest sense for what's been left out and what isn't a fine product of craft or what isn't a fine product of nature. And, due to his having the right kind of dislikes, he would praise the fine things; and, taking pleasure in them and receiving them into his soul, he would be reared on them and become a gentleman. He would blame and hate the ugly in the right way while he's still young, before he's able to grasp reasonable speech. And when reasonable speech comes, the man who's reared in this way would take most delight in it, recognizing it on account of its being akin [γνωρίζων δι' οἰκειότητα]." (401d–402a)[19]

Training in music is precisely training in desire, praise, and blame; this cultivation in taste, in turn, is taken as creating a predisposition for logos. Throughout his description of mimēsis and the supervision of technai, Socrates stresses the relationship between the gracefulness of bodies and artifacts, on the one hand, and logos, on the other. Such bodies and artifacts tend toward articulation. Similarly, Plato's treatment of mimēsis, especially his emphasis on the sovereignty of music, establishes a line of inquiry about the soul that seeks to determine what soul is, such that it is capable of the receptivity that grants mimetic activity its power and that proves to be so intimately influenced by rhythm and harmony. Finally, this discussion combines the pursuit of the psychological line of inquiry with a political line of inquiry, namely, why poets have the particular social power and influence they do. Indeed, the entire discussion is predicated upon the cultural and political capital of poetic artifacts and their producers.

Doctor and Judge

Socrates's purgation of the feverish city takes up the possibilities for unity and fragmentation implicit in the creation of the city in speech, with its 'one person, one job' principle, presents the city as the site in which psuchai intermingle with one another via cultural vehicles and identifies the processes of this interaction as the play between mimēsis and poiēsis. The three lines of thought we have seen emerge from his analysis of mimēsis and poiēsis—the proto-articulate character of bodies and certain cultural artifacts, the receptive character of souls, and the authority of the poets—require the development of some means to evaluate the effects of poetry and other cultural artifacts on the soul. In this early discussion, the dominant metaphor for doing so is that of health. Throughout books 2 and 3, we can see health used as a standard for the assessment of things well beyond the medical art's purview of "the body" established in book 1 (332c).[20] Of course, it is also necessary to note that the precision of the medical art was hardly uncontroversial, and uses of health to describe conditions other than those bodies already had a long history when Plato was writing the *Republic*.[21] This very flexibility informs Plato's development and privileging of medical metaphors.[22] While the *Republic* extends the standard of health beyond the borders of the body, it also purges the medical art itself of what Socrates diagnoses as its decadent and deleterious elements (405a–410a). This is to say, in order for Plato to employ the standard of the medical doctor beyond the limits of medical practice, medicine, like poetry and like the feverish city itself, must be purged.[23]

The culmination of Socrates's purgation of the medical art occurs in the middle of book 3, in which Socrates and Glaucon, having offered a critique of medicine as it is practiced by the dietetic doctors (of which Herodicus is taken as a paradigmatic example, 406a–b), turn to discuss the cleverest and truest doctor. This discussion leads to a comparison with the judge.

"Doctors," states Socrates,

"would prove cleverest if, beginning in childhood, in addition to learning the art, they should be familiar with very many and very bad bodies and should themselves suffer all diseases and not be quite healthy by nature. For I don't suppose they care for a body with a body—in that case it wouldn't be possible for the bodies themselves ever to be, or to have been, bad—but for a body with a soul; and it's not possible for a soul to have been, and to be, bad and to care for anything well." (408d–e)

The doctor's excellence consists of a combination of experience and knowledge that is made possible by the separation between soul and body and the capacity of the doctor to understand things about himself and others from his own experience. The judge's excellence, on the other hand, consists in the ability to cultivate knowledge in the absence of experience, an absence made necessary by the effects of one soul on another:

> "A judge, on the other hand, my friend, rules a soul with a soul, and it's not possible for it to have been reared and been familiar with bad souls from youth on, and to have gone through the list of all unjust deeds and to have committed them itself so as to be sharp at inferring from itself the unjust deeds of others like diseases in the body. Rather, it must have been inexperienced and untainted by bad dispositions when it was young, if, as a fine and good soul, it's going to make healthy judgments [κρινεῖν ὑγιῶς] about what is just. This is exactly why decent men, when they are young, look as though they were innocents and easily deceived by unjust men, because they have in themselves no patterns of affections similar to those of bad men." (409a–b)

While the doctor's art is shaped by a distinction between soul and body, and thus between what treats and what is treated, the judge's art is shaped by the effect of souls on one another, and by an absence of distinction between what treats and what is treated.[24] But it is also necessary to note that in the end, it is the standard of the doctor, health, which takes precedence and is applied to both the work of the doctor and that of the judge.[25]

Socrates's distinction between the doctor and the judge suggests two things about the psychological investigations that are to follow. First, while the use of a medical vocabulary is presented as a means to evaluate the conditions of city and soul, its limits are hinted at as well. Socrates laments the development of a subtle medical vocabulary (405c–d). What is needed, this passage suggests, is a sufficiently subtle vocabulary for conditions of viciousness. It is in the absence of such a vocabulary that Socrates makes use of the idiom of health, whose limits will be made more apparent presently in the dialogue. Second, in submitting both treatment and judgment to the standard of health, Socrates intertwines the art of the judge and that of the doctor. As we will see, Socrates's and Glaucon's efforts to create images of the most just and unjust lives and to discern which is best makes use of the hybrid medico-juridical practice whose possibility is broached here. The necessity for such a hybrid account is made more apparent when we consider whether it is possible to cultivate a sufficiently subtle understanding of viciousness as to be able to choose between vicious and virtuous lives without oneself being infected by viciousness. If the answer to this is no, and if we follow the description of the judge, the suggestion is that in cases in which one has already been exposed to viciousness, rendering judgment on the choice-worthiness of lives is only possible if one is able to discern and contend with the patterns of injustice one already possesses, that is only if one is capable of judging oneself. Such a self-diagnostic capacity resonates with Socrates's depiction of the clever the doctor, whose capacity to treat depends upon his acute awareness of his own corruptability. How such a hybrid practice of judging and treating stands with respect to the practice of philosophy is a question that will receive further investigation.

Conclusion

The defense of the just life that Glaucon and Adeimantus request of Socrates requires a complex developmental psychodynamics of remarkable depth and subtlety. Because such an account is not without reflexive effect on the viewer, this task requires Socrates and his interlocutors to create the conditions in which such viewing can be made possible, while limiting its deleterious effects (quarantining or anesthetizing this vision). Socrates's strategy for dealing with all that is required by the demand to produce the most nuanced portrait of just and unjust lives is to shift perspective from the individual soul to the city in an effort to correct Glaucon and Adeimantus's somewhat naive assumption that such figures can occur in the absence of a process of becoming and a place in which such becoming occurs. Consequently, city and soul are not treated as simply analogical, but as entities whose account is coconstitutive; the city, Socrates emphasizes, is the arena in which souls mingle, interact, and transform one another. Mimēsis and poiēsis specify two particularly powerful vehicles of this interpsychic transformation. Health and sickness are used as one means for evaluating the psychic conditions wrought by residence in a city with others, a means that occurs frequently and significantly enough in the *Republic* to merit extended critical consideration of the technē that claims expertise in health. Socrates's purgation of the medical art occurs immediately after his supervision of poetry (thereby suggesting some connection between medicine and poetry) and forms part of the purgation of the feverish city in which they have been engaged for some time now. Finally, Socrates's discussion of the excellences of the doctor and judge illustrates the absence of a sufficiently complex vocabulary for giving an account of viciousness. It also presents the possibility of a hybrid practice relevant to Socrates's and his interlocutors' endeavors and thus worthy of investigation for its relation to what is said about philosophy.

As we have seen, mimēsis and poiēsis operate by galvanizing and transforming one's attachments and attractions; the intimacy of their operation is a function of their ability to speak to and turn what one wants. It is in their praise and blame that poet and audience shape one another's souls and actions. Thus, the multidimensional psychology required by the brothers' requests to Socrates would not be possible without an analysis of desire, and it is to the account of desire and its training that is offered in books 4 and 5 that the next chapter turns.

5 Psychic Fragmentation

While books 2 and 3 provide an account of the vehicles through which city and soul affect one another, books 4 and 5 elaborate upon the complexity that is interior to soul and identify the tense interaction between desire and other elements of the soul as decisive for the unity or fragmentation of both soul and city. Thus, books 4 and 5 contribute to the multidimensional psychodynamics requested in the preceding books by deepening Socrates's and his interlocutors' understanding of what it means for soul to become virtuous or vicious. They do so by focusing upon the general forms of fragmentation and unity to which the human being and human things (including cities) give rise in the course of their respective becomings.

Indeed, I will argue, books 4 and 5 lay the foundation for a catalogue of psychic division, one which seeks to take into account a broad range of manifestations of fragmentation and unity. These books look not only to individual human behavior and the psychic division that can be discerned therein, but also to collective human action and the political formations to which it gives rise—viewing the city as a field in which division and unity are made manifest—and beyond even human political activity to the varieties of beings themselves and the vision of dissolution and unity provided by an exploration of the ontological status of things.

In doing so, books 4 and 5 mark out the differing stances toward desiderative life that provide, in turn, the basis for distinguishing kinds of life. Book 4's analysis of the form of desire, discussion of the soul's parts, and characterization of their organization as resembling health or disease sketch out a set of desiderative comportments.

The forms of fragmentation and unity made possible by these differing orientations toward desire are made more explicit in book 5's account of the training in desire that is implicit in the argument for the equal training of men and women, made explicit in the effort to produce a community of pleasure and pain, and crystallized in the distinction between the lover of sights and the lover of wisdom. This distinction, in turn, sets the stage for the more elaborate ontology and philosophic portraiture of books 6 and 7. This is to say, the description of the soul's erotic inclination toward Being in books 6 and 7 has its roots in the analysis of desire and its training provided in books 4 and 5.

Moreover, the vision of psychic complexity that an analysis of desire permits, a vision enhanced by the analogy between health/disease and virtue/vice, presents the soul as an entity whose capacity for division is included in what it means for it to be (another way of formulating soul's unique plasticity). Ultimately, this character of soul will give rise to conditions of unity and fragmentation which exceed the descriptive and evaluative capacities of the trope of health and disease.[1] Thus, the seeds for the critique of health and sickness as standards for soul are sown, even as they are used to provide conceptual tools for evaluating the effects of psychic fragmentation.

In order to make good on these claims, this chapter begins by drawing out the preliminary account of desiderative life embedded within book 4's analysis of the form of desire and discussion of parts of the soul, paying particular attention to the implications of its comparison between desire and knowledge (part 1). It then turns to analyze the analogy between health/disease and virtue/vice that conclude this book, marking the manner in which the discussion of soul's parts augments the evaluative framework of health and disease begun in books 2 and 3 by treating both conditions of health/disease and conditions of virtue/vice as a function of the relation between parts, a relation determined largely in response to the pushings and pullings of desire (part 2). This account enables a description of kinds of lives to proceed by way of the identification of differing orientations toward desire, orientations that are established over time and are responsive to various forms of training and education, a few of which are explored in book 5's infamous three waves. Consequently the chapter then turns to this discussion to mark out the training in desire described in book 5, highlighting the forms of psychic fragmentation and unity to which this training gives rise and focusing especially on the differing compartments toward desire described in the distinction between the lover of sights and the lover of wisdom (part 3). This distinction, in turn, will serve the larger project of philosophical portraiture by providing the preliminary terms by means of which books 6–9 present the most just and unjust lives, a presentation whose analysis will form the subject matter of the next chapter.

The Form of Desire

Book 4 opens by placing a few finishing touches upon the city in speech, and then moves quickly to discern what wisdom, courage, moderation, and justice are, determining each on the basis of the class structure outlined in books 2 and 3. Praise for the principle of specialization on which this structure relies is sung early on in book 4. Socrates observes that the maintenance of the class structure made possible by the noble lie "was intended to make plain that each of the other citizens too must be brought to that which naturally suits him—one man, one job—so that each man, practicing his own, which is one, will not become many but one; and thus, as you see, the whole city will naturally grow to be one and not many [τοῦτο δ ἐβούλετο δηλοῦν ὅτι καὶ τοὺς ἄλλους πολίτας, πρὸς ὅ τις πέφυκεν, πρὸς τοῦτο ἕνα πρὸς ἓν ἕκαστον ἔργον δεῖ κομίζειν, ὅπως ἂν ἓν τὸ αὑτοῦ ἐπιτηδεύων ἕκαστος μὴ πολλοὶ ἀλλ εἷς γίγνηται, καὶ οὕτω δὴ σύμπασα ἡ πόλις μία φύηται ἀλλὰ μὴ πολλαί]" (423c–d). Such a practice is taken to combat the divisive effects of wealth and poverty outlined in the preceding pages of book 4 and to produce both unified individuals and unified cities.

As books 4 and 5 unfold, the theme of becoming one or many receives increased attention as the forms of these becomings (and their conditions for possibility) come to light (see especially 443c–e). This interest in becoming and the discussion of parts of city and soul are mutually reinforcing insofar as the *achievement* of oneness or the lack thereof is a task for variegated entities. Socrates's and his interlocutors' discussion of the nature of desire and its effects on the soul serves to illuminate the factors involved in attaining unity or failing to do so.

The claims made about the nature of desire in *Republic* 4 are already well-trod, if also controversial, territory.[2] I will here simply highlight a few features of the discussion most germane to the general trajectory of conversation, and will approach this discussion less for what is says about desire as such than for its particular contribution to the account of desiderative life that runs (in more and less explicit terms) throughout the dialogue. Having outlined the various virtues and vices of the city, Socrates and Glaucon turn in the latter part of book 4 to consider whether the structure of the soul mirrors that of the city. In the course of this conversation they agree that there is a form (εἶδος) of desire (437d) and set about examining this form. The subsequent exploration of what desire is relies heavily upon Socrates's invocation of the experience of desiring and his treatment of hunger and thirst as the most vivid (ἐναργεστάτας) of desires (437d).[3] It results in a provocative sketch of the world inhabited by the desiring human being, one which lays the foundation for the ensuing discussion of kinds of lives by highlighting the variety of orientations one can have toward one's desires, asserting that this orientation is decisive for the kind of character, the turn of soul, one possesses, and laying the foundation for charting the transformation of individual desires and appetites into sustained dispositions and habits of desiring.[4] It is also a preliminary analysis, one which is complicated and deepened throughout the subsequent books of the dialogue with the introduction of destinctions between, for instance, necessary, unnecessary and lawless desires.

Beyond the obvious point that this analysis furthers the analogy between city and soul, three elements of this account are essential for understanding its role in the larger concerns of the dialogue. The first is Socrates's attribution of a formal character to desire (437d). One need not assume a developed technical sense of "form" in order to see that in describing desires as having an εἶδος, Socrates is attributing to them a degree of coherence that allows them to form a kind and that renders possible an account of what they are. While certain modes of desiring (and also certain desires) will be associated with the furthest remove of rationality in books 8 and 9, the *need* to clarify the manner in which one's desiring life could lead to such excesses is a function of the formal characteristics of desire itself, characteristics which also provide the condition for such clarification.

Second, as the conversation continues it becomes clear that the coherence of desire is bound up with its being one of those things that, like knowledge is, "such as to be related to something" (438a–b), and specifically with the manner in which desire allows access to the world. Desiring, willing, and wanting reach out toward and disclose a world in such a manner as to engender in the desirer an affirming and acquisitive stance: "For example, won't you say that the soul of the man who desires either longs for what it desires or embraces that which it wants to become its own; or again, that, insofar as the soul wills that something be supplied to it, it nods assent to itself *as though someone had posed a question* [ὥσπερ τινὸς ερωτῶντος] and reaches out toward the fulfillment of what it wills?" (437c, my emphasis).[5] Desire inaugurates an interrogative context enveloping both desirer and world, one to which the desirer responds in the affirmative.[6] Moreover, in conjoining affirmation to acquisition Socrates sufficiently complicates the notion of acquisition at work here to leave room for a desiderative orientation that neither destroys what it acquires nor remains unaffected by its acquisition (that not only takes but is taken); that is, he leaves room for what he will presently describe as the philosopher's desire for knowledge and the tyrant's possession by Eros.

Third, the world that desire discloses, as Socrates will go on to explain, is a world ordered in parts, wholes, and kinds. Desire desires all of that of which it is the desire; for example, thirst desires all drink, hunger desires all food. While Socrates insists that the particularization of desire occurs because of conditions external to the desire itself, in being *of* something (food, drink, etc.), in stretching out toward all that could be subsumed within that something, desire discloses not only an all, but also parts and kinds. Desire, like knowledge, illuminates kinds, extends the desirer toward things on the basis of these kinds, and does so in such a manner as to be capable of undergoing particularization.[7]

These three features of desire—its formal character, its affirming/acquiring character, and its tendency toward wholes and kinds—mark a kinship with knowledge that renders possible not only knowledge of desire but also desire of knowledge.[8] In identifying their shared relational trajectory, Socrates also identifies the condition for the possibility of their harmony as well as their estrangement. This will, as we shall see, prove decisive for the distinction between the lover of wisdom and the lover of sights made at the end of book 5. In looking even further ahead, this analysis of the form of desire sets the stage for the intimacy between desire and knowledge realized in the lover of wisdom as well as their divergence, realized in most radical form by the tyrant.

In the remainder of book 4, the discussion of desire is used to indicate the variegation of the soul on the basis of the experience of simultaneous contrary impulses: the "tending toward" indicative of desire and the "drawing or holding back" which, as the contrary to "tending toward," must be the result of something other than desire, something that will presently be called calculation.[9] The indignation one can aim at the "tending toward" of desire is, in turn, taken to indicate the existence of a spirited element in one's soul distinct from calculation by its presence in children and animals. Thus, the tripartite soul is forged out of tension between one's desires and the stance one takes toward them.[10]

Like the analysis of the form of desire, this account of the parts of the soul provides the basis for a variety of ways of taking up one's desiderative life, planting the seeds not only for an account of pleonexia but also for the lust for learning indicative of the philosopher. By opening up a variety of possible orientations toward one's desiring life whose discernment makes both possible and necessary the discussion of how, if at all, the desiring life of the philosopher differs from that of others, the analysis of desire and description of parts of the soul serve the larger purpose of elucidating kinds of lives. Most immediately, we can see some intimation of the kinds of lives formed by the stance one takes toward one's desires in the description of the just life near the end of book 4, an account which anticipates the presentation of pleonexia as disclosive of desire's capacity for excess (586a-b):

> "And [the calculating and spirited parts of soul], thus trained and having truly learned their own business and been educated, will be set over the desiring—which is surely most of the soul in each and by nature most insatiable for money [ὃ δὴ πλεῖστον τῆς ψυχῆς ἐν ἑκάστῳ ἐστὶ καὶ χρημάτων φύσει ἀπληστότατον]—and they'll watch it for fear of its being filled with the so-called pleasures of the body and thus becoming big and strong, and then not minding its own business, but attempting to enslave and rule what is not appropriately ruled by its class and subverting everyone's entire life." (442a-b)

Socrates continues to draw out the necessity of curbing desire in order to achieve unity and become one, arguing that the just person

> "doesn't let each part in him mind other people's business or the three classes in the soul meddle with each other, but really sets his own house in good order and rules himself; he arranges himself, becomes his own friend, and harmonizes the three parts, exactly like three notes in a harmonic scale, lowest, highest and middle. And if there are some other parts in between, he binds them together and becomes entirely one from many [καὶ παντάπασιν ἕνα γενόμενον ἐκ πολλῶν], moderate and harmonized." (443d-e)

Injustice, in turn, is a faction among the three, and a rebellion of one part against the whole (444b). It is at this juncture that Socrates makes explicit the analogy with health and disease.

Psychic Health and Disease

A reminder of the context of this analogy will help orient our study of it. As we have seen, the valorizations of injustice that Glaucon and Adeimantus voice in book 2 hinge upon the assumption that the wages of injustice, being mandated by the city in the form of laws and by others in the form of bad reputation, are external to the condition of the unjust person and thus impinge upon his freedom. The brothers assert that the person with an unjust soul is capable of flourishing with, and in fact because of, his possession of injustice. Socrates's efforts to persuade Glaucon and Adeimantus that the unjust life is undesirable are bolstered by his ability to sever the connection between injustice and freedom, a connection that, according to the brothers, is asserted from all corners of Athenian society. He crafts a powerful instrument for doing so by an analogy that arises in the course of their observation of justice and injustice in the city in speech. After he and Glaucon have agreed that justice is minding one's own business and injustice is failing to do so, Socrates asserts that what unjust things and actions are has also come to light because "they don't differ from the healthy and the sick; what these are in a body, they are in a soul" (444c). The discussion continues:

> "Surely, healthy things produce [ἐμποιεῖ] health and sick ones sickness." "Yes." "Doesn't doing just things also produce [ἐμποιεῖ] justice and unjust ones injustice?" "Necessarily." "To produce health is to establish the parts of the body in a relation of mastering, and being mastered by, one another that is according to nature, while to produce sickness is to establish a relation of ruling and being ruled by, one another that is contrary to nature." "It is." "Then in its turn," I said, "isn't to produce justice to establish the parts of the soul in a relation of mastering, and being mastered by, one another that is according to nature, while to produce injustice is to establish a relation of ruling, and being ruled by, one another that is the contrary to nature?" "Entirely so," he said. (444c–e)

By aligning injustice with disease, Socrates goes a long way toward persuading his interlocutors that the unjust life is undesirable. The effectiveness of this strategy is made immediately evident by Glaucon's response that the characterization of injustice as a corruption akin to disease renders ridiculous the need to defend the just life (445a–b). Much of the strength of this comparison lies in its resonance with an understanding of disease, pervasive in archaic and classical Greek culture, as imbalance.[11] The description of justice as a proper organization of parts into a whole and of injustice as a rebellion or disorganization of parts invites comparison with such a conception of disease. In fact, by comparing the virtue and vice of the soul with the health and disease of the body, Socrates invokes a broader analogy between soul and body, one whose use was well established.[12] The distinctly political tone of Socrates's characterization of health and sickness would have been particularly familiar to his interlocutors, as the assertion of a parallelism between the organization of the body and the organization of the city is at least as old as Alcmeaon of Croton's characterization of health and disease as *isonomia* and *monarchia* respectively.[13] Thus, Socrates's comparison in book 4 plays upon a series of associations prevalent in the larger cultural and intellectual context of Athenian life, associations which cast the comparison as a perfectly reasonable clarification of just and unjust actions, given the definitions of justice and injustice he and his interlocutors have agreed upon. Further, the analogy's emphasis on the *production* of health, disease, virtue, and vice accords with the role that Socrates, Glaucon, and Adeimantus have adopted toward the city that they create in speech, namely, as its founders and lawmakers (379a, 380c, 425d, 456b–c). At the same time, this emphasis on production and making, on poiēsis broadly conceived, highlights the soul's malleability and susceptibility to poiēsis. By doing so, the analogy connects the dialogue's investigation of the influence of poetry on the soul with its clinical evaluative framework.[14] Both of these rely on the soul's capacity to be changed, altered, worked over, and transformed. Indeed, such a capacity is expressly presumed in this analogy, as it is presumed by the very task that Glaucon and Adeimantus set out for Socrates.

What is thus gained in this analogy is a concrete way of speaking about an elusive and mysterious subject, namely the effects of justice and injustice on the soul. Whereas previously Socrates had been at a loss as to how to defend the just life against the unjust life (368b), now he and his interlocutors have an abundance of terms for describing the effects of injustice on the soul.[15] In fact, Socrates's particular construction of this analogy reduces the difference between injustice and disease to a difference between soul and body; as he puts it, health and sickness differ from justice and injustice only insofar as the former are conditions of body and the latter are conditions of soul (444c).

However, exactly how soul and body differ from one another is left undetermined in this comparison.[16] The analogy between injustice and disease that Socrates has outlined thus far provides a complex manner of speaking about the soul but at the same time fails to firmly establish the status of this vocabulary. Because the only meaningful way to distinguish between injustice and disease that is given here (that is, the difference between soul and body) is never made clear, a certain degree of confusion threatens whatever aid this vocabulary may provide in understanding the effects of injustice on the soul. As long as the difference between soul and body remains unclear, the complexity of this vocabulary is purchased at the expense of its precision. In fact, a certain lack of precision is precisely what Socrates warns Glaucon they risk in their investigation of whether the soul has parts (435c–d).

The problems with book's 4 medical analogy are symptomatic of a larger tension in the dialogue between describing the soul and granting it ontological priority over the body. In accepting Glaucon and Adeimantus's request to defend the just life by showing the effects of justice and injustice on the soul, Socrates's defense of justice commits him to giving an account of the conditions to which the soul is subject. In order to offer the richest account of these conditions, Socrates is compelled to come up with a subtle and complex means of speaking about the soul. He is afforded just such a vocabulary by describing the soul in the terms of its embodiment and speaking about it as though the soul itself were a living body.[17] This manner of conceiving of the soul has the added benefit of resonating with an analogy between soul and body that, as we have seen, was prevalent throughout Athenian culture. By focusing upon the presumed symmetry between soul and body, Socrates is afforded a culturally salient purchase on the enigmatic operations of the soul, one to which he avails himself frequently in the *Republic*.

If we pause for a moment to look further ahead, throughout the rest of dialogue the phenomenon of embodiment will continue to present itself as a paradigm of unity out of complexity whose fate is subject to the better and worse maintenance of the ordering of its parts. Appeals to embodied existence are made as appeals to that which can provide a nuanced vocabulary for understanding the soul. Thus, one reads of a thirsty soul, a hungry soul, a desiring soul, a soul that moves, sighs, is pained and pleased, is emptied and sated. This bodily vocabulary is perhaps best exemplified in the image of the soul in book 9 as a combination of many-headed beast, lion, and human (588b–e). However, we also find it prevalent wherever the discussion hinges on the nurturing and education of young souls[18] (in this context, Socrates is particularly fond of comparing young souls to seeds),[19] and it is obtrusive in the myth of Er, wherein, for instance, souls are described as emerging from the earth covered in dust (614d) and as having their flesh flayed (616a). The entire educational program offered in books 6 and 7, with the characterization of education as a turning of the soul, locates the soul squarely within the sphere of becoming and among things that grow.

The problem that this bodily vocabulary poses for the *Republic* should be familiar from our study of the *Phaedo*'s presentation of the body-loving soul, namely, that it is enormously complicated by the relationship between living and the soul that is suggested in other parts of the dialogue.[20] Insofar as the soul is responsible for the life of the living body, describing the soul as though it were a living body inserts the soul into the very terms by means of which it is described. Such a manner of thinking about soul risks equating it with a living body and obscuring the unique relationship between soul and life asserted elsewhere in the dialogue.

Moreover, as in the *Phaedo*, we cannot manage these risks by dismissing this vocabulary as "merely" metaphorical.[21] In order for the *Republic*'s educational program to make sense, and for the question of the proper mode of education to be relevant, there must be a very literal sense in which the soul provides an essential vehicle for human maturation.[22] Whether and how this maturation is similar to, and different from, the maturation of other growing things, like seeds, requires explanation.

At the same time, *that* the soul's role in maturation is distinct from the body's is implied whenever Socrates asserts the priority of soul over body. He does so on multiple occasions in the *Republic* (see especially 403d–e, 445a–b, 536e, and 585a–586c).[23] We thus encounter in the *Republic* the same profound tension we observed at work in the *Phaedo* between the terms frequently used to describe the soul, in which the soul is spoken of as though it were a living body, on the one hand, and the ontological status granted to the soul, in which the soul is characterized as superior to the body, on the other. This tension is in large part a function of a lack of clarity about the relationship between the living body and what Socrates calls the region of the bodily or body-like (532d).[24]

The danger in accepting this lack of precision lies in the possibility of forgetting the tentative character of their discussion about the soul. To fail to recognize the proximate nature of this way of speaking would be to mislead oneself about the nature of one's understanding of the soul.[25] Put another way, an uncritical comparison between vice and disease risks an unwarranted optimism about one's knowledge of the soul. In book 4, Socrates is not called to task for this lack of clarity, nor does it prohibit Glaucon's acceptance of the idea that injustice is in some way akin to disease and justice to health. In looking ahead, Socrates and Glaucon are eventually forced to acknowledge this problem when they must evaluate their account of the tyrant, as this account compels them to confront a difference between vice and disease that will prove profound and irreducible. However, as we will see, while they will have to recognize the limits of the health/disease analogy, what is unique in Plato's construction of the diagnostic perspective that utilizes this analogy (a construction that began, as we have seen, with the distinction between the doctor and the judge in book 3) is precisely its self-critical inflection. The eventual critique Socrates and Glaucon offer of their perspective on the soul, a perspective gained by the use of medical concepts, is already inscribed within the clinical comportment Plato has developed. This clinical comportment is the hinge upon which their critique turns. Before we can follow this turn in the account of the tyrant, however, we need to gain some understanding of the character against whom the tyrant is to be measured, namely, the philosophic ruler. And before we do this we must chart out the elaborations upon psychic fragmentation that precede it. To return to the conclusion of book 4, Socrates observes that the health/disease analogy provides him and Glaucon with a perspective from which they can survey not only the forms of virtue, but the various forms of vice, four of which merit further consideration (445c). However, before he can elaborate, he will be required to return to the mode of life of the guardians outlined at the end of book 3 to address some concerns of Polemarchus and Adeimantus. In doing so, he is given the opportunity to delve a bit deeper into the possibilities of unity and fragmentation to which cities as well as individuals are subject.

Training in Desire

Book 5 picks up where book 4 left off, with Socrates's attempt to describe the forms of corruption to which both cities and souls are subject. However, Polemarchus and Adeimantus intervene, objecting to Socrates's failure to provide a more detailed account of the community of women and children within the guardian class, and inaugurating the discussion that Socrates will organize around the imagery of three waves. In the course of his discussion of these three infamous waves—the training of men and women in common, the community of women and children, and the necessity of philosophic rulers for a good city—Socrates returns to the theme of becoming one or many articulated in book 4, and expands the scope of possibility for such becoming. Thus, while ostensibly book 5 provides an elaboration upon certain features of the purged city in speech—the city capable of providing an analogue to the soul's wisdom, courage, moderation and justice—the detail it provides of this city's structure complicates the analogy by marking out conditions of unity and fragmentation that soul and city produce in one another. As we will see, these conditions are bound up with an initial means of attaining unity broached in book 2 (the "one person one job" principle) and with the necessity for negotiating and training one's desires.

Equal Training

In the course of Socrates's argument for the merits of training men and women in common, we find a return to the discussion of the role of nature in organizing the city. As we noted in the previous chapter, phusis functions in the city as a differentiating force, assigning people different tasks on the basis of a propensity for that task. His discussion of the first wave provides a more thorough description of what it means to be naturally fit for a task—to be fit for a deed by nature means to possess ease of learning with respect to it and to have a body that cooperates with one's thought (455b–c)—and a refinement of the sense in which nature differentiates with respect to the city. While Socrates would agree that men and women differ with respect to their nature, he maintains that the fact that women give birth is not sufficient to bar them from the work of the city, from performing the deeds meant to respond to human need (451d). Doing so, asserts Socrates, would be akin to distinguishing between the nature of the bald and the long-haired and refusing to allow them to practice the same art (454c). The ridiculousness of the second example is a more explicit indication of the failure of the first, namely that in appealing to nature as that which differentiates people according to deeds, they "didn't refer to every sense of same and different nature but were guarding only that form of otherness and likeness which applies to the pursuits themselves" (454c). Thus, with respect to nature so conceived, nature suited for a task, there is no relevant difference between men and women in the city, save their relative strength and weakness (451e, 455c, 456a). Whatever differentiating work nature does for the city, it is not based upon sexual difference. Nature emerges from this discussion as a grammar, a population of different sets of differences. The city confronts this field of differences with a set of needs that must be fulfilled and deeds that must be performed. Socrates and his interlocutors' task is to discern the particular set of differences relevant to the city, a set dictated by the demands of technē; indeed, this task is only possible if nature is such as to have already been infused with technē. Insofar as it is the performance of these tasks that makes a person and city a one, nature maintains some relevance to the achievement of selfsameness, but its relevance is found in its illumination of differences and similarities with respect to the performance of a broad range of deeds. Socrates thus implies that to deny women the opportunity to pursue tasks for which they are suited is to deny them the primary vehicle for achieving oneness or unity within the city and to deny the city the full constellation of capacities possessed by women. At the same time, to relegate women to the status of the weaker is to call into question the ability to take full advantage of this vehicle and to overlook to role of the city in determining what constitutes weakness and strength. Socrates is not called upon by his interlocutors to address this point.[26]

Such a construction of nature with respect to the city allows Socrates and Glaucon to conclude that the current practice of not rearing and educating women in common with men is against nature, while their own law would be according to nature: "Then we have come around full circle to where we were before and agree that it's not against nature to assign music and gymnastic to the women guardians." "That's entirely certain." "Then we weren't giving laws that are impossible or like prayers, since the law we were setting down is according to nature [κατὰ φύσιν]. Rather, the way things are nowadays proves to be, as it seems, against nature [παρὰ φύσιν]" (456b–c). Socrates's point here is that an appeal to phusis is not adequate grounds for arguing against equal education and work. For our purposes, however, what is perhaps most significant about this passage is that the now familiar use of nature to critique custom needs to be read with the particular inflection that Plato has given to phusis, that is, phusis already permeated by deeds, pursuits, undertakings, many of which are themselves circumscribed by technē. Thus, his argument for the equal training of men and women offers an elaboration of the possibilities for fragmentation and unity adhering to the performance of work in the city and determined by the city's divison of labor. It also provides a glimpse of the reformulation of the relationship between phusis, technē, and politikē that occurs throughout the dialogue.

The Community of Pleasure and Pain

In the second wave, we see the possibilities of becoming oneself or fragmenting more explicitly extended beyond the individual to the city. In the course of arguing for the community of women and children, Socrates and Glaucon put forward a model of civic unity that adds another layer to their illustration of psychic division:

> "Have we any greater evil for a city than what splits it and makes it many instead of one? Or a greater unity than what binds it together and makes it one?" "No, we don't." "Doesn't the community of pleasure and pain bind it together, when to the greatest extent possible all the citizens alike rejoice and are pained at the same comings into being and perishings?" "That's entirely certain," he said. "But the privacy of such things dissolves it, when some are overwhelmed and others overjoyed by the same things happening to the city and those within the city?" "Of course." "Doesn't

> that sort of thing happen when they don't utter such phrases as 'my own' and 'not my own' at the same time in the city, and similarly with respect to 'somebody else's'?" "Entirely so." "Is, then, that city in which most say 'my own' and 'not my own' about the same thing, and in the same way, the best governed city?" "By far." "Then is that city best governed which is most like a single human being? For example, when one of us wounds a finger, presumably the entire community—that community tying the body together with the soul in a single arrangement under the ruler within it—is aware of the fact, and all of it is in pain as a whole along with the afflicted part; and it is in this sense we say that this human being has a pain in his finger. And does the same argument hold for any other part of the human being, both when it is afflicted by pain and eased by pleasure?" (462a–d)

The model of civic unity here, the unity of soul and body, shifts the operative analogy from that between city and soul to one between between city and human being. What would be the civic correlates of the soul and body whose community produces the single human being?²⁷ In broadening the field of manifestations of unity and fragmentation from individuals to cities themselves, and in comparing the city to a living being, this passage furthers the dialogue's presentation of the city as a psychological phenomenon.

Moreover, the explicit concern with what the guardians say and call their own in this conception of civic unity is an extension of the training in desire involved in supervising the poets and craftsmen for the sake of controlling the effects of mimetic activity in books 2 and 3. The community of pleasure and pain is a community of affect and desire. The training invisioned here intertwines desire with perception and speech; that is, it is not simply a matter of what citizens want, but also what they perceive to be and call their own and others'. Thus, the community of pleasure and pain includes a marked aesthetic component.

The training in speech as well as desire continues to be emphasized throughout the discussion of the community of women and children, as in the following exchange between Socrates and Glaucon:

> "Can you say whether any of the rulers in the other cities is in the habit of addressing one of his fellow rulers as his kin and another as an outsider?" "Many do so." "Doesn't he hold the one who is his kin to be his own, and speak of him as such, while the outsider he does not hold to be his own?" "That's what he does." "What about your guardians? Would any of them be in the habit of holding one of his fellow guardians to be an outsider or address him as such?" "Not at all," he said. "With everyone he happens to meet, he'll hold that he's meeting a brother, or a sister, or a father, or a mother, or a son, or a daughter or their descendents or ancestors." (463b–c)

And again:

> "So, as I am saying, doesn't what was said before and what's being said now form them into true guardians still more and cause them not to draw the city apart by

not all giving the name 'my own' to the same thing, but different men giving it to different things—one man dragging off to his own house whatever he can get his hands on apart from the others, another being separate in his own house with separate women and children, introducing private pleasures and griefs of things that are private? Rather, with one conviction about what's their own, straining toward the same thing, to the limit of the possible, they are affected alike by pain and pleasure." "Entirely so," he said. "And what about this? Won't lawsuits and complaints against one another virtually vanish from among them thanks to their possessing nothing private but the body, while the rest is in common? On this basis they will then be free from faction, to the extent at any rate that human beings divide into factions over the possession of money, children and relatives?" (464c–e)

What the guardians share is the very conviction about what is their own, and this conviction spills over not only into their own character as guardians, but into the character of the city as a whole. Note also that the body remains the only irrevocably private object, the only thing left to an individual to possess, and that this privacy is implicitly tied to mortality itself. It is not the privacy of the body that concerns Socrates here but the privacy of loyalty, the privileging of love of self over all others, as well as the splitting of thumos caused by competing loyalties and conflicting allegiances. The community of pleasure and pain will also include a community of anger and allegiance.

On the basis of Socrates's defense of the community of women and children, he and Glaucon agree that the best city would be organized in the manner that they have been describing. They then turn to discuss the manner in which such a city would wage war. In the subsequent distinction they draw between faction and war there is another account of civic fragmentation, or rather a distinction between civic fragmentation and "extramural" estrangement and animosity:

"It appears to me that just as two different names are used, war and faction, so two things also exist and the names apply to differences in these two. The two things I mean are, on the one hand, what is one's own and akin [τὸ μὲν οἰκεῖον καὶ συγγενές], and what is alien and foreign [τὸ δὲ ἀλλότριον καὶ ὀθνεῖον], on the other. Now the name faction is applied to the hatred of one's own [τῇ τοῦ οἰκείου ἔχθρᾳ], war to the hatred of the alien [τῇ τοῦ ἀλλοτρίου]." "What you are saying," he said, "is certainly not off point." "Now see whether what I say next is also to the point. I assert that the Greek stock is with respect to itself its own and akin, with respect to the barbaric, foreign and alien." "Yes," he said, "that is fine [καλῶς]." "Then when Greeks fight with barbarians and barbarians with Greeks, we'll assert they are at war and are enemies by nature [φύσει], and this hatred must be called war; while when Greeks do any such thing to Greeks we'll say that they are by nature [φύσει] friends, but in this case Greece is sick and factious, and this kind of hatred must be called faction." (470b–d)

The aggression described in this passage is somewhat tempered by Socrates's subsequent account of what he describes as a more gentle way of waging war, but only somewhat. Perhaps Socrates is attempting to galvanize Glaucon's and Adeimantus's pride in order to reveal a certain love for the city, and then attempting to turn that love away from a hatred of what is alien. It seems more likely that Socrates is capitalizing upon a nascent metaphysical tendency in the kalloi kagathoi, specifically in its need for drawing distinctions between one's own and others.[28] However, with the return of the standard of nature in navigating the relevant distinctions (friend and enemy), this passage also returns to a certain contingency to nature that was implicit in the recognition that nature included many sets of differences and similarities. As we have seen, in his argument for the common training of men and women, the differentiating and differencing function that nature serves in the city is extended to a larger claim about nature as housing a variety of kinds of differences, at least one of which is more relevant for the city than others—at least one of which, when applied to the city, can somehow prove to be, paradoxically, less "according to nature" than the other (456b–c). The nature that can differ with respect to itself makes more pressing the question of the extent to which nature can supply the terms needed to ensure a flourishing city, and also blurs the very distinctions between one's own and others. As we shall see in chapters 6 and 7, the insufficiency of the medical analogy calls into question the extent to which nature can operate as a normative standard for human action.

In the move from the first to the second wave we have seen the intertwinement of personal and civic fragmentation. In Socrates and Glaucon's discussion of who the philosophers are, required by the infamous third wave, we can see their exploration of fragmentation extended to the realm of becoming itself, and can note the development of an account of ontological fragmentation.

The Lover of Sights and the Lover of Wisdom

When Socrates turns to clarify whom he means by "philosopher" in order to defend his claim that cities will not flourish unless they install the philosophically inclined as rulers, he begins by reminding Glaucon of one feature of desiderative life that emerged earlier in their conversation: "Will you need to be reminded," I said, "or do you remember that when we say a man loves something, if it is rightly said of him, he mustn't show a love for one part of it and not for another, but must cherish all of it [Ἀναμιμνῄσκειν οὖν σε, ἦν δ ἐγώ, δεήσει, ἢ μέμνησαι ὅτι ὃν ἂν φῶμεν φιλεῖν τι, δεῖ φανῆναι αὐτόν, ἐὰν ὀρθῶς λέγηται οὐ τὸ μὲν φιλοῦντα ἐκείνου, τὸ δὲ μή, ἀλλὰ πᾶν στέργοντα]?" (474c). Glaucon's confusion about this reminder suggests that this tending toward a whole or all marks a relatively new way of construing desire's form. However, Socrates persists in presenting this claim as an extension of their previous analysis.[29] Socrates's explanation of this point to Glaucon also makes clear that the tendency toward wholes that is characteristic of desire is also a tendency toward insatiability. Lovers of boys, for instance (explains Socrates), love all boys in the "bloom of youth" (474d and e). The effect that this character of love has on the lover is the divergence of his desire from broader social constructs of what is beautiful or fine: the lover goes to great lengths to provide justifications for his love when the object of this love is not conventionally beautiful (474d–e).

This illustration of love sets the stage for the claim that what one desires has a profound effect on how one will be affected by one's desires. What one loves can put one more or less at odds with the evaluation of what is worthy of adoration, either in one's own assessment or that of others. The insatiability of desire attains expression in the instability of one who makes certain desires definitive of his or her life; that is, it becomes a defining feature of the life of anyone who describes him or herself as a lover. This is as true for the philosopher as for anyone else: "the one who is willing to taste every kind of learning with gusto, and who approaches learning with delight, and is insatiable, we shall justly assert to be a philosopher, won't we?" (475c). Insofar as desire's tendency toward all of something is also a tendency toward excess, the philosopher, like any lover, appears to be an excessive being. The image of the philosopher we receive at the end of this discussion is of a personality infused with an insatiable lust for learning, whose eros, in extending to all of learning, is, as Paul Ludwig aptly describes, "profligate and promiscuous,"[30] and who is distinct from the lover of sights and sounds only by the class of objects to which this love is directed: the philosopher is the lover of the sight of truth (475e).

These self-consciously enigmatic lines require far more discussion than can be given here. I limit myself to a more general observation that what is at stake in the difference between philosophers and lovers of sight is not whether eros infuses and colors their lives—both are erotic creatures, both are defined by their loves. What distinguishes them is a matter of how they take up their desire and understand their loved object.[31] Lovers of sight affirm that desire discloses an all but deny that their desire discloses a whole; rather, they are content to delight in the many beloved things presented to them by their love and to set about in the acquisition of these many beautiful things. Like the lover of young boys, such a person resigns himself to the possibility of mortification by his desires insofar as he will desire instances of a love object against which he will also chafe.[32] Such lovers fail to capitalize upon the formal character of desire; they do not treat their desire or its objects as objects of understanding as well, resigning themselves thereby to a desiderative life whose pleasure is tempered with frustration.

According to this account, philosophers differ from the lovers of sights in their acknowledgment that their love is directed at a whole, and attempt to investigate this whole. Thus, philosophers differ from the lovers of sights on the basis of their attempt to understand what is being disclosed to them by desire. This attempt shifts the object of their desire from becoming to Being. In identifying this object, and distinguishing between it and that in which the lovers of sights and sounds delight, Socrates draws a distinction between, on the one hand, knowledge and Being, and, on the other, opinion and what neither *is* nor *is not* (what becomes). Much metaphysical weight hangs on this distinction, and both it and who the philosopher is require the extensive development that will come in the following books. From the perspective of the psychological investigation of the dialogue, the philosopher's desire, a desire for Being, will reveal a radical possibility for unity within the very excessive nature of the philosopher's love precisely because the object of this love merits such desire. The philosopher's insatiability is warranted by the worthiness of her object. Thus, the philosopher has something to teach about soul; philosophic natures disclose soul's capacity for unity on the basis of its excessive love, provided this love is turned in the right direction. The most radical form of fragmentation is risked, in turn, by the training of this excessive love elsewhere. The next chapter will follow the illustrations of psychic unity and fragmentation that are provided by the portraits of the philosopher and the tyrant.

Conclusion

I began this chapter by asserting that books 4 and 5 contribute to the psychodynamics begun in books 2 and 3 by offering a catalogue of psychic division. The vision of becoming one that is introduced early on in book 4 and explicitly tied to the "one person, one job" organizing principle of the city implies also a particular form of disorganization whose primary effect is psychic fragmentation. The emphasis on becoming one or failing to do so develops throughout books 4 and 5 in the form of a sustained meditation upon the varieties and depths of unity and fragmentation: the balanced order of the unified individual is overcome by the vice and injustice in the soul of the individual, the harmonious chorus of the unified city is countered by the faction or strife within cities, and the philosopher's focused and ardent pursuit of Being finds its counter in the diffused and dispersed acquisitions of the lover of sights. This discussion deepens our understanding of psychic plasticity by opening up to reflection the question of what soul must be in order to sustain itself through radical change.

All of these forms of fragmentation provide different iterations of psychic division. At the level of the individual, this is most obvious in the depiction of soul as that which can come to be divided against itself insofar as its parts are not harmonized. However, to the extent that natural tendency toward a deed includes psychic as well as (or perhaps more so than) physical composition, a failure to discern and perform that deed for which one is naturally suited is a failure to heed psychic disposition toward a deed and thus also a form of psychic fragmentation that effects both city and individual. The community of pleasure and pain can only be achieved by giving citizens a training in desire, loyalty, perception, and speech, that is, in shaping their souls in such a manner as to make them capable of affirming that what is their own is held in common. As such, it intertwines the unity of citizen and city. That the most vivid form of this affirmation is held only by one part of the city does not change its significance as a manifestation of unity. Finally, the distinction between many fine things and the fine itself illustrates a division between Being and becoming with implications not only for ontology but also for the condition of soul. The soul's implication in the pursuit of Being will be more explicitly spelled out in book 6, whose image of the divided line includes a list of affections of soul that allow access to a variety of beings. I add only that the seeds for this correspondence are sown in the discussion at the end of book 5 that distinguished the philosopher from the lovers of opinion on the grounds that philosophers love and ardently pursue what *is* while the lovers of opinion ardently pursue the many things that become.

Books 4 and 5 demonstrate that there is something essential and peculiar about the soul's ability to sustain itself in its fragmentation. Indeed, it is this ability that indicates both a distinction between soul and body and the insufficiency of the analogy with health and disease. At the start of book 4, the "one person, one job" principle is treated as a preliminary way of opening up this insight into the soul's unique relationship to its own fragmentation—the human suffers from this fragmentation but soul is not destroyed by it. Throughout the discussion of soul's partition and the other ways in which psychic division is illustrated, there runs a tacit assertion that soul is that which includes its fragmentation in what it means for it to be. That is, soul is that entity most capable of being alien to or estranged from itself. However, this analysis also suggests that soul's endurance of its division is of a different sort than the endurance of the human being with a divided soul. Indeed, this analysis of psychic fragmentation opens up a certain indifference of soul to the flourishing or happiness of the individual, and suggests that the analysis of the individual soul will only ever produce an incomplete psychology. Some scale larger than that of the individual is necessary, therefore, in order to understand soul. In turn, those individuals with a grasp of this larger scale are more precise students of soul.

These observations return us to the question of whether the philosopher has a privileged position with respect to soul itself, a question I address more directly in the next chapter with a discussion of philosophic nature, its corruption, and the course of philosophic education. It is at this level that the question of the philosophical status of psychology is most pressing; that soul can gain access to Being tells us something about soul, but does it tell us anything about Being? Put another way, must the student of Being become a student of soul? In taking the human's desiderative life as the field upon which human excellence stands or falls, books 4 and 5 lay the foundation for these questions; their development in books 6–9 is taken up in the next chapter.

6 Philosophy in the City

As we have seen in the previous chapter, in book 5 Socrates explores the forms of fragmentation and unity to which soul and city are subject and introduces a distinction between desiderative orientations that illuminates two courses of life, that of the lover of wisdom and that of the lover of opinion. By the end of book 9, Socrates and his interlocutors have seen this distinction developed into that between just and unjust lives and have had their judgment sufficiently trained to discern their differences with respect to happiness and to choose between them. In the intervening books, Socrates elaborates upon the possibility of psychic unity presented by the properly educated philosophic nature in terms that emphasize the training of this nature's desire (books 6–7) and returns to analyze in detail the corrupt forms of city and soul he mentioned at the end of book 4, concluding with the soul of tyrant, whose depravity provides the terms by means of which the most unjust life is envisioned (book 8–9). This analysis adopts a decidedly clinical stance toward both city and soul, even as it produces an account that calls into question the evaluative efficacy of health and sickness, and culminates in the complex image of soul that allows Socrates and his interlocutors to observe what the advocate for the unjust life is really arguing for. Moreover, in these books we see the city in speech and the city of speakers collide in the enigmatic figure of Socrates, who both seems to include himself among anomalous occurrences of those living in corrupt regimes who nonetheless are able to keep company with philosophy in a worthy way (496c), and yet engages in an analysis of the transformations to which cities and soul are subject, an activity that cannot be easily circumscribed within the single-minded pursuit of Being described in books 6 and 7.

Thus, I will argue, books 6–9 complete the philosophic portraiture of just and unjust lives begun in book 2, deploy the clinical stance developed over the course of the previous books in order to diagnose and judge the forms of life it describes, and also broach the limits of this very evaluative framework, sowing the seeds of its critique in the very subtlety with which they analyze the unjust life. They thus conclude the work begun by the creation of the city in speech by illuminating the implication of the city of speakers in their construction. This chapter charts and explores the effects of this implication; it first draws out the possibility of psychic unity presented by the focused desire of those whom Socrates describes as possessing a natural proclivity for philosophy (part 1) and examines the realization of this unity in the properly educated philosophic nature (part 2); it then observes the emergence of the portrait of the perfectly unjust life from out of the discussion of degenerate regimes and souls, tracing the decidedly medical tenor of this account and the manner in which its clinical diagnostic stance rebounds upon the city of speakers (part 3). Finally, it turns to the judgment of lives in order to observe the effects of this reflexive action (part 4).

Philosophic Natures

Book 6 begins with a reiteration of the characteristics of the philosopher agreed to in book 5, placing emphasis on the philosophers' erotic leanings.[1] Socrates and Glaucon remind themselves that philosophic natures are "always in love with that learning which discloses to them something of the being that is always and does not wander about, driven by generation and decay [μαθήματός γε ἀεὶ ἐρῶσιν ὃ ἂ αὐτοῖς δηλοῖ ἐκείνης τῆς οὐσίας τῆς ἀεὶ οὔσης καὶ μὴ πλανωμένης ὑπὸ γενέσεως καὶ φθορᾶς]" (485b). They agree that, like the lovers of honor and erotic men (φιλοτίμων καὶ ἐρωτικῶν), philosophers love all of that which they love (485b). They agree that philosophers hate (μισεῖν) the false and cherish (στέργειν) the truth (485c). In order to drive home this point, Socrates repeats that just as a lover cares for "everything related and akin" to his beloved, so must the philosopher love truth, that which is most akin to wisdom (485c). They agree also to the insatiability of such a character: "the man who is really a lover of learning must from youth on strive [ὀρέγεσθαι] as intensely as possible for every kind of truth" (485d). They also agree upon a facet of the insatiability of desire that has to yet be drawn out, namely that desire focused toward one thing weakens with respect to other things, "like a stream that has been channeled off in that other direction" (485d).

Insofar as the philosopher is successful in channeling her desires toward learning, Socrates supposes that those desires "would be concerned with the pleasure of the soul itself with respect to itself and would forsake those pleasures that come through the body" (485d).[2] Consequently, such a person would be moderate, and neither a lover of money nor illiberal. Moreover, such a character will be courageous because it possesses an understanding "endowed with magnificence and the contemplation of all time and all being" (486a),[3] a contemplation which liberates it from the fear of death. In fact, to a character endowed with such an understanding, the significance of human life itself recedes into the background. They agree that such a nature will be just and tame (486b), will learn easily (486c), will have a strong memory (486c–d), and will possess an understanding endowed with measure and charm, one which "grows by itself in such a way as to make it easily led to the idea of each thing that is" (486d).

Socrates maintains this emphasis on the erotic character of the philosopher when he turns to give the more elaborate account of philosophic natures, their corruption, and the form of education proper to them that is required by Adeimantus's charges of their uselessness and viciousness (487d). For instance, Socrates begins his defense of the philosopher by reminding Adeimantus that

> "it is the nature of the real lover of learning [φιλομαθής] to strive for what is; and he does not tarry by each of the many things opined to be but goes forward and does not lose the keenness of his passionate love nor cease from it [ἀλλ᾽ ἴοι καὶ οὐκ ἀμβλύνοιτο οὐδ᾽ ἀπολήγοι τοῦ ἔρωτος] before he grasps the nature itself of each thing which is with the part of the soul fit to grasp a thing of that sort; and it is the part akin to it that is fit. And once near it and coupled with what really is, having begotten intelligence and truth, he knows and lives truly, is nourished and so ceases from his labor pains, but not before [ᾧ πλησιάσας καὶ μιγεὶς τῷ ὄντι ὄντως, γεννήσας νοῦν καὶ ἀλήθειαν, γνοίη τε καὶ ἀληθῶς ζῴη καὶ τρέφοιτο καὶ οὕτω λήγοι ὠδῖνος, πρὶν δ᾽ οὔ]." (490b)[4]

The unity of the philosopher's soul is achieved not in the absence of erotic inclination but precisely in its single-minded focus. Indeed, as we shall see, the philosopher's erotic tendencies bring him into close proximity to the tyrant.[5] The chief difference between the philosopher and the tyrant lies in what they love.

The account that Socrates offers of the corruption of philosophic natures results in an emphasis upon the need such natures have for a particular kind of nurturing and education. While Socrates's infamous third wave asserts the dependence of the flourishing of the city upon the coincidence of philosophy and political power, his account of philosophic natures asserts the dependence of these natures on a particular political organization. Philosophic natures are corrupted precisely by the very qualities that make them philosophic if they are not raised in a political environment suited to them (491b). The city is the extraindividual element in which the philosophic individual comes to be. A corrupt city creates a perverse and perverting environment in which what would count as a benefit becomes a corrosive agent. Socrates offers as an example of this corruption the "greatest sophist," that is, the collection of opinions about what is praiseworthy and what is blameworthy that are expressed in public gatherings in such a manner as to transform the natural landscape into a cultural one, as when

> "many gathered together sit down in assemblies, courts, theaters, army camps, or any other common meeting of a multitude, and, with a great deal of uproar blame some of the things said or done, and praise others, both in excess, shouting and clapping;

and, besides, the rocks and the very place surrounding them echo and redouble the uproar of blame and praise. Now, in such circumstances, as the saying goes, what do you suppose is the state of the young man's heart? Or what kind of private education will hold out for him and not be swept away by such blame and praise and go, borne by the flood, wherever it tends so that he'll say the same things are noble and base as they do, practice what they practice, and be such as they are?" (492b–c)[6]

Philosophic natures, Socrates implies, are particularly vulnerable to this corrosive environment and thus particularly dependent upon the kind of regime in which they find themselves. If they are to come to philosophy and not something else, they must be raised and educated within a particular civic structure by particular institutions, customs, and laws. Conversely, it is in the city's best interest to bring philosophic natures to philosophy and to take philosophy in hand, insofar as the work that the corrupted philosophic nature sets about doing can be extremely damaging to the city: "And particularly from these men come those who do the greatest harm to cities and private men, as well as those who do the good, if they chance to be drawn in this direction" (495b). Thus, city and philosophy stand as interdependent and intertwined. In order to respond to Adeimantus, Socrates returns his focus to the cultural environment in which souls are nurtured or deformed. This focus is maintained in the lengthy discussion of philosophic education that is to follow and that permits a critique of the manner in which education in philosophy is "currently" taken up (497b–498c).

Socrates exempts himself from the corruption that attends to the current form of education in philosophy, and reserves the possibility of divine intervention as a cause for the emergence of true philosophers even in such an environment (496a–e, 499b), philosophers who would not owe a debt to the city for their practice of philosophy (520a–b). However, he maintains that if the city is to avoid the dangers of failing to properly educate philosophic natures, and if philosophy is to avoid the slander brought upon it by the corruption of philosophic natures, then the city must make its peace with philosophy, and philosophers, to judge from the compulsion to return to the city (499b, 519c–520b), must have some part in this. That philosophy can, with divine dispensation, crop up even in corrupt cities, should not, on its own, be read as an assertion of the ultimately transpolitical ends of philosophy without careful consideration of the work that Socrates himself is doing in discussing with Glaucon and Adeimantus what form of life is best.[7] Either Socrates should not be taken as a philosopher of the sort described here (and there are, as we shall see, reasons for claiming this), or what one takes philosophy to be must include the work that Socrates and his interlocutors are doing upon one another in this dialogue, work that includes very careful and detailed descriptions of variant and volatile things like cities and souls. Even the manner in which Socrates characterizes the effects of the corrupt city on the philosophic nature emphasizes a certain political dimension of the philosophic natures' turn toward or away from philosophy. Such turns are a matter of navigating what is one's own and what is foreign, what is friend and what is foe. Because no current city is worthy of philosophy "it is twisted and changed; just as a foreign seed sown in alien ground [ὥσπερ ξενικὸν σπέρμα ἐν γῇ ἄλλῃ] is likely to be overcome and fade away into the native stock, so too this class does not at present maintain its own power but falls away into an alien disposition [εἰς ἀλλότριον ἦθος]. But if it ever takes hold in the best regime, just as it is itself best, then it will make plain that it really is divine as we agreed it is and that the rest are human, both in terms of their nature and their practices." (497b-c)

These lines cast the subsequent account of philosophic education as an account of the optimal conditions for philosophic flourishing, a flourishing which is itself treated as a condition of unity and selfsameness made possible by soul's kinship with being. This is to say, the description of philosophic flourishing is also a description of one form of psychic unity and selfsameness. This is so because the philosopher's mimetic activity is trained on the right objects, the philosopher "sees and contemplates things that are set in a regular arrangement and are always in the same condition—things that neither do injustice to one another nor suffer it at one another's hands, but remain all in order according to reason—he imitates them and, as much as possible, makes himself like them" (500c). It is the philosophers, concludes Socrates, "keeping company with the divine and orderly who become orderly and divine, to the extent that is possible for a human being" (500c-d).

The rule of the philosopher is characterized by her wiping clean the dispositions of human beings and then, with a double gaze, making those humans as dear to the gods as possible, looking off to what is eternal and changeless as well as to what is variant and transforming: "in filling out their work they would look away frequently in both directions, toward the just, fair, and moderate by nature and everything of the sort, and, again toward what is in human beings; and thus, mixing and blending the practices as ingredients, they would produce the image of man, taking hints from exactly that phenomenon in human beings which Homer too called god-like and the image of god" (501b).[8] The philosopher's knowledge of the human things will be of particular interest to us in the following investigation of the illustration of psychic unity that Socrates's account of philosophic education provides. Consequently, we will need to follow not only what is said of philosophic education but also the conditions and self-descriptions of those doing the describing.

It is in the course of Socrates's account of philosophic education that he delivers the three famous images of sun, line, and cave, images whose depth and capacity to inspire thought make any claims to a comprehensive treatment beyond the scope of a single book. For the purposes of the present study, we will direct our focus mainly to what these three images tell us about the soul. All three images speak to soul's desire for the good, soul's access to Being, and soul's turning toward Being as a model of human education. In doing so, they locate philosophical activity within both the context of human desire and the larger structure of reality. Throughout these images, soul's complete and total turning toward Being, a turning most vividly exemplified and accomplished by philosophic natures, provides a vision of the accomplishment of oneness and selfsameness. In the next section I will follow Socrates's lead in taking the art of counting as common to all kinds of art, thought and knowledge (522c) and thus as revelatory of the aim of philosophic curriculum, and will focus upon the educative import of counting in order to illustrate a few peculiar and essential features of the accomplishment of unity in the philosophic soul. I then turn to the illustration of psychic fragmentation provided by the portrait of the tyrant, noting along the way the discussions of Socrates's and Glaucon's ability to offer these accounts with which Plato punctuates these passages.

Philosophic Education

Halfway through the seventh book of the *Republic*, Socrates and Glaucon turn to marking out the education of the guardians, beyond the childhood pastimes of gymnastic and music. They are specifically interested in determining what course of study would direct the guardians' souls toward Being. This is no small matter. What they are discussing is treated as a turning of the soul that would comprise an education likened to an apotheosis, an ascent to the sight of what *is*, "just as some men are said to have gone from Hades up to the gods" (521c). In the course of their quest for such a study, Socrates suggests that they look into counting and number, "the lowly business of distinguishing the one, the two and the three" (522c), since counting "probably is one of those things we are seeking that by nature lead to intellection; but no one uses it rightly, as a thing that in every way is apt to draw men toward being" (523a).

As Socrates elaborates upon this statement, he accounts for the importance of number on the basis of a distinction between two kinds of objects of sensation: "some objects of sensation [ταῖς αἰσθήσεσιν] do not summon the intellect to that activity of investigation because they seem to be adequately judged by the senses, while others bid it in every way to undertake a consideration because sense seems to produce nothing healthy" (523a–b). Objects of sensation that do not summon the intellect are adequately judged by the senses because they do not give over to their opposites. The perception of these objects is uncomplicated and lacking in confusion. The objects of sensation that do summon or evoke the intellect are those not adequately judged by sense and that do give over to their opposites. The perceptions of these objects are, not surprisingly, complicated and confusing.

In order to make the difference between these two kinds of objects of sense clear, Socrates offers the example of three fingers, which he introduces by stating, "these [οὗτοι], we say, would be [ἂν εἶεν] three fingers—the smallest, the second, and the middle" (523 c). While this example consists of body parts that presumably Socrates and his interlocutors all possess, Socrates does not next ask Glaucon to look at Socrates's or his own or anyone else's fingers. Socrates does use the demonstrative οὗτοι to suggest "these things here"; however, his use of a potential optative, ἂν εἶεν, "would be," suggests that Socrates is more interested in directing Glaucon's thought than his gaze. Thus, Socrates does not ask Glaucon to *look* at anyone or anything at all. Instead, Socrates states, "*Think* [διανοοῦ, in the imperative] of them while I am speaking *as if* [ὡς] they were being seen up close" (523c, my emphasis). Thus far, the course of this conversation suggests that moving from the visible to the intelligible entails less a transcendence of the features of embodied life than a change in the way one comports oneself to the position one is already in.

To continue with the example, Socrates points out that when considered alone, any one of these fingers is adequately judged to be a finger by the senses.[9] There is nothing in any one finger alone that confuses the person observing the finger. However, when one comes to determine the relationship between the fingers with respect to bigness and smallness, the very same finger must be determined to be both small and big, whereupon the soul is thrown into a state of confusion. On the one hand, the perception of a finger is an uncomplicated perception of a single object. As Socrates states, "the sight at no point indicates to the soul that the finger is at the same time the opposite of a finger" (523d). On the other hand, the comparison between fingers produces the perception that the finger, which is perceived as a single object, is also something that is small and something that is large. Socrates asks, "Does the sight see their bigness and littleness adequately, and does it make no difference to it whether a finger lies in the middle or on the extremes?" (523e). This question indicates that the singularity and simplicity of the perception of the finger is challenged by the multiplicity of the perception of its size. The finger is both big and small. The unity of the finger has been threatened by the variance of its size, by the contention between the bigness of the finger and the smallness of the very same finger. Were it not for the dual senses of the finger's singularity and of its multiplicity, of its stable and its variable nature, there would be no confusion of the soul. The fluctuation between large and small would not be a problem were the senses not simultaneously perceiving a unity. Consequently, sight cannot adequately discern the size of the finger, it cannot determine how big or small the finger is. It is not sight that determines the inadequacy of its judgment with respect to the size of a finger, nor is it sight that is confused. It is the soul that undergoes the effects of the perception(s) of the size of the finger. The soul maintains and is the repository of these conflicting perceptions.

At the same time, because the unity of the finger persists, the soul is not drawn into questioning what the finger is. The soul is not confused about the ontological status of the finger. Rather, precisely because the finger presents itself as a one, the soul becomes confused about what the big and the small, or the soft and the hard, are: "Isn't it necessary that in such cases the soul be at a loss as to what this sensation indicates by the hard if it says that the same thing is also soft, and what the sensation of the light and of the heavy indicates by the light and heavy, if it indicates that the heavy is light and the light heavy?" (524a). It is on the basis of its confusion about the meaning of heavy (if the same thing can be heavy and light) or big (if the same thing can be big and small) that the soul is compelled to summon calculation to determine whether heavy and light are one or two, and it is at this point that one finds oneself forced to ask what the heavy and the light or the big and the small are (524b–c). The selfsameness of the finger, its persistent singularity, confronts the soul with the dilemma of a one that appears to be both heavy and light, both big and small. It is this dissonance between its apparent oneness and its multiplicity that leads to inquiry into the nature of the one:

> "For if the one is adequately seen, itself by itself, or is grasped by some other sense, it would not draw men toward being, as we were saying about the finger. But if some opposition to it is always seen at the same time, so that nothing looks as though it were one more than the opposite of one, then there would now be need of something to judge; and in this case, a soul would be compelled to be at a loss and to make an investigation, setting in motion the intelligence within it [κινοῦσα ἐν ἑαυτῇ τὴν ἔννοιαν], and to ask what the one itself is. And thus the study of the one would be among those apt to lead and turn around toward the contemplation of what is." (524e–525a)

There are several possible responses to the confusion of the soul produced by the eyes' unhealthy judgment of the finger, two of which correspond to affections of the soul belonging to two regions in the intelligible realm. For one, the soul could summon the intellect and try to determine whether or not the finger is large or small. In doing so, the soul would make use of calculation, in which technē, thought and knowledge (τέχναι το καὶ διάνοιαι καὶ ἐπιστῆμαι), participate (522c), in order to determine something about the finger in question. As a second possibility, the soul could summon intellect to investigate the nature of the one itself. Presumably, such investigation would pave the way for dialectic, and marks the most philosophic response to confusion because it draws the soul to the contemplation of Being.[10] Ontology thus emerges as the appropriate philosophic response to the confusion arising from out of competing sensations. It does so because what is given to us in our sensations is a world of countable things. Put differently, ontology is tied to the study of number on the basis of the protean character of the bodily.

Finally, we should note the curious nature of Socrates's description of this ontology. By Socrates's account, the investigation of the one that turns the soul toward being is a function of a collision between medical and juridical events. Socrates states that the eyes do not sufficiently discern (κρινόμενα) the size of the finger, and in failing to do so, they produce nothing healthy (οὐδὲν ὑγιές) (523b). The entire circuit that has been established between fingers, eyes, and soul now risks infection on the basis of the discernment of the eyes. The fingers not only persist in their individual simplicity and communal complexity, but they also call for a court of appeals and seek better witnesses than the eyes. The intellect is summoned as a judge and doctor to render a sufficient verdict and to stave off infection.[11] It is precisely because the soul is confused and in danger of infection that the possibility of ontology unfolds through what we are led to believe is the therapeutic and just investigation of the one. The soul's turn toward Being is motivated by this risk of infection.[12] Socrates does not tell Glaucon to disavow the perception of the finger, but to heed what sensation tells him about it, namely that it is somehow both a unity and a multiplicity. Thus, when it comes to pursuing a study capable of turning the soul toward what *is*, it is not a matter of eschewing sensation, but rather of paying sufficient attention to it. While Socrates asserts that dialectic does not rely upon anything sensed (511b–c), we must keep in mind that dialectic arrives at the end of a process which includes the careful attention to, and articulation of, sense perception (511b, 532a).

This discussion of counting sets the stage for the subsequent identification of the other forms of study capable of seducing the philosophic soul to Being, and anticipates the account of dialectic, the most advanced and difficult component of philosophic curricula, which consummates the increasingly intimate relation between the soul of the philosopher and Being. Once Socrates has finished his account of the proper education of philosophic natures, he can return to the account of degenerate regimes and kinds of soul he enumerated at the end of book 4 and work his way to the most corrupt of figures, the tyrant.

The Tyrant

Socrates inaugurates his discussion of degenerate regimes by adopting a playful poetic conceit. Speaking for and as the Muses, and thus in high-tragic talk, Socrates claims that the cause of the dissolution of the city lies in its generated and composite nature: "A city so composed is hard to be moved. But, since for everything that has come into being there is decay, not even a composition such as this will remain for all time; it will be dissolved" (546a). As Socrates elaborates, what will trigger the decay to which this city is doomed on the basis of its composite nature, is a failing on the part of its leaders to properly calculate the "prosperous birth and barrenness" of humankind (546b). The infamous nuptial number provides a mathematical expression of what will eventualy fail to be properly calculated and inaugurates a discussion that follows the course of the city's decay. One effect of this failure is the "chaotic mixing" of various kinds of character, which "engenders unlikeness and inharmonious irregularity" (547a). As offspring degrade in quality, so too does the leadership and education in the city, which, in turn, ensures further degradation of character for both leaders and city. It is this degradation that can be charted as the progression from aristocracy to timocracy to oligarchy to democracy to tyranny.[13]

We gain much in our understanding of this account of the initial stages of civic corruption by looking at what it enables in the ensuing conversation. The coherent course of decay is traced through a series of regimes and corresponding arrangements of soul and results in a portrait of the life of the tyrant, presented as the image of the perfectly unjust life. The correspondence between regimes and souls is not merely a function of the analogy between soul and city asserted in book 2, but is requisite for the portrait of the perfectly unjust life because, as Socrates insists, such a life is not fully visible without granting it the possession of political power (578b–c). Once such a life is visible, Socrates and Glaucon are then in a position to judge it in comparison with the perfectly just life outlined in the preceding books. It will thus be necessary for us to delve into the analysis of regimes and souls in some detail. Doing so requires some brief consideration of the controversy surrounding the status of this discussion.

When Socrates introduces the four regimes to be analyzed, he locates them within Glaucon's realm of experience both historically and linguistically. The regimes to which he refers are "the ones having names" (544c), including the regime of Crete and Sparta (what is to be called the timocracy or timarchy) as well as the oligarchy, democracy, and tyranny. As the discussion continues, it becomes clear that their order is not simply one of degrees of remove from the best human regime but also one of generation, as one regime grows out of another regime according to a discernible course of decay.[14] The discussion purports to give a genealogical account of these regimes, following the transformation of one regime into another.

Much depends on how we interpret the temporality of this progression. Aristotle's famous critique of this discussion in his *Politics* is based upon his observation that, historically speaking, there is nothing necessary about the progression that Socrates identifies.[15] Oligarchies have emerged out of democracies as well as the other way around, and tyranny often breeds nothing but further tyranny. Attempts to rescue Plato from this critique have varied but have tended toward the claim that Plato has his Socrates abstract from the possibility of radical changes of regime due to natural or human catastrophe in order to chart the inevitable[16] course of decay belonging to a created composite entity, in this case the city.[17] The discussion of regimes would then be a discussion of what, under the best of circumstances, would be the course of destruction of even the best city. As R. L. Nettleship puts it, books 8 and 9 "put before us an ideal history of evil, as the previous books put before us an ideal history of good."[18]

Nettleship's use of the phrase "ideal history" should be sufficient warning that the extent to which the discussion of regimes is intended as an account of past events is not without question. It is thus no surprise to find commentators differing on what they take the philosophical status of the discussion of regimes to be. For some, the discussion is Plato's contribution to a philosophy of history.[19] For others it marks an early foundation of political science.[20] Those who favor the latter approach tend to reject the progression of regimes as a chronological progression,[21] although this is not universally the case.[22]

This is not the place for a full consideration of the issues surrounding this longstanding debate. There is, however, one dimension of Socrates's treatment of regimes that is particularly germane to the present study, namely the frequency with which Socrates appeals to medical terminology. Throughout the discussion of regimes, Socrates uses medical terminology in order to cast the city's devolution as a function of disease (see, in particular, 544c, 563e, and 564b).[23] Any consideration of the historical status of the discussion of regimes should keep in mind its medical tenor. The discussion of regimes is more like a case study designed to elucidate the unimpeded course of a disease for diagnostic purposes than an account of the events befalling a particular past regime. Thus, in considering the discussion of regimes, we would do well, to paraphrase Taylor, to avoid confusing symptomology with biography.[24]

This is to say that the governing idiom of the discussion of regimes is neither simply historical nor exclusively political, but medical. Thus, this discussion is not reducible to a philosophy of history or to a political science narrowly conceived; it provides an account of psycho-political pathology, a diagnosis (and perhaps prognosis) of city and soul. The progression of types of regimes and arrangements of soul is a progression of successively sicker and more moribund conditions.

Regardless of one's stance on the accuracy of this discussion's depictions of sources of change in particular regimes or the theoretical viability of Socrates's political diagnostics, it is necessary to note the rhetorical efficacy of the diagnostic stance that Socrates has adopted here. As we will see, the descriptions of familial and civic dynamics resonate with Glaucon and Adeimantus; they are not simply persuaded by Socrates, they are enthusiastically convinced.[25] Adopting this diagnostic perspective further enhances Socrates's authority in the eyes of his interlocutors.[26]

Socrates's description of the disintegration of the best city into four lesser regimes, his political pathology, hinges upon an inverse correlation between desire and calculation that can be found in all of the degenerate regimes. The timocrat is marked by a desire for honor that impedes his cultivation for argument (548e–549a). The oligarch uses his capacity for calculation in the service of his desire for money (553b–d). The democrat comprises a tense truce of necessary and unnecessary desires accomplished by the further subservience of calculation to desire (560d–561e). The tyrant is defined by the absolute rule of desire and subjugation of all other concerns to the *eros* that has been made ruler of his soul (572e–573a): "but love [ὁ Ἔρως] lives like a tyrant in him, in all anarchy and lawlessness, and, as a monarch, will lead him who has it, *just like a city*, to every reckless act by which he will feed it and the clamorous mob around it" (574e–575a, my emphasis). This love is the perfect device of control; it unceasingly drives the tyrant to fulfill it, sapping all of his resources, and leaving him with nothing left to do anything else (specifically leaving him with precious few resources with which to cultivate a capacity for calculation). Further, this love is the least likely to fulfill itself, thus guaranteeing the distraction of the tyrant in perpetuity. The tyrant represents the fullest realization of the inversion between calculation and desire: he has the greatest desires and is the most impotent with respect to fulfilling them. His love can do nothing for him; it is a desire that renders him as dependent on other desires and people as it is insatiable and overweening.[27]

Rather than seeing himself as the puppet of Eros, the tyrant understands his desires to be his servants and moreover believes that they can be entirely fulfilled by the acquisition of things in the world (577d–579e). Thus, the tyrant treats the world as containing only objects for his potential consumption. That such consumption will never fully sate his desires, and that his desires themselves will cause him pain as well as pleasure, is a knowledge to which the tyrant is not privy. Thus, the impotence of the tyrant with respect to the fulfillment of his desires is counterbalanced by the terrible effectiveness with which he operates in the world.

Indeed, what is most disturbing about the account of the tyrant offered in book 9 is that this incapacity to fulfill his desires is coupled with the absolute license offered the tyrant to engage in attempts at such fulfillment. These attempts are not only doomed to fail in advance, but are predicated upon taking things from others—their property, their dignity, their lives. What has been destroyed in the tyrant soul is precisely its capacity to be unified and whole. However, the shattered, fragmented soul is not without its own means for operating in the world. The tyrant's incapacity to respond to the demands of eros does not render him powerless to wreak havoc; if anything, it drives him to commit increasingly atrocious acts. For this reason, Socrates counts as most wretched not simply the one who possesses a tyrannical nature, but the one who, in addition to possessing such a nature, is then given the most means to enact his perpetually frustrated attempts to fulfill his desires by finding his way into the rule of a city (578b–c).

The wretchedness of the tyrant provides a counterimage to the flourishing of the unjust person figured by Glaucon and Adeimantus in book 2; its persuasiveness is in part a function of the clinical orientation by means of which it is developed.[28] However, it also provides a poignant indication of the need to distinguish between vice and disease. Throughout the frequent references to health and sickness in books 3 and 4, disease is presented as a persistently degenerative entity. According to such a conception of disease, while it is certainly possible to be ill without showing any symptoms of illness and without even knowing that one is ill, eventually, without treatment, diseases either get better on their own or kill the people who have them.[29] The nature of the tyrant's "disease," however, is such that while it discourages the tyrant from seeking treatment (573a–b), no resolution to the disease occurs on its own. The tyrant neither gets better (ceases being a tyrant) nor is the death of the tyrant necessarily forthcoming.[30] As this account of the tyrant chillingly demonstrates, the tyrannical soul does not cease to be when it becomes corrupted. Mad, at war with itself, pained and vicious, the tyrant soul remains a force to be contended with nonetheless.

The endurance of the tyrant in the face of his own corruption makes clear the irreducibility of vice to disease. While they may be analogous, the viciousness of the tyrant's soul well exceeds the terms of disease and gestures toward the limits of this analogy. Failing to acknowledge this difference results in failing to understand tyranny. Yet, as we have seen, Socrates leaves the difference between vice and disease underdetermined in the comparison that he draws between them in book 4. Consequently, this account of the tyrannical soul poses a pressing difficulty for Socrates's earlier comparison between vice and disease. It also places Socrates in a dilemma. The analogy he had used so effectively to dissuade Glaucon and Adeimantus of the opinion that the unjust life is the most desirable life has now proven insufficient to account for that figure who epitomizes the unjust life, the tyrant. By creating an uncritical analogy between vice and disease, Socrates risks overlooking the distinctions between disease and injustice that explain why the presence of doctors is not sufficient to guard against tyranny. Some means beyond the vocabulary of health and disease is needed in order to account for the effects of vice on the soul if Socrates and his interlocutors are to avoid being rendered speechless in the face of tyranny. Socrates's analysis of the tyrant demonstrates the need for a more refined conception of vice than that offered by the comparison between vice and disease.[31] As we shall see in the next chapter, book 10's discussion of immortality comes to the aid of Socrates and his interlocutors by venturing just such a conception. The seeds for this approach, however, are sown in the judgment of lives with which book 9 concludes, in which Socrates and his interlocutors find it necessary to turn their clinical gaze toward themselves, and so it is to this discussion that we now turn.

Judgment of Lives

Socrates's account of the tyrant culminates in three judgments about the tyrant's happiness, during the course of which Glaucon concludes that the life of the tyrant is the least desirable of lives (576d–588a). These judgments, and indeed the account of the tyrant and the review of regimes preceding it, rely upon a particular perspective that Socrates characterizes as viewing the city and the soul "as a whole" (576d–e, 579e). The holistic view of city and soul that Socrates and Glaucon have gained is a function not of their remove from what they are observing, but of their immersion in it; they view the tyrannical city by "creeping down [καταδύντες][32] into every corner and looking" (576d–e). The judgment of the tyrannical soul is reserved for one who "is able with his thought to creep into [ἐνδύς] a man's disposition and see through it—a man who is not like a child looking from outside and overwhelmed by the tyrannic pomp set up as a façade for those outside, but who rather sees through it adequately" (577a). Socrates continues:

> "And what if I were to suppose that all of us must hear that man who is both able to judge and has lived together with the tyrant in the same place and was witness to his actions at home and saw how he is with each of his own, among whom he could most be seen stripped of the tragic gear; and again, has seen him in public dangers; and since he has seen all that, we were to bid him to report how the tyrant stands in relation to the others in happiness and wretchedness?" "You would," he said, "be quite right in suggesting these things too." "Do you want us," I said, "to pretend [προσποιησώμεθα] that we are among those who would be able to judge and have already met up with such men, so that we'll have someone to answer what we ask?" (576e–577b)

This passage invites a kind of intimate viewing of tyranny.[33] Rather than dissuade Glaucon from intimacy with tyranny, Socrates purports to provide it for him (all the while creating a portrait which will actually be the most effective antidote to the attraction to tyranny), although with several layers of insulating narrative. The insulation is provided by a variety of distancing moves, by adopting a poetic perspective carved out of medical, mathematical, and legal tropes. It plays upon the experience and the self-diagnostic capacities of the doctor, as well as the distancing capacities of the judge's knowledge. Socrates's imputation of their ability to take on this hybrid persona to a certain poetic operation, "pretending," reminds us of the voice of the Muses with which Socrates has been speaking since the start of his account of corrupt regimes. The scene of pretending, of fantasy, is a necessary conceit to permit observation (and thus experience) and judgment. Socrates and Glaucon have not escaped the mimetic danger here; rather, the discernment of the tyrant's life has also prompted them to look not simply at the tyrant, but at their own image of the tyrant, their own preconceptions of and dispositions toward tyranny. Their judgment of the tyrant will also be a judgment of their own perspective on tyranny.

In developing this scene of judgment, mathematics provides a distancing resource, a means to isolate oneself against contamination by the thing being studied. The mathematical calculation of the tyrant's remove from true pleasure gives depth and shape to the tyrant's life, providing the figure by means of which they can creep into the disposition of the tyrant; it corrects the facile, two-dimensional portrait of the tyrant offered in book 2. Something similar is going on with the nuptial number, whereby the way is prepared for Socrates and Glaucon to investigate disease and decay of city and soul without themselves becoming diseased and corrupted because of the antiseptic mathematical introduction to the conversation. But of course, they are diseased and corrupted because of the city in which they have been born and the regime by which they have been educated (specifically, by the poetic content of their educations) so that the number also inaugurates a context in which they can examine themselves. This self-examination or self-diagnostic ability is figured in the discussion of the doctor, as that which in fact makes a doctor "clever." Thus, the number not only provides a context in which to distance themselves from decay, it also opens up a discussion in which the diagnostic tools for examining their own poetic dispositions are developed. It even suggests the affinity between poetry and mathematics by reminding them of their common musical heritage.[34]

Having constructed images of the perfectly just and unjust lives, analyzed them, and judged them, Socrates and Glaucon turn to construct the crowning achievement of their hybrid poetics: an image of the soul that would allow them to make manifest what is really behind the assertion that the perfectly unjust life is best (588b–e). The complicated image that they produce of a many-headed beast, a lion, and a human all bound together so that from the outside they appear to be a single human, provides them with the means to describe both the attainment of unity and the failure to do so. With this image in mind, according to which choosing the unjust life is tantamount to cultivating what is worst in one's soul at the expense of the best, Socrates and Glaucon turn to outline the way of life of the just person. They conclude that, because such a person attends always to the condition of his soul, looking "at the regime within him [πρὸς τὴν ἐν αὐτῷ πολιτείαν]" (591e), and allowing this concern to govern his acquisition of money and honor, he cares not for his "fatherland" (πατρίδι) (save by some divine coincidence [ἐὰν μὴ θεία τις συμβῇ τύχη] [592a]) but only for this city, the regime in his soul (592a–b). Thus, the rejection of concern for the πατρίς does not include a rejection of politics; rather, it reframes the object of political concern and the bearer of a politeia to include soul. This is another expression of the approach to politics that has been at work all along as the "art of ruling" and of the city as the conglomerate of what rules and what is ruled. It is the case that the conclusion in book 9, that one should focus concern on the city that is the soul, risks a form of quietism, insofar as it advocates eschewing public life in order to cultivate a condition of soul. However, in assessing these lines, we should note that the dialogue does not end here. Instead, book 10 returns to the city of speakers to consider in greater detail the effects on the soul of particular institutions and people.

Thus, while it is with their thought that they investigate the tyrant, the perspective informing this investigation is not one of noetic distance but noetic engagement. Were we to keep within the distinctions introduced by the divided line, we would have to say that throughout books 8 and 9 Socrates and Glaucon direct their thought not to what is eternal and changeless, but to what is variant and volatile, in this case the transformations and corruptions to which cities and souls are subject. Their discussion in book 9 does culminate in their recognition of the possibility that the best city supplies a pattern for the soul rather than for any existing human city (592a–b). However, as we have seen, whatever critical and contemplative purchase Socrates and Glaucon have won in order to allow them to come to this conclusion has been carved out of their persistent recognition of the interdependence between city and soul.[35] While it may be possible for a soul to be organized in a manner far superior to that found in any city, in most cases this is not possible without the aid of the very city whose regime would be overcome. Throughout the *Republic* we are shown that, for better or for worse, the life of the philosopher is bound up with the affairs of the city.

Socrates's and Glaucon's noetic immersion in cities and souls is dictated by the characterization of both soul and city as capable of becoming unified and fragmented. Because the philosophic nature can be trained by a course of education in which its eros is channeled and its phronēsis turned toward Being, the philosopher acts as a manifestation of unity and self-sameness. Because the soul of the tyrant has many parts, many "corners" around which to creep, one would be misled and fail to see the soul as a whole if one observed the tyrant only from the outside. The accounts of the philosopher and of the tyrant share this conception of the soul's plasticity. It is this plasticity that motivates Socrates to return, at the start of book 10, to a consideration of poetry. As he states, their identification of the forms of the soul underscores the importance of their earlier censure of poetry (595a). In the course of the critique of mimēsis that follows, Socrates and Glaucon are drawn further into a critique of their own perspective on the soul. The following chapter will chart this self-critical turn, and its implications, in detail.

7 Politics and Immortality

Book 10 opens with Socrates's observation that their most recent comments have illustrated the correctness of their earlier critical assessment of poetry. He then levels a charge against the imitative arts as such: they "seem to maim the thought of those who hear them and do not as a remedy have the knowledge of how they really are" (595b). According to this assessment, the lovers of poetry[1] are lovers of something that disfigures them, and moreover does so without announcing these effects. Indeed, it is precisely the lack of transparency regarding poetry's ontological status and effects, its lack of provision for knowledge of what it is and does, that Socrates attempts to remedy in the subsequent discussion of what mimēsis is. This is to say that book 10, which concludes with the myth of Er, begins with a call for a poetry that is able to account for itself, a dialectical and self-critiquing poetry.

Throughout the first half of book 10, Socrates's critique of poetry takes as its justification the tendency of poetry to foster[2] one part of the soul to the detriment of others, even in the souls of the decent (605c). The figure he summons to illustrate this danger is that of a bereaved and decent father who, having lost his son, does battle with himself, struggling between a desire to deliberate and set his affairs aright, on the one hand, and a desire to indulge in lamentation, nourishing the part of him that wants to mourn, on the other (603e–604d). Even decent people, concludes Socrates, are tempted by the displays of lamentation in tragedy to luxuriate in mourning (605c–d).

Socrates and Glaucon are afforded this grasp of the souls of the decent by the thoughtful immersion that also provided them with an intimate view of the souls of the corrupt. The end of this account makes explicit their own implication in the discussion of mimēsis with which book 10 begins. Agreeing that they would be willing to offer protection to poetry if it were able to defend itself from the charges which they have leveled against it (607c–d), they turn to outline the stance toward poetry required in the absence of such a defense. This stance includes explicit instruction to themselves:

> "just like the men who have once fallen in love with someone, and don't believe the love is beneficial, keep away from it even if they have to do violence to themselves; so we too—due to the inborn love of such poetry we owe to our rearing in these fine regimes—we'll be glad if it turns out that it is best and truest. But as long as it's not able to make its apology, when we listen to it, we'll chant this argument we are making as a counter charm, taking care against falling back again into this love, which is childish and belongs to the many." (607e–608b)

Thus, Socrates and Glaucon conclude their investigation of mimēsis by turning their critical gaze upon themselves, recognizing their own investment in poetry and the demands placed upon them by the critique they have just offered. This is to say that the opening discussion of book 10 returns to the self-critical and self-diagnostic stance that Socrates and his interlocutors have been compelled to adopt at decisive junctures in their previous conversation. This stance is maintained throughout book 10, and, when coupled with their intimate grasp of psychic plasticity, results in a direct critique of the perspective of the soul that they have developed during the course of the dialogue. We see this coupling emerge in their return to just and unjust lives and the wages and rewards appropriate to them, a task which includes a discussion of the immortality of the soul.

Immortality

Socrates's account of the immortality of the soul in *Republic* 10 is one of the strangest and most vexing passages in the entire dialogue. It has plagued those commentators who pay it close attention[3] and has been described, to take a few examples, as, "one of the few really embarrassingly bad arguments in Plato,"[4] "perfunctory and weak,"[5] and "far-from-cogent."[6] Even the most sympathetic readers note the ineffectiveness of its demonstration and call into question the seriousness with which such a demonstration is intended.[7] Despite Eric Brown's compelling defense of Plato against these criticisms,[8] the validity of the argument is, for a number of commentators, less troubling than its apparent incompatibility with the rest of the dialogue.[9] R. C. Cross and A. D. Woozley go so far as to claim that the soul's immortality stands in "irresolvable contradiction" with the account of the soul given in book 4.[10]

However, the incompatibility between the discussion of the soul's immortality and the accounts of the soul given earlier in the dialogue is made clear in the *Republic* by Socrates himself, who observes, immediately after the discussion of immortality, that while he and his interlocutors have gone through the affections and forms of the soul in its human life, they have failed to arrive at a determination of what the soul, in its true nature, is (611a–612a).[11] Their investigation of the soul, with its emphasis on the soul's complex structure and its assertion of the soul's immortality, has won them not a grasp of the soul itself, but a perspective from which they can now critically asses this investigation.

In fact, it is precisely the dissonance between the assertion of the soul's immortality and the earlier assertion of the soul's complexity that dissatisfies Socrates (611b). As we have seen, this is not the first time in the *Republic* that Socrates has expressed doubt about his and his interlocutors' treatment of the soul; uncertainty pervades even the dialogue's most detailed discussion of the soul's structure (435c–d).[12] The discussion of immortality, like the critique of mimēsis, prompts Socrates to return to a self-reflective and self-critical consideration of his and his interlocutors handling of the soul.

Consequently, we can neither ignore Socrates's dissatisfaction with the accounts that he and his interlocutors have given of the soul, nor can we assume that the incompatibility of these accounts renders incoherent all that has been said about the soul in the dialogue. By staging the failure of certain attempts to arrive at a satisfying account of the soul, Plato presents his readers with a self-critical dimension within the *Republic*. Whatever one's doubts about their discussion's strength as a demonstration of immortality, they are not grounds for dismissing the discussion as irrelevant or superfluous without a thorough investigation of the role of the discussion in this self-critical dimension. The relevance of the discussion of immortality to the concerns that animate the dialogue is directly apparent if we set aside the expectation of receiving a perfectly adequate account of the immortality of the soul and attend instead to the service it offers to Socrates's critical assessment of the accounts of the soul he and his interlocutors have given.

More specifically, I will argue that the discussion of immortality in book 10 acts as a corrective to the uncritical analogy between vice and disease established in book 4 (see chapter 5). The limitations of this analogy are already suggested by the account of the tyrant in book 9, whose viciousness defies reduction to disease. Book 10's attempt to demonstrate the soul's immortality on the basis of its capacity to endure its own viciousness explicitly illustrates the politically and philosophically salient difference between vice and disease. In so doing, it addresses the tension between book 4's comparison between vice and disease and book 9's account of the tyrant. We will also find that the discussion's identification of the unique nature of vice hinges upon its focus on the interaction between souls within the city. As a result, the discussion of immortality finds evidence for the soul's deathlessness in the political life of the person. Socrates adopts this focus because it is uniquely suited to persuade Glaucon that care for the soul cannot occur independently of care for the city.

* * *

Initially it seems as though, in order to investigate soul's immortality, Socrates and Glaucon must take leave of the immersed perspective on the soul that enabled their intimate view of the philosopher and tyrant. Surveying the benefits of justice requires, Socrates states, a shift in perspective from one lifetime to "all time" (608c).[13] And indeed, he goes on, in the myth of Er, to discuss the fate of the soul after a single lifetime.

However, the myth of Er occurs only after Socrates and Glaucon have agreed that the soul is immortal, and this agreement comes after a discussion not of eternity but of the effects of various kinds of corruption on a community of things.[14] To briefly summarize the rest of their discussion, after Socrates and Glaucon agree upon an initial delimitation of good (τὸ ἀγαθόν) and evil (τὸ κακόν), they focus their attention on evil, giving a series of examples of evil things in order to refine their understanding of the operation of evil (608e–609a). They agree that these kinds of evils are naturally connected (σύμφυτον) to the things they affect, and that if something is not destroyed by the evil that is naturally connected to it, then for such a thing there is no destruction (609a–b). They then narrow their focus to the evils that belong to the soul, the vices, and determine that in fact the vices do not affect the soul in such a manner as to utterly destroy it, appealing twice to the Athenian practice of executing criminals as evidence of this difference (609b–610e). They conclude that since the soul is not destroyed by the evils that are naturally connected to it, there is nothing that can destroy the soul, and thus the soul is deathless (ἀθάνατον) (610e–611a).[15]

This discussion hinges upon the identification of a difference between the effects of vice on the soul and the effects of disease on the body. The effects of vice on the soul become apparent only when Socrates and Glaucon attend to the interactions between souls, a view that is afforded by the city. In fact, the disclosure of the nature of vice turns upon one particular means that one particular city has for contending with vice. The perspective that is required to understand the rewards of justice (and the full effects of justice and injustice on the soul) begins with a turn not toward the soul's eternal life but toward its political life. In the discussion of immortality, the variant and transforming city, and not a changeless eternity, is the arena wherein the full effects of justice and injustice on the soul can be seen.

This focus on the variant, the quotidian, and the particular is evident in the exchange that begins this discussion. Socrates reports this exchange as follows:

> "Do you call something good," I said, "and something bad [Ἀγαθόν τι, εἶπον, καὶ κακὸν καλεῖς]?" "I do." "Do you think about these things just as I do?" "How so?" "Everything that destroys and corrupts is bad, and what saves and benefits is good [Τὸ μὲν ἀπολλύον καὶ διαφθεῖρον πᾶν τὸ κακὸν εἶναι, τὸ δὲ σῷζον καὶ ὠφελοῦν τὸ ἀγαθόν]."[16] "I do," he said. (608d–e)

The casual nature of this construal of good and bad is striking. A discussion of what the Good is occupies a large portion of book 6 and is preceded by a disclaimer in which Socrates emphasizes his and his interlocutors' limited capacity to discuss the Good (506d–e). In book 6, in fact, Socrates offers a formulation very similar to the question posed above.[17] However, while this statement in book 6 is followed with an observation that they also assert there to be a Good itself, in book 10 no such turn from what is said about good things to what is said about the Good itself is made. In this discussion, Socrates and Glaucon do not shift perspective from the particular to the formal. Instead, they turn to delimit good and bad things on the basis of their effects on other things that are capable of faring well or poorly.

Thus, the noetic engagement with political and psychic transformation that characterizes Socrates and Glaucon's perspective in books 8 and 9 is maintained even in their discussion about the soul's immortality. In fact, this perspective is decisive for the structure of the discussion and helps explain some of the elements that most plague its readers. Its focus on vice, its brevity, its reliance upon the ethical underpinnings of the dialogue, it assertion of evils that are naturally connected to things, its use of the execution of criminals as evidence of the soul's immortality all make more sense when we view the discussion of immortality as an extension of the concerns and interests that frame Socrates's account of the tyrant. The necessity of such an extension is a function of the misunderstanding of vice that is risked in an uncritical comparison between vice and disease; such a misunderstanding interferes with the task to which Socrates has committed himself, namely the demonstration of the effects of injustice on the soul. In order to fulfill his obligation to Glaucon and Adeimantus, Socrates must indicate the divergence between vice and disease. The discussion of immortality accomplishes this task by bringing what has been learned of vice in the analysis of the tyrant to bear on the comparison between vice and disease. It is thus inextricably tied to the task that Socrates accepts in book 2.[18] Its ethical import is evident in its indication of the need to cultivate a vocabulary of viciousness that is not reducible to one of disease. Its ability to do so is predicated upon its focus on the interaction between soul and city. Thus, its ethical import is conjoined to its political perspective. In order to make this clear we will trace in some detail the discussion's illustration of the difference between vice and disease, its reliance on the role of the city in order to demonstrate this difference, and the salience of this demonstration to the concerns raised by Glaucon.

Disease is introduced in the discussion of immortality as one example among several of kinds of evils:

> "Do you say there is some bad and some good for each thing? Just as ophthalmia for eyes and disease for the entire body [σύμπαντι τῷ σώματι], blight for grain, rot for wood, rust for bronze and iron, and as I am saying, there is for nearly everything some naturally connected badness and sickness for each thing?" "I do," he said. "Is it not the case that whenever some one of these attaches itself [προσγένηται] to something, it makes [ποιεῖ] the one to which it attaches itself defective, and at the end dissolves and destroys the whole thing [ὅλον διέλυσεν καὶ ἀπώλεσεν]?" "How could it not?" (609a)

There are two primary indications that this passage speaks to concerns raised earlier in the dialogue. For one, the focus in this passage on the production of good and bad conditions resonates with the emphasis on poiēsis in the vice/disease analogy in book 4. Here, this stress on poiēsis is furthered by the conception of good and bad as that which attaches itself to a thing. When what is bad (κακόν) for a thing attaches itself to the thing, this badness then produces or engenders (literally, makes), the thing to which it is attached defective (πονηρόν). Thus, badness functions by means of attachment and production; that is, it functions by means of a certain poiēsis.

Second, Socrates's characterization of the relationship between evils and things as one of "natural connection" links this investigation of evil to the distinction between nature and law drawn much earlier in the dialogue, first by Thrasymachus in book 1 (343b–344c) and then refined by Glaucon in book 2 (358e, 359c). Both Thrasymachus and Glaucon suggest that an antagonistic relationship exists between nature and convention, such that what is naturally good—the exercise of one's power over others—is directly opposed to what is conventionally good—the limitation of the exercise of one's power over others. According to this characterization, being subjected to law is alien to the natural good that is the expression of one's power. Socrates's invocation of natural goods and evils here brings the distinction between nature and convention into play in this discussion and sets up the reconfiguration of this relationship which will occur during the course of the conversation.

Socrates's account of natural goods and evils in the present passage has been the source of intense scrutiny and criticism. To be sure, we will continue to be frustrated by apparent inconsistencies throughout this conversation if we take Socrates to mean that each thing has one and only one thing that corrupts it. In a few lines Glaucon will list a number of corruptions for the soul (609b), and Socrates will offer a series of examples of corruptions of the body (610a–b). Further, as has been noted by a number of commentators, any one of these things can be destroyed by multiple different objects and events.[19] Finally, Socrates addresses what role a variety of things can have in destroying any one thing by carefully delimiting the manner in which the various instances of corruption may and may not communicate with one another (609e–610c). In fact, Socrates addresses death by violent means directly as evidence that the soul's corruption does not tend necessarily toward its destruction nor that of the person (610c–d).

This list of corrupting agents and that to which they are naturally connected are instances of the more general operation of destruction that Socrates and Glaucon have identified at 608d. Insofar as Socrates's main concern at this juncture is to elaborate upon the activity of tò kakóv in order to determine the manner in which vice operates on the soul, he can afford a certain casual indifference to the names of particular instances of this general activity. Thus, while his display of this indifference has been the source of much controversy, I maintain that Socrates's concern here is not to show that each thing has one and only one form of corruption, but that destruction itself operates with a certain general coherence and consistency that can be identified.[20] The examples Socrates offers are given as particular instances of the kind of global destruction that he and Glaucon have agreed is the characteristic work of evil. His characterization of them as naturally connected evils deflects the significance of what each thing's natural corruption is to the question of what it is that makes that thing be subject to good and bad conditions. Whatever makes it a thing subject to these conditions is what also dictates that it have a specific mode of degradation and loss of integrity. According to this reading, an evil is naturally connected to something when it degrades the thing's capacity to be what it is. An alien evil would be something that degrades some object, but does not do so when attached to another object.[21] Socrates's indifference to the names and numbers of particular natural corruptions is a function, then, not of incoherence but of his interest in outlining a larger logic of destruction.

According to this reading, the passage suggests that the destruction of wood by fire is an accelerated instance of the same logic of destruction at work in the deterioration of the wood by rot. As we shall see, Socrates presently makes disease a paradigm of this mode of destruction. The ultimate point of this series of examples is to illustrate the difference between the general mode of destruction common to complex and bodily things and the general mode of corruption applicable to souls. Certainly, this does suggest that even the global logic of destruction with which Socrates and Glaucon begin the discussion will require some revision, but this is precisely what is accomplished over the course of the conversation.

In fact, this list of examples with which we have been dealing is the first movement toward a specification of one general kind of destruction. At this juncture in the discussion, Socrates's investigation of the bad is tied to a taxonomy of things whose overarching organizational principle merits discussion. Socrates's reliance on familiar objects (bodies, eyes, grain, wood, iron, and bronze) whose differences are not immediately problematic serves a strategic function by suggesting that one need not investigate whether a more pressing ontological distinction between these things exists in order to discern their illustration of a course of destruction. Further, there is a tacit hierarchy at work for the first two objects. The disease of the eyes stands to the disease of the living body as part to a whole, just as eye stands to living body as part to whole. Socrates's reference to the wholeness of the body emphasizes this relationship (609a1). While this hierarchical relationship is not explicitly established for the rest of the members, all of the remaining things listed carry some connotation of their significance for humans in particular: σῖτος and ξύλον carry connotations of products that have been worked over by humans[22] which connect them to the final two examples, iron and bronze, as these become useful through the intervention of some action. Finally, eye and body share with grain and wood the fact that both are living, while iron and bronze share only their complex, bodily composition.

Because the examples that Socrates has provided of things that undergo destruction are also examples of things possessing complexity and bodily composition, the order of destruction that Socrates outlines here calls attention to the manner in which complex, bodily objects decompose: a disintegration of their wholeness. The complexity of these objects invites comparison with the complexity that has been attributed to the soul. At the same time, however, this comparison is confounded by any presumed ontological distinction between soul and body. It is noteworthy, then, that Socrates does not initially draw such an ontological distinction, but rather invites Glaucon to consider whether corruptions of soul operate in the same way as these other corruptions (609b–d). In doing so, he allows the difference between soul and body to be suggested by the difference that will emerge between vice and disease.[23] Thus, this list allows Socrates to draw the soul's complexity into question. If it can be shown that the soul does not function in the same way that other complex things do, then the nature of the soul's complexity must be reexamined. It also allows Socrates to broach the question of the soul's relationship to the bodily, insofar as the banality of these examples highlights the presumed difference between soul and body by provoking one to wonder whether and how soul's difference from body is any more significant than the eye's difference from iron.

Finally, it is significant that Socrates includes in this list both living and nonliving things. In a discussion aimed at discerning the deathlessness of the soul, it is interesting that the first general structure of destruction offered pertains to both what is living (and therefore capable of death) and what is nonliving (and therefore incapable of death). Such a list thus locates death within a larger context of destruction and poses the question of how death does and does not differ from blight and rust. In this context, the banality of the examples prompts consideration of the place of death among a plurality of forms of destruction. While the particularity of iron's erosion may be much less individualized than the particularity of the demise of, for example, Achilles or Socrates, the suggestion is that all of these are instances of the same kind of destructive behavior about which we have more or less sophisticated vocabularies, depending upon our investment in the object suffering destruction. By beginning with a broad context of destruction, the passage invites us to consider death as it relates to destructibility as such.[24]

The location of death within the context of destruction has implications for the characterization of disease operative throughout the dialogue. We have already noted that in 609a1–3 Socrates speaks of disease as one example of the general destruction wrought by τὸ κακόν. When, in 609a3–4, Socrates extends sickness to nearly all things, he associates disease not only with the living body but with nonliving bodily things. Socrates makes of disease a paradigm of bodily corruption, a paradigm not limited to the living body, but also not operative outside of the larger category of the bodily. Disease, then, names that kind of evil which attacks the wholeness of the body and is indicative of the evils that attend to all bodily and complex things.[25] If allowed to go unchecked, disease dissolves the community of parts that make the living body what it is and leaves a corpse in the place of the living body. The decaying body is indeed an appropriate example of the utter destruction of a complex object. The corpse is not a simple object but a collection of parts lacking in unity. What is missing from it is not its complexity but its organization; what has been lost is not simply a part of the body but the whole that is the living body itself.[26]

Of course, disease only produces a corpse if it does not get better; the possibility that a disease may be diverted from its course is not addressed in this discussion. Socrates and Glaucon treat sickness not only as a paradigm of bodily destruction but also as though it were a condensed or intensified activity of dying.[27] By emphasizing the relationship between disease's utter destruction of the body and death, Socrates makes clear the importance of bodily dissolution for the living person. However, the close association between disease and the logic of destruction proper to bodily, complex things poses problems for the association between disease and death as such. While iron may suffer utter destruction in a manner exemplified by disease, we would be stretching "death" nearly to the point of meaninglessness to assert that iron dies. Until Socrates has clarified the relationship between bodily dissolution, epitomized by disease, and the death of the person, any assertion of the body's mortality and the soul's immortality remains unpersuasive.[28]

However, in keeping with the nature of his obligation to give an account of the effects of justice and injustice on the soul and furthermore to defend the just life, Socrates is more concerned at this juncture with the life and death of living people than with explicitly charting the difference between eye, body, wood, iron, and soul according to the metaphysical distinctions introduced in the image of the divided line, even if he relies on his interlocutors' assent to these distinctions in making his case now. For this reason he is willing to rely upon a series of connections aligning disease with both what is bodily and with death itself, which then allows his own interlocutors' experience of the difference between ophthalmia, rust, and injustice to speak for itself. That is, Socrates exploits the connection between bodily and psychical plasticity at the same time that he undercuts it. His suggestion to Glaucon is this: even if we posit neither more nor less controversial a distinction between soul and body as between eye and iron, the difference between the body's corruption and the soul's corruption is profound. Socrates thereby reverses the importance of the distinction between soul and body and the distinction between vice and disease; whereas in book 4 the difference between vice and disease was a function of the difference between soul and body, now it is suggested that the difference between soul and body is most clearly seen and called for by the difference between vice and disease. He is willing to rest on this series of distinctions only because of the nature of his obligation to Glaucon and Adeimantus. That this is his main concern, and that the soul's immortality is demonstrated as a side-effect of this concern, is attested to by the structure of the final leg of the conversation, and helps make clearer two moves that Socrates makes in particular: his specification of the mode of exchange between natural and alien evils and his focus on the role of the city in contending with vice.

In the final part of the discussion of immortality, Socrates asserts that the exchange between kinds of corruptions is such as to limit a causal relationship between the corruption of the body and the corruption of the soul. His argument begins, again, with what could be taken as a banal distinction between two things, this time between body and food. The corruption of food cannot be said to cause the destruction of the body unless it engenders disease in the body (609e–610a). That rotten food does have a hand in the physical degeneration of the person who consumes it is hard to deny, but Socrates's point here is simply that it does not necessarily do so. Thus, the extent to which rotten food acts as an agent of the body's destruction must be limited to the extent to which it introduces disease into the body. Socrates generalizes this specification of exchange from the relationship between food and body to the relationship between body and soul: the corruption of the body cannot be said to cause the corruption of soul unless it engenders injustice in the soul (610a–c). The body's corruption does not necessarily do so, as is quickly and decisively asserted by Glaucon. "On the contrary," he said, "no one will ever show that the souls of the dying become more unjust through death" (610c).[29]

This way of proceeding implies that the limitation of exchange between body and soul requires no more controversial a difference between body and soul than that between body and food.[30] The agreement that the corruptions of the body are not sufficient to cause the corruptions of the soul[31] suggests that no manipulation of a person's body will necessarily result in a change in the condition of a person's soul. Neither doctors nor trainers are sufficient to contend with injustice; something other than physical alteration is necessary to do so. Were we tempted to ask what the psychical equivalent of rotten food is, we are given an answer to this question in the account of the degeneration of souls in books 8 and 9, wherein psychical degeneration is a function of the interaction between familial, civic, and individual structures that impede the optimal relationship between desire and calculation (491c–492c, 495a). Thus, Socrates's elaboration of the mode of exchange between bodily and psychical evils calls upon Glaucon's tacit acknowledgment of a distinction between disease and vice. It does so in a manner that commits Glaucon to the assertion that human viciousness is not necessarily limited by human finitude.

This same concern is exemplified in Socrates's focus in the final part of this discussion about the role of the city in contending with vice. When Socrates and Glaucon turn their attention to the evils that are naturally connected to the soul, they begin by identifying them as the vices that they had discussed earlier in the dialogue: injustice, licentiousness, cowardice, and lack of learning (609b).[32] Socrates directs Glaucon not to be confused into conflating the death that is caused by disease with the death of a criminal who has been caught at the hands of city: "And reflect, so that we are not deceived by thinking the unjust and foolish person, whenever he is caught doing an injustice, is then destroyed by his injustice, which is defectiveness of soul" (609b). Rather than fall prey to this deceptive conflation of two different kinds of death, Socrates directs Glaucon instead to consider the vicious soul in the same way that they have considered the diseased body, asking: "Do injustice or the other vices, being in it, by being in and besieging, ruin and wither it, until leading it to the point of death, separate it from the body?" (609d). Glaucon concludes that this is not the case.[33]

Speaking about death in this manner allows Socrates to emphasize what he seems most concerned with here, namely the capacity for people with vicious souls to remain not only active in the city, but in positions of power. As a combination of soul and body, the living person can be corrupted either by a corruption of body, which leads to the separation of soul and body (death), or by a corruption of the soul, which, as Glaucon has agreed, does not lead to death. Socrates's point here is that not only does vice not destroy the soul, neither does it make the soul unable to interact with the body, which is to say, neither does it make the unjust person unable to function in some fashion. Socrates thus reminds us of that quality of injustice that was so disturbingly demonstrated by the tyrant: its endurance.

In fact, Socrates invokes the corrupt but enduring tyrant throughout his reference to the criminal. The death of the criminal at the hands of the city cannot be taken as analogous to the death of the body by disease because the death of the criminal is a function not simply of his injustice, but of his having been caught. Thus, his injustice does not directly lead to his death. At the same time, the corrupting influence of injustice functions regardless of whether or not the criminal is caught. The identification of injustice as a form of evil that corrupts without destroying requires Socrates and Glaucon to acknowledge two orders of evil: those that corrupt and destroy utterly, like disease, and those that corrupt but do not destroy. While disease tends toward the death of the person, injustice does not necessarily do so.

The significance of the distinction between these two deaths is profound. What stands between the death of the body by means of disease and the death of the criminal by means of execution is the entire structure of law and enforcement set into place by the city. Whenever the city intervenes in the life of the unjust person, the city attests to the difference between injustice and disease; insofar as injustice is tied to the soul and disease is tied to the body, the city's treatment of criminals comprises a tacit assertion of the distinction between soul and body.

The figure of the executed criminal is taken to be so indispensable a testament to the radical difference between vice and disease that Socrates invokes it a second time in this discussion. He turns to assess the status of the counterclaim to the assertion that the soul must be immortal because its natural evils do not kill it. One who would make the claim that the sick or dying person has become unjust in order to avoid conceding that the soul is immortal would have to also claim that "injustice is fatal to the one who has it, just as disease is, and that, since its nature is such that it kills, those who have it die, those with more sooner, those with less in a more leisurely fashion; but it is not as it is now whereby the unjust are killed through this injustice [διὰ τοῦτο], but by other people [ὑπ ἄλλων] establishing a penalty" (610c–d). Socrates sees this position to be refuted on the grounds that it is so opposed to common experience as to be immediately worthy of rejection. As with the warning not to confuse the death of the criminal with the death of the diseased, Socrates employs the execution of criminals as illustrating a tacit awareness, embodied in the Athenian legal system, of a distinction between vice and disease and thus between body and soul.[34] He uses this awareness as evidence of the absurdity of the idea that people are killed off by injustice as they are by disease. Within this formulation, to assert that there is no distinction between the execution of the criminal and death by disease would be to deny the role of city and law in contending with injustice. Moreover, to overlook the role of the city in the demise of the criminal is to fail to attend to the unique character of vice. Further, it results in repressing the phenomenon that so powerfully colors Glaucon's speech in book 2, the seemingly flourishing unjust person.

At stake in these two references to the execution of criminals is nothing less than the demarcation of political life as such with respect to the realm of nature. To fail to distinguish between injustice and disease is to risk blurring any boundary between polis and phusis. Socrates has risked precisely this consequence in his employment of an analogy between vice and disease, one which left undetermined the difference between the two. His invocation of the city's practice of executing criminals, therefore, reasserts a boundary between polis and phusis. This boundary, however, is one in which the law of the city acts as a prosthesis for the unlimited character of vice. Because vice does not incline toward the same end that diseases do, which is to say because vice, while operating as a form of corruption for the soul, does not tend toward the utter destruction of the individual who possesses the soul—the city must step in to act as a prosthetic limit that compensates for the vice's lack of finitude.[35] According to this formulation, the vicious soul gives home to a form of corruption that does not limit itself. The corrupt soul is fragmented, dissolute, but yet persists in this condition without being utterly destroyed. Indeed, the actions of vicious souls are granted an uncanny endurance, one that extends well beyond the life of the vicious individual. Thus, insofar as the soul houses vice, the soul has an ambivalent and potentially monstrous effect on human beings.

It is only after the unique nature of vice is brought to light and the necessary role that the city must play in contending with vice is revealed that Socrates and Glaucon are compelled to agree that the soul is immortal. As Socrates puts it, "Therefore, if it is destroyed by no single evil, neither its own nor an alien one, it is clear that it necessarily is always [ἀιὲ ὀν]; and if it is always, then it is deathless [ἀθάνατον]" (610e–611a). This is a less than glorious immortality to say the least. The soul is immortal, it seems, insofar as there is nothing that can kill it.[36] The soul is immortal not because of its grasp of forms, not because of its kinship with the divine, not even because it is a source of motion; rather, it is so because its viciousness does not destroy it. Its viciousness does not even serve to separate it from the body, and it is the endurance of the unjust person that, to repeat, seems to be what is most important to Socrates at this point, while the immortality of the soul appears to be an implication of this endurance. The evidence of this endurance that he employs, namely the necessity of the city to intervene in the life of the unjust person, attests to this overarching concern with the effects of injustice on the soul. Such effects can only be fully seen, therefore, when the city is taken into account. Put otherwise, the deathlessness of the soul on the basis of its capacity to endure its corruption is a view of immortality that is afforded by a political perspective.

However strange this approach to immortality may be, it must be noted that this perspective is uniquely suited to persuade Glaucon. Glaucon began this discussion by drawing an image of the happy tyrant, unscathed by his injustice and hampered from the free display of his power only by the limiting effects of city, law, and reputation. The analogy between vice and disease shattered the conception that the soul is not negatively impacted by its injustice but failed to go far enough in providing an account of this impact. As we have seen, in the discussion of immortality Socrates maintains the focus on the relationship between city and soul that we noted in books 8 and 9, and turns to illustrate the distinction between vice and disease. He aligns disease with what is bodily, complex, and mortal, and juxtaposes this with the limitless character of vice. Socrates limits the causal relationship between corruptions of body and the vices of the soul and asserts instead the necessity of the city for contending with vice. What possesses vice is denied any native or natural destruction and requires the intervention of law. He uses the execution of citizens as evidence both of the unique nature of vice and of the city's awareness of this unique nature.

By illustrating the awareness of a need to distinguish between soul and body that is embedded within the Athenian legal system and by employing this awareness as evidence of the soul's immortality, Socrates radically shifts the burden of proof. One who would deny the immortality of the soul is committed to denying the role of law in contending with vice, and must therefore come up with an alternate means of conceiving of the distinction between vice and disease or deny that there is such a distinction and thereby deny the traumatic endurance of the tyrant.

However, the role of law in contending with vice has been emphasized by Glaucon from the very start of the discussion of just and unjust lives. Thus, by asserting a distinction between vice and disease and by appealing to the necessity of civic intervention in order to bring about an end that can occur without intervention in disease, Socrates accomplishes two things. First, he attests to the validity of Glaucon's initial emphasis on the role of law in limiting injustice. The immortality discussion, in effect, takes up the suggestion that the unjust person flourishes and transforms this flourishing into an endurance that attests to the soul's immortality. However, whereas Glaucon (and Thrasymachus before him) had conceived of the relationship between nature and law as one of antagonism, Socrates and Glaucon have now replaced this with one of prosthesis. Law acts as the prosthetic limit to a kind of evil that corrupts without destroying. Thus, second, Socrates shows Glaucon the interdependence between the condition of the human soul and the condition of the city; one cannot care about one without caring about the other.

The evidence Socrates produces for this interdependence between city and soul is not found in dialectical demonstration nor in religious doctrine but in the practices of the city of which Glaucon is a citizen. The degree to which Glaucon has been convinced by this evidence is made clear in his agreement that injustice does not kill its possessor:

> "By Zeus, then injustice won't look like such a very terrible thing if it will be fatal to the one who gets it. For it would be a relief from evils. But I suppose rather that it will look, all to the contrary, like it kills other men, if it can, but makes its possessor very much alive and, in addition to alive, sleepless. So far surely as it seems, does its camp lie from fatality." (610d–e)[37]

This statement exemplifies the transformation that Glaucon has undergone from his initial position on injustice: he moves from being one who could easily supply a defense of the unjust life (one for whom tyranny holds a certain attraction) to one who views injustice not as a sign of strength but as a condition of corruption from which one should seek liberation.[38] Socrates's description of the excessive quality of vice separates it out from all other agents of corruption that Socrates and Glaucon have identified and convinces Glaucon that there are worse evils than death. The structure of the discussion of immortality is indispensable in bringing this about.

The soul's endurance in the face of its corruption also provides the grounds for a critique of the specific prosthesis that Socrates and Glaucon have identified. While the discussion about the immortality of the soul indicates the need to establish a prosthetic limit to the corruption of the soul, it has also called into question what form this prosthesis should take. The distinctly political dimension of the soul's immortality suggests that killing the tyrant will not get rid of the factors within the city that produced the tyrant. Far from providing an endorsement for capital punishment, this discussion points to the insufficiency of the prosthesis devised by the city, and suggests that the only thing that can contend with tyranny is a transformation of that within the city which makes the life of the tyrant appear desirable.[39] Such a transformation would necessarily involve an understanding of the elements of the soul that are persuaded by the life of the tyrant. Thus, the discussion of the immortality of the soul offers a tacit critique of the execution of criminals as a means for contending with injustice, and affirms the need to critically evaluate those social and political institutions which valorize tyranny. Specifically, such an activity, as the *Republic* offers it, requires a radical critique of poetry. The irreducibly poetic tenor of the dialogue's end, however, recommends against reading this as an indication that Plato treats the asserted connection between tyranny and tragedy as obvious and uncontroversial.

* * *

As an analysis of vice, the discussion of immortality's focus upon the city makes sense. As a discussion of immortality, however, this perspective is indisputably odd. Yet its oddness is not a function of its lack of connection to the concerns that animate the rest of the dialogue; rather, its oddness derives precisely from its connection to the concerns that animate the rest of the dialogue. Its employment of a political perspective is carefully crafted to convince Glaucon not only that the just life is better than the unjust, but that a consideration of the condition of souls is a necessary part of the rule of cities. However, Glaucon's acceptance of this as a display of immortality need not be our own. While the discussion corrects the misunderstanding of the soul that an uncritical comparison between vice and disease risks, it remains unpersuasive that this correction should involve an acceptance of the soul's immortality. If this were all the *Republic* had to say about the soul, its treatment of soul would be deeply dissatisfying. But, of course, the dialogue does not end with this discussion of immortality; in

Glaucus

After their rather complicated discussion of the immortality of the soul, Socrates and Glaucon assess their previous psychological investigations, and decide they have come up lacking.[40] Here is how Socrates diagnoses their condition:

> "Now we were telling the truth about it as it looks at present. However that is based only on the condition in which we saw it. Just as those who catch sight of the sea Glaucus would no longer easily see his original nature because some of the old parts of his body have been broken off and the others have been ground down and thoroughly maimed by the waves and at the same time as other things have grow on to him—shells, seaweed, and rock—so that he resembles any beast rather than what he was by nature, so, too, we see the soul in such a condition because of countless evils. But Glaucon, one must look elsewhere." (611c-d)

When Glaucon asks where, Socrates states:

> "To its love of wisdom, and recognize what it lays hold of and with what sort of things it longs to keep company on the grounds that it is akin to the divine and immortal and what is always, and what it would become like if it were to give itself entirely to this longing and were brought by this impulse out of the deep ocean in which it now is, and the rocks and shells were hammered off—those which, because it feasts on earth, have grown around it in a wild, earthy, and rocky profusion as a result of those feasts that are called happy. And then one would see its true nature—whether it is many-formed [πολυειδής] or single-formed [μονοειδής], or in what way it is and how. But now, as I suppose, we have fairly gone through its affections and forms [πάθη τε καὶ εἴδη] in its human life." (611e-612a)

It is tempting to view this passage as providing yet another image of the soul, like that provided at the end of book 9. However, this temptation should be avoided. The image of Glaucus in book 10 is not reducible to an image of the soul. Rather, it is an image of the *sight* of the soul. That is to say, it is an image of viewing itself. Or, rather, it is an image of the particular viewing of the soul that has been available to Socrates and Glaucon, and has been operative in their discussions about the soul throughout the dialogue.[41] It is thus an image that incorporates a representation of those who are making the image. Socrates and Glaucon are likened, in their sight of the soul, to men who see the sea creature Glaucus. The soul is likened to the body of this creature, which has been maimed by the waves and by its converse with the sea, losing parts of itself and gaining others through its residence in water and its ingestion of earth. The likening of the soul to the body of Glaucus here is a means of commenting upon the likening of the soul to the body overall, and indicates that this likening will ultimately fail to offer a true account of the soul. Such attempts, it would seem, locate the soul in a murky environment in which the view of it cannot be anything other than distorted. What must be overcome is precisely this distorted view, and the accretions of opinion about the body as well as the soul that belong to this view—opinions that the body is obvious, that it is self-evident, that it does not demand inquiry. So long as the soul is seen as a body of some sort, and so long as the bodily is seen as the realm of the self-evident and unquestionable, the soul will not be seen in its truth. These sorts of bodily discourses of the soul have resulted at this point in the dialogue in an aporia about what the soul is.

However, this aporia is itself brought out by means of a logos about the soul that embodies in speech the soul and the sight of it. The enterprise of explaining the soul through the body is critiqued at the same time that the capacity of embodied and embodying discourse to critique is revealed. Thus, Socrates and Glaucon are able, through this image of their own viewing of the soul, to diagnose the very position from which they have operated in their discussion of the soul thus far. A new discourse on the soul is not, as of yet, attempted here; rather, Socrates creates an image of the very discourse about the soul that has resulted in aporia. In the breakdown of the bodily discourse of the soul a critical capacity has emerged that would finally permit the question of the soul's nature to be posed and heard in its pressing urgency. While the insufficiency of conceiving of the soul as made up of parts was suggested by the logos about the immortality of the soul (611a–b), the capacity to see wherein this insufficiency lies is given here through an image of viewing. It is only with the understanding of their position which this image offers that the question of whether the soul is single or complex, one-formed or many-formed, can be asked. And the answering would seem to require not only the winning of a certain perspective, but a kind of relocation of the soul, and a critical, deconstructing work on the soul as it appears now—a viewing of the soul "out of the deep ocean" and if "the rocks and shells were hammered off" (611e).[42] Such a relocation is reflexive; it would have to involve a relocation of those who are themselves viewing the soul.

The loving of wisdom of the soul presents a view of the soul's image if it were out of the ocean and without its wild earthy, rocky accretions. We might ask how Socrates and Glaucon would be able to view this condition of the soul. The suggestion would seem to be by their own love of wisdom. It is not clear, however, that this is a view afforded by book 10 of the *Republic*. Yet, the *need* for such a view is offered, as is the need to pose the question of what the soul is. The *Republic* does not go on then to offer a "disembodied" vocabulary for the soul. Instead, the *Republic* ends with myth. As we will see, Socrates's shift to the register of myth does not mark a shift to contemplate the soul in its truest nature. Rather, the myth he tells remains squarely within a concern with the human things, a concern enhanced by a sense for their cosmic context.

Er

What Socrates and Glaucon have won in their critical engagement with their own discussion of soul heretofore is a transformed vision of human life, augmented and made more vivid by a sense of its limits and of the context in which it unfolds; the myth expresses and expands this vision. It forms an essential part of Socrates's and Glaucon's efforts to return to justice and injustice the wages they are owed, a return that is presented as an enactment of justice.[43] It's telling is made necessary by their limited grasp of the nature of the soul: the prizes awaiting the just after they are dead "should be heard so that in hearing them each of these men will have gotten back the full measure of what the argument owed him" (614a).[44]

In turning to Er's tale, Socrates and Glaucon acknowledge their need for the eyes and ears of another.[45] Plato thereby underscores the limitation of their grasp of the soul and their need for others, a need to which Socrates gives expression in the interjection he offers halfway through his telling of the myth (618b–619a). This is to say that the myth of Er serves a prosthetic function: it simultaneously supplements their account of the wages and rewards of justice and injustice, augments their conception of what is necessary in order to live well, and extends their understanding beyond the scope of a single life to include a plurality of lives and the community of souls contained therein. It allows, thereby, a vision of the human things as such. This, in turn, makes it possible to direct a critical gaze at one's life as a whole, a gaze which requires acknowledgment of other lives and nonhuman forces, that is, a gaze which locates "the human" within the context of "the animal" and "the cosmos."

Its dramatization of the choice of lives outlines the disposition, the turn of soul, necessary to choose well by marking out the impediments to this choice. In doing so, the myth of Er provides a meditation upon the irreversible effects of action, the nature of human vulnerability and the contingency of human happiness. Because the choosing of a life always occurs unannounced, with a soul already shaped, in the middle of things, within seemingly small and banal decisions, and among the influence of others, the spectacle of choosing lives is also a spectacle of life in the city. Both culminating vision and continuation of inquiry, the myth directs our attention to what must be done granted the human vulnerability it marks out, that is, the demand to act in the face of the inexorable consequences of these decisions and actions, consequences which will always stretch further, and into more obscure regions, than the human mind can grasp at the time in which it must decide.

The myth of the earth in the *Phaedo* describes an earth capable of bearing the human things, that is, capable of enacting a kind of justice. The myth of Er offers a cosmos similarly inclined, in which we can discern the necessity of enduring the effects of one's actions.[46] However, while the myth in the *Phaedo* presents the rewards and punishments to which souls are subject on the basis of their actions—processes figured by the unique geographic features of the earth whose descriptive capacities we have drawn out—the myth of Er's focus on the events leading up to and after reward and punishment recommends a different landscape, a change of scenery. While the *Phaedo* describes an earth in three dimensions, and hovers between its various regions, the *Republic* concludes with an account of a plain. This landscape affords a view of the spectacles staged upon it, spectacles of voyaging out and returning, of greeting, storytelling, and delight, of sorrow and fear, of choice and ratification. Indeed, the plain is uniquely suited to provide a vision of the collective as well as the individual. It resonates not only with the perspective of children on horseback observing the theater of battle (467d–e), but also with the plain of Ilium itself.[47]

If the myth evokes the scene of battle, however, it is a battle not over territory but over the kind of life one is to lead.[48] One's ability to wage this battle is presented as a function of one's actions and experiences.[49] At the same time, as we shall see, its presentation of the choice of lives is not a simple determinism. Rather, the constraints and impediments it identifies—a lack of practice in labors, for instance, or a reliance on habit and failure to be sufficiently estranged from oneself to know oneself—create the conditions within which choice can occur. The landscape of Er's tale marks out the shifting terrain of choice, one whose contours are forged by tension and over time. An analysis of the four movements in which the myth of Er unfolds—the scene of judgment; the description of Necessity, her spindle, and her daughters; the spectacle of choosing lives; and the journey to the plain of Lēthē—will sharpen our understanding of these contours. We will thereby be better able to discern the myth's contribution to the dialogue's investigation of soul.

The Scene of Judgment

Having died in battle, Er's soul departs from his body and accompanies many others to "a certain demonic place" in which souls circulate between four openings, two in the earth and two in the heaven. The souls in Er's company submit themselves to judgment and then embark on their journey through the opening appropriate to them, carrying the signs of their judgment. The unjust—bearing signs on their backs like a burden legible to those behind them—leave through the downward left opening. The just—sporting signs like ornaments announced to those before them—exit through the right upward opening. The judges assign to Er the role of messenger and charge him with viewing what occurs in this place.

After observing the judgment of souls, Er is treated to the sight of the festive return of souls, who, having undergone their punishment and reward, greet one another and tell their tales, a telling which inspires lamentation on the part of those whose tales are filled with suffering, having undergone a thousand-year term of punishment. Er's tale does not linger over these stories (save for one) but moves on to describe the allotment of punishment and reward. The calculus by means of which the terms of punishment and reward are decided employs the human life as the unit of measurement: souls are punished for unjust deeds ten times over, "that is, they were punished for each injustice once every hundred years; taking this as the length of a human life, in this way they could pay off the penalty for the injustice ten times over" (615a–b). Presumably, just souls are rewarded by the same measure of time, residing in a place of "inconceivable beauty" (615a) for one thousand years.[50]

Like the *Phaedo* myth, punishment is meted out by residence on some place, and the categorization of souls includes both those exemplary souls and those who, because of the magnitude of their misdeeds, are deemed incurable. The tyrant Ardieaus, and others like him, men of the sort whom Glaucon and Adeimantus had presented in book 2 as luxuriating in their power and strength, are denied entry to the passageway that conveys souls from beneath the earth to the meadow and instead are bound, flayed, and thrown into Tartarus. Isolated from other kinds of souls and unaware of themselves as incurable, Ardiaeus and his companions are treated to a set of punishments falling outside of the usual calculus and are denied return to the meadow on which the other souls mingle and to a choice of lives. This account is made more terrible by the fear of the soul recounting Ardieaus's fate that he be similarly judged; that is, he does not know if he is incurable until he has been told so by the roaring of the mouth or its silence.

Necessity and Her Daughters

After seven days on the plain, the souls continue their journey, arriving on the fourth day at the spindle of Necessity, suspended in a light stretching though heaven and earth. The souls are treated to the display of cosmic motion, orchestrated by the turning of this spindle, whose whorl contains eight orbits, each accompanied by their Siren and surrounded by Necessity's three daughters, the Fates (Lachesis, Clōthō, and Atropos) responsible for its turning. Clōthō, singer of what is, uses her right hand to turn the outer revolutions of the spindle; Atropos, singer of what will be, uses her left hand to turn the inner revolutions; and Lachesis, singer of what has been, has a hand on each.

Socrates's description of the spindle's shape, color, and motion emphasizes its achievement of unity and wholeness with multiplicity in a manner that resonates with the *Phaedo*'s presentation of the equanimity and wholeness of the earth. With respect to its shape, the eight whorls nested within one another form a single whorl.[51] With respect to its color, Er's description specifies the interaction between whorls that contributes to their forming a whole.[52] With respect to its motion, Socrates recounts a turning of a whole that is itself comprised of parts moving in the opposite direction.[53]

As a figuration of the existential conditions of human life, this description of the work of the Fates marks out the decisive, inescapable role of the past. Lachesis has a hand in the turning accomplished by both her sisters, that is, what has been is at work both in what is and what will be. Indeed it seems that what will be is irreversible precisely because it is determine by the past—Lachesis grants her sister Atropos the force implied by her name. It is Lachesis who holds the pattern of lives, and it is Lachesis's speech, delivered by her spokesman, that instructs souls to chose a life, exhorting them not to blame the gods on the grounds that their choice is their own, and that virtue is without a master (617d–e). The role that the myth marks out for Lachesis suggests that the effects of one's actions reverberate upon one's future self by shaping and restricting one's capacity to choose; indeed, as Ardieaus's fate asserts, our actions can so compromise our self-awareness as to make choice impossible. This privileging of the past, this emphasis on the role of what has been to determine what is and will be, is evident throughout the description of the choosing of lives.

The Spectacle of Choosing

Upon delivering the speech of Lachesis, the spokesman casts the lots that determine the order of choosing among the souls gathered there. By marking out a time of choosing that is unimpeded by others, thereby avoiding a mad scramble for lives, the contrivance of the lot calls attention to the act of choosing itself. What is being chosen, the patterns of lives (βίων παραδείγματα), are greater in number than the souls doing the choosing and include the lives of animals as well as the varieties of human lives. I take this point to be instructive of the difference that is assumed here between human and other animal life: human life is such as to have variety within the species; animal life as taken to be such as to have variety only between species—the suggestion is that the unit of choice for the human life is an individuated course of life, while what is chosen in the animal life is the life of the species. But of course, the human life can only be so individuated if it is to have a pattern, that is, if it is to be iterable. How a set of possibilities for human life differs from both the individual who will be living the life, and the animal whose individual life is treated as entirely coextensive with the life of the species, is not addressed explicitly here, but that such a difference is at work is evident.[54]

The factors that grant to a life its particular pattern include political standing, reputation, beauty, strength, and capacity. The patterns cohere on the basis of the interaction between features marked out by body and polis, by the setting into time of beauty, political office, family, strength, etc. These patterns of life, then, hold together for viewing the time in which a life unfolds. It also takes time to discern them, however, and, as we shall see, a failure to do so results in making a poor choice. The conceit of these patterns has been at work in the dialogue all along as it is precisely the kind of life possessed by the just and unjust that Socrates and his interlocutors have been attempting to observe. Presumably, these patterns represent variations on a theme of just and unjust lives, held together into a coherent whole (a whole guaranteed, as we shall see, by the role of the daimon accompanying each pattern). It is worth noting that a philosophic life is not specified in the kinds of lives mentioned, but neither is a just life, and I take these two omissions to be a function of the dialogue's alignment of a philosophic life with a just life and of the presentation of these lives as variations of just and unjust lives.[55]

Finally, Socrates distinguishes between patterns of life and ordering of souls, noting that an ordering of souls is not included in the choosing depicted here, "due to the necessity that a soul become different according to the life it chooses" (618b). I take this to be a decisive confirmation of soul's plasticity and reflexivity: the soul that does the choosing will be made different by the choice. This may also shed further light on why a philosophic life is not specified among the types of lives: insofar as philosophy is a certain turn or condition of soul, it would not be chosen any more than an ordering of soul is chosen. This suggests that the turn of soul that is philosophic must be achieved in the course of one's life and according to the political environment in which one finds oneself, a suggestion consistent with the discussion of the philosophic nature and its corruption in book 6.

After describing the factors that give a life its pattern, Socrates pauses his recounting of Er's tale in order to observe that they have arrived at a lookout from which they can survey what constitutes "the whole risk for a human being." This interruption confirms and sharpens the tale's focus on this-worldly pursuits. This choice of lives is best conducted by one who can, "to the neglect of other studies, above all see to it that he is a seeker and student of that study by which he might be able to learn and find out who will give him the capacity and the knowledge to distinguish the good and bad life, and so everywhere and always to choose the better from among those that are possible" (618b–c). How are we to read this greatest risk, this study to which we are exhorted, to the neglect of all other studies, especially in light of what book 6 presented as the greatest study (the study of the good)?

There are several details of this passage that need to be taken up in responding to this question. For one, what is at stake here is not the good itself, but the good or bad life, and even this choice is tempered to the better and worse on the basis of the limits of the possible.[56] What this student will take into account, the combinations which she must learn to discern and judge, seems distinctly different from the philosophical curriculum outlined in book 7 because of its orientation not toward Being but toward becoming (and becoming in the most pressing of senses, that is, one's own becoming). These conditions include beauty, wealth, habit, birth, private station, ruling office, strength, capacity with respect to learning, all the things that are "connected with a soul by nature or are acquired" (618c–d).[57] Only in taking these things into account will she be able "to draw a conclusion and choose—in looking off toward the nature of the soul—between the worse and the better life, calling worse the one that leads it toward becoming more unjust, and better the one that leads it to becoming juster" (618d–e). The knowledge of the nature of the soul is in the service of the choice of lives, a task requiring thoughtful immersion in the realm of becoming (with all of the factors that accompany this becoming), one which reiterates the noetic immersion required of the judgment of lives in book 9.

Second, the study Socrates marks out, a study of who will be able to aid one in discerning and choosing a good life, seems to be distinct from the knowledge that such a person would be able to impart. This is an odd distinction. After all, if one could identify the teacher, couldn't one also identify what is taught? Why must one seek the study that will reveal the teacher, rather than simply pursuing the knowledge itself? What is being recommended here is a course of study in where, and with whom, to place one's trust. Glaucon and Adeimantus have, from the beginning, placed their trust in Socrates, as the one person from whom they might hear a defense of justice and the just life in themselves

Politics and Immortality | 159

(see, for instance, 367a–e). Perhaps Socrates is now exhorting them to examine this trust and make sure it has been well placed. At the very least, he is emphasizing to Glaucon the need that Glaucon has of another. Far from advocating a turn away from the company of others in order to investigate Being, Socrates exhorts Glaucon to seek out that study that would indicate to him with whom he should spend his time.

Socrates returns to relate Er's tale, offering a series of examples of choices. Lacking practice in labor and philosophy, having become virtuous not by reflection but by the luck of having been born into an orderly regime and thus having habituated himself to virtue, the first soul to choose is overwhelmed by folly and gluttony, chooses too quickly, and selects a tyranny. The role of chance in this choice is conspicuously limited. If anything, this soul was benefitted by chancing upon the first lot, but the point seems to be that this would be a benefit only if the soul were disposed to choose well, which it is not. This first example emphasizes the particular vulnerability to which humans are subject. The dominant forces shaping the context of choice here are a function of the soul's lack of cultivated reflective capacity and lack of training in labors; in fact, the latter is a function of the former, as the former led to the soul's reward for having just habits.[58] That is, the landscape of choice is defined by enduring features of the person's life and the affect of his actions, features that are worn on the soul, so to speak, and that affect the soul's choosing, creating the conditions in which, overwhelmed by passions, its rushes to a decision.[59]

The influence of prior experience (of what has been) on choosing is further evinced by the next set of examples: Orpheus chooses the life of a swan out of hatred for women, Thamyras's soul chooses to become a nightingale; swans and other musical animals choose to change to the lives of humans;[60] Ajax's souls chooses the life of a lion and Agamemnon's the life of an eagle, both out of hatred of humankind; Atalanta's soul opts for the life of an athletic man; and Odysseus's soul, having been cured of the love of honor, rejects public life and selects the life of a private man "who minds his own business" (620c). An analysis of the dominant passions at work in these choices is revealing. Most of the changes from human to animal life are motivated by a sickened evaluation of humanity, resulting in misogyny (Orpheus) and misanthropy (Ajax and Agamemnon). The choice to move from animal to human life is made by musical animals, suggesting that a human life would give greater expression to musical impulses. Atalanta's choice is a function of a desire for honor; Thersites's foolishness results in the choice of an ape; and Odysseus's choice is a result of overcoming the very love of honor that motivates Atalanta's choice.

Socrates concludes this portion of Er's tale by observing that, "from the other beasts, similarly some went into human lives and into one another—the unjust changing into savage ones, the just into tame ones, and there were all kinds of mixtures" (620c–d). This ceaseless circulation attests to the permanence of deeds and passions even in the face of the radical transformations of sex and species. The mingling of lives under the power of the past highlights the passions, the habits, and the deeds that remain the same. At this juncture, personal identity and soul itself seem as stand-ins precisely for the permanence of these passions and actions.[61] Soul is treated here as the repository of deeds, as holding a record of one's actions and passions, as bearing through time the indelible marks of what one has done and suffered.

The spectacle of the choice of lives identifies a particular bind for human beings. On the one hand, we are, in our daily decisions and actions, always choosing a kind of life. On the other hand, we are also always living out the consequences of the decisions and actions we have made. This latter dimension of life means that no clean break with ourselves is possible; yet, the former suggests that the possibility of choosing differently is always before us. A reflective awareness of ourselves, one which would have to involve undergoing estrangement from ourselves, presents the fullest expression of choice to which humans can aspire. It is in this capacity for self-estrangement that Er's tale finds salutary effects for philosophy. As it is presented here, philosophy benefits the choice of lives by countering a blind trust in habit, guiding one's passions (guarding against being overtaken by folly and gluttony) and by helping one take one's time with choosing. There is some dissonance between this account of the measuring and checking benefits of philosophy and the insatiable lust for wisdom earlier attributed to philosophic natures in books 5–7; perhaps this is why the tale reserves happiness and a smooth journey to one who "philosophizes in a healthy way [ὑγιῶς φιλοσοφοῖ]" and, in addition, does not chose the last lot (619d-e).[62] In the myth of Er, even philosophy itself must be measured by the standard of living well.

Once souls have selected their patterns of life, their choice is ratified by Atropos, and the souls are assigned the daimon that will assure the adherence of their life to the chosen pattern. They then pass beneath the throne of Necessity and on to the final part of their journey.

The Plain of Lēthē

Making their way to the scorching plain of Lēthē, the souls in Er's company are faced with another choice—how much water to drink from the river of Carelessness—a choice which highlights the enduring effects of prudence and the lack thereof. The results of this choice, however, are underdetermined in Er's tale. Perhaps they would be felt in one's capacity for anamnēsis later in one's life. As it stands in Er's tale, upon drinking, each soul forgot everything (621a). We are not told whether they will remember that they were carried off to their birth, "each in a different way," shooting like stars (621b). The myth is thus as much a tale of beginnings as ends; its purported description of events beyond the limit of death (and thus beyond the furthermost reaches of human understanding) is also a concern with the start, the source, the archē of life, or at least the archē of the particular features of lives, the source of that which grants to life its coherence and sense as a whole, all of which are treated as occurring before (and in some sense outside of) the details of birth.

Socrates concludes his telling of the myth with the following words: "And thus Glaucon, a tale was saved and not lost; and it could save us, if we were persuaded by it, and we shall make a good crossing of the river Lethe and not defile [μιανθησόμεθα] our soul" (621b–c).[63] After Socrates points out the effects of being persuaded by the myth, however, Plato concludes the dialogue by having Socrates specify what they should be persuaded of by Socrates himself:

> "But if we are persuaded by me, holding that soul is immortal and capable of bearing all evils and all goods, we shall always keep to the upper road and practice justice and prudence in every way so that we shall be friends to ourselves and the gods, both while we remain here and when we reap the rewards for it like the victors who go about gathering in the prizes. And so here and in the thousand year journey that we have described we shall fare well." (621c–d)

The dialogue leaves us, then, with the question of what, if any, distance lies between Er's myth and Socrates's exhortation.

Socrates's claim about the soul here—that is it capable of bearing all good and all evil—is a succinct specification of the effect that psychic plasticity has on human life. Because soul is such as to endure all evils and all goods, human happiness is only possible by training, by cultivating both knowledge of the nature of the soul and a condition of soul whereby one can choose one's actions well. The myth of Er thus sharpens the understanding Socrates and Glaucon have of the task with which human life is charged.

My emphasis on the this-worldly focus of the myth begs the question of in what sense, if it all, the myth emerges out of the claim that the soul is immortal. However, our discussion of the argument for immortality has altered the sense of this very claim by revealing a similar this-worldly trajectory in its assertion of the potentially deleterious effects of the limitless nature of soul on human life and the need for city to step in with law (and now myth) to provide prosthetic limits for soul.[64] Insofar as the argument for immortality claims that the capacity for virtue and vice in human life points beyond itself, to the effects of such actions on the lives of others and on human community as a whole, it refines and augments the sense of the city held by Socrates's interlocutors and by Plato's readers. Socrates's subsequent critique of their vision of soul leading up to this argument (that this vision is flawed) and conclusion that they have given an account of the soul in its human life both announce that and can only occur because human life gestures beyond itself. However, this gesture is precisely what makes most pressing the need to consider the city, that is, the need to consider the conditions in which one chooses a life. And it is to this need that the myth of Er responds, with its depiction of the actions and passions that shape one's life. According to Er's tale, while residence in an orderly city may not, on its own, guarantee that one takes up just actions by choice and not simply by habit, the capacity to do this requires a city that accommodates a cultivation of self-estrangement and self-analysis.

By this reading, the myth's focus on the impediments to choosing well and the irreversibility of action provides its own prosthetic limit to the souls of its listeners, one which augments their vision of the city and of the nature of human action and choice by clarifying their understanding of human vulnerability and the constraint to which we, in our happiness or lack thereof, are subject. The only measure for such a limit is the life to which it gives rise. As with any prosthesis, the measure of its worth is found in the extent to which it can be taken up and used for living. I take this to be precisely the point Socrates makes in his identification of the greatest risk to human beings: the value of knowledge, even knowledge of the soul, must be measured in the service it offers life. His concluding observation that soul is capable of bearing all good and all evil serves as a final reminder that the soul's peculiar limitlessness makes human happiness contingent not only upon human choice, but also upon the community within which the capacity to choose well is cultivated or hampered.

Conclusion

Like the *Phaedo*, the *Republic* is concerned with illuminating and evaluating kinds of lives. Its contribution to Plato's psychological investigations consists in its sustained meditation upon the complex soul and the varieties of psychological phenomena such a study unearths. In creating the portraits of philosophic and tyrannical lives as the two poles of psychic unity and fragmentation possible for human beings, it describes the conditions (internal and external) of soul's transformation, illustrates the impact on and implications these have for human political life, and offers a glimpse into the innermost workings of the human soul.

Doing so requires Plato to cultivate a vocabulary capable of both describing and evaluating psychic states. His careful employment of the language of medicine offers him a particularly powerful means of doing so. However, as we have seen, the depth of the dialogue's analysis of tyranny also reveals the limits of even this vocabulary, and leaves its interlocutors with an acute sense of the limits of their investigation. Plato documents the results of this self-critical and self-diagnostic stance with some care; denied an authoritative perspective on soul, Socrates and his interlocutors avail themselves of the tale of another, one which reminds them of the stakes of their entire conversation.

The inadequacy of the medical model for understanding and evaluating conditions of soul also reveals the inadequacy of an appeal to a phusis conceived in opposition to nomos in regulating human behavior. By uncovering the excessive, limitless character of psuchē, the analysis of the tyrant thus also marks out the work of the city in providing prosthetic psychic limits by its laws and myths. It thus challenges the characterization of the relationship between phusis and nomos as necessarily antagonistic.

The analysis of the philosophic nature and its corruption supports the need for a refigured conception of the relationship between phusis and nomos. It also illuminates a deep interdependence between philosophy and city. The medical/juridical hybrid practice with which Socrates and his interlocutors operate in order to arrive at their conclusion about which life is best, as well as their acknowledgment of the limitations of their own purchase on the soul, gestures toward the work of philosophy in the city, a work that requires the cultivation of the self-diagnostic stance we see illustrated in the final book of the dialogue.

Finally, the *Republic* expands its interlocutors' conception of what constitutes psychic phenomena well beyond individual human behavior, and reveals the intimate intermingling of the psychological and the political. When Socrates speaks of the city that is the soul, and locates the paradigm of its politeia beyond the πατρίς, he draws out the connection between the refiguring of polis (with its laws and technai), phusis (with its differences) and cosmos, and the expansion of political and psychological phenomena. His purpose in doing so—to provide his interlocutors with some means to determine how to lead their lives—places this meditation firmly in the city wherein these speakers are ensconced.

As we shall see in the next section, the *Laws* shares with the *Republic* an interest in the relationship between polis, phusis, and cosmos. But where the *Republic* expands political phenomena to the soul, the *Laws* offers us a vision of a psuchē for whom both cosmos and city are epiphenomena. Thus, while the *Republic* provides us with a psychic politics, the *Laws* presents cosmological and political phenomena alike as branches of psychology. It is to the *Laws*' account of this prodigious and excessive psuchē that we turn now.

PART III

Laws

THE *Laws* is often treated as Plato's illegitimate child—awkward, crude, embarrassing, a progeny best kept upstairs and out of sight when company is over. Although some of this attitude can be attributed to a variety of prejudices about who Plato is and what his work means, the generally negative reception of the dialogue is not simply a function of scholarly foibles. The *Laws* is a prickly, complex, confusing composition which frequently returns its readers' attention with mortifying and violent prescriptions against a variety of behaviors. For instance, few pieces of legislation match the sweeping scope and chilling tone of an observation the Athenian Stranger makes in book 9, namely that they will need to create penalties whose harshness "must, so far as possible, fall in no way short of the punishments in Hades" (881b).[1] A variety of interpretive strategies can be drawn from the history of philosophy to address this call to create a Hades on earth.[2] However, that some caution is warranted in interpreting these lines, as well as the dialogue as a whole, is signaled by the fact that the actual range of penalties the Athenian goes on to outline for the crime at issue here (assault on a parent)—exile, rustication, and banning from the city's sacred places (881d)—fall short of the violent and grotesque punishments depicted in Plato's own accounts of Hades in other dialogues.[3] Without question, it would be a mistake to make light of exile. Nevertheless, it seems worthwhile to mark a distinction between the violence of exile and the flaying, branding, crushing, burning, and freezing done to souls in Hades.[4] If banishment from the city is to be conceived, like the penalties in Hades (854e), as worse than death, it would be worth our time to investigate the conception of the city that informs this perspective. Put another way, Plato's *Laws* provides us not only with information about Plato's conception of the work of the law but also about his conception of the human beings to whom it is designed to speak and the city wherein it operates.

Indeed, law, city, and human being are inextricably intertwined throughout the dialogue. In between the inscription placed on the wall of a citizen's phratry indicating his or her birth and the erasure of that inscription upon his or her death,[5] there is not a single aspect of the Magnesian citizen's life that is untouched by law. Much of this intimacy is a function of the model for unity that the city upholds, namely, that citizens become one body, whereby "eyes, for instance, and ears and hand seem to see, hear and act in common" (739c).[6] Such a conception of unity invites the medical inflection that is given to legislating in its service to the political art, an art which has its end in the care (θεραπεία) of the soul (650b), and especially to that best practice of legislation, namely, the appending of persuasive preludes to the laws (a practice arrived at on the basis of a demarcation of two different forms of medical treatment [719e–720e]).

This intimacy between law and life is given some theoretical basis[7] very early on in the dialogue, in a passage initially intended to help explain what it might mean to say that one can be superior or inferior to oneself.[8] Suppose, suggests the Athenian, that all living beings are playthings of the gods (θαῦμα μὲν ἕκαστον ἡμῶν ἡγησώμεθα τῶν ζῴων θεῖον), and are constituted by the tense interaction between an array of demands and capacities, figured as sinews or cords, like pleasure and pain, hope, confidence, and "the golden and sacred pull" of calculation, which, when it becomes the common opinion of the city, is called law (644d). It is this final cord that should at all costs be followed, and, because of its gentleness, must be assisted against the more violent draws of the other cords.

Chapter 8 discusses further the implications of this image for the dialogue's conception of human nature. For now, I would like to focus upon its implications for legislative practice. The effect on the dialogue as a whole of such an understanding of law is hard to overestimate. If the law is the externalization of internal calculation, and this capacity for calculation is what is best in the soul of each individual, then the city, or more precisely its code of laws and its politeia contain the primary support of soul's betterment. In the *Laws*, nomos expresses and reinforces what is best in the soul; a legislation of profoundly intimate character is thereby taken to be justified. Moreover, humans' need for law is demonstrated in the most forceful terms. To be most or best of what one can be requires the strengthening feature of law. To the extent that the city houses laws, the city is the place in which humans realize themselves most fully.[9] To be a citizen is thus to be most oneself. This, of course, is only the case if the laws do indeed express logismos, and I take the correlation between logismos, nous, and the divine, as well as the grounding of Magnesia's legislation in divine nous, to be the Athenian's effort to offer an assurance of this.[10] At the same time, to be oneself is to recognize oneself as in need of the city, and in need of the support to one's logismos provided by the law. Within this formulation of person and law, to understand oneself is to acknowledge that one belongs to the gods and to the city.

This broader claim of the city's ownership of citizens and their investment in the city as that in which they will come to be themselves forms the background against which the allowance for and allotment of private property in Magnesia is to be read. Certainly, the importance (or even sanctity) of ownership is stressed throughout the dialogue, especially in those sections concerned with penal law, wherein taking what belongs to another is presented as a paradigm of wrongdoing (884a, 913a). However, this emphasis is accompanied by an equally pervasive and sustained reflection upon (and attempt to instantiate) the right attitude toward property (an attitude that prizes the attainment of virtue over that of wealth and that is thus willing to give up property for the good of the city)[11] and the civic allotment of fixed property and income. This is to say that while the citizens of Magnesia may hold private property, this permission is granted along with a radical reconfiguration of what constitutes "ownership." A variety of laws and customs limit what the citizen may do with his or her body, property and wealth, for example, prohibitions on travel (950d–951a), funerary law (958c–960d), inheritance law (923c–925d), allocation of orphans (926d–928d), size and constitution of neighborhoods (736d–738b, 740b–741c, 848c–849a), laws pertaining to the size and constitution of one's family (773a–d, 740b–741b, 783d–784d, 928d–929d), limitations on the amount of wealth one can accrue (741e–742b), and laws against suicide (873c–d). Thus, while the *Laws* permits the ownership of private property, it so mutates what constitutes "ownership" as to render it hardly private at all, and as to constantly remind citizens that they themselves are the property of the city.

Such a reconfiguration of ownership serves the larger model of civic unity that we identified above, a model whose more radical features can be drawn out by comparison with the *Republic*. While the *Republic* recognizes the body as one, perhaps the only, irreducibly private property (464d), the *Laws* promotes a vision of civic unity in which even the body is shared (739c–d). To be sure, this vision is qualified for a city made of humans and not the children of gods (739e), but it is less qualified than one might think: the manipulation of what a citizen sees and thinks when she is seeing is presented as part of the legislative project, and the imagery of the city as composing a single body returns in book 12 to aid in the description of the work and membership of the infamous Nocturnal Council (961d, 964e–965a, 969b–c). The "publicizing" of the body is accompanied by a "communizing" of the soul that has perhaps its most direct expression in the dialogue's claim that the law is the external expression of the soul's logismos.

Indeed, these two intertwined concepts—that law is the externalization of the best human impulse (logismos) and the mutation of ownership such that the human is first and foremost owned by city and gods—circumscribe human life within the task of discerning what is most one's own (what is οἰκειότατον). Throughout the *Laws*, human excellence and viciousness are measured in terms of this task; the varieties of human acquisition and obedience, in turn, mark varieties of failures and successes at it. Moreover, the *Laws* is concerned to mark out the role of the city in the human's discernment of what is and is not her own. The project of citizenship includes inculcating a particular orientation toward the city, the divine mind (to which law and logismos belong), and oneself. That this project will also include a particular stance with respect to the soul and will involve a relatively elaborate psychology is suggested as early as book 1 with its characterization of politics as care for the soul (650b). The Athenian's observation, at the start of book 5, that the most divine possession a citizen has is her soul because it is most her own (726a) not only signals the dialogue's reformulation of what constitutes property but also draws into sharp relief its enigmatic elision between what is θειότατον and what is οἰκειότατον, between what is most divine and what is most one's own.[12]

This conception of the relationship between the laws of a city and its citizens has profound effects on the structure and form of the dialogue as a whole, three of which I would like to highlight. First, there is an emphasis on the eruptions, spontaneous and cultivated, of order in human life evinced by phenomena like dance, technical calculation, a general tendency away from unjust actions and toward the company of the just, a distaste for imbalance and predilection for elegance.[13] Second, we find a corresponding emphasis on the impediments to the development of these expressions of order into fuller realizations and expressions of logismos in human life, impediments like the excessive love of self (731e), the inability to conceive and prioritize the common good (875a–c), and the tyranny of pleasure, pain, hope, anger, and fear (863e). All of these are treated as examples of the failure to properly navigate what is one's own and as further illustrating the need human beings have for the law. Third, this account of the relationship between law and citizen provides the impetus for the development of a marked aesthetic component to citizenship and its cultivation. The demands of civic unity require the citizen to perceive the laws, herself, and her fellow citizens in a particular way. Creating citizens means, for the Athenian, creating a certain view of the city; it is the work of politics and legislation to instill this view. Thus, we find throughout the dialogue the presentation of the laws as beautiful (as like a beautiful painting [769c–e] or poetry [811c–e]), of the lawgivers and gods as craftsmen and artists, and of the citizens as performing through their actions, their passions, their perceptions, and their expressions, the work that is the city.[14] This is to say that the *Laws* describes a poetics of citizenship; it includes also a corresponding rehabilitation of perception. Traces of this aesthetic component are at work in the prelude to the atheist in book 10: the conflict between the atheist and the lawgiver is introduced as a difference about what one sees when one looks to the heavens; the sight of the orderly motion of the planets can act as evidence of the gods' existence only if one has been trained in a particular way.

Indeed, what the citizen thinks and feels about the city, and about his or her place in it, is of particular importance to the *Laws*' conception of legislation. Throughout the dialogue, the Athenian Stranger asserts that proper citizenship includes certain attitudes, beliefs, opinions, and feelings about the city, all of which coalesce into a particular condition of soul. Moreover, the *Laws* is a dialogue acutely aware of the influence on human action had by certain beliefs in the soul. An entire doxology about the nature of the soul and about Hades itself will prove influential in creating and fostering civically salutary psychic conditions. Plato's infamous employment of the language of medicine to characterize the work of the laws, language which we have seen play a critical role in the *Republic*, is in part a function of his focus upon the condition of the soul of the citizen. This is to say that Plato's therapeutic conception of law is inextricably linked to his psychology. We can see in the laws of Magnesia an attempt to "teach" people how to think and feel about the city. We can also discern in its penal laws the effort to treat conditions that obscure, mutilate, or disrupt the cognitive and affective states conducive to good citizenship. Plato thus allots a dual educative/therapeutic function to the law. In the following chapters, I am interested in the specific mechanisms, the "lessons" and treatments, of this therapeutic education.

Were one to wonder how the citizen is to conceive of the specific service the law offers human life, one would be well served by attending to the prelude that the Athenian delivers in connection with the law concerning wounds. The law is necessary, proclaims the Athenian, because "no man's nature is naturally able both to perceive what is of benefit to the civic life [εἰς πολιτείαν] of men and, perceiving it, to be alike able and willing [δύνασθαί τε καὶ ἐθέλειν] to practice [πράττειν] what is best" (875a). According to this formulation, the law would act as a correction to a certain human shortsightedness with respect to civic life, and as a supplement to human incapacity and unwillingness to act according to the benefit of civic life. The law both corrects mortal vision and extends or refines mortal capacity for action—it serves a prosthetic function. Indeed, as we shall see, the *Laws*' account of the relationship between soul and law will provide a paradigmatic instance of the prosthetic function we have been highlighting.

The Athenian attributes a certain blindness even to the law itself, observing that law and ordinance (τάξιν τε καὶ νόμον) "see and discern the general principle, but are unable to see every instance in detail" (875d). Indeed, among the arsenal of techniques and instruments needed by the legislator in order to counteract the desires for food, drink, and sex that can lead to hamartia, for instance, law is listed as only one of the three greatest forces (783a). The other two, fear and true account, mingle with some frequency in the preludes themselves, as we will see.[15] We might imagine then that just as law corrects human vision with respect to the good of the entire politeia, the preludes attached to law supplement the law's own blindness to particularity (thereby serving their own prosthetic purpose) and do so by speaking to the legislated herself and making her an ally of the law.[16] If this is the case, then our understanding of the preludes must be informed by a grasp of the people to whom the preludes are delivered. In other words, the preludes, like the Platonic dialogues themselves, are decisively shaped by the perspectives of their interlocutors. As André Laks has observed, no matter how far these preludes may stray from resembling the kinds of conversations Plato depicts Socrates having throughout the dialogues, "the Socratic model of a dialectical conversation constitutes the horizon within which the theory of legislative preamble must be situated."[17]

The *Laws* provides several accounts of what it is in human nature that leads to the blindness and incapacity that is to be supplemented by the law and its preludes.[18]

Indeed, an entire psychology[19] is constructed and given to the legislator, beginning with the image of the human as a puppet suspended from multiple cords (664e), one which corresponds to the account of soul encapsulated within many of the preludes that are to be delivered to the citizens. The following three chapters aim to discern the conception of soul that is at work in the *Laws*' accounts of what it is necessary for citizens to think and feel about the city and what role the city plays both in human life and in the cosmos as a whole. Doing so will make explicit the *Laws*' characterization of the city itself as a psychological phenomenon and demonstrate the dialogue's intertwining of political, philosophical, and psychological inquiry. Chapter 8 offers a sketch of the conception of human psychology that the *Laws* offers to the legislator and argues that the combination of nomos with the preludes' curious mixture of muthos and logos serves the legislator in producing a community of pleasure and pain by regulating affect and opinion. This combination is evident in the discussion of penal laws pertaining to impiety and murder in books 9 and 10, wherein particular beliefs about action, the immortality of the soul, and the nature of justice are advocated precisely for their ability to inspire obedience to law. Chapter 9 argues that these particular pieces of legislation comprise a collusion of nomos, muthos, and logos that aims at correcting the shortness of vision and incapacity to act according to the good of civic life that the Athenian suggests is indicative of human being. They do so by inspiring an affective comportment toward the good of the city as a whole.[20] Chapter 10 then focuses in greater detail upon the preludes against the impious in order to draw out the account of soul and the account of city, the psychology and politics, contained therein, and to argue that both are designed to function as a prosthetic vision of the good of the city.

8 Psychology for Legislators

In the first book of the *Laws*, the Athenian Stranger and his interlocutors turn to discuss the best form of civic education, one that would provide for the well-being of citizens. They conceive of education in terms that merit comparison with *Republic*: education is a matter of becoming good (634e, 644a), and requires a training in pleasures and desire (643c) that includes the turning of one's erotic impulses toward that which one is studying (643e). In the *Republic*, as we have seen, it is the plasticity of young souls that is taken to recommend the supervision of poets and the determination of which tales are suitable to tell. In the *Laws* the first detailed account of psychic plasticity, that is, of the factors that shape the soul and give character to a human life, occurs in the form of an image introduced in order to clarify the Athenian's assertion that those capable of ruling themselves are good, while those incapable of so ruling are bad (644b): the infamous image of the living being as a puppet of the gods (644d–645c). What unfolds in the course of this image-making is an account of the legislative subject, the being for whom laws are enacted.[1] This being is constituted by the tense interaction between an array of demands and capacities, figured in the image as sinews or cords. Several of the most powerful of these cords are described as follows: pleasure and pain, two "foolish and antagonistic counselors" (644c); opinions (δόξας) about the future, hopes, which, when they anticipate pain are called "fear" and when they anticipate pleasure, "confidence"; and calculation (λογισμός), capable of determining which opinions are good and which are bad (644c–d). Populated by a plurality of competing affections, the human being is a loose and tenuous conglomerate whose actions are the result of a tense mechanics of pulling and pushing. One such cord—calculation—is capable of adjudicating between the competing demands of the others and directing action on the basis of the good. However, this particular cord exerts its attraction and influence in a gentler manner than the others, and thus requires aid. When calculation becomes the shared opinion of the city, it is called law (644d, 645a).[2]

Several features of this image prove decisive in clarifying the conceptions of human nature and law that dictate the dialogue's particular approach to legislation. First, what emerges as most characteristically human from the perspective of the lawgiver is the encounter between pleasure and pain, along with a certain human capacity to weigh these two against a now and a later and a better and a worse. We may call this combined sense of time and value, this combination of doxa and logos, a "measuring capacity" for the purposes of discussion, but only provided we do not import into this a rigid distinction between cognition and affect. Indeed, a second significant feature of this image is its characterization of hope, confidence, and fear as opinions. Because these opinions arise as effects of one's encounter with pleasure and pain, they are presented as epiphenomena of this very encounter. Calculation in turn finds its task in measuring these epiphenomena against the good and the bad. The centrality of pleasure and pain to human life is alluded to earlier in the *Laws* in a description that emphasizes their excessive nature: pleasure and pain are "two fountains which gush out by nature's impulse" (636d–e). The main labor put before the human is thus less an overcoming of lack or need than a negotiation of abundance. Human life is carved out of the excessive and potentially overwhelming phenomena of pleasure and pain.[3] Human happiness, in turn, depends upon creating some measure to one's pursuit of pleasure and avoidance of pain. Law emerges as assisting in this effort.

Third, the intimacy between law and human life mentioned in the introduction to this section receives fuller explanation in this characterization of the law as the externalization of calculation and as an aid in the realization of a human capacity for self-rule. According to this model, the city, as the legislating unit or scene of legislation, is necessary for human happiness in that it supports the human impulse most capable of negotiating a measured pursuit of pleasure and avoidance of pain. By means of its laws, the city assists the human in ruling over herself.

Finally, the Athenian insists that it is necessary for the private individual to "grasp the true account [τὸν μὲν λόγον ἀληθῆ] of these inward pulling forces and to live in accordance therewith" just as it is necessary that the city make this account "a law for itself" and be guided by it in its intercourse both with itself and with other cities (645b). The necessity that individuals have some understanding of their own psychical condition and thus also have some grasp of the need they are in for law as a helper to them informs the various descriptions of human nature and the causes of its hamartia and hubris that follow. This is to say, fostering an understanding of one's soul is one goal of both the preludes and the laws. Moreover, since lawgivers and citizens alike are to share a true account of the psychical constitution of human beings, the psychology for legislators also marks out a psychology for the legislated.[4]

How this shared true account is delivered, on the other hand, admits of some variance, as we will see in our discussion of a few specific preludes in chapters 9 and 10. For now, it suffices to note that it is precisely in their consideration of how a law is to be conveyed that the Athenian and his interlocutors identify the need for and develop the practice of appending preludes to laws. Their own conviction about the merits of the prelude is won by the Athenian's appeal to two forms of medical practice: that of the free doctors who attend to citizens and employ an account designed to tame the sick with persuasion (720d) as well as orders for treatment, on the one hand, and that of the servants of these doctors who treat slaves, employing, like tyrants (720c), only orders, on the other. He develops from out of this model two forms of legislation, the single and the double, giving an example of each for Magnesia's marriage laws (721b–c).[5] The Athenian then links the persuasive speech of the double form of legislating to the preludes that are delivered prior to speeches and songs (722d–e), and advocates for the mixture of preludes and law on the grounds that such a mixture favorably disposes the citizen to the law (723a).

This interweaving of medical and political activities should by now be familiar to us on the basis of our discussion of the role of medicine in the *Republic*. In the *Laws*, this interweaving is already at work in the presentation of politics as a therapeia of the soul. The discussion of the preludes deepens this conception of politics by casting the relationship between legislator and legislated as akin to that between doctor and patient. Moreover, the gentleness of the prelude, as distinct from the violence of the law (722b–c), aligns the prelude with the gentle regulative form of calculation within the soul. In looking further ahead, this alignment makes more natural the connection the Athenian will eventually draw between receiving the law and being educated—the laws, as the greatest poetry the city produces, are themselves a primary form of education (817a–d).[6] It also anticipates the Athenian's acknowledgment of the law's blindness to particularity (875d), a blindness for which, presumably, the preludes compensate, and paves the way for the alignment of injustice, disease, and blight as all instances of pleonexia (906b–c).[7]

To return to the immediate context, we note that with their agreement to append preludes to certain laws,[8] the Athenian and his interlocutors agree to begin their legislating anew, and to finish off the prelude that their previous conversation had been composing without them knowing it (723d–e) by moving from legislation regarding the proper attitude toward the gods to considering how a citizen should comport himself toward his soul, his body, and his possessions. The lengthy prelude the Athenian composes at the start of book 5 does just this, allowing us to analyze more closely the conception of soul that citizens are to maintain.

Book 5 begins with the following observation: "Of all a man's own belongings, the most divine is his soul, since it is most his own [πάντων γὰρ τῶν αὑτοῦ κτημάτων μετὰ θεοὺς ψυχὴ θειότατον, οἰκειότατον ὄν]" (726a). This description of soul stands out for its strange mixing of banality (soul is referred to by the same term one would use to describe a household implement), significance (soul is most one's own), and divinity (soul is most divine). It suggests that what is most one's own also belongs to another (the gods). That is, what makes a person most him- or herself is not something to which he or she can lay claim as sole owner. Because this conception of soul falls within a theology that sees the gods as causes only of the good, this claim about what is one's own suggests that viciousness is a certain failure with respect not only to the city and the gods, but to oneself. Such a conception of what is one's own can be more or less individually inflected and can signify more or less specificity across social, political, and biological valences. What is one's own can refer to what is most Socrates's or Glaucon's, but it can also refer to what is most human and to what is most alive. In any of these cases, however, this particular vision includes a disinvestment in one's "ownership" of what is most one's own. And I take this to be saying more than simply that the individual human being is the being at stake for herself, that she is a question for herself. I take it to be saying that the individual never *is* without the operation of entities which she is not.

For those who are not convinced that it is of utmost importance to honor one's soul and that doing so requires one to acquire what the legislator determines to be good and avoid what he determines to be bad, the greatest judgment awaits: "to grow like unto men that are wicked, and, in so growing, to shun good men and good counsels and cut oneself off from them, but to cleave to the company of the wicked and follow after them" (728b).[9] This presentation of the effects of wrongdoing places heavy emphasis on the community to which one commits oneself in the performance of certain deeds. This community is a penalty precisely because, in becoming like those who are "wicked," one fosters a predilection for the company of other wrongdoers and cuts oneself off from companionship by which one would be better served. This emphasis on the community that is formed by one's actions resonates not only with the myth of the *Phaedo* and with Socrates's exhortation in the middle of the myth of Er, but also, as we shall see, with the vision of the afterlife given in one of the preludes against impiety in book 10.

After this initial sketch of the psychic sources of human action and the need to append preludes to the laws, the dialogue eventually turns to identify those internal conditions of soul that cause wrongdoing and thus that should be legislated against. Given both the centrality of the soul to the legislative project and the medical inflection of the dialogue, the Athenian's etiology of wrongdoing consists of an account of pathological conditions of soul. The excesses to which pleasure and pain push the human, along with the more and less effective capacity to weigh these against a sense of time and value, feature prominently in the psychic pathology that unfolds, wherein we encounter a host of epiphenomena in the same family as hope and fear.

For instance, in book 5 we read that the cause of all hamartia lies "in the person's excessive love of self" (731e). The problem with this love of self is that it promotes a warped sensibility, a myopia, and even a blindness, about what is good and bad (731e).

The overestimation of the value of oneself that attends upon excessive self-love is also a source of that most dangerous form of ignorance, namely, mistaking one's ignorance for knowledge (732a).[10] Thus, excessive self-love is problematic because of the damaging effect it has on one's judgment.[11] Because of this inflated sense of self-value, one comes to have a misguided opinion about one's own place and worth.

This blinding by excess receives further elaboration in book 9, wherein self-interested grasping is identified as rendering even one who is capable of recognizing the good of the city incapable of performing that good. Such a person's mortal nature "will always urge him on to grasping and self-interested action [πλεονεξίαν καὶ ἰδιοπραγίαν], irrationally avoiding pain and pursuing pleasure," thereby corrupting both himself and the city (875b–c). Again, the human being must negotiate between a variety of tendencies toward excess, in this instance a desire for self-perpetuation, a desire to extend what is one's own and to unfold oneself out boundlessly.[12]

Indeed, book 9 brings to fruition the *Laws*' portrait of human nature and the vicissitudes to which it is subject—its tendency toward excess, blindness, and diffusion, along with the fragility of its unity and character—by defining injustice and producing a taxonomy of corrupt conditions of soul. Early on in book 9, the Athenian and his interlocutors address themselves to a problem that has plagued them for several books, namely, their desire to maintain both some notion of voluntary wrongdoing and the claim that no one willingly does injustice.[13] The Athenian's solution to this dilemma is to distinguish between injury, which is a result of some action, and injustice, which is a condition of soul that may or may not be the source of the injurious action (860d–863a). Injustice names that condition of diffusion characterized by a tyranny (τυραννίδα) in the soul of, "passion [τοῦ θυμοῦ] and fear and pleasure and pain and envies and desires" (863e), whereas the rule in the soul by the opinion of the highest good (τὴν δὲ τοῦ ἀρίστου δόξαν) (864a) constitutes a condition of the opposite sort, even if the person with such a condition should somehow do damage to another. In legislating against injustice, the law will have to overcome the tyranny of a variety of the soul's most powerful "sinews" in order to legislate in favor of an opinion about the good.

The subsequent taxonomy of wrongdoing that the Athenian and his interlocutors produce consists of five classes (πέντα εἴδη 864b]) of psychic conditions that cause hamartia. It also encapsulates much of what has been said throughout the dialogue about the roles of pleasure, pain, and opinion in human life. The first class, identified as painful, is that of anger and fear (θυμὸν καὶ φόβον); the second kind consists of pleasures and desires; and the third consists of hope and untrue opinions about what is good (ἄριστον) (864b). The Athenian divides this last kind into three,[14] producing five kinds in all: (1) anger and fear; (2) pleasure and desire; (3) hope; (4) simple ignorance; and (5) double ignorance. The Athenian introduces one further distinction concerning the manner in which acts are performed; namely, whether the act is done publicly or privately and in secret (864c).

Granted the distinction between injury and injustice, the legislator is now charged with two tasks: first, addressing and setting aright the injury; second, diagnosing and, when possible, treating the soul of the offender. In other words, this distinction allows the legislator to separate out the interests of the victim (and his or her family) from the needs of the offender and, most importantly, to attend to both for the sake of the welfare not just of citizens but also of the city itself. In locating the desires, interests, and anger of the victim within the realm of recompense and setting aright, the Athenian both establishes limits to the claims of injured parties and provides specific means to acknowledge and recognize the nature of the offense against them. In identifying the need of the offender for treatment, he shifts the conceptual framework of legislation from punishment to a rehabilitation based upon the complex psychological model established for this purpose and the diagnostic skills that will be required of the legislators. Thus, the anger of the victim ceases to be the single-most influential factor in legislating.[15] However, the fact that it is still possible to deem certain offenders incurable, a diagnosis which is taken to recommend the permanent "removal" of the offender, should serve to remind us that in the final analysis it is the good of the city that is maintained above all else.[16] Both the recompense for injury and the diagnosis and treatment of the soul of the offender are undertaken for ensuring the endurance of the city itself.[17]

The instruments for attempting these dual tasks—setting aright the injury and treating the unjust—are multiple: purifications, payments, exile, scourging, exposures, and death. In developing these penalties, Plato had at his disposal a system of Athenian penal law whose elements and institutions he borrowed as well as transformed. With respect to homicide laws in particular, Athenian legislation encapsulated two parallel mechanisms for contending with wrongdoing, mechanisms whose relationship was not always seamless: one, which we have encountered in our study of the *Phaedo*, a broadly religious conception of the pollution (miasma) that attends certain deeds and can adhere to places and personages beyond those of the immediate doer, accompanied by rituals for the purification of this pollution; and two, a set of more or less formal legal processes and institutions.[18] In light of Robert Parker's compelling collection of evidence that the more ancient religious conceptions of pollution and purification practices were waning in influence during Plato's lifetime, Plato's maintenance of these practices in particular begs explanation. Setting aside, as beyond the scope of the present inquiry, the question of whether all forms of legislation modeled upon a conception of the health of the citizen are inherently conservative, I am inclined less toward Parker's suggestion that the *Laws*' use of these practices speaks to its "profound religious conservatism" and more toward Saunders's assertion that Plato harnesses these practices for the sake of a radical legislative agenda.[19] The conception of pollution and the regulations for purification that are operative in the *Laws* are not simply expressions of a religiously or theologically inflected model of civic hygiene; they are also mechanisms for acknowledging and contending with the uncanny and traumatizing endurance of violent deeds. Thus, they operate by means of the implicit phenomenology of violence we described in our study of the *Phaedo*. I maintain that Plato includes acts of purification as part of his penal law precisely because of the orientation toward violence they offer. What Plato finds useful about these practices is the attitude toward violent action that they encapsulate, an attitude that emphasizes the collective implication of the entire city in the commission of violent deeds, a sense that the effects of such deeds, as J. P. Vernant describes, "cover a field of action in which the constituent parts and moments are connected."[20] In order to see this, we will turn in the next chapter to look at a few specific instances of Plato's penal law.

Before doing so, we should pause and summarize the portrait of human nature, and its pathologies, that the Athenian gives the would-be legislator. Pulled and drawn in a variety of different and often contradictory directions by myriad forces, the human being comprises a tenuous and fragile unity won by means of negotiating these forces, whose competing demands and excessive nature constantly threaten to overthrow this unity and compel it toward diffusion. One such force, calculation, has the power to determine the merit of the various directions in which the others pull and draw the individual, and is thus a significant aid to the successful negotiation of these forces. However, because of its gentleness, calculation requires assistance to accomplish the coalescence of forces and defense against diffusion that is productive of unified humans. Law is the name granted to externalized calculation. Without the assistance of law, the human being is led into a variety of more or less diffuse conditions in which she is expended and blinded by the pursuit of pleasure and the avoidance of pain. Psychic pathology consists in those conditions of soul, like excessive self-love and boundless acquisition (pleonexia), which promote this diffusion and are inextricably bound to injustice, conceived as the tyranny of a variety of psychic forces.

In order to counter these forces, the law must engender and foster citizens' sense of themselves as living in the context of the city, bound by limits and answerable to others. The laws must aid in contracting citizens' esteem of self and expanding their sense of the effects of their actions. This is to say that the laws must foster in citizens a more exact grasp of themselves as socially and politically constituted.

It seems to me unwise to assume that the tension at work here—that laws which, as we will see, employ a variety of threats about the afterlife are intended to promote that most philosophic of ideals, self-knowledge—is lost on Plato. Rather, I take the distance between this ideal and the attitudes and affects promoted by the preludes we are about to examine to tell us more about what Plato believes is necessary for fostering self-knowledge in acquisitive, foolish, and self-absorbed characters. If we are going to hold Plato responsible for pathologies that he engendered, then we should also look at the pathologies to which he was reacting. The descriptions in the *Laws* of an overblown sense of self and a restless desire for acquisition are not so distant from the famous description of the Athenians that Thucydides places in the mouths of the Corinthians: "they were born into the world to take no rest themselves and to give none to others."[21] Of course, neither Plato nor Thucydides has a disinterested perspective on the psychai of Athenian citizens. Nevertheless, a generous critical evaluation of the beliefs espoused in the preludes should take into account their function within the *Laws*' interest in what is required to get people who are flirting with injustice to see themselves as answerable to others. A few examples of the preludes employed in Plato's penal law should make this function clear.

9 Psychology for the Legislated

The Athenian's turn to penal law begins with a lament that such legislation is necessary in Magnesia (853b). However, he quickly acknowledges that they are humans legislating for humans, and that the account of human nature and the human soul they have been developing reveals the necessity for laws of the sort they are about to create. The structure of these laws is informed by another early agreement, namely, that the account of the soul that informs the legislators' approach to legislating is to be shared with the legislated (645b–c). As we have seen, the preludes that are appended to laws are treated as a powerful vehicle for conveying this civically salutary conception and attitude toward soul. This chapter will argue that the preludes attached to penal law are particularly vivid instantiations of this psychology for the legislated. We will begin with the prelude to temple robbing, a piece of legislation which directly precedes and motivates the distinction between injury and injustice that so shapes Magnesian homicide law, and which promotes precisely the attitude toward violent action that is encapsulated by the religious language of pollution. From there we will move on to discuss the legislation pertaining to homicide and the impiety of the young in order to analyze the implicit accounts of soul contained therein.

Temple Robbing

The Athenian begins the prelude to be administered to the would-be temple robber with the following words:

> "By way of argument and admonition [διαλεγόμενος ἅμα καὶ παραμυθούμενος] one might address in the following terms the man whom an evil desire urges by

day and wakes up at night, driving him to rob some sacred object—'My good man, the evil force [ἐπιθυμία κακὴ] that now moves you and prompts you to go temple-robbing is neither of human origin nor of divine, but it is some impulse bred of old in men for ancient wrongs unexpiated [οἶστρος δέ σέ τις ἐμφυόμενς ἐκ παλαιῶν καὶ ἀκαθάρτων τοῖς ἀνθρώποις ἀδικημάτων], which courses around wreaking ruin [περιφερόμενος ἀλιτηριώδης]; and you must guard against it with all your strength." (854a–b)

In presenting the temple robber's temptation as a function not of human or divine sources but of the endurance of deeds that have not been properly expiated, Plato is playing upon the broader religious attitude toward the effects of violence identified above. The prelude's description of those tempted by temple robbery as being pursued, gadfly-like, and haunted by these deeds both presents this temptation as coming from the outside—and thus as an object for observation, analysis, and even avoidance—and emphasizes the importance of properly dispensing with certain actions. Failing to do so creates precisely the context in which one is tempted to perpetuate further acts in need of expiation. Thus, a certain economy of deed is suggested by this prelude, as is the capacity of these deeds to exceed their doer. Indeed, the entire prelude reduces the agency of the would-be temple robber by emphasizing the excessive and enduring character of the kinds of act he is contemplating; the endurance of passion and action we have seen given expression in the myth of Er is appealed to here as a means of persuasion. In the face of the autonomy of these deeds and the possibility of contributing to this economy, the prelude goes on to advise the person tempted by temple robbery to supplicate the gods and seek the company of good men, eschewing at all costs the company of the bad; if this is insufficient to guard against temptation, he must remove himself from the human community entirely by taking his own life (854b–c).[1]

Having broached the appropriateness of death as a means of dealing with the crime of temple robbing, the Athenian pronounces incurable the citizen who fails to guard himself sufficiently against this temptation and assigns to him the penalty of death, "the least of evils" (854e). The pronouncement of this penalty does not occur without some anxiety, and the next several pages of the dialogue contain the more extensive discussion of punishment,[2] which results in the distinction between injury and injustice and leads to the laws against homicide.

Homicide

The homicide laws are divided into three main groups that display a range of possibilities opened up by the distinction between injury and injustice: (1) accidental and involuntary homicide; (2) homicide in anger; (3) voluntary homicide. In the penalty of exile for involuntary homicide, the Athenian deploys the language and mythic tradition surrounding pollution and purification as part of the process of setting aright, one which acknowledges and recognizes the excessive nature of violent acts. In turn, the legislation concerning homicide committed in anger displays the diagnostics and therapeutics of soul that Plato's Athenian has been outlining. In creating a category that allots a special place to deeds committed in anger—and thus in granting a special status to anger—Plato demonstrates his focus on treating the soul of the offender for the sake of the city rather than punishing the offender for the sake of the victim. More intentional than accident but less intentional than choice, anger possesses a tractability and volatility that makes it powerful, but also shapeable.

Finally, the legislation pertaining to voluntary homicide illustrates the effects of a diagnosis of incurability. In dealing with these cases, the Athenian feels compelled to reiterate the psychology developed earlier and identifies desire, love of honor, and fear as psychic structures particularly implicated in the deeds which they are now to legislate (869e–870d). He follows this reiteration of psychology for the legislator with a return to the psychology espoused to the legislated, and carves this second psychology out of mythic sources:

> "Concerning all these matters, the preludes mentioned shall be pronounced, and, in addition to them, that story which is believed by many when they hear it from the lips of those who seriously relate such things at their mystic rites,—that vengeance for such acts is exacted in Hades, and that those who return again to this earth are bound to pay the natural penalty,—each culprit the same, that is, which he inflicted on his victim,—and that their life on earth must end in their meeting a like fate at the hands of another. To him who obeys, and fully dreads such a penalty, there is no need to add to the prelude by reciting the law on the subject." (870d–871a)

Like the prelude against temple robbing, this prelude gives primacy to the deed at the same time that it requires the potential doer of the deed to consider himself not as an agent but as a patient. The circulating of unexpiated wrongs referenced in the prelude to temple robbing receives its mirror image here as the potential return of a deed to its doer. While Hades names one site of punishment, the site of return (the scene of the deed's revisitation) is this-worldly in the sense that it gives shape to the life to which the soul of the doer is returned. Thus, in addition to suffering in Hades, the enduring soul must suffer in the life to which it moves next. Such a life is less a second life than a reiteration of the first, with one major change of character—the agent has become the patient. In this prelude, both Hades and manner of life share the character of providing a site for the return of the deed. Indeed, the prelude presents a more radical version of the myth of Er's vision of the manner in which one's actions and passions define the shape of one's life, a version which (at least in the case of potential homicides) locates the possibility of choice of lives only in the choice of whether or not to perform an action whose recursive effects are indelible, automatic, and utterly determinative of one's form of life.

The one for whom this prelude proves unpersuasive, once convicted, shall be put to death, and, adds the Athenian, "he shall not be buried in the land of the victim, because of the shamelessness as well as impiety of his act" (871d). Refusing burial in the land of the victim denies to the corpse a place in communion with the victim, as the doer has denied to the victim the continuance of his place in human community.[3] It is to this extent a ritualized instantiation of the very return of the deed that is threatened in the prelude.

This interaction between prelude and penalty is even more evident in the special case of the voluntary murder of parents. This case presents a hyperbolic version of voluntary murder, one which fully conjoins impiety and violence (and thus reveals the close relationship between the two that has been assumed throughout book 9). In delivering the prelude to the law concerning this sort of murder, the Athenian observes:

> "we must again recite the story we uttered a moment ago, if haply anyone, on hearing us, may become more strongly disposed in consequence voluntarily to abstain from murders of the most impious kind. The myth or story (or whatever one should call it)[4] has been clearly stated, as derived from ancient priests, to the effect that Justice, the avenger of kindred blood, acting as overseer, employs the law just mentioned, and has ordained that the doer of such a deed must of necessity suffer the same as he has done: if ever a man has slain his father, he must endure to suffer the same violent fate at his own children's hands in days to come; or if he has slain his mother, he must of necessity come to birth sharing in the female nature, and when thus born be removed from life by the hands of his offspring in afterdays; for of the pollution [μιανθέντος] of common blood there is no other purification, nor does the stain of pollution [μιανθὲν] admit of being washed off before the soul which committed the act pays back murder for murder, like for like,[5] and thus by propitiation lays to rest the wrath of all the kindred. Wherefore, in dread of such vengeances from heaven a man should refrain himself." (872e–873a)

As with voluntary murder in general, the prelude invites the potential patricide or matricide to consider his deeds from the perspective of the patient rather than the agent. Here, however, the explicit reference to pollution, which acts as a visceral attestation to the need for a penalty of return and which remains not only indelible but communicable to others until expiation occurs (in turn implicating the community that does not facilitate expiation), underscores the injury to the community committed by such a murder. This communal injury, this context of collective implication and responsibility, is emphasized ritualistically in the penalty assigned to the one convicted of shedding the blood of a parent:

> "and if any man be convicted of such a murder, and of having slain any of the persons named, the officers of the judges and magistrates shall kill him and cast him out naked at an appointed cross-roads outside the city; and all the magistrates, acting on behalf of the whole state, shall take each a stone and cast it on the head of the corpse, and thus make atonement [ἀφοσιούτω] for the whole state; and after this they shall carry the corpse to the borders of the land and cast it out unburied, according to law." (873b)

The treatment of the corpse distinguishes between the penalty for the killing of a parent in anger (death) and the voluntary killing of a parent (death and stoning of the corpse). The stoning of the corpse, the need of the entire city to atone for the deed, attests to the deed's excessive character as well as to the injury that is done to the city, but also to the implication of the city in its commission. In light of what is said about the head elsewhere in the dialogue (see 961d), stoning the head of the corpse amounts to impugning that organ to which the laws, preludes, and education designed by the legislators should speak—that receptacle of the preludes' address—and thus to impugning the city's failure to have persuaded this person to act otherwise. The denial of burial is a refusal to grant a place to the life of one who commits such a deed; it is a sign that the person has forfeited his dearness to the gods. Because of his actions, his corpse has ceased to be the "soulless altar to the gods below," a status which funerary law exhorts the city to extend to the corpse of the law-abiding citizen (959c–d).

The trope of pollution and purification is useful to Plato because it highlights the endurance of action and soul, the acknowledgment of which is needed in order to provide citizens with some sense for the good of the city and, moreover, to shape their desires and their fears to act accordingly. Thus, the language of miasma, like the accounts of vengeance accomplished both in Hades and by means of reincarnation, promotes a conception of and comportment toward action (that is, an ethics and a psychology) that not only extends citizens' sense of the city, but also alters their understanding of their place in it. This ethics and psychology is duplicated in the prescriptions for the treatment of criminal corpses: the need of the city itself to seek atonement for the crime of killing a parent, and the refusal of burial, the refusal to grant a place that would allow the deceased some endurance in memory—and thus some permanence in the civic economy of honor—attest to the extension of the effects of these deeds well beyond the doer. They bring to the fore the very context in which the deed was committed and which it deforms. The expulsion of pollution, indeed the entire framework of pollution and purification, reconfigures the way in which one thinks about oneself and one's actions. As a potential doer, one comes to see oneself from the lens of patiency more than agency, as being overpowered by the excessive effects of certain deeds and as in need of protection from this.

Impiety

We noted in the introduction to our study of the *Laws* the political significance of impiety. Indeed, the attempt to ground Magnesia's laws in divine nous renders impiety an attack against the very foundation of the city. The course of civic life and education outlined in the legislation of the dialogue's central books attempts to shape how Magnesia's citizens conceive of and behave toward their own and can thus be presented as combating this general, diffuse impiety. The impious addressed in book 10 are those who, having been given the education outlined in the previous books, prove hardhearted to the attempts to shape their character or have otherwise been persuaded to reject their civic training. Their specific impiety, that of the young, finds its source in three beliefs, and it is in the treatment of these beliefs that the Athenian feels compelled to offer the account of the soul that occupies much of the book. In light of the above comments, the therapeutic thrust of the preludes delivered to the impious in book 10 is found in their attempt to correct the way in which several species of the impious think about what is their own. They do so by offering a cosmology in which they present what is most one's own as an offshoot of a much larger and potent cosmic force. Chapter 10 will focus on the content of these preludes; the remainder of the present chapter charts out the people to whom they are delivered and the penalties to which they are attached.

The significance that impiety has for the legislative project of the dialogue advises careful attention to the people to whom these preludes against impiety are addressed. Given the Athenian's description of the impious in book 10, this entails grasping a turn of soul possessed not only by charlatans, sophists, tyrants, and demagogues (908d), but also by those young people whom the Athenian describes as akin to the gods and as lovers of justice (899d, 908b-c). This is a curious cast of characters to say the least, one that has some bearing on Plato's conception of the role of the philosopher in the city.[6] The Athenian's description of the people to whom the preludes are delivered, as well as the cultural milieu in which they operate, suggests that an investigation into what must be told to the impious about the soul will make a significant contribution to understanding Plato's conception of the relationship between philosophy and politics. In the rest of this chapter, we will focus on developing a clear sense for who these impious are and a general conception of how their preludes operate as part of Magnesia's penal law. We will then turn in chapter 10 to examine in greater detail the account of soul promoted within these preludes and the effect that this psychology is to have both on the impious and on the broader concerns of the dialogue.

Near the end of book 10, the Athenian identifies six classes of impiety to be distinguished because they require penalties that are "neither equal nor similar" (908b). In discerning who falls into these classes, we may take as a preliminary description those whom the Athenian identified at the start of the book as prone to particularly grave offenses, namely, the young. Further valuable information about these young people and those by whom they are influenced is given in the Athenian's early admonition (παραμύθιον) of the impious, wherein he offers a general diagnosis of impiety: "No one who believes, as the laws prescribe, in the existence of the gods has ever yet done an impious deed voluntarily, or uttered a lawless word: he that acts so is in one of these three conditions of mind—either he does not believe in what I have said; or, secondly, he believes that the gods exist, but have no care for men; or thirdly, he believes that they are easy to win over when bribed by offerings and prayers" (885b). The Athenian's response to Klinias's question of how one is to contend with these beliefs defines a certain posture which they must adopt toward the people who possess such beliefs. Like the good doctor described in book 4 (720c-e), they must listen to them (885c). But here there is a discursive disruption, as this posture is made possible only by a kind of speaking, the speaking for the legislated; the voice to which the Athenian claims they must listen is his own.[7] In order to listen to the legislated, the Athenian must address "himself," that is, he must address the persona that he has adopted as the legislator, by taking on the persona of the legislated, who are addressing the legislators. That is, the Athenian must both give and receive the demand of the legislated. Thus, it is by merit of a certain discursive gymnastics and ventriloquism that this scene of address is created.

The image of themselves that the Athenian gives to the impious is hardly flattering. The tone he attributes to them is mocking and demanding; he answers it by addressing them as children and telling them that their views are neither novel nor radical (888a–c). However, the legislated are not without talents in rhetoric and public debate. The demand that they make of the Athenian both appeals to the model of legislation that he has adopted and attempts in turn to translate this model into the idiom of the court. The legislated charge the legislators with deceiving people by using groundless arguments for the sake of manipulating citizens (886e), and demand that they prove the existence of the gods (885e).[8] When Klinias suggests that proving the existence of the gods is as simple as pointing to the heavens, and attributes impiety to a simple inability to master one's desire for pleasure (886a–b), the Athenian finds it necessary to complicate this diagnosis of impiety. He does so by calling attention to a broader cultural and political landscape in which impiety is allowed to flourish, a landscape beset, according to the Athenian, with "a very grievous unwisdom [ἀμαθία] which is reputed to be the height of wisdom" (886b). In elaborating upon this "unwisdom," the Athenian outlines and diagnoses a context in which the theologies produced by ancient poets have not only failed to provide a check to the pursuit of pleasure, but have also created a class of individuals who, in rebelling against them, propound a cosmology that fosters akrasia by asserting there are no gods.[9] Thus, the stance of the atheists must, according to the Athenian, be viewed in its reactive connection to a particular kind of theology.

This is a shrewd strategy on the part of the Athenian. By locating the position of the atheist within a particular cultural and intellectual framework, and specifically as a reaction to (and thus as something dependent upon) a particular theological context, the Athenian sets the stage for the putting-in-place of the atheist that is continued in the prelude delivered directly to him. Moreover, he also signals to his interlocutors that any attempt to contend with the beliefs that produce impiety must not only replace akratic cosmology with some other form of cosmology, but must also replace archaic theology with some other theology. That is, akratic cosmology will be replaced by noetic theology.

The Athenian's preliminary exchange with the impious tells us that the impious are the inheritors of this cultural landscape, of this constellation of beliefs in which a particular vision of the gods provokes a conception of nature purporting to refute any such vision and to resent its advocacy as a manipulative deception tricked out in specious argumentation. This exchange conveys the sense that many of the impious are predisposed to argument (even if this manifests itself as a love for eristic) and thus that the preludes to these people can take the shape of something akin to dialectic.[10] However, for the purposes of the present investigation, I will focus less on the dialectical or argumentative character (or lack thereof) of these preludes and more on how their substance is fitted to the psychic condition of the person they are addressing. Given this general introduction to the impious, we can now inquire into the specific conditions of soul of the atheist, the deist, and the one who claims that the gods can be bribed (the traditional theist, following Robert Mayhew's classification).[11] Because the prelude delivered to the atheist is the longest and is that upon which the other two preludes are based, my focus here is on this prelude's relationship to its recipient, followed by a sketch of what the other two preludes must correct in their recipients.

The Atheist

The belief that engenders the turn of soul of the atheist turns out to be a misconception of what constitutes the "first cause of becoming and perishing in all things" (891e). The atheist falls prey to a widespread misunderstanding about psuchē, one that attributes to it a later generation than that of the body (892a). The cosmology to which the atheist is victim is one in which things come to be primarily by the interaction between phusis, whose primary manifestations are soulless bodies of earth and fire, etc. (889b); tuchē, which governs the mingling of these natural forces (889b–c); and technē, which provides a secondary and lesser source of things (secondary because later, and lesser because it receives what is good about it from nature) (889a). Legislation, especially legislation that asserts the existence of gods, acts counter to the "natural" tendency to dominate: "as to things just, they do not exist at all by nature, but men are constantly in dispute about them and continually altering them, and whatever alteration they make is authoritative, though it owes its existence to art and the laws, and not in any way to nature" (889e–890a). Thus, the atheist is persuaded by sophists who align law with technē against nature, and who, on the basis of this antagonism, chart out a politics that valorizes injustice under the rubric of living a natural life.

Because his beliefs about the nature of the cosmos entice the atheist toward impiety, the "cure" or treatment for this psychic condition must involve a set of counter-beliefs, an alternate cosmology to the akratic cosmology. In his response to this cosmology and the politics that it suggests—and thus in his antidote to the condition of soul fostered by such a cosmology—the Athenian tacitly accepts the general vision of phusis had by the atheist, namely that phusis is the "production of things primary" (892c). Where the atheist errs, however, is in what he considers such primary things to be: "That which is the first cause of becoming and perishing in all things, this is declared by the arguments which have produced the soul of the impious to be not first, but generated later, and that which is the later to be the earlier; and because of this they have fallen into error regarding the real nature of the divine existence" (891e). This is to say that the Athenian will assert that it is the soul (what the atheist had aligned with technē and with later and secondary creation) which is responsible for the first productions, and thus it is the soul that should be called by the atheists most natural (892c). The pharmacological move to be found in the logos that follows resides in its radically reconfiguring the relationship between phusis, tuchē, and technē such that the motions of soul—phenomena like joy, sorrow, hatred, love, reflections, memories, opinions true and false,[12] phenomena manifest in phusis and technē alike—are the primary workings of the cosmos. These motions are responsible for the generation and dissolution of all things. In this alternate cosmology, the operation granted to tuchē by the atheist's cosmology—the combination of elements into things—is instead a function of the presence and absence of mind. Moreover, law, like soul itself, will speak to the inadequacy of the presentation of the relationship between phusis and technē as antagonistic. This antidote to atheism functions only by the assertion of some provocative claims about the origin and nature of soul. These will be discussed in chapter 10; for now it is sufficient to note that the prelude to the atheist concludes by setting down certain limiting conditions: either the atheist must show that soul is not older than body, or he must believe in and honor the gods (899c).

The Deist

The preludes to the deist and to the one who claims that the gods can be bribed explicitly build upon this account of psuchē and cosmos by drawing out the implications for human life of an ordered and mindful cosmos overseen by rational gods. However, the condition of soul of the one who believes that the gods neglect human affairs is somewhat different from that of the young atheist. This potentially impious person is driven not by a denial of the gods, but by a certain bind, a certain incapacity to square his belief in the gods with his perception of the apparent flourishing of unjust people. Here is how the Athenian characterizes such a person, or rather, here is the portrait that the Athenian gives to this person of himself:

> "My good sir [ὂ ἄριστε],"[13] let us say, "the fact that you believe in gods is due probably to a divine kinship drawing you to what is of like nature, to honor it and recognize its existence; but the fortunes of evil and unjust men, both privately and in public—which, though not really happy, are excessively and improperly lauded as happy by public opinion—drive you to impiety by the wrong way in which they are celebrated, not only in poetry, but in tales of every kind." (899d–e)

While the atheist has fallen victim to a vision of the cosmos handed to him by certain sophists, the person who fears neglect from the gods is a victim of his own observations and of the many stories and songs that valorize an unjust life. There is a powerful resonance here between the Athenian's description of the soul of this young person and Plato's depiction of Glaucon and Adeimantus in *Republic* 2.[14] Here, as in the *Republic*, the truly enigmatic human phenomenon is the person who seems to have a natural love of justice, a passionate predisposition toward measure and harmony.[15] The occurrence of such a human, against all tendency toward pleonexia and excessive self-love, is the phenomenon that most begs philosophical attention and inquiry.

And here, as in the *Republic*, attempting such an account requires the employment of a vast conceptual apparatus, involving not only arguments about the nature of the gods' rule over the cosmos, but also a vision of theodicy offered as a supplemental and necessary charm. The details of this account will be explored in the next chapter. For now, let us simply observe that the prelude must contend with the impression that injustice pays, and I take the necessity of adding the discursive supplement of the charm to the prelude to signal Plato's acknowledgment of the power and traumatizing force of this experience. According to the Athenian, what the deist lacks, and what the prelude and its supplementary charm are intended to provide, is a vision of the expiation of unjust deeds. They do so by means of an elaborate spatial metaphor in which theodicy is figured as the movement of souls to appropriate places and is governed by the cosmic law of "like to like." Throughout this prelude and charm, the tropes of ownership and kinship play a decisive role: as both the property of the gods and as kin to the gods by merit of their possession of soul (902b),[16] humans should be assured of the care and attention of the gods who, in their solicitude of what is their own, are exemplars of ownership.

The Traditional Theist

The one who believes that the gods can be bribed is also one who has fallen prey to stories about the gods from both poets and prose writers. Like the deists, these impious people are misled by their own conception of divinity. However, the conception of the gods had by such people so far surpasses in depravity the claim that the gods neglect humans as to make Klinias describe those who hold this opinion as the worst and most impious people (907b). The opinion about the gods that sparks Klinias's ardent, zealous condemnation is presented by the Athenian as likening gods to guardians and those who bribe them to wolves: "it is just as if wolves were to give small bits of their prey to watch-dogs, and they being mollified by the gifts were to allow them to go ravening among the flocks" (906d). Such a person takes the gods to be more corrupt than those human practitioners of technai who manage to fulfill their duties without succumbing to corruption. Their discussion of the people who hold these views of the gods also has a maddening effect on the Athenian and his interlocutors themselves, driving them to a passionate and contentious denunciation of such people that violates their earlier agreement to tame their thumos (887c–888a) and argue against the impious dispassionately, a failure to which the Athenian calls their attention (907b–d). Beyond the preludes already delivered to the atheist and the deist, little hope is held out for convincing this person otherwise. The law prohibiting the possession of private shrines (909d–e) which concludes book 10 seems designed with this particular form of impiety in mind, suggesting that with this person the limits of persuasive argument have been reached.

Frank and Ironic Impiety

There remains one more criterion relevant to the legislator's discernment and treatment of impiety, the distinction between the "frank" (παρρησίας [908c])[17] and the "ironic" (τὸ εἰρωνικὸν [908e]) impious person, a distinction perhaps most clearly illustrated in its demarcation of two kinds of atheist:

> "For while those who, though they utterly disbelieve in the existence of the gods, possess by nature a just character, both hate the evil and, because of their dislike of injustice, are incapable of being induced to commit unjust actions, and flee from unjust men and love [στέργουσιν] the just, on the other hand, those who, besides holding that the world is empty of gods, are afflicted by incontinence in respect of pleasures and pains, and possess also powerful memories and sharp wits—though both these classes share alike in the disease of atheism, yet in respect of the amount of ruin they bring on other people, the latter class would work more and the former less of evil." (908b–c)

It is from out of the class of the ironic impious that one finds diviners and jugglers, tyrants, demagogues, and generals, "those who plot by means of peculiar mystic rights of their own, and the devices of those who are called sophists" (908d). With respect to both the deist and the one who believes that the gods can be bribed, the ironic or acute forms of their impiety turn their victims into "ravening beasts" who

> "besides holding that the gods are negligent or open to bribes, despise men, charming the souls of many of the living, and claiming that they charm the souls of the dead, and promising to persuade the gods by bewitching them, as it were with sacrifices, prayers and incantations, and who try thus to wreck utterly not only individuals, but whole families and states for the sake of money." (909a–b)

This passage draws together again both those who believe in the gods' neglect and those who believe the gods can be bribed, a sobering reminder of the depths to which even those who possess some "natural" kinship with the gods (899d) can fall if their corruption is not checked.

Indeed, this distinction between frank and ironic impious people would not be possible if the only cause of impiety was akrasia, which is why the Athenian corrects Klinias's claim that it is only a weakness with respect to pleasure and pain that causes impiety. By pointing to the persuasive power of the sophistic position on the cosmos, the Athenian sets the stage for the corruption of those who, while, and perhaps because, they naturally love justice, are traumatized by the apparent flourishing of unjust people and are thus vulnerable to the arguments of the sophists about what is natural and about the falsehood of justice. What Klinias's somewhat naive diagnosis fails to consider is the more dangerous possibility that even people predisposed to love justice and the gods can be turned away from both; what Klinias fails to discern is the *array* of impious people (the jarring connection between the sophist, the charlatan, and the people persuaded by each) and the work of a variety of cultural and political factors in producing this array.

Consequently, the preludes must be constructed with an eye to individual psychology and social institution alike. Much of the work done by the preludes to the impious consists in pointing out the psychic condition of the person to whom they are addressed and locating this person within a larger framework, a framework that requires of the person certain metaphysical, theological, and cosmological commitments attested to by the very kind of person many of the impious are. In presenting their psychic conditions and the inclinations that arise from them as part of a larger psychic structure that exceeds them, the prelude attempts to put the impious in his or her place, as it were, a gesture that grants two things: the security of theodicy that the deist desires[18] and a kind of self-knowledge and humility that the atheist and those who believe the gods can be bribed are taken to lack. Insofar as this lack can be seen to stem from, or be a manifestation of, excessive self-love (τὴν σφόδρα ἑαυτοῦ αἰλίαν), whose warping effect on judgment the Athenian has previously emphasized (731e), the Athenian's comment that such preludes will make the impious more disposed to hate themselves (ἑαυτοὺς μισῆσαι [907c]) is revelatory of the intended therapeutic thrust of these preludes and the specific psychological and cultural context in which they are operating.

For the frank impious person, the antidote lies first in pointing to the existence of people who, like themselves, do have a natural love for justice and order and then on playing up the metaphysical and cosmological implications of such a love. The strategy which the prelude employs is to show frank impious people that they are not at home in the very cosmology they espouse; their predisposition toward justice and order cannot be explained by the beliefs they have claimed as their own. This is especially true for the frank deist, whose attention is to be turned from the apparent flourishing of unjust people (the phenomena that causes this person so much torment) to the remarkable emergence of those naturally predisposed to love justice.[19] The Athenian presents the prelude's cosmology as able to account for *both* pleonexia and a natural predisposition toward justice. The atheist's cosmology, on the other hand, can only account for pleonexia; it is bereft of tools to offer a satisfactory explanation of an innate love of justice and related phenomena like the eruptions of order seen in children at play and by all humans in dance. Its only resource for explanation here is chance, and the Athenian is gambling that once the impious have been recognized as having a place in an orderly cosmos, for many of them this recourse to chance will appear symptomatic of an impoverished account.

The penalties that the Athenian goes on to assign to impiety, penalties which are supposed to reflect the taxonomy of impiety that the Athenian has produced, imply that not all people tempted by impiety will be persuaded by these preludes. According to the Athenian, as there are three causes of impiety (the three beliefs discussed above) and two kinds of impiety that result from each (frank and ironic), there are six classes (γένη) "which require to be distinguished, as needing penalties that are neither equal nor similar [οὐκ ἴσης οὐδ' ὁμοίας]" (908b). Since imprisonment is imposed in all cases of conviction for impiety, the differences between these classes will be a function of the location and conditions of their imprisonment. This, in turn, is possible because there are three kinds of prisons in Magnesia: the public prison near the agora where most "criminals" are housed; the reformatory (σωφρονιστήριον) located near the assembly room of the Nocturnal Council; and the third, called "retribution" (τιμωρίας), located in the wildest and most isolated part of the country (908a). The "frank" impious people, people who are suffering from "folly being devoid of evil disposition and character [ὑπ' ἀνοίας ἄνευ κάκης ὀργῆς τε καὶ ἤθους]" (908e), and who require "admonishment and imprisonment [τὸ δὲ νουθετήσεως ἅμα καὶ δεσμῶν (908e)], are to receive a penalty of no fewer than five years in the reformatory, where they will be visited only by members of the council asked to "minister to their soul's salvation by admonition" (909a). Those who appear to be reformed after the period of their incarceration are allowed back into Magnesian society; those who are convicted a second time are put to death (909a). The "ironic" impious people, those who are like "ravening beasts" (θηριώδεις [909a]) and for whom, according to the Athenian, even two deaths is not enough (908e), are to be imprisoned in the countryside and refused any visitors whatsoever, receiving only a food ration determined by the law wardens. While it is not explicitly stated in this passage, that they are to be imprisoned until death is strongly suggested both by the absence of any specification as to a means for or result of their rehabilitation and by the legislative detail that should such a person have children, those children are to be received by the guardian of orphans from the day of their parent's conviction (909d). Upon death, these impious are denied burial; instead, their bodies are to be thrown outside the borders of Magnesia, with a penalty of impiety for anyone who dares to bury them, enforceable by anyone who chooses to prosecute (909c). Thus, two deaths are indeed allotted to these people: the symbolic death of imprisonment in the most isolated place—and under the most isolating of conditions (marked by the appropriation of the convict's offspring and reiterated in the denial of burial)—and physical death.

The Athenian's delivery of the penalties to the impious, his "interpretation" of the law regarding impiety (907d), is incomplete. It specifies not six, but two, main different kinds of punishments, those for the frank and those for the ironic. Perhaps we are to infer that, for the classes of the frank impious, distinctions will be drawn in terms of the length of time incarcerated. Nevertheless, the Athenian fails to follow through with the demand to produce six separate penalties (908b). This apparent lapse reminds the reader that all of this legislation occurs under the specter of its failure. The same reminder lies in the admission that repeat offenses are possible, in the suggested impossibility of rehabilitating three of these classes, and in the limitation placed on oath taking in book 12 (948d–e), a limitation which bodes poorly for their efforts to stem the tide of impiety. As we move on to discuss in more detail the account of soul that is hoped to render these punishments superfluous, we should have in mind already the admission of the possibility (and even the likelihood) of its failure.

10 Psychic Excess

Early on in the lengthy prelude addressed to the would-be atheist, the Athenian makes a statement about soul whose ambiguity and profundity beg comparison with that fateful description of the good from *Republic* 6 as "beyond being" (ἐπέκεινα τῆς οὐσίας) (509b). If, observes the Athenian, soul can be shown to be generated prior to things like fire and air, then "it would be most correct to say it to be διαφερόντως φύσει" (892c).[1] As the adverbial form of διαφέρω, διαφερόντως means primarily "differently from." It is often used (in conjunction with a genitive) to indicate "above," and this specification to its kind of "difference from" recommends the adverb's use to indicate "especially," "pre-eminently," or, as Bury renders it, "superlatively." To claim that psuchē is διαφερόντως φύσει is to suggest that psuchē has being as both surpassingly and superlatively natural, which is to attribute to soul a deeply ambiguous relationship to nature.

This is a fruitful ambiguity, one in keeping with the general tenor of the discussion of soul in book 10. The Athenian's characterization of the soul as exceedingly natural is contingent upon both a conception of phusis and a demonstration of soul's generation, a showing of its priority with respect to genesis. In fact, genesis and phusis are brought into an intimate relationship in this passage because the atheist's conception of phusis, as the Athenian describes it, is precisely as γένεσιν τὴν περὶ τὰ πρῶτα (generation or coming-to-be of things primary) (892c). As we have seen, the Athenian does not expressly challenge this general formulation of phusis; instead, as the prelude develops, he attempts to reconfigure the atheist's conception of the relationship between phusis and psuchē by asserting that soul is the primary cause of all motion. In doing so, the

Athenian attributes to soul generative capacities whose magnitude and scope blur the distinction between psychology and cosmology.

The shape that the Athenian's contention with impiety takes in book 10—namely, the development of an account of soul aimed at the impious as an antidote to their impiety—attests to the political efficacy of "psychology." At the same time, the particular account of soul that the Athenian produces, with the excesses it attributes to psuchē and their cosmic significance, offers a commentary on the cosmological status of the laws under which the polis itself operates, and by which its citizens are to be treated. Thus, the account of soul produced in book 10 has significant implications for the *Laws*' overarching conception of the role of the polis in the lives of the humans who are its citizens and the cosmos in which it stands.

The influence it exhibits over the remaining books of the dialogue attest to its importance. When, in the final books of the *Laws*, the Athenian Stranger and his interlocutors discuss how the wardens of the law are to be educated, they agree that no one who has not labored over things divine should be admitted to the ranks of the Nocturnal Council (966d). They identify two agreements that have emerged from their previous discussion as most conducive to belief in the gods: that psuchē is the oldest and most divine of those entities whose motion receives genesis, and that nous is the source of the orderly motion of the stars (966e). The Athenian's expression of the first of these two agreements, however, contains one of the most vexed statements about soul to be found in the Platonic corpus. It renders extremely difficult the attempt to understand its relationship to its companion, their agreement about "the ordering of the motion of the stars and all the other bodies under the control of reason, which has made a 'cosmos' of the All" (966e). I offer below the Greek text, followed by a handful of translations.[2] The Athenian and his interlocutors maintain that ψυχή:

ὡς πρεσβύτατόν τε καὶ θειότατόν ἐστιν πάντων ὧν κίνησις γένεσιν παραλαβοῦσα ἀέναον[3] οὐσίαν ἐπόρισεν

> R. G. Bury: "is the most ancient and divine of all the things whose motion, when developed into 'becoming,' provides an ever-flowing fount of 'being.'"
>
> Trevor Saunders: "is far older and far more divine than all those things whose movements have sprung up and provided the impulse which has plunged it into a perpetual stream of existence."[4]
>
> Thomas Pangle: "is the eldest and most divine of all the things which are provided with ever-flowing existence by a motion that receives its coming-into-being."

The obscurity of this statement receives slight clarification by the gloss that the Athenian gives a few lines later: "It is impossible for any mortal man to become permanently god-fearing if he does not grasp the two truths now stated, namely, how that the soul is oldest of all things that partake of generation, and is immortal, and rules over all bodies—and in addition to this, as we have often affirmed, he must also grasp that reason which controls what exists among the stars, together with the necessary preliminary sciences" (976d). Here, however, the difficulty of conceiving the relationship between soul's rule of bodies in general and mind's rule of heavenly bodies is pronounced.[5] Coming to some understanding of the relationship between these two claims—the one about the soul and the other about mind—is the most immediate animating concern of this chapter.[6]

The earlier discussion of psuchē and nous to which the Athenian alludes in book 12 occurs in the course of the lengthy preludes delivered against impiety in book 10. In fact, the discussion of the education of the law wardens in book 12 is decisively shaped by the concern that the citizens holding this position be the least likely to succumb to impiety. While the average citizen might be allowed to follow only the letter of the law (966c), law wardens should know the truth about things divine and should be impervious to the three opinions identified in book 10 as productive of impiety in the young (885b).

By the end of the dialogue, the project it undertakes is radically incomplete. The Athenian and his interlocutors have yet to arrive at a detailed account of the education proper to the guardians of the laws, and have thus failed to provide the sustaining and preserving force necessary, according to the Athenian, for any such task to come to completion (960b). Magnesia's susceptibility to the plague of impiety that has afflicted other cities is implied by the limitation on oath-taking that the Athenian feels compelled to institute (948d–e). Such legislation does not cast an optimistic light on the efficacy of the preludes delivered to the impious in book 10, but does suggest that we must look there for some clarification of the obscure statements made about the soul and its relationship to mind in book 12.

This chapter returns to the preludes against impiety in book 10 in order to investigate in greater detail the relationship between what it asserts about soul and what the dialogue envisions the work of the city to be with respect to the cosmos as a whole. I will argue that the people to whom this cosmology is administered, that is, young people susceptible to arguments that lead to impiety, possess a constellation of qualities which the Athenian is eager to harness for the good of the city and which he believes can cause the city great damage if they are not so directed. The psychology is designed to reconcile these people to citizenship by altering their view of the work proper to the city and their own implication in this work. It does so by presenting soul as the prodigious and excessive cause of all motion and mind as the limit which soul takes upon itself in order to produce orderly motion. The city emerges as the place in which the motion proper to mind is translated into human action and life; human action and life are in turn presented as requiring this extraindividual entity for their completion and happiness. Thus, to return to the passage so puzzling to translators and commentators alike, the priority of soul's motions as a source of ever-flowing being is the first of a pair of cosmological concepts (the direction of mind in the orderly motion of the heavens is the companion) designed to entice the would-be impious person to love the city and to reconcile him or her to citizenship.

***

It would be useful to remind ourselves of the essential features of the Athenian's portrait of the young and potentially impious citizens to whom book 10's preludes are addressed. The impious of book 10 are young, scornful of their education and of the civically sanctioned sources of authority (their parents, other family members, and their elders), and certain of their convictions. Some of them are willing and likely to speak out publicly about their suspicions and beliefs, while others will hide these beliefs and instead manipulate others. For these reasons, they all pose a threat to civic unity. They also request to be persuaded about the truth and hold the legislator to his own stated investment in persuasion. Many of them have a facility for argument and persuasion themselves, and some of them also have a natural love of justice. The impious includes a group of people and a constellation of qualities (stated interest in the truth, facility with argumentation, sharpness of wit, strength of memory, charisma, kinship to the divine) that resemble the philosophic natures described in the *Republic*. The legislator is particularly keen to cultivate and harness these qualities in the service of the city, but also recognizes the harm that is done to the city if he fails to do so.[7] The question that the Athenian and his interlocutors must address is: Can those possessing these natures be reconciled to citizenship? The preludes they deliver to them are designed to do just this.

Because the beliefs productive of impiety in the young are adopted not only through personal weakness but also through a variety of cultural and political factors that grant them persuasive power, the preludes must speak to individual psychology and social institution alike. Much of the work done by these preludes consists in locating the impious within a cosmic structure that places demands upon them. This is to say that the preludes begin their therapeutic work through the very manner in which they address their recipients. The Athenian speaks to all three kinds of impious people in such a manner as to call into question their grasp of reality. The atheist is treated as a rebellious child whose views on the gods and the heavens are neither novel nor likely to stand the test of time (888a–c).[8] The deist's belief that in the apparent flourishing of the unjust he sees, "as in mirrors" (905b), the indifference of the gods to human affairs is criticized as lacking the proper scale and knowledge upon which to base judgments of happiness and unhappiness (899d–900c, 904e–905c). The assumptions about the gods made by those who maintain their tractability are treated as not only false but crass (906d–907b). These strategies of address set the stage for the substance of the preludes, to whose analysis we will turn presently.

It is also worthwhile to remind ourselves that the clinical context of the account of soul in book 10—its occurrence as a prelude and thus as a form of treatment—advises against assuming that it simply contains a statement of what Plato takes to be true about the soul. Rather, the safer assessment to make about the preludes is that they tell us quite a bit about what Plato suspects it is necessary for citizens to believe about the soul, given the political and cultural landscape that has produced the particular condition of soul and set of beliefs the Athenian has just described. This is not to say that Plato is "lying" or is not concerned with the truth.[9] In fact, given the resemblance that some of these potentially impious people have to some of the young men he depicts as particularly philosophically leaning elsewhere in the dialogues, there is reason to believe that Plato constructs the Athenian's "answers" to the impious with particular care. Nevertheless, the curious clinical operation granted to the preludes ties their claims to a particular set of concerns in a way that asserts their immersion within a political environment, not their transcendence of it. Granted the strong political inflection of the preludes in general, it is necessary to ask how we might locate the role of the polis in the relationship between psuchē and cosmos that the preludes assert against impiety. Investigating this question will give us a sharper sense for the vision of health informing the very legislative structure that recommends the use of therapeutic preludes.

As we have seen in the previous chapter, in his prelude to the atheist, the Athenian does not take substantive issue with the atheist's conception of phusis as generation of things primary (892c), but rather with what he takes the primary things to be. In reversing the order given to bodily and psychic things, and thus refiguring the relationship between phusis, technē, and tuchē asserted by the atheist, the Athenian is required to make some remarkable claims about the nature of the soul. The Athenian himself signals this by noting the strangeness and difficulty of their discourse (891d–e) as well as the pervasive ignorance about soul and its origin (892a–b). The cosmic priority which this account grants to psuchē asserts that it is by merit of psychology, or, better, psychogony, that the existence of gods can and must be gleaned from the motion of the heavens. It is this psychogony that is to defeat the incredulity of the atheist by providing an alternate cosmology. The conception of soul, the psychogony and psychology, that the Athenian maintains as capable of combating the atheist's cosmology, and the relationship between soul and mind promoted therein, is decisive for the therapeutic operation of the prelude. It is thus necessary to examine what the Athenian claims one must believe about soul in order to excise atheism from it.

In this prelude, the generative power of soul is a function of its alignment with a kind of motion, an alignment accomplished by appeal to the phenomenon of living being itself. The Athenian presents the kinetics at the heart of this prelude by identifying ten kinds of motion and ordering them according to a hierarchy in which that motion which is capable of moving itself and others is granted the highest honor and conceded to be the motion that causes all others. The Athenian then connects this "self-movement" with psuchē by securing agreement from his interlocutors that: (*a*) the condition of things capable of moving themselves is that of being alive, and (*b*) being alive is also attributed to the operation of soul (895c).[10]

Armed with the account of soul as "self-movement," the Athenian draws out several of its implications: soul is the cause of motion and change in all things (896b);

soul is the oldest (πρεσβυτάτη) of all things generated (896b);[11] soul is prior to body (896b); the "things" of soul are also prior to body (896c–d); soul is the cause of all things, including opposites like good and bad (896d); and the soul controls heaven (896e). As the Athenian elaborates upon how soul causes motion, he and his interlocutors agree that there must be at least two kinds of soul, good soul (soul in cooperation with [προσλαβοῦσα] mind) and bad soul (soul consorting [συγγενομένη] with anoia) (896e–897b). In attempting to determine which kind of soul governs heaven, they investigate which motion is proper to mind, an investigation which requires the creation of an image. Revolution's tendency toward selfsameness recommends it as the best image for the motion of mind (898a–b);[12] as this motion is also most characteristic of the motion of the heavens, they conclude that it is good soul or several good souls that govern the heavens. This conclusion is further illustrated by a consideration of how good soul might govern motion in which the movement of the sun is taken as caused by its soul (which implies that the sun and other heavenly bodies are not soulless) and is indicative of the movement of the cosmos as a whole. They conclude their discussion of the sun's motion by stating that the sun, like the cosmos itself, is moved by a good soul and agree that this soul is a god (899a–b).

The emphasis placed throughout this prelude on the excesses that attend to psuchē and their cosmic effects is decisive for its therapeutic operation. The pervasive ignorance about the soul and its origin (892a–b), the Athenian's characterization of their discourse about the soul as alien and unfamiliar (see 891d, their logos is ἀηθεστέρων and 891e, the logos is οὐκ εἰωθότα) as well as violent (892e–893a),[13] and the account of soul as self-movement (896a) all attest to a certain limitlessness of soul. Indeed, to define soul as self-motion is to attribute to soul an ecstatic character that, as Aristotle observes,[14] renders such an account nearly nonsensical. Nevertheless, this definition and the excess it implies are, in fact, in keeping with the general portrait of the soul that the Athenian has been drawing. A psychology predicated upon self-motion is a psychology of ec-stasis. This ecstatic quality of soul, in turn, gives us some indispensable information about the relationship between soul and mind in the *Laws*.

The ensuing discussion of soul's motion also contains numerous illustrations of this excessive character. The Athenian describes soul's motion as, for instance, infinitely malleable (894c), infinitely excellent (894d), exceedingly effective (894d),[15] and as graspable by mind alone (898e). What mind can tell him and his interlocutors is that there are three ways in which soul might move the body of the sun: psychic infusion, psychic occupation, or some other surpassingly wondrous capacity. Soul either

> "exists everywhere inside of this apparent globular body and directs it, such as it is, just as the soul in us moves us about in all ways; or, having procured itself a body of fire or air (as some argue), it in the form of the body pushes forcibly on the body from outside; or, thirdly, being itself void of body, but endowed with other surpassingly marvelous potencies [ἔχουσα δὲ δυνάμεις ἄλλας τινὰς ὑπερβαλλούσας, θαύματι ποδηγεῖ], it conducts the body." (898e–899a)

The very mind through which they describe these possibilities is itself a source of excess, as is illustrated in the impossibility of describing the movement of reason without an image: "In making our answer let us not bring on night, as it were, at midday, by looking right in the eye of the sun, as though with mortal eyes we could ever behold reason and know it fully; the safer way to behold the object with which our question is concerned is by looking at an image of it" (897d).[16]

Perhaps the most telling illustration of psychic excess, however, is found in the Athenian's account of the motion for which soul is responsible—that is, all motion.[17] Indeed, the prodigious operation of soul is such as to shatter soul: in order to describe the kind of motion that the heavenly bodies conduct, the Athenian finds it necessary to split soul into *at least* two, good soul and bad soul (896d–897b).[18] Thus the soul's excesses comprise also a deficiency, insofar as they require the supplement of mind in order to produce the motion that is observable in the heavens (897b).

We are now in a better position to discern the relationship between soul and mind that is presented by these preludes. The excessive and prodigious acts of soul require a limit if the cosmos is to be orderly and best; the name given to this limit is mind. However, what I find most remarkable about this need for supplement is that soul also invites supplementation: it receives mind as something that is fitting to it, that discloses something about it, that brings to light its capacities, and that augments those capacities.[19] As such a limit, mind would do nothing but enable soul to take on the full variety of forms of motion of which it is capable, and thus this limit is somehow both "external" to it and intimately related to it, intimately its own.[20] Such an enhancing and augmenting limit would act not merely as an *addition* to soul, but as a *prosthetic* to soul. Soul, endlessly malleable, endlessly plastic, endlessly transforming, tends toward prosthesis. Or, to speak more precisely, we could say that soul tends toward prosthetic limits. Mind and its closely related phenomenon, law,[21] are precisely such enhancing and augmenting limits.

To contextualize this claim, recall that the Athenian has described a cosmos for which an assertion of antagonism between phusis and technē, an assertion made by the atheist, is ill-suited because it denies the generative force of soul and the effects of this force. He has also given an account of soul as having been separated into at least two by the excessive and prodigious generation of which it is the cause. While soul can operate without mind, consorting with mindlessness, when soul receives mind, mind provides soul with those limits that allow soul to render its motions orderly.[22] Mind thus has a unique relationship to soul, and I have tried to capture the nature of this relationship with the notion of the prosthetic function (as enabling limit) mind supplies to soul. Further illustration of this prosthetic function can be seen if we turn our attention from the life of the cosmos itself to the character of human life.

The ecstatic character of cosmic soul belongs to living beings as well, insofar as their living is aligned with self-motion, and bears, furthermore, on the very structure of legislation in the dialogue itself. Indeed, it is nomos that helps to bring out the insufficiency of the rigid and antagonistic distinction between phusis and technē, and that operates with the limiting function granted to mind.[23] The clinical function reserved for both law and prelude, emphasized whenever the curative capacity of voicing the law and prelude is observed, attests to law's prosthetic character.[24] What is it that grounds the therapeutic operation of the prelude, what vision of health, if it is, in fact a health of the soul and thus a health of that which cannot be circumscribed by phusis alone? From what the Athenian has said thus far, there is no such absolute ground, and thus the standard of health must be replaced by a vision of human flourishing that is somehow imposed upon soul in the form of prosthetic limits like mind and law.[25] There is at least one important difference among the disease, plague, and injustice which the Athenian presents as all instances of pleonexia (906b–c):[26] diseases and plagues operate within the limits imposed upon them by their "bodily" nature, even if that limit is conceived simply as mortality itself. Injustice does not operate within the same limits, as is evinced by the fact that people who "catch" injustice do not necessarily die from it, and may even appear to flourish from it, to return to the experience that so traumatizes the one who believes the gods neglected human affairs. If injustice, unlike disease, is a corruption that does not carry its own limitation, then human soul is in need of prosthetic limits in order to assure some end to human corruption. Laws are such prosthetic limits. At the same time, the Athenian's cosmology presents such a vision of human flourishing as not simply imposed on soul but invited by soul, just as mind is both somehow external to but also intimately related to soul. The *Laws'* construction of the soul's relation to mind, then, bears a striking resemblance to its construction of the citizen's relation to the city. Both cosmic and individual soul must actively take mind as an ally; for human beings, doing so requires, or at least is greatly facilitated by, a good city.

Such an understanding of the relation between person and city is in keeping with book 1's characterization of law as externalized calculation, and has two important implications for our understanding of the dialogue's psychological investigation. First, it refines our understanding of the *Laws'* emphasis on the need humans have for a city. As the vessel or vehicle of the law, city emerges as that arena in which human beings flourish or flounder, maturate or fail to mature, as that which is outside of the individual human yet allows the human to be most human or to cultivate what is best in herself. Second, it further refines our understanding of the significance of property and ownership in the dialogue, along with the dangers of pleonexia. The desire to own property is treated as a flawed attempt to comprehend how one is divested of oneself, how one can be outside of oneself, an attempt which erroneously concludes that the acquisition of property is perfecting and completing. The careful management and allocation of "private" property (and as we have seen, in Magnesia property really seems to be private in name only, given the limitations of what one may do with "one's" property) is an attempt to overcome this understanding of the possession of property as a "cure" for being outside oneself and to replace ownership (as a means of compensating for a perceived lack) with the dialogue's construction of piety (as a means of accepting that the tools of one's betterment lie outside of oneself).

The vision of theodicy in the charm that supplements the prelude to the deist offers further evidence of soul's tendency toward prosthesis. By means of an elaborate spatial metaphor, the charm delivered to the deist figures theodicy as the movement of souls to appropriate places, a movement conducted by the divine and governed by the cosmic law of "like to like."[27] The specific operation of this charm is to present an account of the cosmos in which theodicy is assured by topography, that is to say, in which souls receive what is appropriate to their condition by being moved to appropriate places. The Athenian presents the belief in the soul's residence in a place as necessary if one is to discern an outline (τύπον ἴδοι) of the truth[28] and give an account of life as regards happiness and unhappiness (λόγον συμβάλλεσθαι περὶ βίου δυνατὸς ἂν γένοιτο εἰς εὐδαιμονίαν τε καὶ δυσδαίμονα τύχην) (905c). As we have seen, in book 12, the soul's priority, immortality, and rulership over all bodies are among the things one must grasp in order to rule (967d–968a). If some opinion about the soul must be supposed in order to discern a trace of the truth, to contribute a logos about happiness and unhappiness, and to rule the city, then an inquiry into the soul involves an inquiry into the fundamental conceptual framework that informs ontology,[29] ethics, and politics. Whatever the specific contributions such a psychology makes to these activities, whatever specific scope or significance it has for each of them, the study of the soul is the study of an entity the belief in which is fundamental to them.[30]

The lengthy charm from 903b–905d develops a psychic topography which unfolds, dreamlike in its condensation of images and displacement of desires, by utilizing a variety of mythic tropes in order to fulfill the wishes of one who wants to be assured of the suffering of the impious. Such a person can be consoled by the belief that:

> "inasmuch as soul, being conjoined now with one body, now with another, is always undergoing all kinds of changes either of itself or owing to another soul,[31] there is left for the draughts-player no further task,—save only to shift the character that grows better to a superior place, and the worse to a worse, according to what best suits each of them, so that each may be allotted its appropriate destiny." (903d)

The Athenian continues: Recognizing that all action both involves soul and contains much that is good and bad, and that when generated (γενόμενον) soul and body are indestructible (ἀνώλεθρον) but not eternal (οὐκ αἰώνιον) (904a), the god,

> "designed a location for each of the parts wherein it might secure the victory of goodness of the whole and the defeat of evil most completely, easily and well. For this purpose He has designed the rule which prescribes what kind of character should be set to dwell in what kind of position and in what regions; but the causes of the generation of any special kind he left to the wills of each one of us men. For according to the trend of our desires and the nature of our souls each one of us generally becomes of a corresponding character. . . . All things that share in soul change, since they possess within themselves the cause of change, and in changing they move according to the law and order of destiny; the smaller the change of character, the less is the movement over surface in space, but when the change is great and towards great iniquity, then they move towards the deep and the so-called

lower regions, regarding which—under the names of Hades and the like—men are haunted by most fearful imaginings, both when alive and when departed from their bodies." (904b–d)

Because all "internal" transformation is repeated in "external" motion, there is no interior depth that is not made apparent by one's location. No one, according to this account, has a secret condition of soul; over time all souls migrate to that place appropriate to them.[32] Thus, a plurality of places would also provide a way of speaking about and discerning kinds of souls. And we should not ignore the strangeness of these places, as the Athenian makes reference not only to Hades but also to the variety of bodies a soul will occupy. As with the myth in the *Phaedo*, both body and region emerge as "places" of the soul insofar as they mirror the souls' character and provide means for speaking about the variety of these characters.[33] The Athenian concludes this psychic topology by addressing those who claim the gods neglect human beings in the grandiose voice of the gods, and states the divine decree that, "as thou becomest worse, thou goest to the company of the worse souls, and as thou becomest better, to the better souls; and that, alike in life and in every shape of death, thou both doest and sufferest what it is befitting that like should do towards like" (904e).

Throughout this prelude and charm, the tropes of ownership and kinship play a decisive role: as not just the property of the gods (902b) but also as kin to the gods by merit of their possession of soul (726e, 906a–b),[34] humans should be assured of the care and attention of the gods. What the god imposes upon human life is the gravitational pull of souls upon one another and toward regions appropriate to them. Thus, this discursive supplement includes a legislative prosthesis: a certain order of movement is imposed upon the soul in the form of the law "like to like," but imposed by those entities who are themselves presented as among the highest manifestation of soul's reception of mind.[35]

This law of "like to like" and the ambiguity attendant upon it—that it is presented as both a function of the god's activity and of the character of soul itself—illustrates the manner in which nomos fluctuates between phusis and technē and thus exhibits soul's excessive character and its need for prosthesis. Several other formulations of the "like to like" law in the dialogue aid in measuring the full significance of this prosthetic. For instance, what is described in book 10 as the action of a god needs to be measured with the characterization of the same state of affairs as automatic earlier in the dialogue. In book 5, the Athenian observes that few people notice the greatest judgment against wrongdoing (κακουργία): "to grow like unto men that are wicked, and, in so growing, to shun good men and good counsel and cut oneself off from them, but to cleave to the company of the wicked and follow after them; and he that is joined to such men inevitably [ἀνάγκη] acts and is acted upon in the way that such men bid one another to act" (728b). Here, the law of "like to like" ensures the inevitability of psychic decay, such that corrupt souls gravitate toward other corrupt souls, eschew the better, cleave to the worse, and act according to the community with which they have surrounded themselves. This passage treats the pull of like to like, the propensity of soul to flock to those like itself, as automatic.[36]

In the prelude delivered to the one contemplating the murder of a parent in book 9, the Athenian employs an ancient "account" in which expiation for the murder of a parent is only attained when "the soul which committed the act pays back murder for murder, like for like" (873a). Here, as with book 10, the law of "like to like" is presented as a formulation of divine justice. Another version of this law occurs in book 8, namely that like is friends with like (837a–b). But the addition of attraction (philia) in this passage, as distinct from the simple association asserted in books 9 and 10, creates a crucial difference between these two "versions" of the ancient rule, a difference to which the Athenian attests when he notes in book 4 that like is attracted to like only among those who are measured (μετρίῳ); for those who lack measure no amity, no friendship is possible (716c). This statement should be weighed against the Athenian's assertion in book 5 that the greatest penalty for wrongdoing is that it makes the wrongdoer more like bad men and puts him in their company (728b–c).

The play between necessity and contingency in these passages suits a therapeutic purpose: it erodes an illusion of self-sufficiency while also fostering a sense of responsibility for the collective; that is, it adjusts a vision of the city. The Athenian is asserting both the irreducibility of human community (the unjust reside in a community, even if they do everything they can to deny that this is the case) and the contingency of the particular character of such communities (the formation of just or unjust communities is at least in part a function of the commission of just and unjust actions). While the association between similars is treated as inevitable, and will in book 10 function as an effect that attends upon the commission of deeds and acts as an automatic penalty for wrongdoers (they must suffer one another's company), that the company or community so forged would be one of friendship is possible only in the absence of wrongdoing (or the presence of measure). The community of souls may be amicable or acrimonious, but necessary nevertheless.

This point is essential in navigating the description of theodicy in book 10, in which a discussion of "physical" space mutates into an emphasis on psychic conglomerates. Insofar as the charm conflates the places appropriate to souls with the community of like souls, "Hades" emerges as signifying the city itself, and city as the scene of the soul's reception of its prosthetic limitation/augmentation. Thus, psychic topography becomes psychic politics. The ultimate result of the legislation against impiety is the allocation of different kinds of impious people to particular kinds of "places," namely prisons (908e–909d). In this sense, the penalty performs in deed what the charm asserts in speech, and creates a this-worldly Hades, a Hades on earth, which would be in keeping with the chilling call in book 9 to create laws on earth that fall in no way short of those in Hades (881b).[37]

It is, however, important to keep in mind that a Hades on earth is deemed necessary because of the particular conception of soul that is at work in the dialogue, a conception in which soul's excesses are not *necessarily* limited by any mandate to promote human flourishing. The locus for such a mandate is the city itself, and thus the city is the place in which soul receives prosthetic limits. In this sense, there is no grounding for psychic prosthesis, for psychic health, outside of the particular political and cultural constellations of particular cities. The specific character of human dwelling and flourishing is, therefore, radically contingent. At the same time, however, such a mandate can be more or less amenable to the soul; there are better and worse prostheses, and the limitless malleability of soul seems also to be precisely that which invites prosthesis. What is emerging here, I submit, is an outline of politics not as the effort to approximate an ideal, but as the effort to devise ever more subtle psychic prostheses, an effort that would involve critical engagement with particular laws and with the practice of legislating itself.[38] This is to say that the scene of psychic phenomena is not simply cosmic, but also deeply political. Both a cosmology and a politics are outlined in the psychology that the Athenian produces in order to convince the impious that there are gods who care for humans and cannot be bribed.

Such a cosmology and politics involves a particular vision of the relationship between psuchē and polis. The psychology at work here provides an image of the city as that arena of human striving wherein human action and psychic condition reciprocally affect one another and coalesce into the character, not only of the individual but of the city itself. It provides a panoptic view of the city as the living medium of action. This psychology is thus an instrument of the *Laws'* legislative effort to make citizens identify with the city itself, to take on its body as their body, its psychic structure as their psychic structure, to see themselves as the sum of the community that their actions help to foster. What such a vision of the city offers the impious in particular is the "assurance" (which the Athenian suggests will seem assuring or threatening, depending on the kind of impious person one is, but therapeutic in either instance) of a this-worldly automaticity of punishment. It does so by presenting the city as the place wherein collectives of human souls form communities of better and worse, thereby providing the environment in which the soul gravitates toward that which it most resembles. Thus, the "like-to-like" law, at once a function of the gods' mindful intercession in the world of human affairs, and an attestation to the tendency toward mind within the human soul, is treated as an impulse toward that revolving, selfsame motion of the heavens, itself the best likeness of the movement of mind.

We are now in a position to summarize how these preludes reconcile their recipients to citizenship. On the surface level, they are reconciled to citizenship insofar as the city in which they are citizens is conceived as having value only to the extent that it is grounded upon and imitates the mind of the divine and they are now convinced that the gods exist, care for human matters, and cannot be bribed. But we also have gained a deeper sense for what this, and the city itself, means. The city imitates the mind of the divine by instantiating, as far as possible, the law of like-to-like; that is to say, by enacting the movement of mind in the lives of the citizens and the institutions, legislation, and architecture of the city. Citizenship becomes a matter of perceiving in a certain way as well as thinking and acting in a certain way. Its value is secured by the work that it does to instill divine/cosmic rationality into the lives of humans. In taking up citizenship, people up take up the task of participating in that being (the city) which delivers divine cosmic order and motion to human life.

The Athenian's preludes attempt to seduce the impious to citizenship by providing a cosmology in which the work of the city is needed, in which the limitlessness of soul as well as the negative effects on human (and cosmic) flourishing of this limitlessness are recognized. It is, moreover, a cosmology in which the limiting of psuchē by mind requires perpetual enactment and instantiation, and where the scenes of this enactment include human political life. The city is capable of realizing the nous that is immanent in human life (traces of which can be seen in dance, in the innate love of justice, in technē, etc.) by providing limits to the excessive and prodigious operations of soul.[39] This account of excessive soul and regulating mind, when seen in conjunction with the earlier account of law as the external expression of that which logismos is the internal expression, helps explain the *Laws*' insistence on the need which the human being has for the city. The human needs the city to be who she is in the best and truest sense. The need of cosmic psuchē for limitation is also true of human psuchē; just as cosmic psuchē can take mind as its ally, so can human psuchē. The human psuchē does so most fully, as we have seen, when it submits itself to laws that are externalized expressions of its own capacity for calculation.[40] Thus, the role of the city is to provide prosthetic limits to the human soul by means of its laws, customs, institutions, etc. In doing so, it translates or applies orderly cosmic motion to human affairs and thus assures the flourishing of the whole. The preludes attempt to convince the impious that they should care about this because their own lives will attain greater perfection in participating in the political project that is the preserving of the city. What is most one's own is also what belongs to the city; to love oneself is to love the city.[41] Thus, the *Laws*' account of psychic excess presents the city as necessary to human life and determines its role as instantiating the orderly motion of the cosmos within human affairs. What the *Laws* takes itself to attempt is less an ethics to be appealed to in the absence of good political institutions[42] than a politics to be appealed to as the most vivid instantiation of the best possibilities of human life.[43]

* * *

By the end of the *Laws*, we find that its legislative project remains radically and necessarily incomplete. In their discussion of the infamous Nocturnal Council, the Athenian and his interlocutors agree that they cannot adequately legislate for the law wardens, a body which must, when it has been properly formed, legislate itself (968c). While the general schema for forming this body has been given in outline, the details of its education (that is, who should receive it, in what its studies consist, and for how long they should be studied) cannot be prescribed in advance (968c).[44] Consequently, concludes the Athenian, "although it would be wrong to term all these matters 'indescribable [ἀπόρρητα], they should be termed 'imprescribable' [ἀπρόρρητα], seeing that the prescription of them beforehand does nothing to elucidate the question under discussion" (968e). Insofar as the Athenian and his interlocutors do not arrive at a detailed account of the education proper to the guardians of the laws, they have failed to provide that sustaining and preserving force necessary, according to the Athenian, for any task to come to completion (960b). In assessing the significance of this failure, we would be well served to recall that the installation of law wardens is an essential feature of the legislative experiment undertaken in the dialogue, as is indicated by the remarkable image used to describe this very project.

The image occurs in book 6, just after the Athenian and his interlocutors have given a general outline of Magnesia's courts and as they turn to discuss its law wardens. Noting that the work of the painter is without limit (οὐδὲν πέρας), that is, it never reaches a point in which the picture "admits of no further improvement in respect of beauty and lucidity" (769a–b), the Athenian draws out the implications of this interminable character in order to extend it to the act of legislation itself:

> "Suppose that a man should propose to paint an object of extreme beauty [ὡς κάλλιστον ζῷον], and that this should never grow worse, but always better, as time went on [καὶ τοῦτ' αὖ μηδέποτε ἐπὶ τὸ φαυλότερον ἀλλ' ἐπὶ τὸ βέλτιον ἴσχειν τοῦ ἐπιόντος ἀεὶ χρόνου], do you not see that, since the painter is mortal, unless he leaves a successor [εἰ μή τινα καταλείψει διάδοχον] who is able to repair [ἐπανορθοῦν] the picture if it suffers through time [ἐάν τι σφάλληται τὸ ζῷον ὑπὸ χρόνων], and also in the future to improve it by touching up any deficiency left by his own imperfect craftsmanship, his interminable toil will have results of but a short duration [σμικρόν τινα χρόνον]." (769b–c)[45]

While there is not here sufficient space to do this image justice, I would like to highlight a few of its features for the sake of suggesting one direction of future investigation. First, the primary emphasis of this image is less on painting as a form of likening or imitating (which could then be extended to legislation as also a form of likening or imitating) than on how to compensate for the fallibility of the painter. Nothing is said of the beautiful object beyond the emphasis on the extremity of its beauty (perhaps we are to think of it as simply divine). The superlative nature of its beauty is treated as capable of coming to expression in a painting that never grows worse and only better, that is, in a painting that has found some means to compensate for its own mortal tendency.[46] The image focuses on the need of the painter to acknowledge his limitations and to educate others who would be capable of compensating for his own fallibility and mortality. The beauty of the painting is not a function of a single genius, but of a community of artists, each of whom is able to acknowledge his own limitation and the collection of which is able to compensate for one another's failings and to preserve one another's excellences. When applied to the act of legislating, the result of this image is an acknowledgment of the limits of any particular legislator and an exhortation to train future legislators:

"you cannot suppose that any lawgiver will be so foolish as not to perceive that very many things must necessarily [ἀνάγκη] be left over, which it will be the duty of some successor to make right [ἃ δεῖ τινα συνεπόμενον ἐπανορθοῦν], in order that the constitution and the system of the state he has organized may always grow better, and never in any way worse [ἵνα μηδαμῇ χείρων, βελτίων δὲ ἡ πολιτεία καὶ ὁ κόσμος ἀεὶ γίγνηται περὶ τὴν ᾠκισμένην αὐτῷ πόλιν]." (769d–e)

Second, the Athenian's elaboration on this model of legislation attributes a dual corrective and preserving activity to the work of the law wardens: "suppose then that a man knew of a device [τίς τινα μηχανὴν] indicating the way in which he could teach another man by deed and word to understand in a greater or less degree how he should conserve or amend laws [ὅπως χρὴ φυλάττειν καὶ ἐπανορθοῦν νόμους], surely he would never cease declaring it until he had accomplished his purpose" (769e). This correcting as well as preserving activity would have to include the cultivation of a robust critical capacity that imparts to the law wardens resources for determining what is worth preserving and what must be corrected. Provided the legislator educates other legislators and equips them with this critical capacity, the mortality of the legislator need not condemn the politeia to decay. Or, put another way, the education of legislators is taken to limit the effects of the mortality of any one legislator; the work of a community of legislators will act as a prosthetic to the failings and mortality of any one legislator.

Finally, this prosthesis has a reproductive quality as well, as evinced by the Athenian's conclusion of this discussion: "since we are in the evening of life, while those compared to us are youthful, we should not only legislate, as we say, ourselves, but also make legislators, as well as Law-wardens, of these very same men, so far as we can" (770a). The education of the law wardens turns them into legislators; in educating law wardens to legislate, the legislators are reproducing themselves. All legislators participate in a single perpetual, corrective, and preserving legislative process.

Book 12's discussion of the Nocturnal Council should thus be read with this image of a self-critiquing and reproducing legislative practice in mind. The installation of the council, as that entity capable of preserving the city and assuring the perpetual beauty of its politeia, is presented as the culmination of the entire legislative project. The Athenian's description of this council, with its rehabilitation of perception by means of the unity of thought and perception that it envisions through the image of the head, in which eyes and mind act in concert (964e–965a), is the "crowning" achievement of a model of citizenship in which the psuchai of citizens are to be calibrated to create a whole, unified, rational living being.

The strangeness of this particular vision of the ensoulment of the city, and of the enterprise undertaken by the *Laws* in general, is made more evident by comparing it with the *Republic*. The subtlety and richness of the *Republic*'s discussion of cities paves the way for its reformulation of politics as operative in both city and soul and its subsequent exhortation to attend to the politeia of one's psuchē (592a–b). The *Republic*'s overarching focus on psychic politics presents the exemplary status it grants to philosophy as a function of philosophy's purported ability to successfully instantiate and preserve the politeia that is most illustrative of human beings' divine kinship. I would thus agree with G. R. Ferrari's assessment that in the *Republic,* the city "at its best supports its philosophic class; but except in this sense, the city does not philosophize."[47] I submit, however, that the *Laws* contemplates the reversal of this state of affairs, that it develops a conception of the city as capable of becoming beautiful and approximating the divine, and that it considers individual souls as material and engines for this civic process. In the *Laws,* Plato allocates to the city that action which, in the *Republic,* is best accomplished by the philosopher: becoming godlike. The *Laws* envisions not a city of philosophers but a philosophizing city.[48]

The failure of the dialogue's legislative enterprise should tell us something about Plato's assessment of the possibility of such a city. Nevertheless, the seeds of this failure should not go unnoticed. One reason the Athenian gives for his and his interlocutors' inability to arrive at an education proper to the guardians of the laws is the radical novelty of the characters they are describing. The result of the education and upbringing they can outline but not describe in detail in advance would be law wardens, "the like of whom we have never before seen in our lives for excellence in safeguarding" (969c). The best that they can determine at this point is that what is required to form the legislative body that their city needs "is teaching by means of prolonged conferences [διδαχὴ μετὰ συνουσίας πολλῆς]" (968c). I take the reticence in legislating advised by the novelty of these characters to be a crucial feature of the dialogue's overall approach toward legislation. Like the good doctor, the legislator renders unnecessary the imposition of his work. That this reticence marks an acknowledgment of the limits of human legislation on the part of the founders of Magnesia themselves, and a turn away from legislation and toward discernment and conversation, that is, teaching with extensive interaction, stands as a significant statement about the *Laws*' conception of politics as "therapy" of the soul.

Conclusion

The failure that marks the end of the *Laws* can also been seen as extending to the psychological investigation of all three of the dialogues we have been studying. With respect to an account of soul, the three dialogues we have investigated are aporetic. This aporetic dimension opens up for philosophical reflection the work that is accomplished by belief in the soul (specifically by belief in an immortal soul) and explores the significant political and philosophical implications of psychology. As we have seen, Plato's analysis of vice hones this aporia by calling attention to the soul's unique relation to its own corruption. Riddled with dissent and scarred by its actions, the vicious soul presents a fundamental enigma for Plato, namely, that of an entity whose capacity to endure its own fragmentation is contained within what it means for this entity to be. Plato's attempt to configure this capacity as a certain limitlessness of soul, that is, his thematization of vice as pleonexia decisively shapes his understanding of another expression of this limitlessness, soul's immortality. How a thing can be both a complex entity and deathless remains for Plato a living question without clear or solid resolution.

However, as the critical character of Plato's evaluations of his accounts of soul suggest, the aporetic dimension of Plato's psychology includes a diagnosis of itself, a sense of the limits and flaws within the conversation that led to aporia, and that fuel the inquiry by opening up avenues for further thought. Platonic aporia is not simply skeptical but also provocative and creative. It allows us to deepen our grasp of the questions that gave rise to the aporetic impasse. As we have seen, the critical iconography Plato employs in his investigation of soul in the *Phaedo*, *Republic*, and *Laws* gives rise to its own critique and to the dialectical mythology by means of which the limits of investigation and its stakes are explored.

Working within traditional language and images, Plato turns them on themselves, revealing both their possibilities and their limitations (as, for example, his demonstration of the inadequacy of health as a standard for human life). The result of these efforts is less a method than a practice, that is, the cultivation of a critical stance whose object is human political life, taking the polis as the place in which human life emerges and shapes itself by the interactions between psuchai that it makes possible. It thus gives rise to a very particular and powerful form of analysis, the reflexive and self-critical analysis of human political life with respect to the actions and passions, the excellences and atrocities to which it gives expression. Both a theoria of the polis (a vision of the city) and a psychoanalysis (an evaluation of the soul), Plato's psychological explorations outline a critical theory that is also a way of life.

Notes

Introduction

1. The translation is that of Lamb (1927), the Greek text that of Denyer (2001); I accept Denyer's arguments for Platonic authorship of the dialogue.
2. We must maintain also the possibility that these are two ways of saying the same thing. The dialogue's conclusion, in which Socrates and Alcibiades exchange roles and the lover becomes the beloved, underscores the sense in which the differences between individual souls fade when soul as such is the object of consideration.
3. He does so in order to stress that while their conversation is in words, their interaction is between their souls; nevertheless, in order for logos to provide the medium for this interaction, logos must speak to the soul, a point Socrates emphasizes in the next line, observing that, in using words, he is conversing with Alcibiades, not with his face (130e).
4. Conceived in the broadest of senses and with the ambiguity of the genitive fully intended, that is, a logos about psuchē and a logos that belongs to psuchē.
5. The demands of euphony are real, however, even granted this inadequacy. For this reason, throughout this book, I will use "psychology" as shorthand for "account of the soul" without intending to assume a particular form or content to such accounts and while acknowledging that there are good grounds to wonder whether we can gather any systematic "theory of the soul" from Plato's dialogues that matches the contemporary meanings of "psychology." Similarly, I will accept the standard rendering of "soul" for psuchē and "mind" or, occasionally, "reason" for nous as simply the closest approximations in English currently recognized, while also agreeing that such renderings are flawed.
6. In contemporary scholarship, Norbert Bloessner's work offers a particularly rigorous challenge to the assumption that Plato has a "psychology" at all (Bloessner 1997 and 2007).
7. As well as criticizing the accounts of others (see, for instance, Socrates's critique in the *Phaedrus* of the way in which the term "immortal" is commonly used [246b]).
8. This tentative and exploratory character has not always been given the sustained attention it deserves in the scholarship on Plato's psychology. Instead, Plato's assertions about soul have often been treated as doctrinal, and their ambiguities as fatal. This trend is particularly evident in early and mid-twentieth-century Anglo-American scholarship (see, for instance, Burnet [1916]; Guthrie [1978]; Cherniss [1954]; and the translations and commentaries on the *Republic* by Cornford [1941] and Paul Shorey [1956]). Robinson (1995) is in many ways an exception to his trend, although Robinson maintains the tendency to draw conclusions about coherence without giving sufficient attention, in my opinion, to the possibility that a term's polysemy may have been precisely why Plato chose it, and to have resonances that do not survive translation. See note 19 below.
9. For instance, the image of the soul in the *Phaedrus* is introduced by the qualification that only the gods can speak of soul as it is; humans must make do with a likeness (ἔοικεν) (246a). The myth that concludes the arguments for immortality in the *Phaedo* also contains a careful qualification of its account of the soul's afterlife (114d). Even the extensive discussions of soul that occur in the *Timaeus* unfold within the context of a "likely story" (τὸν εἰκότα μῦθον) (29c–d).
10. Indeed, the much-maligned discussion of immortality in *Republic* 10 is based upon the dialogue's attempt to demonstrate the unique nature of soul's viciousness. For a defense of the relevance and significance of this discussion, see chapter 7 of this book.

11. Scholars have long pointed out that what Plato means by immortality is far from clear, a fact of which Plato himself seemed quite well aware. Much of the controversy hinges on two points of contention. The first is whether Plato exploits the ambiguity between two connotations of athanatos (divine and deathless) to such a degree as to render his claim that soul is "immortal" meaningless. The essays contained in the third section of Wagner (2001) provide a helpful summary of the ambiguity that adheres to Plato's description of soul as immortal and the scholarly consternation it has caused. For a concise discussion of this ambiguity in the context of the *Symposium*, see O'Brien (1984). The second is whether Plato believes soul as a whole is immortal or just the calculating part. See especially the classic treatment of this issue in the context of the *Republic* in Szlezak (1976). See also Annas (1981, 312); and Reeve (1988, 111). The amount of attention paid to the personal versus nonpersonal immortality debate strikes me as at least in part a function of concerns that Plato may not share insofar as they are informed by a tradition which, while certainly appropriative of Platonic text, is not one under which he can be entirely subsumed. At the very least, what Plato means by immortality, what he does with it, and what he takes it to imply both conceptually and ethically needs to be investigated without the personal/impersonal immortality debate placed front and center.

12. See, for instance, the characterization of thought as silent conversation with oneself (*Theaet.* 190a; *Soph.* 263d-e), and of learning as depending upon the soul's capacity to be confused and to house multiple competing impressions and motivations (*Phdo.*, 74b-75b; *Rep.* 523a-525a), which is in turn connected to the accounts of soul as partite in nature in the *Republic*, *Phaedrus*, and *Timaeus*. Morevoer, in the *Theaetetus*, opinion is presented as the cessation of division, and thus as the cessation of thought, the calcified remnant of the practice of dialogue (190a).

13. The most vivid discussion of which is the *Republic*'s account of the tyrant, whose cruelty is a function of his possessing a soul so fragmented as to be incapable of achieving its desires while still able to drive the tyrant to vicious deeds (571a-575a).

14. See, for instance, *Phaedrus* (245c-249d); and *Laws* (895e-896a).

15. See, for instance, *Republic* (353d); and *Laws* (895c).

16. As David Claus has persuasively argued, the influence of medical and sophistic conceptions of soul therapy on Plato's accounts of soul merits particular emphasis: "The Platonic use of ψυχή in the earlier dialogues involves the moralization and revaluation of many traditional contexts of ψυχή, but the decisive early use is here taken to be moralization of the psychosomatic ψυχή of fifth-century medical and sophistic soul therapy" (1981, 182–83). Claus then concludes: "The Platonic use of ψυχή in the early dialogues is in fact radically at odds with traditional uses, and Plato himself repeatedly makes us aware of this. It is also true, however, that by the late fifth century an important confluence was beginning to be seen between ψυχή as the archaic 'life-force' with its traditional psychological characteristics and ψυχή as a naturalistic 'life-force' whose psychological behavior could be rationally predicated and controlled" (183).

17. The influence of the *Republic*'s efforts to view the soul *as* the city have, at times, obscured this (see Ferrari [2005]).

18. This is Robinson's (1995) list. Plato inherited many of these senses (see Dodds [1971, 179]). General treatments of ancient psychology can be found in: Green and Groff (2003); Bremmer (1983); Rohde (1950); Snell (1982); and Everson (1991). For Plato's relation to these, see Solmsen (1983); and for general discussions of Plato's psychology, see the four chapters on Platonic psychology in Benson (2009); and Allan Silverman's chapter on psychology in Shields (2003, 130–44).

19. As has been one dominant scholarly tendency. Robinson (1995) provides a particularly succinct formulation of this argument. Robinson views the ambiguity between psuchē as life force (a conception that Robinson reads as morally neutral and as responsible for what he calls purely "biological" life) and psuchē as a moral agent (operative whenever Plato treats the soul as a primarily rational or cognitive entity) as spilling over into a critical ambiguity adhering to Plato's conception of life, the same ambiguity at work in his use of eu prattein (namely, that between living well understood as living in a morally

upright manner and living well in the sense of living prosperously) (see Robinson [1995, 35–39, 152–53]; as well as Shorey [1933, 482; and 1956, 100]). As will become clear, I have reservations about whether it is appropriate to attribute to Plato a firm distinction between "biological" and "rational" or "cognitive" concerns—it cannot simply be assumed that living things do not strive toward reason or have a rational trajectory for Plato; if we are to take seriously Timaeus's claim that the kosmos itself is alive, we must concede that Plato at least flirts with this possibility—nor am I convinced that Plato has a sense of purely biological life at all; "biological life" is a phrase that may be meaningful to us, but would have been very close to redundant in the Greek at least with respect to human life (although whether this is only true for human life is the matter of some debate [see Findlayson's (2010) critique of Agamben's (1998) construal of the distinction between bios and zōē]).

20. Indeed, there are a number of passages throughout the dialogues that suggest that the confluence of living and ruling is precisely one of the enigmas human life presents to philosophic reflection. When, for instance, the Athenian Stranger remarks upon the wonder-provoking spontaneous eruption of order in dance and in those people who seem to have a natural love for justice (*Nom.* 664e–665a, 899d, 908b–c), or the Eleatic Stranger wonders at the strength and endurance of a city in the face of the many threats to its integrity (*Pol.* 302a), or Socrates marvels at the emergence of young people who have managed to avoid adopting the opinions about justice and injustice held by their peers and superiors, or at the occurrence of philosophic natures even in corrupt regimes (*Rep.* 367c–368b, 496a–e), Plato both highlights the provocation to thought made by these phenomena (What must human being, city, and philosophy be such that they exhibit these capacities?) and sets them up as standards by which to judge their respective account. Any adequate treatment of the human being, the city, and philosophy must include an analysis of these phenomena.

21. Plato may not go so far as Isocrates and describe the politeia of a city as its psuchē (7.14), but his descriptions of city as a living being do come close to such a claim.

22. In Plato's *Symposium*, Diotima includes laws in her list of the children of psuchē (209a–e).

23. It is also consistent with figurations of legislation in the dialogues. I have in mind here in particular the *Protagoras*, in which dikē is presented as a gift from Zeus meant to correct Epimethean shortsightedness in denying humans any means to defend themselves (321c–322c), and the *Laws* (see chapter 10 of this book). The idiom has been taken up by Freud (1961), for whom it bears the tension between the necessary and the ornamental, as well as a variety of other cultural and literary theorists and philosophers, many of whom emphasize precisely the term's ambiguity. For an early application of the idiom to media theory, see McLuhan (1964). Derrida's sustained meditation on the logic of the supplement employs the trope of prosthesis as well in a variety of texts (see esp. Derrida [1998]). The impact of the idiom on deconstruction has been long-standing (see Stiegler [2001]). On the various uses of prosthesis in architecture, see Wigley (1991); and Wills (1995). For more critical assessments of the use of prosthesis, see Jain (1999) and, more recently, Smith and Mona (2006); and Brill (2011).

24. See, for instance, *Ap.* 23a–b; *Rep.* 500b–c, 604 b–c, 608b–c; and *Nom.* 803b).

25. For an interpretation which connects a number of otherwise divergent scholarly approaches to Plato, see, for instance, Bobonich (2002); Ludwig (2007); and McNeill (2010).

26. See Annas (1982); Sedley (1991); D. White (1989); Burger (1984); and Dorter (1982).

27. A digression often seen as stemming from a variety of more or less problematic stances toward mortality: religious conservatism, mysticism, bad faith, cynical demagoguery. Popper's (1971) critique of Plato is perhaps the most extreme form of this criticism; Annas's (1981, 349) description of the myth of Er as a "vulgarity" and "painful shock" is often pointed to as representative of a milder form of this trend in scholarship.

28. Hence the frequent attribution of the myth to another source, for example, Er, people by whom Socrates has been persuaded, etc.

29. See, in particular, the pivotal recent studies of Brisson (2000); Morgan (2000); and Partenie (2009); along with the earlier studies of Stewart (1905) and Futiger (1930).

30. Of which Morgan (2000) is exemplary.

31. Baracchi's (2001) treatment of the myth of Er is especially thought-provoking, as is Fussi's (2001) treatment of the *Gorgias* myth.

32. Sedley 2009, 51.

33. The dialogues have a variety of ways of referring to "kinds of lives"; as, for example, an "arrangement of life [τὴν τοῦ ζῆν παρασκευήν]" (*Pol.* 307e); "patterns of lives [βίων παραδείγματα]" (*Rep.* 617d); and "ways of life [τὰ τῶν βίων . . . σχήματα]" (*Nom.* 803a).

34. I will argue presently that accounts of the relationship between logos and muthos in the dialogues, especially those that treat the myths as delivering a theory or doctrine rather than engaging in inquiry, often overlook this critical dimension. For a helpful review of several more prominent approaches to Plato's myths, although one which assumes a few of the claims I will challenge, see Catalin Partenie's introduction to his edited collection (Partenie 2009, 1–27).

35. And thus bring to bear on them the recent work done on Plato's use of myth more generally (see esp. Morgan [2000]).

36. Nightingale 2002. I would add to Nightingale's excellent analysis only that the eschatological myths draw out not only the extrahuman context in which the individual human life unfolds, but also the extraindividual context; that is, they figure not only the cosmos but also the city.

37. For Plato, the comportment that people have to their own mortality is of interest to both politics and philosophy: politically speaking, it affects the way people behave toward one another and the city; philosophically speaking, fear of death can impede philosophical reflection. The dialogues present a number of attitudes toward mortality, including the denial of death, a posture to which Plato gives poetic expression in the *Phaedo*, for instance, in Socrates's account of those sorrowful souls who refuse to acknowledge their separation from body and who haunt the graveyard, unwilling to leave the side of their former companion (108a–c). Cephalus's account in the *Republic* of his friends who, having denied the existence of any cosmic judge of their actions in their youth, are stricken with anxiety and fear in their old age offers another example of the effects of the denial of one's mortality (330d–331a).

38. Perhaps the fullest expression of this collusion between muthos and nomos can be found in the disturbing fusion of myth and law for which the Athenian calls in the *Laws*; it will be necessary, he asserts, to formulate laws that will create a Hades on earth in order to persuade the most recalcitrant souls against the commission of evil deeds (881a–b). The function the Athenian attributes to such laws, namely to act as an antidote to bellicose and acquisitive natures, suggests that for Plato it is the city and not the soul that secures the cohesion and endurance of the individual. For further discussion of this issue in the *Laws* see section 3 of this book.

39. See for instance, *Phaedo*, 114d–115a; *Rep.* 618b–e; and, to the extent that discerning happiness and unhappiness are bound up with philosophy, *Nom.* 905c.

40. Indeed, in the *Phaedo* this exemplarity is pointed out as part of an outline of the philosopher's capacities with respect to the study of Being rather than the study of soul.

41. It is not listed among the studies making up the curriculum for philosophic natures in *Republic* 7, for instance, even though in book 10 an understanding of the nature of the soul is presented as necessary in order to choose one's life well. For discussion of the relationship between these two passages, see chapter 7 of this volume.

42. See, for instance, Gonzalez (1995 and 1998); Nightingale (1996); Sallis (1996); Gordon (1999); Levin (2000); Russon and Sallis (2000); Blondell (2002); and Hyland (2004).

43. Of the five dialogues in which detailed eschatological myths appear (*Phaedo, Gorgias, Phaedrus, Republic, Laws*), the *Gorgias* myth, while rich and provocative, is relatively short, and the *Phaedrus* myth occurs in the middle of the dialogue. The *Timaeus* presupposes a for- and afterlife of soul, but does not go into great detail about either. A comprehensive study of Plato's afterlife myths would have to address all of these, but such a study is beyond the scope of this book.

44. *Politics* 2.6.1264b26–27.

45. To be sure, a firm distinction between pollution and purification on the one hand, and sickness and disease on the other cannot be presupposed in classical Greek culture, much to the chagrin of the authors of Hippocratic texts like "The Sacred Disease." Nevertheless, the attempt to distinguish the medical art from ritual purification stands as one of the persistent themes in a number of Hippocratic texts and was an intellectual movement of which Plato was a keen observer, as we will see.

46. Cornford 1941, xxvii.

47. See fn 11 above.

48. Solmsen (1942, 192–93).

Part I

1. Wagner (2001) contains several of the most influential critical assessments of these arguments. See also Beck's (1999, 132–38) discussion of Socrates's own awareness of the inadequacy of the logoi. At the same time, there are a number of defenses of the arguments' collective validity (see, for instance, Dorter [1977]; Pakulak [2003]; and Lesser [2003]). Nevertheless, H. G. Gadamer's assessment of the four logoi is particularly succinct and representative: "the *Phaedo*'s poetic power to convince is stronger than its arguments' logical power to prove" (Gadamer 1980, 22).

2. See Edmonds's assessment of *Phaedo* commentary as regards its concluding myth (Edmonds 2004, 160). There are, of course, exceptions to this absence of discussion (see, for instance, Dorter [1982]; Burger (1984); D. White (1989); Annas (1982); and Sedley (1991). Sedley argues that the myth fulfills the expectations of a teleological explanation of the earth established in Socrates's autobiographical speech in the middle of the dialogue. However, Gail Fine's response to Sedley (Fine 1991) persuasively calls into question the validity of Sedley's assertion of the intended expectation of a teleological account; moreover, Sedley deals almost exclusively with only the first third of the myth. I find David White's account of the myth as fulfilling the teleology hinted at in Socrates autobiography compelling (D. White 1989, 221–69); however, Fine's response to Sedley also applies to White. Further, White makes little of the critical component of the myth to which I would like to draw attention.

3. References to *peithein* abound in the dialogue (see, for instance, 70b, 77a, 77e, 83a 88c, 88d, etc.). While the *Phaedo* is not generally studied for its relevance to Plato's work on rhetoric, the relationship between rhetoric and the soul is emphasized in the *Phaedrus* (270c–274b), particularly as regards the need for a rhetorician to be a student of the types of souls. The prominence the *Phaedo* gives to the investigation into soul, the taxonomy of souls it attempts and its emphasis on persuasion recommend an inquiry into the *Phaedo*'s rhetorical dimension.

4. For instance, Socrates fears that his and his interlocutors logos about the immortality of the soul has passed away and must be brought back to life (89b–c); further, he offers an account of the dangers of misology (89d–91c), and shares his interlocutors' concern (although for different reasons) that philosophical logos will die with him (76b, 91a–c).

5. See Ronna Burger's discussion of the myth of Theseus in framing the dialogue (Burger 1984, 17–22).

6. This is not to say that there is no difference between logos and muthos, but rather that it is ill-advised to valorize one over the other because neither logos nor muthos is authoritative to the degree that both have been taken to be. As I hope to show, the two supplement one another.

7. As Gadamer has pointed out, we gain much in our understanding of the structure and style of these four logoi by viewing them as responses to Plato's own suspicions about the capacity of both the scientific discourse of mathematics and the rhetorical displays of the sophists to yield accounts of the soul (Gadamer 1980, 21–28). I would simply add that the critical engagement Gadamer attributes

to the four logoi is also present in the myth of the earth and that it is this critical stance that draws the two modes of discourse together.

Chapter 1

1. Indeed, as I hope to make clear, Plato's treatment of the theology that helps to open up the dialogue's investigation of soul suggests that unmediated access to soul is impossible; soul cannot be investigated directly, but must be viewed through some image or even a variety of images. At the same time, this state of affairs only punctuates the importance of making explicit the border and limits of the images with which one is operating in order to avoid mistaking one's view as unobstructed or unmediated and perhaps even to refine it.

2. There are many grounds to compare the defense Socrates gives to his friends in the *Phaedo* with the defense he gives to his Athenian jurors in the *Apology*, in which Evenus makes an appearance, not the least of which is their complementary accounts of Socratic piety as inexplicably tied with testing, inquiry, and investigation (see *Ap*. 21b, 22a, 23b, 23b–c). All citations of the *Phaedo*, unless otherwise noted, are taken from the Brann, Kalkavage, and Salem translation (1998).

3. This hesitation also invites comparison with another character whom Plato depicts confronting his own mortality, Cephalus. Indeed, Cephalus's piety stands in stark contrast to the depiction of Socratic piety in both the *Apology* and *Phaedo*.

4. For a lucid (although firmly developmentalist) discussion of the issues informing Plato's presentation of Socrates's position on suicide, especially regarding the impact these issues have on the claim frequently made that Cebes is objecting to a contradiction Socrates has produced, see Miles (2001). As will become clear, despite my agreement with Miles's assessment that this passage is born out of a tense engagement with Pythagoreanism (257), I am not entirely convinced that Plato's engagement with Pythagoreanism can be so clearly distinguished from a theorizing of Plato's own for which he finds Pythagorean imagery useful and thus that that he chooses to call Pythagorean.

5. Socrates's response to Cebes's admission that he had heard such things but has not yet heard an adequate account of them is instructive. Socrates tells Cebes, "But you should take heart [προθυμεῖσθαι], maybe you'll hear something" (62a).

6. The extent to which Philolaus's cosmology is in keeping with the teachings of Pythagoras himself, however, continues to be a source of debate. The most definitive and widely adopted case for the denial of scientific and philosophical teachings to the historical Pythagoras is made by Walter Burkert (1972). More recently, Charles Kahn has made a compelling argument for a more positive portrait of Pythagoras scientific and mathematical achievements (2001).

7. And here one should avoid assuming that the principle of this unity could be reduced to either mathematics or ethics; nor should one assume that one was necessarily ancillary to the other in Plato's thought. I would add that the challenge that many dialogues pose around this question is to think of both as emerging from a single source.

8. It is possible that we are to read in this willingness a rejection of the silence demanded of initiates in the earliest form of Pythagoreanism known to us, or perhaps the tacit claim that Socrates and his interlocutors have now moved beyond the position of initiates. While both of these suggestions are possible, we should note the playful tenor of Socrates's engagement with his interlocutors.

9. The dubiousness with which Socrates treats what is considered the most characteristically Orphic component of this tradition is significant; Socrates describes the account of the Mysteries as "a grand one and not easy to make out" (62b).

10. This assertion of the gods' care for and ownership of humans merits comparison with the accounts of the nature of the gods' care for humans in the *Euthyphro* and the *Laws*.

11. In emphasizing the distance Plato suggests between Socrates and the true-born philosophers described in this section of the *Phaedo*, I diverge from Vasiliou's (2012) claim that Socrates is presented as a representative of this group. As will become clear, I argue that the Socrates of the *Phaedo* has his eye on embodied philosophy, and an interest in this-worldy philosophical community, to a greater extent than Vasiliou allows.

12. That Pythagoras's capacity to impart to his followers a manner of living was particularly impressive to Plato is suggested by the fact the Pythagoras's espousal of a way of life is emphasized in the only direct reference to Pythagoras in the Platonic dialogues (at *Republic* 600a), prompting Kahn to speculate that "Pythagorean society may well have served as inspiration for the educational institution that Plato in turn was to organize in the Academy" (Kahn 2001, 10). Robert Parker attributes similar significance to the Pythagorean way of life as of particular interest to Plato (Parker 1996, 281–307).

13. LSJ, s.v.

14. In Homeric vocabulary, thumos was one way of referring to the heart. In modern Greek, it simply means anger. In both cases, thumos has close ties with that particularly ineluctable connection between soul and body that is at play when one becomes spirited; thus, προθυμία calls to mind the thumoeidetic or spirited dimension of soul described at length in the *Republic*.

15. This notion of getting in touch with philosophy in the right way is a bit odd, to say the least. As the defense progresses, the notion of getting in touch with philosophy becomes increasingly problematic, as it is precisely in his turn away from the senses and toward thought that the philosopher pursues the truth of which he is the lover. Early on, then, the inadequacy of the concepts available to Socrates and his interlocutors announces itself at the same time that the kernel of truth these concepts attempt to express is acknowledged and explored.

16. Pakulak (2003) argues that Socrates's defense does comprise an argument for substance dualism. I maintain, however, that given the evidence highlighted above, Plato deliberately distances Socrates from the "true-born" philosophers whom he describes in this defense. The relationship between soul and body presented in the defense is interrogated and critiqued throughout the rest of the dialogue.

17. For similar treatments of Socrates's discussion of the "true-born" philosophers, see Burger (1984, 37–50); and Sallis (2002).

18. That the eventual discussion of this description will play in particular upon the words they use to describe and account for death is hinted at in the somewhat awkward way Socrates introduces it, namely, his asking Simmias whether they can agree that there is some thing called death (64c).

19. At 67d, he refers to this formulation as "what goes by the name" of death, but of course this is not the same as a definition and Socrates formulates the phrase in the interrogative.

20. Explicit discussion of the temporally prior condition of community between body and soul is given in the third logos (82e–83a).

21. The "itself by itself" formulation is first used in their agreed definition of death, the separation of soul and body such that each are alone themselves by themselves.

22. The play between touch and sight that occurs here and throughout the dialogues suggests also an intimacy between epistemology and ethics.

23. Parker 1996, 121. Evidence of this expressive character of the contact evoked here through reference to touch and to pollution and purification can also be seen in ancient Greek attitudes toward homicide, a deed that institutes a polluting context into which all parties related by the deed are drawn and affected (Parker 1996, 108–9). Within such a conception, the deed inaugurates a community and creates a kind of space. Vernant (1990, 134–54) also emphasizes the instituting character of homicide as the Greeks conceived of it: "The effects of the defilement thus cover a field of action in which the constituent parts and moments are connected. In the case of murder, for example, the miasma is embodied in all the beings or objects that are involved in the crime:

the murderer, the weapon, the blood, and the victim. If the crime is of a sacrilegious nature, the uncleanliness, in the form of a loimos, may even embrace an entire territory, causing the women to be infertile, the herds to be barren, and the children to be born deformed. The objects on which the power of the daimon works comprise a whole more or less extensive system of human, social, and cosmic relations the order of which has been upset by the sacrilegious disruption. Basically, it is this disorder that the defilement makes manifest through all the various concrete forms it adopts."

24. For instance, in the case of pollution by a corpse, there is strong evidence to suggest that it is the dead person's blood relations, and not just those in the house with the corpse, who are polluted (see Parker [1996, 39–40]); granting his reticence to draw final conclusion because of lack of evidence, it is nevertheless the case that actually having touched the corpse is not necessary to be polluted by it, entering the same social space as the corpse is sufficient. Vernant (1990, 131–32), too, in arguing against the positivist model of pollution promoted by Moulinier, emphasizes this communicative character: "Thus, 'physical' dirt, in the sense understood by Homer and Hesiod, can itself only be understood within the framework of religious thought. A 'besmirchment' seems to indicate some contact that is contrary to a certain order of the world in that it establishes communication between things that ought to remain quite distinct from each other. Such a contact is the more dangerous the more powerful the objects concerned."

25. See Vernant 1990, 134–35.

26. In this passage, Socrates also characterizes the body as shaking the soul up in its communion with her, another emphasis on the body's capacity to affect the soul.

27. If we keep in mind the characterization of the Athenian people that Thucydides attributes to a Corinthian envoy to the Spartans, we can imagine many examples of such a way of life in Plato's Athens.

28. Parker 1996, 281–82.

Chapter 2

1. This temporal structure is emphasized by the repetition of πάλιν, which appears three times in as many lines.

2. A Socratic homecoming (see Gordon [2012]).

3. Further, the extension to all animal and plants in the passage cited above is very similar to a move Eryximachus makes in the *Symposium* (186a–b).

4. An antagonism attested to by Hippocratic texts like "On the Sacred Disease."

5. In the fourth logos, Socrates will clarify the discussion of contraries in the first logos by describing it as a discussion of things with contraries and not of contraries themselves. This character is left undetermined in the actual discussion itself, which furthers the sense of interlocking relationship between the four demonstrative logoi.

6. As we shall see, Socrates's awareness of this lack is indicated by the attention erotic engagement receives in the second logos.

7. This is not to assume that there is no erotic tinge to Simmias's and Cebes's relationship; the point here is that by merit of their being peers, their friendship does not have the formal pederastic structure of ἐραστής and ἐρώμενος.

8. The implication David Sedley takes this indifference to have for traditional construals of Platonic metaphysics is significant, namely that the Form-particular relationship is not dependent on resemblance (Sedley 2006, 318–21). The significance of the progression of examples for Plato's psychology is relevant to our present inquiry. I will argue that not only does the erotic example illustrate recollection from a non-resemblance-based relation, but also that the entire progression

poses a question that Socrates will explore as this conversation continues; namely, what resemblance- and non-resemblance-based relationships might have in common such that they both give rise to recollection.

9. Note this language of "we claim" again as though Socrates is drawing out from Simmias a kind of creed and gesturing toward their own community. But note also the interrogative at the end.

10. LSJ, s.v.

11. Sedley calls attention to the uniqueness of this formulation (Sedley 2006, 324–26). I maintain that part of its role in the *Phaedo* is to further "naturalize" the human soul by claiming a kinship between its striving after being and the striving of all things, which in turn furthers the suggestion that the philosophical soul is at home in the cosmos.

12. For an account of the breadth of erotic phenomena across several dialogues, see Gordon 2012.

13. LSJ, s.v.

14. τῷ μὲν θείῳ καὶ ἀθανάτῳ καὶ νοητῷ καὶ μονοειδεῖ καὶ ἀδιαλύτῳ καὶ ἀεὶ ὡσαύτως κατὰ ταὐτὰ ἔχοντι ἑαυτῷ ὁμοιότατον εἶναι ψυχή, τῷ δὲ ἀνθρωπίνῳ καὶ θνητῷ καὶ πολυειδεῖ καὶ ἀνοήτῳ καὶ διαλυτῷ καὶ μηδέποτε κατὰ ταὐτὰ ἔχοντι ἑαυτῷ ὁμοιότατον αὖ εἶναι σῶμα.

15. By a vocabulary of the mortal and bodily, I have in mind the use of words and concepts that denote a complexity and variety of conditions (for instance, those of diseases and the desires like hunger and thirst that are most associated with embodiment) that are rendered senseless or nearly senseless without reference to the body.

16. I do not mean to suggest that Socrates presumes a robust conception of forms at this stage in the *Phaedo*. Dimas (2003) argues that rather than employing the forms as part of the proof for the soul's immortality, Socrates attempts to demonstrate both the immortality of the soul and the ontological status of the forms in the dialogue. For my own purposes, it is sufficient to note that the affinity between eternal and changeless ideas and the soul, whether that affinity be established on the basis of the *assumption* of the former, or in *conjunction* with an assertion of the former, suggests the possibility that an investigation of forms is sufficient to yield an account of the soul. As I go on to argue, it is precisely this suggestion that is called into question by Socrates's account of the exchange between body and soul.

17. Cass Weller concludes that, given the soul's capacity to be affected by the body, we must assert that the soul is "two-faced" (Weller 2001, 38).

18. Even then, there is no guarantee that this concern will be resolved. The incompatibility of the soul's complexity and its deathlessness have plagued assessments of Plato's assertions of the soul's immortality throughout the dialogues (see the introduction to this volume).

19. That in doing so Socrates and his interlocutors will become victims of the very associations and affinities they have been articulating is suggested by Plato when he has Socrates and Cebes limit the distinction between visible and invisible to a human context and perspective (79b), and of course how they could have any other perspective is a question the dialogue also poses.

20. That there is some sliding here between being in the company of gods and becoming godlike has not escaped commentators' notice and will reappear more sharply in the myth, at which point it will receive further attention.

21. See Gillespie (1912).

22. In fact, this grammatical structure is deployed not only to render body sufficiently stable as to have things that are "like" it, but also that entity Socrates closely aligns with body, earth, as in the γεῶδες, "earthy" (81c), and one condition of the body-like soul, its resemblance to shadow, σκιοειδῆ, "shadowy" (81c–d).

23. Thus, what had supplied grounds for the likeness between soul and body, namely plasticity, is now revealed as of a sort to prohibit reduction of soul to body. Eventually, corrupted bodies are destroyed. The same cannot be said about the soul.

24. By this reading, souls' residences in Hades and their transmigration to bodies appropriate to them are presented less as two competing (and contradictory) models of what happens to soul after death than two attempts to provide as subtle an account of differences of psychic condition as possible. For further discussion of the status of these two tropes and their reception in the scholarly literature, see chapter 3.

25. This description of the lovers of learning eschewing the company of those not like them, coming as it does from a man whom Plato frequently depicts engaging in conversation with people who hardly resemble such lovers, is another distancing gesture that calls into question whether Socrates himself fits the portrait he gives of the lover of learning.

26. Thus, while this passage suggests the possibility of soul gaining direct access to itself, this possibility exists only with the cooperation of the body and by means of training, which in turn requires a community of a certain sort.

27. The gentleness of philosophy is juxtaposed with the punishment for wrongdoing undergone by souls that refuse the benefits of philosophy and persist in their love of the body.

28. This description of the greatest evil should be compared with Socrates's later portrayal of misology as the greatest evil (89d).

29. On the broader significance of personification for Plato's psychology, see Kamtekar (2006).

30. Socrates's characterization of the soul inflicted with a love for the body and its fate begins by drawing upon the Homeric tradition of depicting the soul as the miserable and wretched eidolon of the person, visible but impotent. However, his account of the variety of animals into which once-human souls are born draws upon a tradition at least as old as Pythagoras (although where exactly this conception of transmigration originated is notoriously difficult to trace with certainty) and somewhat at odds with the Homeric depiction. For a concise discussion of the distinction between Pythagorean and Homeric conceptions of soul, see Kahn (2001, 18). In general, the suggestion that some souls have a difficult time dying and making their way to and through Hades has broad mythical support, see Edmonds (2004, 171).

31. I have argued that a similar state of affairs exists in the *Republic* (Brill 2007).

32. But we must also note that this will not involve a release from residence in some place (see discussion of relevant passage in myth of the earth in chapter 3).

33. To care for logos is to care for yourself and others, to care for human community. This in turn suggests that concern for logos involves a care for the city, and thus that the philosopher is not a misopolist.

34. I am thus in agreement with Frede's (2001, 289) argument that Socrates does not refer here to "fire" and "snow" as immanent forms but as tangible, visible things.

35. "So it's the case about some things of this sort, that the Form itself isn't the only thing worthy of the form's name for all time; there's also something else, something that is not the form but, whenever it is, always has the shape [τὴν μορφήν] of that form" (103e).

36. "It's apparent those contraries aren't the only thing not to admit one another—there are also all those things which, not being contrary to one another, always contain contraries. Nor are these like things that admit whatever look is contrary to the look in them; instead, whenever that look comes at them, they perish [ἀπολλύμενα] or give way" (104b) .

37. We might be tempted to add that were Socrates to strictly hold to what was agreed earlier he would have to add that the soul cannot admit death without "perishing" presumably in the sense of ceasing to be a soul, but we can begin to see the unique and vital ambiguity here. David Bostock calls attention to this ambiguity and considers it fatal to the argument, insofar as it assumes that it has shown that the soul is both immortal and imperishable, but really has only argued for the former (Bostock 1986, 52–53, 189–93). Bostock goes on to say that the ease with which the soul's imperishability is accepted is a function of the difficulty of conceiving of something that is both immaterial and not living, a "soul-corpse" as he calls it (19). Weller (2001, 45) echoes this concern.

When we take the ethical concerns of the dialogue into account, however, the soul's corruption by viciousness does provide an approximation of Bostock's "soul-corpse." The problem, of course, is that the vicious soul does not cease to be operative in the world. However, this is precisely an argument for the need to cultivate a more precise vocabulary of viciousness. This dimension of the *Phaedo*, its call for an account of the soul's corruption as distinct from its destruction (possible or impossible), connects the *Phaedo* with the immortality discussion in book 10 of the *Republic* (608c–611a).

38. Now that he has defined death as the contrary of life, we can see another ramification of the absence of such an account. Conceived as the contrary of life, thanatos can refer to what was once living but is no more; however, it can also refer to what was never living and would normally not be referred to as dead, things like rocks, mud, rain, etc. The absence of a direct discussion of how the living body stands with respect to the bodily continues to haunt this discourse, in this instance by imbuing thanatos with an extremely problematic ambiguity. For Bostock (1986, 52–53, 189–93), this ambiguity in Plato's use of thanatos is fatal. I am suggesting instead that Plato is aware of the problems this ambiguity creates. This is precisely why he has Socrates express some dissatisfaction with the logoi that he and his interlocutors have produced and follow these up with a similarly qualified muthos.

Chapter 3

1. "And he should sing, as it were, incantations [ἐπᾴδειν] to himself over and over again; and that's just why I've drawn out the story for so long" (114d); such stories are worth listening to (110b).

2. In responding to Hackforth's (1972, 186) characterization of the myth of the earth as a presentation of the immaterial in material form, Dorter (1982, 165) observes that it is rather more the case that the myth presents an image of the life of the soul while connected to the body, thereby presenting "the timeless in temporal form, or the implicit present in an explicit future." Aherensdorf (1995, 193) offers a similar account of the myth as more concerned with this-worldly affairs than with other-worldly affairs. I am deeply sympathetic to both of these readings. My point is rather that the myth's presentation of what Dorter calls the "implicit present" occurs not primarily through a discussion of time but through an account of place. Socrates's focus on place here marks this myth off from Hesiod's tale of Four Ages and the myth in the *Statesman* and connects the myth of the true earth with the *Republic*'s famous image of the cave.

3. As Sallis (2002, 122) has noted, that we are to wonder how seriously to take this disparagement of the earthy is suggested by Plato's emphasis early in the dialogue on Socrates's contact with the earth; when Socrates is released from his chains, he plants his feet on the earth, where they remain for the rest of the conversation (61d).

4. W. D. Geddes maintains that this passage is an allusion to the ritual sacrifice to Hecate that was made at crossroads (142]), but see Dorter (1982, 170).

5. For a discussion of the mythic tradition from which Plato is drawing here, see Edmunds (2004, 188–90). By citing as evidence particular practices, Plato signals that Socrates's criticism of Telephus does not involve a complete rejection of religious practice, but neither does it simply affirm this practice. We have here an example of Plato's critical appropriation. It is as though he is saying, "insofar as you participate in these rites, you are already committed to the belief that the ways to Hades are many." And what is behind this claim is the notion that not all fates in Hades are the same. Socrates takes this to mean that there are real differences between conditions of soul and that these differences are at least in part a function of one's actions.

6. For a helpful account of the agonistic dimension of myth telling, see Edmunds's introduction to his study of Greek conceptions of the afterlife (Edmunds 2004, 1–28).

7. Part of the significance of this passage is the degree to which it calls into question and submits for critical assessment all that Socrates and his interlocutors have discussed and agreed upon throughout the dialogue. It emphasizes the need for repeated and consistent examination of these accounts, as Socrates himself suggests (106b, 114d–e).

8. Annas (1982) asserts that the cosmological elements of this myth are in tension with the depiction of final judgment in the myth. According to Annas, the problem with this tension is that it results in two competing conceptions of punishment. On the one hand, the trope of reincarnation suggests that embodiment is punishment for the possession of a corrupt soul and the myth's claim that only philosophic souls will be allowed to persist in a disembodied state proposes disembodiment as their reward (114c). On the other hand, the specific character of the earth suggests a form of punishment on the basis of the experiences that souls undergo while disembodied. When combined, these two forms of punishment suggest that no matter how thorough the punishment one undergoes while disembodied, all but a very few souls will then undergo that added insult of returning to bodies. Annas sees this somewhat pessimistic view as a mean between the optimistic final judgment scene in the *Gorgias* and the heavier pessimism of the myth of Er in the *Republic*, where very little room is left open for individual souls to change the outcome of their lives. This is a compelling and provocative comparison. However, it does not take into account the work that the description of regions of the earth does; namely, it provides yet another means of describing different kinds of soul and emphasizing the variety of forms of viciousness. In the myth of the earth, the theme of reincarnation is alluded to, but it is by no means the central theme of the myth. Gallop (1975, 224), like Annas, maintains that what is said in the myth is incompatible with the theme of reincarnation utilized earlier. However, by my reading, since the main work of the theme of reincarnation was to supply Socrates with some means of distinguishing between kinds of souls, a robust account of reincarnation is no longer needed in the myth of the earth because its work is done instead by a description of regions of the earth. Rather than attributing this difference between accounts of punishment to Plato's pessimism, I suggest that it calls into question the sense in which embodiment should be considered punishment. This move is appropriate given that Socrates maintains that these philosophical souls who have been "freed" from embodiment do indeed continue dwell somewhere (114c). Even if we take Socrates's reticence to describe these dwellings as an indication that they in particular are not easily spoken of in the terms of physical regions, he maintains the appropriateness of conceiving of such souls as dwelling and thus maintains the suggestion that whatever their abode is like, it is appropriate to their condition.

9. Damascius's attempted refutation of those who claim that the earth Socrates speaks of in this myth is really form and those who claim it is really nature is instructive as regards these dual ethical and geological registers. According to Damascius, Socrates's description of parts of the earth as whiter than chalk and his account of the temperate climate of this earth militates against construing this earth as form, while his description of it as the abode of blessed souls and as inhabited by gods militates, in his opinion, against construing this earth as nature (see section 504 [p. 254] of L. G. Westerink's translation [1977]).

10. Dorter (1982, 175) also notes the sympathy between the zoology present in the discussion of reincarnation and the geology offered in the myth of the true earth.

11. Initially Socrates focuses equally upon both time and place: death is not a freedom from time; the souls of the dead must go on a journey utilizing particular paths led by particular guides and reside in a particular place, but they must do so for a particular allotted time and are returned after a particular and long allotment of time.

12. Note the resonance with the account of soul's judgment in *Gorgias*, in which differences of body, wealth, and family are not treated as relevant to the judiciary process, whereas differences of region are (524a).

13. Socrates explicitly calls attention to the fact that this is the soul he described previously (see 108a).

14. Notice the conjunction of confusion, wandering, resistance, force, necessity, and isolation.

15. ἁλουργῆ; from ἁλουργής, ές (ἅλς, ἔργω): wrought in the sea, sea-purple, i.e., genuine purple (Plat); ἅλς, ἁλός, ἡ: the sea (Hom), also described in this passage as "wondrous in beauty" (θαυμαστὴν τὸ κάλλος).

16. It also extends purity and beauty to bodily things (see Stern [1993, 167]).

17. See reference at fn 9 above.

18. Τὰ κοῖλα from τὸ κοῖλον, a substantive form of the modifier κοῖλος, "hollow," which, in archaic poetry, often describes an object in which something was hidden or concealed, as with the description in the *Odyssey* of the hollow horse by means of which Argive troops gained entrance to Troy (4.277, 8.507); and with Hesiod's description in the *Theogony* of the hollow fennel stalk in which Prometheus hid the fire he had stolen from Zeus (569). In classical tragedy, Euripides used the term to refer to the hollows of the body (*Phoenissae*, 1411). See LSJ, s.v.

19. I take the imagistic character of this description of the earth's hollows to be implied by Socrates's reticence to insist that this description by which he has been persuaded is true and his emphasis instead that it or some account like it seems to be the case (108d–e, 114d).

20. The comparison between a perspective on the soul and a spectacle from the sea is one to which Socrates avails himself in the *Republic* as well (611b–612a). On this image, see Burger (1984, 194–95, and the reference to *Republic* 10 at 268 n. 17); and Brill (2005, 297–315).

21. This same word is used again by Plato in *Laws* 12 in a particularly curious passage, for a discussion of which see chapter 10.

22. This imagery of a baseless, foundationless flowing and of a motion that partakes of chance, begs comparison with the discussion of chora in the *Timaeus* as the errant cause, the receptacle of being.

23. For a more extensive discussion of the connection between Socrates's description of the rivers that run beneath the earth and the passions of the soul, see Burger (1984, 197–200).

24. The examples Socrates gives here are informative: "for example, those who've practiced some violence against father or mother under the influence of anger [ὑπ' ὀργῆς] and live out the rest of their lives in repentance, or those who became homicides in some other such way" (114a). In the *Laws*, Plato will create a category of misdeed, homicide in anger, which, according to Saunders, was without precedent in Athenian law (866d–e).

25. On the question of why some souls would be burned and others frozen, Edmunds notes that it is likely that this distinction plays upon a mythic tradition now lost to us (Edmunds 2004, 213), while Burger emphasizes the reference to a variety of pathē made by the names of these rivers, and suggests that the effects of the rivers resonates with the effect of these pathē (Burger 1984, 197–200). I add only that insofar as anger would be associated with heat, it makes sense that those who committed patricide and matricide in anger would find themselves in Pyriphlegethon.

26. Annas (1982) offers a particularly clear discussion of this problem.

27. The impure do not find fellow travelers or guides, not even, it would seem, among other impure souls, souls to which they are akin. Socrates specifies that the impure soul wanders around alone and perplexed for a set period of time before going on its journey (108b–c).

28. If we consider the discussion of "true" rhetoric in the *Phaedrus*, the offender will be successful only insofar as he has understood the truth of the matter, the condition of the soul of the victim, and understood and employed the kind of logos that will persuade this particular kind of soul (273d–e). The offender must become an expert in both psychology and logos itself. Placing the redemption of the offender in his ability to persuade his victim locates the redemption of the offender in his ability to come to some understanding of the truth, of his victim, and of the manner in which to speak to this victim.

29. As we have seen, the assertion of a connection between aggressor and aggressed is not without support in other facets of Greek society, especially in the religious beliefs about the context of

impurity that pervades the act of homicide (see references to Parker [1996] and Vernant [1990] in the discussion of the third logos in chapter 2).

30. "So each of the elements has gotten a judge in its favor, except earth; no one has declared in favor of it, unless someone has said the soul is composed of all the elements, or is all of them" (405b8). The translation is that of Joeseph Sachs (2001).

31. Brann, Kalkavage, and Salem 1998, 18.

32. See, for instance, the Hippocratic text "On the Sacred Disease."

Part II

1. In this passage, Cephalus is unsure whether the shift from indifference to concern is a function simply of waning faculties due to old age, or to a privileged perspective on matters pertaining to Hades due to proximity to death; his point is simply that having had money relieves him from some of this concern because his wealth has enabled him to escape some of the motivation for wrongdoing. And in order to make this point, he attends to the discomfort experienced by many of his friends about actions that they have committed throughout their lives. Thus, Cephalus's description of his friends is an account of a particular condition of reflection about one's life, one that is not conducive to restful or peaceful leave-taking, but instead makes one watchful, ruminative, and anxious. Such an introduction to ψυχή gives prominence to the therapeutic trajectory that we have outlined, in which belief in soul (or lack thereof) is closely related to comportment toward death. Accordingly, it is significant to note Cephalus's point that his friends had given no thought to these issues of the end and the afterlife before, and it is only their proximity to death that makes them heedful of stories about the afterlife (330d–e).

2. How different a register and what the significance of its difference may be is discussed in chapter 7.

3. Such a frictive use of images, in which a variety of images are used against one another for the purposes of elucidation, is figured in the image of two sticks rubbed together for the purpose of producing light (434e–435a).

4. I am convinced by Andrea Nightingale's description of Plato's appropriation of theoria for his account of philosophic apprehension of the forms, and my understanding of the role of viewing in the *Republic* owes much to this study (Nightingale 2009, esp. 109–16). My point here is simply that there are more forms of viewing at work in the *Republic* than the theoric contemplation of forms. Moreover, I do not mean to assume that in presenting this variety of gazes Plato depicts Socrates and his interlocutors as having attained all of them. It is precisely their failure to do so that prompts the critical discussion of book 10.

5. In both of these cases, this immersion and depth are necessary to see the city (576e) and soul (579e) as a whole. Unless otherwise noted, all translated citations of the *Republic* are taken from Bloom (1991). Citations of the Greek text are from Burnet's edition, Oxford Classical Texts, *Platonis Opera*, vol. 4 (Oxford: Oxford University Press, 1902).

6. This oscillation is related to the turning that is the motion privileged with respect to soul's education in book 7 (518c–d, 521c).

7. Robinson 1995, 33. See the discussion of Robinson's assessment in the introduction to this volume.

8. And here again we confront a fundamental question: Is Plato concerned with philosophy for the sake of human life, or is he concerned with human life for the sake of philosophy?

9. Whether this passing away takes the form of a destruction of the character of a life (e.g., one can set out to have a just life and end up destroying this character) or simply of the mortality of the individual living that life (e.g., this particular just or unjust life will not be again) will

need to be determined, as will the relationship between kind of life and the patterns of life (βίων παραδείγματα) that are chosen in book 10's myth of Er (617d).

10. It is also important to keep in mind the experimental and qualified character of the city/soul analogy, a character maintained even at the judgment for which the analogy was designed (see 577d: "If, then, a man is like his city ...").

11. Or, at least, the *Republic* broaches this possibility, while, I will argue, the *Laws* develops it further (see chapter 10).

12. "For if one assumes that psychology is individual psychology, the *Republic* will then look like it is composed of various bits—among them, a psychology and a political theory—and there will inevitably be a question of how they fit together. In Plato's psychology, as I understand it, this question should not arise. For psuchē-analysis and polis-analysis are, for Plato, two aspects of a single discipline, psychology, which has as its core the relation between inside and outside. What holds the *Republic* together is Plato's understanding of what holds people and polis together" (Lear 1992, 186).

13. Any assessment of the causal relation between city and soul in the *Republic* is well served by considering G. R. Ferrari's (2005) careful demarcation of the city/soul analogy from such an account. Ferrari does agree that there is a causal account; his point is that this analysis is outside of the purview of the task he has taken on of elucidating the analogical aspect of the city/soul coupling in the *Republic* (2005, 79), a point with which I agree.

14. This, in turn, will require a serious and extended consideration of ruling and attaining political power.

15. See Ferrari (2005, 77).

16. The controversy surrounding Plato's attribution of "kinds," "forms," and "parts" to the soul is well documented in Shields (2010) and has bearing upon the debate surrounding the relationship between the discussion of epithumia in book 4 and the forms of corrupt souls in books 8 and 9. I reserve discussion of this complex issue for the analysis of book 4's account of epithumia in chapter 5. See especially the section entitled "The Form of Desire" and note 4.

17. See the discussion in the introduction to this volume.

18. A point emphasized by the list of things that must be discerned in order to choose, a list Socrates interrupts his telling of the myth of Er to produce. In choosing a life well, one must, "know the effects, bad and good, of beauty mixed with poverty or wealth or accompanied by this or that habit of soul; and the effects of any particular mixture with one another of good and bad birth, private station and ruling office, strength and weakness, facility and difficulty of learning, and all such things that are connected with a soul by nature or are acquired" (681c–d).

Chapter 4

1. The brothers' tendency throughout this early discussion to treat person and soul as interchangeable makes the eventual conclusion in book 10, that soul exceeds the life of the individual, significant to them.

2. This is in part due to both brothers' assumption that being unjust means having an unjust soul.

3. The close connection between a kind of viewing and the brothers' demand to make a display of just and unjust lives in order to defend the just life is again asserted in Socrates's initial characterization of the qualities that this investigation requires: "It looks to me as though the investigation we are undertaking is no ordinary thing, but one for a man who sees sharply" (368c).

4. That all of these assumptions will be explored and questioned in the subsequent conversation by means of images is a sign of the subtlety of the iconography at work in the dialogue.

5. This is what the thought experiment that Glaucon connects to the ring of Gyges tale is supposed to show: "give each, the just man and the unjust, license to do whatever he wants, while we follow and watch where his desire will lead each. We would catch the just man red-handed going the same way as the unjust man out of a desire to get the better [διὰ τὴν πλεονεξίαν]; this is what any nature naturally pursues as good [ὃ πᾶσα φύσις διώκειν πέφυκεν ὡς ἀγαθόν], while it is law [νόμῳ] which by force [βίᾳ] perverts it to honor equality" (359c).

6. It is just this coming into being that Socrates emphasizes in his initial formulation of the city/soul analogy: "'If we should watch a city coming into being [γιγνομένην] in speech,' I said, 'would we also see its justice coming into being [γιγνομένην], and its injustice?' 'Probably,' he said. 'When this has been done, can we hope to see what we're looking for more easily?'" (369 a–b); note the emphasis on genesis of justice and injustice as well as the claim that once this genesis has been observed, they will have a better chance at viewing just and unjust lives.

7. Thus, technē involves some kind of relationship to the fine.

8. This model of disfigurement comes up explicitly in the discussion of philosophic natures, which stresses the danger of people coming to philosophy who are not suited to it, both as accounting for why people hold philosophy in contempt but also, more importantly, as an occurrence that results from truly philosophic natures abandoning it and going off to do things likely to cause harm to the city (495a–e).

9. A point made explicit near the start of book 4 (423c–d).

10. I am indebted to Stephen Halliwell's astute and careful discussion of the complexity of Plato's understanding of mimēsis, especially to the variety of degrees of mimetic receptivity (Halliwell 2002, chaps. 1–4).

11. Following Lear (2011), focused absorption in the performance of a role need not imply deep identification with one's character, although it certainly can result in this. The effect the mimetic artist has on his audience is not necessarily the same as the effect that playing this role has on the artist.

12. Indeed, as Halliwell (2002, 52) points out, the practice of reading aloud further blurs the distinction between artist and audience.

13. While I do not want to belabor one of the most controversial and frequently noted features of the *Republic*, the firm, if also regretful expulsion of the tragic poets from the city should be read within the context of this broad construction of mimēsis.

14. This supervision occurs alongside the use of craft, technē, and poetry as means to envision the work of the city; for instance, the guardians are to be "craftsmen of the city's freedom [δημιουργοὺς ἐλευθερίας]" (395c). See also the characterization in book 6 of the philosopher king wiping clean a tablet and drawing and painting to produce the "image of man," and being a "painter of regimes" (501a–c); see also Socrates's characterization of their own work as a kind of painting at the start of book 4 (420c–e), and again in the discussion in book 5 of whether the best city is possible (472c–e).

15. That all of the technai and artifacts listed in this passage, as well as the body itself, are treated as manifesting grace and gracelessness comprises both their usefulness (for philosophy) and the need Socrates has for addressing them. This should be compared with the emphasis on spontaneous and cultivated eruptions of order in the *Laws* 664e–665a; 899a, 908b–c.

16. Compare this with the landscape that reflects the community of praise and blame in book 6, 492b–d: the rocks that echo the cheers and boos of the crowd iterate the entire framework of values and desires in the city (the entire cultural artifice). Thus, the spatial metaphorics works in both directions: artifact is figured as landscape and landscape is figured as artifice.

17. The sovereignty of music will also result in the eventual revision of their understanding of the relationship between music and gymnastics; it is not that the former is for the soul and the latter the body, rather, both are for the sake of the soul; overindulgence in either disrupts the best condition of soul (403d, 410b–412b).

18. This reference to harmony laying hold of the soul resonates with the trope of touch and contact developed in the *Phaedo* by means of the language of pollution and purity.

19. Note the language of kinship and recognition on the basis of kinship (a version of "like to like").

20. See, for example, their agreement to study a feverish city rather than a healthy one (372e) and the need to supervise all craftspeople in order to create a healthy environment for the young (401b–d).

21. In the realm of tragic poetry, comparisons between diseases and certain conditions of the soul, often wrought by eros, are too frequent to number here. For a helpful collection of some of the most illustrative of such passages, see Lloyd (2003, chap. 4); and Solmsen (1983). As David Claus has observed, in most of the analogies between soul and body that appear in classical Greek literature other than the Platonic dialogues, "psuchē is to be seen as something influenced, if not created, by analogy to scientific and medical notions of the body, and in this context the interactions of soul and body occur in a naive or pragmatic way that assumes the two parts of the composite to be highly symmetrical, not ontologically or qualitatively different" (Claus 1981, 109–10).

22. The references to medicine in the *Republic* fall into three kinds: First, there is the use of medicine as an example (and a privileged one at that) of technē, and this as representing a body of knowledge and practice teachable to others, directed toward a particular end and answerable to standards defined at least in part by that end. Given the second moment, we could call this the stage of precritical reference to medicine. Second, there is an explicit critique of the practice of medicine, a purgation of medicine that accompanies the purgation of the feverish city. This purgation then makes way for the third kind of reference, the identification of a practice of medicine that proves to be quite useful for also indicating certain dimensions of the role of the philosopher in the city. Once the art of medicine has been purged of deleterious elements, the development of a metaphorics can take place in which health and sickness are used as analogies for virtue and vice. However, the *Republic* also indicates the limitation of this metaphorical or analogical structure by indicating the extent to which disease and vice differ. Thus, just as the medical art is purged before the construction of an analogy between health and virtue, disease and vice, so too is this very analogy, and the adequacy of medical terminology in general, critiqued on the grounds of its limitations for providing an adequate account of conditions of soul. At stake in this discussion is the extent to which "health" and "disease" can provide an adequate means for conceiving of psychic conditions. Both the usefulness and the limitations of this manner of speaking, this medical model, are explored.

23. In fact, the connection between medicine and poetry is made explicit in Socrates's distinction between the true lie and lie in speech, wherein he allocates to the lie in speech a pharmacological function (382a–b). The comparison between medicine and poetry is extended to politics in a subsequent passage in which Socrates further illustrates the work of the lie in speech (389b–c). In addition to drawing out and laying the foundation for a comparison between medicine, politics, and judgment in a manner that inserts a poetic dimension into all three, this passage also sets the stage for the coming analogy between health and vice. In looking ahead, see also 414b–c and 459c–d.

24. The doctor's art employs an unfixed distinction and brings with it some risk, to be sure. The doctor can only use his art if his own sickness does not kill him.

25. The submission of the work of the judge to the standard of the doctor is repeated just a few lines later in a passage that also, for the first time in the dialogue, explicitly broaches the taking of lives as part of the work of the provision of a good city: "Will you set down a law in the city providing as well for an art of medicine such as we described along with such an art of judging, which will care for those of your citizens who have good natures in body and soul; while for those who haven't, they'll let die the ones whose bodies are such, and the ones whose souls have bad natures and are incurable [ἀνιάτους], they themselves will kill?" (409e–410a)

Chapter 5

1. As we shall see, the limits of the language of health and disease in evaluating conditions of soul are suggested in book 4 by Socrates's qualification of the precision of an account of soul that proceeds by way of assigning it parts (435c–d). This qualification returns in book 10 with the claim that they have failed to see the soul in its truest nature (611b).

2. See, in particular, the discussions in Rosen (1965); Kahn (1987); and Ludwig (2007).

3. This focus on hunger and thirst as especially disclosive of eputhumia is more operational than substantive, that is, it is not argued for but rather asserted and put to work. It has led to the general scholarly tendency to distinguish between appetite (as the subject of book 4) and "higher"-order desires attributed to the rational aspect of soul in subsequent books of the dialogue (see Parry [2007] for a particularly succinct argument for this distinction). As will become clear, I take the relation between book 4's analysis of phenomena like hunger and thirst, book 5 and 6's attribution of desire and lust for learning to philosophic natures, and books 8 and 9's identification of the dominant passions of a variety of characters to be part of a single account of desiderative life, one which, as it grows in complexity, reveals the course of transformation from individual appetites and other forms of desire to well-defined proclivities, dispositions, and modes of desiring. I will thus also argue that Plato grants a greater malleability even to appetitive desires than is attributed to him by Lorenz (2006); the depravity of the tryant, for instance, is found not only in his eros, but also in his hunger—there is no food he will not eat (571c–d).

4. In treating this discussion of desire as a sketch of desiderative life that is filled in later in the dialogue, I aim to avoid the problems that arise when one reads the divisions of soul in book 4 as comprising an exhaustive list of necessary parts of the human soul, problems well documented in Shields (2010), and to keep in mind both Plato's reticence to describe these divisions as parts and the tentative character of this account. In treating it also as a preliminary account, I am in agreement with the growing number of scholars who read the divisions of soul in book 4 as continuous and consistent with rather than divergent from those in book 8, 9, and 10, see especially Shields (2010); Singpurwalla (2010 and 2011); Moss (2008); and Whiting (2012). Nevertheless, the difference between the appetitive desires book 4 focuses upon and the dispositions described later in the dialogue is real—Richard Parry's (2007) discussion of this difference is particularly illuminating. My point is simply that the former lay the groundwork for the latter. I am thus sympathetic to Whiting's argument for a hybrid of "realist" (see, for example, Bobonich [2002]; Irwin [1995]; and Lorenz [2006]) and "deflationist" (see, for instance, Robinson [1971]; Cooper [1984]; and Gerson [2003b]) positions with respect to the relationship between book 4 and books 8–9. The tension between these two positions is lessened if we view the *Republic*'s treatment of epithumia as forming a single account of desiderative life that begins with some preliminary distinctions (book 4) and then elaborates on how individual appetites can develop powerful agent-like capacities with the ability to deeply fracture the human soul (books 5–10). Or, as Whiting puts it, contra Annas (1999), these books do not offer, "competing moral psychologies but rather complementary aspects of a single psychology, one intended to accommodate different kinds (or at least different conditions) of soul" (Whiting 2012, 194).

5. I follow James Adam (1965 ad loc.) in maintaining that an insistence on a firm distinction between desiring, willing, and wanting is not reflected in the text.

6. This character of desire is made most explicit in book 5's description of philosophic natures, where it is presented as a tendency toward wholes; further discussion of this aspect of desire will be reserved for an analysis of this account of the philosopher.

7. This capacity for particularization, bound up with the overarching tendency toward kinds and classes of things, furthers the similarity between desire and knowledge that Socrates asserts: "And what about the various sorts of knowledge? Isn't it the same way? Knowledge itself is knowledge

of learning itself, or of whatever it is to which knowledge should be related; while a particular kind of knowledge is of a particular kind of thing" (438c–d). On the relevance of the series of examples of relative difference that occur just before the use of knowledge as an example, I have found Dorter's (2006) commentary useful (see chapter 4).

8. We might even characterize this account as granting a proto-articulate or proto-logical character to epithumia, taking its tendence toward a group or class of things as resonant with the acts of defining and classifying involved in giving a λόγος of something. Or, as Whiting (2012, 185) puts it, even in book 4, Plato, "seems to think a proper upbringing can bring it about that a person's appetites do not simply obey her reason, but spontaneously, as it were, and of their own accord *sing tune with it*" (emphasis added).

9. Socrates suggests that a certain contingency adheres to the exercise of calculation: "Doesn't that which forbids such things come into being—*when it comes into being*—from calculation, while what leads and draws is present due to affections and diseases" (439c, my emphasis). The phenomenological tenor also extends to the discussion of whether spirit is a third part of soul, with its illustration of the battle between Leontius's desire and his spirit (439e–440a), and of the spiritedness of children (441a), animals (441b), and heroes (441b–c).

10. Ferrari's comparison between Plato and Freud on the role of tension in forming parts of soul is apt (see his "The Three-Part Soul" in Ferrari [2007b, 165–201]).

11. While there was some disagreement about exactly what was imbalanced, that disease involved an imbalance between parts was uncontroversial and quite familiar. See Jones's (1929) introduction to the first volume of his translation of the Hippocratic corpus for the Loeb Classical Library.

12. See note 16 of the Introduction.

13. Jones 1929, introduction.

14. The appropriation of medical language in classical tragedy, especially in the work of Euripides, has been well documented by Holmes (2010) and her accompanying bibliography.

15. The degree of subtlety and complexity with which one could refer to diseases is noted ruefully by Socrates in his critique of certain practices of medicine in book 3 (405c–e). Socrates avails himself of this vocabulary when he turns to describe the various regimes and their sources of degeneration (see 552c, 563e, and 564b).

16. That Plato presumes a distinction between soul and body without ever arguing for it is a concern voiced by a number of commentators, such as Annas (1981, 345); Reeve (1988, 160); and Waterfield (1993, 450). Such a presumption is certainly present in Socrates's formulation of the analogy between virtue, vice, health, and disease. However, this presumption was at work, even if only implicitly, in many parts of Athenian culture (and thus was not simply an invention of Plato's). This does not exempt Plato from making the distinction explicit but should inspire a willingness to give him time to make his case. I hope to show that the immortality discussion in book 10 does provide some grounds for distinguishing between soul and body on the basis of their differential responses to corruption (see chapter 7).

17. Plato's use of this trope is well documented in Kamtekar (2006).

18. See, for instance, book 3's discussion of bringing health to young souls (401b–d).

19. See especially book 6's discussion of the philosophic nature (485a–494b).

20. By suggesting the possibility of ruling both according to and not according to nature, and by tying health and disease to these kinds of rule, the analogy flirts with collapsing the distinction between living and ruling. At this juncture in the dialogue, no one directly addresses these questions; however, as I hope to show presently, these questions do not remain unaddressed.

21. Lloyd (2003, 8–9) voices a similar concern with respect to what he considers to be an unhelpful distinction between metaphorical and literal references to health and disease, preferring instead to investigate the "semantic stretch" of these terms.

22. And may fail to do so, an example of which we have in the *Phaedo*, when Cebes characterizes himself and his companions as having something in them that possesses a childlike fear of death (77e).

23. By doing so, Socrates takes leave from at least one prominent cultural conception of the soul. It has been argued that the ontological difference between body and soul was championed first by Plato (see, in particular, Claus [1981, 110]; and Solmsen [1983]). While space limitations prohibit a discussion of this suggestion here, it is important to note that Plato's emphasis on the ontological separation of soul and body would have been a noticeably different approach than that of a number of his contemporaries. However, Socrates does draw our attention to a culturally sanctioned recognition of the difference between soul and body during the immortality discussion, as we shall see below.

24. Resonating with the *Phaedo*'s difficulty surrounding this term. While Socrates tries to elucidate the enigmatic workings of the soul by appealing to a bodily vocabulary, what body is becomes mysterious in that very process.

25. In fact, the effects of this ambiguity are made immediately apparent in the gloss with which Socrates concludes this comparison between health, sickness, justice, and injustice: "Virtue, then, it seems, would be a certain health and beauty and good habit of soul, while vice would be a disease and ugliness and weakness" (444e). The characterization of vice as a kind of disease does not explicitly restrict disease to the body; it thereby decenters the priority of a distinction between body and soul in conceiving of the relationship between vice and disease. Thus, this characterization of vice as a kind of disease is not fully commensurate with the characterization of injustice as analogous to disease. However, both characterizations suffer from a failure to specify the difference between vice and disease, consequently, both characterizations risk an unwarranted optimism about one's knowledge of the soul.

26. Socrates's and his interlocutors' silence on this matter need not be our own, however. For a discussion of the treatment of sexual difference in this passage, see Brill (2013).

27. That it is really the body that takes precedence here is indicated in a gloss to this image which Socrates offers a few lines later: "But we further agreed that the community of pain and pleasure is the greatest good for a city, likening the good governing of a city to a body's relation to the pain and pleasure of one of its parts" (464b).

28. See Ferrari (2005, 15–20) on the connection between metaphysics and Athenian aristocratic ethos.

29. His grounds for doing so can be found in the very basis for his comparison between knowledge and desire (what I have described as the implicit or proto-articulate nature of desire), namely, that desire has a form, and that its form is shaped by that toward which it tends. Desire is somehow classificatory. It is precisely desire's tendency toward a whole or all that is repeatedly emphasized in Socrates's descriptions of this nature (474c, 475b, 476a, 485 a–d, 490 a–b), and what makes pressing the question of the difference between the philosopher and the lovers of sights and sounds as worthy of serious inquiry (476a). Whether Socrates refers specifically to their previous discussion of desire when he asks Glaucon if Glaucon recollects their agreement that desire is of an all is subject to debate. Nicholas White (1979, 154) affirms this reference; Halliwell (1993, 202–3) disputes it. My argument is that book 4's analysis of the form of desire is consistent with this description of the lover, regardless of whether 474c is an explicit reference back to book 4.

30. Ludwig 2007, 209.

31. Following Moss (2008, esp. 47), this could be put another way: the lovers of sight delight in appearances; the lovers of wisdom delight in what is.

32. I thus follow Adam's (1965, ad loc.) reading that the erotic man loves even those things he does not find beautiful and add that herein lies a source of conflict and tension, herein lies his mortification in his desires and his need for a rationalizing vocabulary, herein lie the seeds of the claim that the philosopher's pleasure is "truer" than that of the tyrant.

Chapter 6

1. As a number of commentators have noted (see, in particular, Rosen [1965] and Ludwig [2007]).

2. Here we begin to see the *Republic*'s version of the philosopher's privileged position with respect to soul. Philosophers seek a pleasure that most belongs to soul.

3. The contemplation of all time resonates with the *Phaedo*'s introduction of the myth of the earth; in the *Republic,* attention to all time will return in the immortality discussion.

4. Note the mixing of metaphors between eating or being nourished and giving birth, between consuming and producing. Note too that soul is taken to be akin to being, or at least a part of soul is taken to be akin to being; this evokes the *Phaedo,* but also surpasses it in complexity with the addition of the soul's kinship with Being specified to a part of the soul.

5. Some preliminary handle on the relationship between the philosopher and the tyrant is given in the ambivalent role marked out for phronēsis in book 7 (see 518d–519b).

6. This passage should be compared with its mirror image in the "healthy environment" produced by proper education that is pictures in book 3 (401b–d). Note too the reference to one's heart as though to emphasize what is being appealed to here is not simply or even desire but loyalty and allegiance.

7. That for Plato philosophy has ultimately transpolitical ends is asserted, in different ways and for different purposes and effects, by scholars with otherwise divergent approaches to Plato. See, for instance Paul Ludwig (2007); Bobonich (2002); and McNeill (2010). The extent to which I diverge from them and my reasons for doing so will become evident and will be argued for throughout the next few chapters. That the detail with which Plato treats the subsequent account of corrupt regimes points to a political concern that defies reduction to its sketch of psychological traits is well argued by Ferrari (2005) and Menn (2005).

8. This characterization of philosopher rulers as painters, made explicit at 501c, resonates with a passage from the *Laws* in which legislating is presented as a kind of painting (769a–e).

9. The philosophic significance of the *Theaetetus*'s limitation of the degree of autonomy granted to the senses in this passage is elegantly drawn out by Burnyeat (1976). My interest in this passage is less on the role of the senses than on the effect of soul's confusion in encountering bodily things, namely, the summoning of intellect, and Socrates's treatment of this effect as recommending the study of the one as a study that draws the soul toward Being.

10. A third possibility remains. The soul could simply ignore the confusion it is experiencing and go about its business. While Socrates is speaking about the education of those already determined by nature to be predisposed toward learning, we cannot lose sight of the fact that for a great number of people an equivocation about the size of one's finger is hardly arresting. In fact, the banality of the example of three fingers serves to trace a comic portrait of a philosophic nature so sensitive to the possibility of contradiction in the world that it suffers from any contemplation of one thing among others. The capacity of the philosophic nature to recognize contradiction and betrayal must be counteracted with some sense of what the important contradictions are, lest such a nature fall into the comedy of mourning the loss of cohesion of its finger.

11. The juridical context stands even if one attributes the inadequacy of the initial judgment to the soul itself rather than to the senses (that is, if one operates with the more limited work granted to the senses in the *Theaetetus*).

12. This passage is thus reminiscent of Socrates's observation that there are two disturbances of the eyes: that which occurs when moving from dark to light and that which occurs when moving from light to dark (518a).

13. The debate between Adam and Taylor on whether the principle of decay is within the city or external to it is instructive. Adam maintains that because this city is the perfect city, it could not contain the seeds of its own demise because, "a city which carries within itself the

seeds of decay is not perfect, but imperfect" (Adam 1965, 202). Instead, the number represents the law of necessity to which the entire universe is subject and dictates that the entire universe will undergo changes from better to worse and worse to better. Adam will go on to connect the discussion of two harmonies with the two directions of rotation of the earth and corresponding ages spoken of in the *Statesman*, concluding that Plato has in mind with the nuptial number the number of years counted within each direction of revolution or each age. Thus, the degradation of the perfect city is a function not of any internal principle of decay but of a universal law to which the entire cosmos is subject. Taylor (1939) rejects this reading of the nuptial number, granting it no cosmic significance, and locates the cause of decay within the city on the grounds that cities are generated by humans, and thus by fallible creatures and so consequently will necessarily themselves be fallible and subject to an internal logic of decay. I am sympathetic to Taylor's point that the discussion of regimes is a discussion of a logic internal to this city. In fact, as Glaucon is summarizing Socrates's earlier account of the best regimes, he notes that Socrates characterized the city he and Glaucon and Adeimantus had built as good "in spite of the fact that you had a still finer city and man to tell of" (544a). Nor do I find fully persuasive the comparison Adam draws between the *Republic* and the *Statesman* on this front, nor his description of the discussion of regimes as an early instance of a philosophy of history (Adam 1965, 196, 210). However, I diverge from Taylor's description of this discussion as Plato's philosophy of history (1939, 31).

14. The way for thinking about the progression of one kind of nature into another is prepared by the discussion of philosophical natures in book 6 wherein a philosophical nature that is not properly nurtured and educated is twisted into a person capable of the worst evil and atrocity. The philosophic nature, it would seem, provides the seeds not only for philosophers but for tyrants as well.

15. *Politics*, 1316a1–1316b27.

16. For Taylor, it is a "pure case" (1939, 26–28); for Nettleship (1901, 295), an "ideal" case; for Dorter (2006, 277, 284 n. 28), it is an "idealization" or an "ideal classification." In this note, Dorter rejects characterization of the number as a "historical prognosis" but this rejection is called into question by his own assessment of the discussion in light of European history.

17. Taylor (1939) is one proponent of this defense, as is Adam (1965), although Taylor and Adam diverge on several points, not the least of which is whether the cause of the city's inevitable degeneration is internal or external to the city.

18. Nettleship 1901, 295.

19. Adam (1965), Gomperz, Bury, and Taylor (1939) included.

20. Including Bloom (1991) and Dorter (2006).

21. See, for instance, Cross and Woozley (1964, 283).

22. See Straus (1978, 129–30).

23. The perspective that Socrates adopts throughout this discussion merits comparison with those Hippocratic texts which chart the timeline of a fever or the critical days of a disease, texts like "On Prognosis" and "Epidemics I." There is a deep sympathy in endeavor between Socrates's discussion of the coherent course of civic and psychological degeneration wrought by the estrangement of calculation and desire, and the authors' of these texts discussion of the coherent course of physical degeneration caused by disease.

24. Taylor 1939, 31; see also 29: "The story of successive stages through which the kingdom of philosophers sinks into the final degradation of vulgar 'tyranny' should be read, then, in the same spirit in which we might read a physiologist's description of the typical advance of senile decay." Where Taylor and I differ is in the object of diagnosis. For Taylor, Socrates is using the state of cities to diagnose the conditions of souls (37–38); this allows Taylor to maintain that Plato is indeed offering a philosophy of history (31). I maintain that Socrates adopts a diagnostic perspective for

both city and soul, and thus that it is not history he is interested in for either city or soul, but pathology.

25. As evinced by their frequent use, throughout books 8 and 9, of superlatives, oaths to Zeus, and appeals to ubiquitous agreement to affirm Socrates's claims.

26. This effect enacts the opening argument that the author of the Hippocratic text "On Prognosis" gives in honor of this practice: "I hold that it is an excellent thing for a physician to practice forecasting. For if he discover and declare unaided by the side of his patients the present, the past and the future, and fill in the gaps in the account given by the sick, he will be the more believed to understand the cases, so that men will confidently entrust themselves to him for treatment. Furthermore, he will carry out the treatment best if he knows beforehand from the present symptoms what will take place later" (Loeb, vol. 2, trans. Jones, p. 7).

27. For an illuminating account of the tyrant's depravity, see Ophir (1991, 34–38).

28. The patricidal, friendless, and enslaved tyrant of book 9 merits close comparison with the free and happy unjust person Glaucon describes at 362b–c.

29. Hence Socrates's valorization of the "simple" form of medicine administered to artisans and his criticism of the more "subtle" medicine offered to the rich (405c–407a). Socrates suggests that if a condition is such as to be one with which one can live and work, it hardly merits being called a disease at all. Calling such conditions diseases comes close to calling life, with its discomforts, and death, with its finality, diseases; hence the comical and critical tone of his characterization of Herodicus's attempts to treat the "mortal disease" (406b).

30. Of course, there are instances when an unjust person, like the tyrant analyzed here, is put to death on account of his injustice, or dies because of certain events surrounding his injustice. Socrates and Glaucon will refer to just such a state of affairs in book 10 (610c–e). Nonetheless, all Plato needs in order to make the case that corruption of soul is substantially different from corruption of the body, is to point out that such demise is not necessarily the case. The tyrant is not always utterly destroyed by his own injustice.

31. Again, this contradiction is not of Plato's making alone; its elements were present in Athenian culture at large, as is suggested in book 2 by Glaucon and Adeimantus. By the discussion of immortality in book 10, Socrates has done his best to respond to the requests the brothers make of him and to the various contradictory messages about vice, virtue, and the soul that motivated them. The discussion itself allows Plato to pose the question of what the soul is in the most rigorous of fashions, namely, by revealing the radically ambivalent yet necessary relationship between soul and city.

32. The verb Socrates uses here, καταδύω, evokes the descent (κατάβασις) with which the *Republic* begins.

33. This stripping of the tyrant's tragic gear resonates with the judgment myth in the *Gorgias* in which people must be stripped of their bodies in order for their souls to be judged, and furthermore casts Socrates and Glaucon in the roles of Rhadamanthus and Minos.

34. The argument that follows can be taken in another direction as well: Socrates's ability to present an image of the tyrant is predicated upon his own experience with the elements that lead toward tyranny (with eros in particular); Socrates's diagnostic ability signals his ability to reflect upon and critique himself, especially his own possession of eros. Thus, Socrates is not above the ridiculous and the silly, and his playful framing of the nuptial number is a good indication of this. What rescues Socrates from the merely silly and ridiculous is the same thing that rescues him from the tyrannical elements of his own nature, namely his ability to measure and critique himself.

35. This interdependence is suggested by the parallelism between city and soul in book 2, and is most explicitly indicated in the discussion of philosophic natures in book 6. There Socrates notes that philosophical natures, like vigorous seeds, are capable of both the greatest good or the greatest evil, depending upon the environment (system of education and civic culture in general) in which they are raised (491c–492c and 495a).

Chapter 7

1. A group that would include Socrates and Glaucon, raised as they have been in their particular regime, 607e.
2. Literally, "watering" (606d).
3. Most of the few extant ancient commentaries on the *Republic* had little to say about this particular passage. Averroes (1966, 250) pauses to describe the discussion as "rhetorical or dialectical" and then moves on to discuss the myth of Er. Aristotle focuses his critique in book 2 of the *Politics* on the community of women and children and the eradication of private property (see Mayhew [1997]). The exception to this trend would be the commentary of Proclus, whose fifteenth *Dissertation* does pay some attention to the discussion (see Proclus [1970, 29–33]). Even still, as Adam (1965, 421–22) notes in his edition of the text of the *Republic*, the various works that briefly reference the discussion in some form or another are vast (and often, according to Adam, "unfairly and unintelligently" critical. The sources cited here are a condensed survey of frequently referenced contemporary sources greatly aided by Gerald Press's helpful account of the history of *Republic* interpretation (Press 1996).
4. Annas 1981, 345.
5. Sayers 1999, 158.
6. N. White 1979, 259; see also Winspear (1956, 281); Boyd (1962, 111); and Benardete (1999, 223).
7. See, for example, Reeve (1988, 160); Pappas (1995, 183–84); Bloom (1991, 435); and Roochnik (2003, 121).
8. Brown 2001, 297–322.
9. Annas 1981, 344; Sayers 1999, 158; Nettleship 1901, 355.
10. Cross and Woozley 1964, 120.
11. Certainly, what Socrates means by the soul "in its true nature" is not without controversy. My point here is that at this juncture in the dialogue he is operating with a critical perspective toward his and his interlocutors' previous characterizations of the soul.
12. This uncertainty has not gone unnoticed by scholars; however, in very few cases has a commentator's acknowledgment of Socrates's disclaimers about the precision of their discussion of the soul affected the way he or she reads these discussions and the expectations of clarity and soundness he or she brings to their reading.
13. Note the resonance with *Phaedo* here.
14. That Socrates and Glaucon will remain within a concern for the variant and the volatile is hinted at in the very form of the question about immortality that Socrates first poses to Glaucon. Socrates describes this exchange in the following manner: "'Have you not perceived [ᾔσθησαι],' I said, 'that our soul is immortal [ἀθάνατος] and is never destroyed [οὐδέποτε ἀπόλλυται]?' And he looked me in the face with wonder [θαυμάσας] and said, 'By Zeus, I have not. Can you say this?' 'If I am to avoid injustice,' I said. 'And I believe you can also, for it is nothing hard'" (608d). Socrates's reference to perception, in a dialogue in which its status has been a topic of lengthy and controversial discussion—resulting in the relegation of perception to a position beneath that of thought and contemplation (509d–511e)—suggests that even this account of the soul will have an imagistic quality to it. We should also note that Plato describes Glaucon's response to Socrates's question with a specific perception; Glaucon looks to the face of Socrates and he does so with wonder. Without belaboring this detail, it would nonetheless be remiss not observe that wonder is what Socrates claims in the *Theaetetus* is the start of philosophy (155d).
15. Socrates will then go on to claim that they have also shown that there must always be the same number of souls (611a). Because of space constraints, the comments here are limited to the demonstration of the soul's immortality itself, and do not address this assertion about the number of souls.

16. This translation is my own, as are all of the citations in this section on the discussion of immortality, unless otherwise noted. A number of interesting ambiguities arise in this sentence. For one, depending upon how one distributes the article, πᾶν can function in a number of ways producing a series of variations: "everything that destroys and corrupts [Sachs]," "the evil is entirely what destroys and corrupts [Brown]," "what destroys and corrupts everything [Bloom]." Throughout this passage, Plato plays with the relationship between τὸ πᾶν and τὸ ὅλον, between "all," "every," and "whole" as these are related to complex objects; I have opted for the first construction in order to draw out the resonance that this passage has with the subsequent descriptions that Socrates offers of the work that is characteristic of τὸ κακόν.

Further, this sentence introduces two terms whose difference is subtle but significant. While both ἀπόλλυμι and διαφθείρω can mean to destroy utterly and thus to kill, διαφθείρω also carries with it a sense of corruption. During the course of this discussion, Socrates and Glaucon will determine that the soul is such as to be corrupted without thereby being utterly destroyed, and it is informative to observe the way in which Socrates's choice of words, especially his introduction of terms, plays upon subtle shifts in meaning between killing and corrupting. Throughout this passage I have tried to remain consistent in rendering the variety of terms for negative conditions that Socrates introduces.

17. At 507b, he observes: "We affirm that there are and distinguish in speech many fine things and many good things and the same way for each."

18. I am thus in agreement with both Nettleship (1901, 356) and Brown (2001, 312) that the discussion is not intended as a separable and exhaustive demonstration of the soul's immortality, but as an extension of the ethical concerns of the dialogue. I would add, however, that its contribution and attachment to the dialogue's concern for ethics goes hand in hand with a concern for politics.

19. James Adam offers a particularly succinct version of this concern when he wonders how Socrates would deal with violent destruction, using as an example the destruction of wood not by rot but by fire. Adam's solution to this objection is as follows: "The fact is that Plato's theory of ξύμφυτον κακόν by which and which alone each object is destroyed, if destroyed it be, does not apply except where the object is independent of external influences, and such, throughout the proof, he supposes the soul to be" (Adam, *Republic*, ad loc.; Adam 1965, 424); note the similarity between this stance toward destruction and that adopted in the discussion of degenerate regimes in books 8 and 9. I am inclined, however, to agree with Eric Brown's argument that Socrates is not prohibiting the possibility of one thing being destroyed by a number of other things; to summarize Brown, if something is such as to not be destroyed by its own badness then nothing else can destroy it, but if something is such as to be destroyed by its own badness than all bets are off and any number of other things may destroy it (Brown 2001, 302).

20. It thus resonates with the account of the tendency toward dissolution of all generated things which precedes the discussion of corrupt cities and soul.

21. I am thus in agreement with Brown's assertion that natural corruption refers to a logical connection between something that is essentially such as to be able to be corrupted and that which corrupts it (Brown 2001, 302). As Brown notes, by this reading Socrates includes a course of corruption and decay in what it means for a particular thing to be and attributes a limiting function to nature (2001, 303). This is indeed controversial, but I take it to be in keeping with much of what Socrates has said in the *Republic* about the nature of a great many things, namely, that they suffer the possibility of degradation of their own integrity (see esp. 546a).

22. They can refer to ground corn or grain and firewood, respectively. How all of these things stand with respect to human matters is a question also raised by the next series of things.

23. I take this to be further evidence that Socrates's primary concern here is less with establishing an ontological difference between body and soul than with discerning the differing therapeutic needs of each, a concern resonant, as Claus (1981) has observed, with broader cultural associations.

24. This calls to mind the ambiguity that adheres to the Greek word ἀθάνατος as indicating both what is imperishable and what is divine. We see traces of this ambiguity just after this discussion when, after seeming to take himself to have shown the soul's immortality, Socrates points out that they have yet to really focus on the soul in its kinship with the divine and what is immortal (611e). However, rather than conclude that Plato's employment of this ambiguity is a sign of the incoherence of his argument, we might rather note that he poses the question of how imperishability is related to divinity by asserting the soul's imperishability in the same dialogue in which he suggests the *possibility*, not the guarantee, of souls likening themselves to the divine.

25. This is precisely the characterization of disease that Socrates offers: "the defectiveness of body, which is disease, melts and dissolves body and leads it to the point where it is not body" (609c). This characterization of disease is reminiscent of Socrates's description of disease in book 4: a condition in which the relationship between the parts of a complex entity productive of a healthy whole becomes disrupted (444d).

26. For some interesting suggestions about what the *Symposium*'s discussion of the decomposition of the body can tell us about the question of the soul's fate in the *Republic*, see Baracchi (2002, 129–30).

27. For instance, Socrates offers both illness and slaughter as examples of the same kind of dissolution (610a–b).

28. This point provides another version of the problem that emerged in our analysis of the *Phaedo*'s logoi for immortality.

29. Glaucon's conviction merits emphasis, and may in part be a function of his having taken as a lover a young man with a bodily deformation (402d–e). Socrates's method of argument here is thus particularly suited to Glaucon. We should also note that Glaucon himself suggests that bodily corruption (what had been characterized as disease) is interchangeable with death itself (610c).

30. This passage merits comparison with the *Phaedo*'s model of exchange between soul and body. There, soul becomes body-like. Here, the limits of this transformation are charted.

31. Socrates's limitation of the exchange between bodily and psychical corruptions draws into question the extent to which one can say that body corrupts soul. Of course, this limitation is itself only extended to the corruptions of body—Socrates says nothing here about whether body itself (regardless of whether or not it is corrupted) could corrupt soul. At the very least, Socrates refrains at this juncture from assessing the goodness or badness of the body as such; this is not a restraint he exercises elsewhere in the dialogue (see esp. 585d), and so it should not escape our notice here.

32. This precise list of vices is given earlier in the dialogue in book 4, right before Socrates offers an explicit formulation of the analogy between vice and disease. There it was agreed that vice is a function of the faction between the three parts of the soul such that "the confusion and wandering of these parts are injustice, licentiousness, cowardice, lack of learning, and, in sum, all vice [τήν τε ἀδικίαν καὶ ἀκολασίαν καὶ δειλίαν καὶ ἀμαθίαν καὶ συλλήβδην πᾶσαν κακίαν]" (444b). Glaucon's agreement that these vices are forms of evil indicates that he has shifted from conceiving of injustice as freedom to conceiving of injustice as a form of corruption.

33. Glaucon's conviction at this juncture causes Adam some consternation, as it seems to come not from dialectic inquiry but experience (Adam 1965, ad loc. 609d). See Brown's defense of Glaucon's position (2001, 309). Moreover, Socrates's phrasing of this question, which inserts "separation from the body" in place of "destruction of the soul" has caused some controversy; it provoked J. A. Stewart to assert that Socrates never seriously entertains the possibility of the soul's destruction (see Stewart [1905, 73]). Rosen (2005, 378) makes a similar point, asserting that Socrates "never considers whether the dissolution of the body is not also the dissolution of the soul." However, Socrates's prose suffers more from brevity than from disingenuousness here. He does at least mention the possibility of the soul's destruction at 610a and 601b. I am in agreement with Brown

that his reference to separation is a function of his desire to communicate in a manner that would be familiar to Glaucon (Brown 2001, 308–10). This construal is also the initial formulation of death in the *Phaedo*.

34. Socrates's various references to the execution of criminals are nearly impossible to read without thinking of Socrates's own fate at the hands of the Athenians. There is at least a suggestion here that not only does executing criminals fail to defend adequately against injustice, but that such execution may very well stand in the way of the critique of institutions that would provide such a defense. Whether or not Plato intends this suggesting is a question whose treatment requires more attention than can be given here.

35. Book 2 hints that vice possesses a certain unlimited or excessive quality, where the tension between aretē and pleonexia is characterized in the shift from discussing what is called by Socrates a healthy city and by Glaucon a city of swine, to discussing a luxurious and, according to Socrates, feverish city (372d–e).

36. By characterizing the soul in this manner, Plato gestures toward an impersonal dimension of the soul, a dimension that is furthered in the claim that there are always the same souls (611a). While the soul may be the source of the self, it cannot be reduced to the self; it exceeds the individual person. It is this realization that allows Socrates and Glaucon to agree upon the limitations of their investigation and to characterize the view of the soul with which they have been operating as one of the soul in its human life (612a).

37. Here I defer to Bloom's translation, and return to using this translation for citation throughout the rest of this chapter.

38. Glaucon's conception of death as a liberation from one's own vice is contended with in the myth of Er.

39. I am thus in agreement with Jonathan Lear, who, noting the affinity Plato draws between poets and tyrants, writes, "Plato's point is that if you really want to get rid of the tyrant, you also have to get rid of the cultural vehicles that make him look attractive: you must also banish his poetical counterpart" (Lear 1992, 213).

40. Moline (1978, 20) has identified a similar instance of self-diagnosis and treatment at play in the *Phaedo*.

41. As he has noted (Woolf 2012, 163 n. 25), Raphael Woolf and I agree that the Glaucus image as an image of the psychological *methodology* employed by Socrates and his interlocutors.

42. Such imagery suggests a Socratic version of Nietzsche's famous philosophizing with a hammer.

43. Glaucon explicitly describes their discussion in terms of its justice: 612d (if he doesn't remember their previous agreements he would be doing an injustice [ἀδικοίην]); 612e (what Socrates asks is just [δίκαια]); 613e (what Socrates says is just [δίκαια]). For a discussion of how this context might be tailored to Glaucon's own expectations about the performance of justice, see G. Ferrari (2011).

44. Although, as we will see, details about these rewards are conspicuously absent from the myth.

45. This need is reciprocal; in telling the myth, Socrates saves it, just as, he claims, it could save them (621b).

46. The presentation of this necessity supplies an antidote to the image of the tyrant unscathed by his actions in book 2. The discernment of the effects of one's actions will motivate, in turn, the account of the afterlife in the *Laws* (where we will encounter again the soul that can bear all evil and all good, and the operation of necessity).

47. For a compelling discussion of the martial resonances of the myth of Er, see Baracchi (2002).

48. This identification of the greatest risk resonates with Socrates emphasis, twice, in book 1, on the profound importance of the choice of life (344e, 352d).

49. The other impediment, chance (represented most vividly by the convention of lots that determine the order of choosing) does not make the choice of a good life impossible. Even one who has been given the final choice could still find a decent life (691b). My contention is that the tale assumes the operation of chance as well as necessity, and focuses upon those impediments to choosing well that are in some way up to the one doing the choosing, impediments of which she is somehow the source. The habits and lack of training that affect the choice of the first chooser, for example, are things he has taken on and failed to scrutinze. Thus, while I agree with H. S. Thayer's eloquent emphasis on the role of choice in the myth, I diverge from his account of the myth as presenting the true soul as a "pure chooser," precisely on the grounds that these choices are made by souls still bearing the effects of their previous lives and the terms of their punishment or reward (see Thayer 1988, esp. 372).

50. The silence with which Er's tale passes over the beauties to which these souls are exposed marks a divergence from the detailed account of the lives of the blessed in the myth of the *Phaedo*, a silence that is consistent with the myth of Er's orientation toward the conditions leading up to and after judgment, rather than describing the specific processes by which justice is enacted. That this focus has a certain dissonance with the purported aim of returning wages to justice and injustice has been observed by G. Ferrari (2011).

51. "there are eight whorls in all, lying in one another [ἐν ἀλλήλοις ἐγκειμένους] with their rims showing as circles from above, while from the back they form one continuous whorl [ἑνὸς σφονδύλου] around the stem, which is driven right through the middle of the eighth" (616d–e).

52. In doing so, it also illuminates the essential features of vision as such: brightness, relationality and reflection, similarity and dissimilarity, multiplicity, differences between and within specific colors (note the use of comparatives and superlatives): "the lip of the largest whorl is multicolored [ποικίλον]; that of the seventh, brightest [λαμπρότατον]; that of the eighth gets its color from the seventh's shining [προσλάμποντος] on it; that of the second and the fifth are like each other [παραπλήσια ἀλλήοις], yellower [ξανθότερα] than these others; the third has the whitest color [λευκότατον χρῶμα]; the fourth is reddish [ὑπέρυθρον]; and the sixth is second in whiteness [δεύτερον δὲ λευκότητι]" (616e–617a). On the possible significance of the order in which these colors are mentioned, see Brumbaugh (1951 and 1954).

53. "The whole spindle is turned in a circle with the same motion, but within the revolving whole the seven inner circles revolve gently in the opposite direction from the whole . . . [κυκλεῖσθαι δὲ δὴ στρεφόμενον τὸν ἄτρακτον ὅλον μὲν τὴν αὐτὴν φοράν, ἐν δὲ τῷ ὅλῳ περιφερομένῳ τοὺς μὲν ἐντὸς ἑπτὰ κύκλος τὴν ἐναντίαν τῷ ὅλῳ ἠρέμα περιφέρεσθαι]" (617a–b).

54. It is also consistent with the conception of human nature operative since book 2, that is, as a nature possessing individual, but limited, capacity for deeds, see chapter 4.

55. For a different interpretation of the absence of a philosophic life among the patterns of life listed, see Ferrari (2011).

56. Socrates's focus on good or bad lives recalls the discussion of immortality's account of good and bad things.

57. This suggests that the issue with respect to strength is less the body than the kind of life one can have in particular times and places when one possesses a body of a particular sort.

58. The judgment itself is revealed as lacking in a certain fineness or subtlety.

59. Here there is a resonance with the afterlife tale in the *Gorgias*, in which souls maintain the scars of their wrongdoing as well as, it would seem, the influence of polis, insofar as they are judged according to region (524a).

60. That animals choose as well is less surprising if we keep in mind that their own lives have likely been animated by souls that at other times were human, as, according to their discussion of immortality, there are only a finite number of souls, ceaselessly circulating through bodies and lives (611a). At 620d, Socrates attributes justice and injustice to animal souls as well. But these

details do punctuate the question, raised above, of how, if at all, human life is different from animal life.

61. As we shall see, the *Laws* presents a version of this theme of the power of the passions of the soul.

62. We see here the return of the standard of health, but a standard that has been inflected by the very particular approach toward medicine at work in this dialogue, as we have highlighted in our study of the *Republic*. Again, the difference between this account and the blessings reserved for the philosophic life in the afterlife that are presented in the myth in the *Phaedo* is pronounced, and further underscores the difference in trajectory: while the *Republic* is determined by the task of choosing a life, the *Phaedo* is determined by the task of defending a life that has been chosen.

63. We see here an invocation of the conception of pollution so significant for the *Phaedo*, as we have seen chapters 1–3.

64. Thayer (1988, 380) will go so far as to say the myth of Er is not about immortality at all. In emphasizing the this-worldly concern of the myth of Er, I am offering something like what Stephen Halliwell describes as an allegorical reading, and doing so very much along the lines Halliwell himself suggests (Halliwell 2007, 469). If I am right about the this-worldly trajectory of the discussion of immortality, then the problem Halliwell identifies with an allegorical reading of the myth of Er, that it discards the claim that gave rise to the myth (the claim that soul is immortal) is diminished.

Part III

1. Unless otherwise noted, all citations are taken directly from Bury (1967). Pangle's (1980), Saunders's (1975) and Mayhew's (2008) translations were consulted as well.

2. For instance, we might take a Nietzschean approach, reading these lines as a particularly forceful expression of the vindictive, violent and revengeful tendency toward the spectacle of suffering which Nietzsche finds characteristic of Platonic metaphysics and psychology (Nietzsche 1989). Or, following Giorgio Agamben's analysis of the state of exception, we could conceive of these lines as an attempt to use the threat of the existence of recalcitrant, corrupts souls to establish a perpetual state of crisis and to justify the conferral of absolute authority upon the law wardens (Agamben 1998). Or, we might adopt a less literalist reading of these lines and see in them a description of an essential feature of the city rather than an imperative, a reading I take to be in keeping with Seth Benardete's provocative claim that Hades "is nothing but another name for the city" (Benardete, 35, cited in Burger (2004, 58). If, in following this line of thought, the city is the final scene of judgment and punishment, these lines are simply a call to acknowledge this and legislate accordingly. Such a reading is far more sympathetic to the Athenian's motives; however, it also provides a characterization of the city that risks the possibility of becoming fuel for the legislative violence that the Athenian himself criticizes. This is by no means an exhaustive list; myriad other approaches to this passage could be cobbled together from major figures in the history of philosophy.

3. As Trevor Saunders (1991, 157) has observed, "since this is far less severe than the penalties traditionally associated with the next world, the Stranger's point may well be more *recherché*: just as death is removal from life, so too the penalty in this world will be 'removal from life,' in another sense." But note also: "The penalty is harsher than the fine for *aikia* of Attic law; indeed it is not clear how life in the conditions specified would be possible, though if the offender were a lot-holder he would presumably be allowed to live off its revenues. . . . Perhaps the point is that the offender is beast-like, and should therefore live in the county-side" (ibid., 275; see also 273 n. 33).

4. To this list of violences, we would also have to add the violence of the threat of exile that is made in the annunciation of the law. Throughout this section, I take for granted the violence of the law, the Athenian's frequent assertion of the inadequacy of law, his various critiques of law,

and the more subtle and in some ways more troubling violence that attends even to the "persuasive" preludes. While gentleness is treated in this dialogue as desirable, its legislative instantiation is enigmatic and perpetually incomplete. On the violence of the law, see esp. Laks (2006, 277–78, 286–90).

5. Book 6 concludes with this statement: "For everyone the first year is the beginning [ἀρχὴ] of the whole life [βίου]: it ought to be inscribed [γεγράφθαι] as life's beginning [ζωῆς ἀρχη] for both boy and girl in their ancestral shrines [ἐν ἱεροῖσι πατρῴοις]: beside it, on a whited wall in every phratry, there should be written up the number of the archons who give its number to the year; and the names of the living members of the phratry shall be written always together, and those of the deceased shall be erased" (785b). Note that this "birth certificate" locates the citizen with respect to the gods, family, government, time (the year whose number is given by the number of the archon), and space.

6. The crowning image of this model of biological unity is that of the head, of which the younger members of the synod are the eyes and ears and the elder the mind (964d–965a). This model of civic unity is duplicated in architectural expression by the building of walls in such a manner as to make the entire city into the shape of a single house (779d).

7. Whether this is also an anthropological or more broadly biological basis is a question invited by the Athenian's sliding between speaking about "each of us" and about living beings more broadly.

8. This topic arises in the course of outlining a system of education conceived as a training in virtue (πρὸς ἀρετὴν) (643e), wherein the Athenian asserts that those capable of ruling themselves are good (ὡς ἀγαθῶν) and those incapable of so ruling are bad (κακῶν) (644b). It is in clarifying what he means by this that the Athenian offers the infamous image of living beings as playthings of the gods. He begins constructing the image by attaining agreement about the principle unit or subject of its portraiture: "May we assume that each of us by himself is a one [my replacement of Bury's 'single unit' and Pangles 'one person'] [Οὐκοῦν ἕνα μὲν ἡμῶν ἕκαστον αὐτὸν τιθῶμεν]" (644c). It is worthwhile to note that this assertion of singularity arises within the context of an investigation of rulership; the Athenian develops this image as an account of the legislative subject, the being for whom laws are enacted.

9. Indeed, one significant point of comparison between the *Republic* and the *Laws* lies in their differing emphases on the primary residence of the laws; in the *Republic*, where the analysis of city and soul takes place for the sake of discerning the best life, the residence of laws in the soul receives more emphasis. In the *Laws*, I will argue, the city is the primary home of the laws, although in the present context law itself is viewed as the external expression of what is internally manifest as logismos.

10. On the relationship between nomos and nous, see 713e–714a and 957c. The qualification in this latter passage, namely that the learning pertaining to the laws is sovereign with respect to human betterment if they are set up correctly is important, but maintains the relationship between nomos and nous by shifting the burden from the laws themselves to their instantiation by the legislators. See also the correlation between logismos and nous at 967b. On enslavement to the laws as enslavement to the gods, see 762e. At 741b, the lot distributing property is itself called divine. At 902b, it is agreed that all mortal things are possessions of the gods.

11. Indeed, as Morrow (1993, 101) notes, "Plato asserts that the establishment of a right attitude toward property is the foundation (krēpis) of all legislation, the security of the state." Morrow cites 736a, but we also find this proper attitude encapsulated in the justification for prohibiting the taking of lost, abandoned or buried property in book 11: "For never should I gain so much pecuniary profit by its removal, as I should win increase in virtue of soul and in justice by not removing it; and by preferring to gain justice in my soul rather than money in my purse, I should be winning a greater in place of a lesser gain, and that too in a better part of me" (913a).

12. The enigmatic nature of this relationship is furthered in book 12's funerary laws, in which citizens are exhorted to believe the lawgivers' statement that the soul is, "the being that is really each of us" (959a–b). The laws against suicide are revelatory of this relationship between what is one's own, the city's and the god's; suicide, outside of certain legally recognized contexts, is treated as a rebellious and appropriative gesture. Socrates displays a similar attitude toward suicide in the *Phaedo* wherein he speaks of humans as the property of the gods (62b).

13. The spontaneous eruptions of order in dance, the occasions when someone loves justice and eschews the companionship of the unjust, the care and attention a technitēs has in dealing with his subject matter or performing his art, all speak to some kinship with the orderly motion of the universe. Laks's (2006, 277–78) discussion of the "human prodigy" and especially the significance of dance is quite helpful on this point.

14. We can see the prohibition on the citizens' participation in commerce and paid labor as reserving for them the work that is the city by exempting them from the work of the city.

15. As they do in the Platonic corpus as a whole. It is worthwhile to compare this list with that of the three forces (βιάζοιτ) that compel people to keep sexual laws: reverence to the gods (θεοσεβὲς), love of honor (φιλότιμον), desire (ἐπιθυμίᾳ) for fair form of soul, rather than body (841c).

16. Of course, it is necessary to emphasize the imaginary or fantastic character of this address. Whatever "dialogue" or conversation occurs between the prelude and citizen, it is unlikely to take the shape of the conversation between the Athenian, Clinias, and Megillus.

17. Laks 2006, 289.

18. For instance, excessive self-love, which leads to a conceit of knowledge (731d–e) that, as double ignorance, can produce countless ills (863b–d); desires, spiritedness, pleasures and pain, hopes, false beliefs about the good (around 864dff.), etc.

19. Or, as Kahn describes it in order to avoid comparisons with a "tri-partite" theory of soul, an entire moral phenomenology (Kahn 2004, 362).

20. As Nightingale (1993, 293) concisely puts it, "the preludes are 'doing things' to the citizens."

Chapter 8

1. The Athenian begins his construction of this image by identifying the unit or subject of analysis: "May we assume that each of us by himself is a one?" (644c). I think it worthwhile to note that this assertion of human singularity arises within the context of a specifically juridical investigation. The sketch of the human being that is to follow is one motivated by the question of how best to legislate. The puppet image does not explicitly state that the cords it identifies are in the soul, only that they are in the human being. However, that these cords are psychological phenomena is asserted throughout the dialogue; see in particular the claim shortly thereafter that drunkenness establishes a disposition in the soul (645e), as well as the attribution of pleasure, pain, ignorance, and arguments in the soul at (689a–b), and the discussion of injustice and justice as conditions of the soul in book 9 (863e–864a).

2. At 715b, the Athenian asserts that the laws must look to what is common to the whole city in order to be correct.

3. The mandatory musical performances outlined in book 2 make clear that the citizens' education in pleasure and pain is ongoing, and requires replenishment throughout their lives (see Frede [2010]; and Kamtekar [2010]). While Kamtekar (2010, 143) contrasts the *Laws*' description of the wayward and chaotic tendencies of pleasure, pain, and even calculation in the young (653d–654a and 808d) with the *Republic*'s description of the plasticity of young souls, I assert that the capacity to tolerate these unruly pulls is precisely a function of plasticity.

4. It would be interesting to compare this account of human nature with that promoted by the noble lie in the *Republic*. For instance, while the noble lie is constructed to justify a purported distinction between kinds of people, the puppet image asserts a structure common to all.

5. The prelude he gives in the example of the double form makes claims, not incidentally, about immortality (721b–c). As we will see, the preludes frequently employ some conception of immortality as part of their persuasion.

6. For an interpretation of this much-cited passage, see Laks (2010).

7. For further discussion of this alignment of injustice and disease, see chapter 10.

8. All laws have preludes, but the need to deliver them must be tempered by the individual legislators discernment of when it is necessary to do so (723c–d).

9. The Athenian will go on to distinguish between this judgment, which he calls retribution, and legal penalty, a distinction which anticipates the dual punitive models at work in the Athenian legal system that Plato will make use of in the *Laws* penal legislation, as we shall see toward the end of this chapter and in more detail in chapter 9. For further discussion of the role of divine intercession in this judgment, see chapter 10.

10. The role of ignorance in wrongdoing is prefigured in book 3, in which we read that the greatest ignorance is that evinced by one who hates what he judges to be noble and good and loves what he judges to be bad and unjust (689a). The Athenian continues: "that want of accord, on the part of the feelings of pain and pleasure, with the rational judgment is, I maintain, the extreme form of ignorance and also the 'greatest' because it belongs to the main mass of the soul,—for the part of the soul that feels pain and pleasure corresponds to the mass of the populace in the state" (689a–b).

11. We should compare this claim with one from the *Phaedo*, in which Socrates asserts that pleasure and pain nail the soul to the body and confuse it about what is really worthwhile, making it believe that the cause of pleasure and pain is the most real thing. As with the gushing fountains of pleasure and pain, the problem in the *Laws* is not characterized as an absence or lack of something but as an excess, in this case an excess of self-regard, a mistake about the position one occupies with respect to what is good and bad, too high an estimation of one's value, a failure to conceive of one's own interest within a larger framework.

12. These lines offer a possible index for comparing Platonic and contemporary political philosophy, insofar as they suggest that one primary problem in Plato's political philosophy is overcoming excessive self-love and the unfettered desire for acquisition. While, on the other hand, one primary problem for contemporary (or modern, insofar as this question was first put by Spinoza) political philosophy is how to understand human beings' willingness to fight to the death for their own oppression (see Michel Foucault's introduction to Deleuze and Guattari [1983]). Such a study would invite one to consider the relationship between a political theory that emphasizes human acquisitive tendencies (viewing the human being as the being that acquires) and one that emphasizes human suicidal tendencies (viewing the human being as the being that negates).

13. This is, of course, the Socratic claim.

14. I follow Saunders (1991, 147) in assuming that the Athenian separates them out according to the distinction drawn at 863b–d between simple and double ignorance, double ignorance being the conceit of knowledge.

15. For discussions of the decisive role of the anger of the victim in Athenian penal law, see Saunders (1991); Allen (2000); and Konstan (2003). Saunders (1991, 178) will go so far as to say that with this model of penal law Plato comes very close to eradicating the rubric of punishment entirely.

16. Much of the civic ideology promoted in the preludes in book 10 will be focused upon convincing the citizen that the good of the city is also the good of the citizen.

17. As Margaret Mackenzie's thorough illustration of the *Laws*' emphasis on the good of the city (as distinct from the *Gorgias*'s more limited emphasis on the psychic condition of the criminal alone) makes clear (Mackenzie 1981, 195–204).

18. As Saunders characterizes it, "the position achieved at the end of the *Oresteia* is then in essence what we find in the Athenian homicide law of the classical period: purification rituals and legal processes operate side by side" (Saunders 1991, 71). Chapter 1 of this book deals with Plato's appropriation of the first in the *Phaedo*.

19. Parker 1996, 128. According to Saunders, Plato "has drafted into his law, on a grand scale, a set of beliefs which were probably already waning in his day, interpreted them in accordance with his penology as strictly a demand for recompense, and so used them as a means of reconciliation and restoration of normalcy" (Saunders, 1991, 256). This restoration of normalcy by means of deploying the language, concepts and practices of purification is Plato's attestation to the phenomenological "account" of violence encapsulated within these practices.

20. Vernant 1990, 134.

21. Thucydides 1996, 40.

Chapter 9

1. This attitude toward suicide marks a divergence form the one Plato gives to Socrates in the *Phaedo*; however, its presence here in the prelude suggests it may be used simply to set up the appropriateness of the sentence of death for one who fails to be persuaded by this prelude and acts on his temptation.

2. This discussion begins with the identification of its various kinds: "death, or imprisonment, or stripes, or seats or stations or exposures of a degrading kind at temples or at outermost boundaries, or money-fines" (855c). Punishment so conceived applies a calculus not only to those elements of human life that admit of degree—time, body (both by means of the gradations of pain that can be inflicted and by violation of the integrity of the corpse), honor, money—but to human life itself. Note, too, that the Athenian points out on several occasions that death is not the worst penalty (see, for instance, 854e).

3. There is here an echo of the myth of the *Phaedo*'s separation between the souls of those who have committed homicides and those they have wronged, and the need of these souls to attain forgiveness in order to by received back into the community of those they have wronged.

4. This indifference to whether one describes the tale as a logos or a mythos is significant but certainly not without precedent (see Socrates's characterization of the afterlife tale he offers in the *Gorgias*).

5. The reference to the model of propitiation as "like to like" is particularly interesting here. It will be picked up again in book 10, where we see that theodicy functions by moving souls to the company of like to like (904e–905a), as I will discuss further in chapter 10.

6. After all, if Socrates is any indication, philosophy has a profoundly ambivalent connection to impiety, one that is more directly asserted by the Athenian's claim in book 12 that one source of slander against the philosophers is to be found in the astronomical theories of certain sophists (967c–d). His observation that atheistic beliefs about heavenly bodies are bred in reaction to a certain kind of theology rampant in Athens is also a noteworthy detail of his account of impiety (886b–e).

7. The stance that he will adopt throughout the legislating of impiety, the stance that enables this entire discussion to resemble a dialogue given the limitations of Klinias and Megillus (892e–893a), is that of giving voice to the impious, answering and asking as the impious as well as the legislator. In order to have a substantive dialogue, the Athenian must bifurcate. And what his assertion that they listen to the words of the impious signals to us is that he is now going to adopt the seductive posture and speak in the cloying voice of the one who knows you better than you know yourself.

8. This is to say, the legislated accuse the legislators of corruption. The Athenian and his interlocutors initially accept this context: "Are we to make our defense as it were before a court of impious

men, where someone had accused us of doing something dreadful by assuming in our legislation the existence of gods?" (889e–887a), asks the Athenian and receives a reply in the affirmative. Eventually, the Athenian counters this somewhat aggressive move on the part of the legislated by inverting the charge. He will present the position of the legislated in such a manner as to make them answerable to the charge of corrupting the youth, a reversal made most explicit by Klinias's response to it: "What a horrible statement you have described, Stranger! And what widespread corruption of the young in private families as well as publicly in the states! (890b). This exchange, and the courtroom scene it presents, evokes Socrates's trial and then inverts it.

9. In doing so, the Athenian draws together two figures: those ancient poets who have produced stories about the gods, and contemporary investigators of nature, sophists. While the Athenian exercises some restraint in critiquing the ancient stories of the gods, and states that it is rather the views of the sophist that must be held responsible for the beliefs productive of impiety, the significance of his mention of the ancient composers of theogonies in this context should not be lost on us. The theologies of the ancient poets, suggests the Athenian, actually leads to sophistic, akratic cosmology.

10. The Athenian's description at 891c–d of the atheist's views as not only harmful but erroneous suggests that the prelude to them will be both therapeutic (correcting with respect to health) and also the case (correct with respect to the truth); that these two need not always accompany one another is implied in the *Republic* by the therapeutic function attributed to the lie in speech (382c–d). For a recent treatment of the argumentative status of these preludes, see Bobonich (2002), along with the discussions of this work in Kahn (2004) and Brisson (2005).

11. See Mayhew (2008).

12. 892b, 896d, 897a.

13. Note the difference between the address to this atheist, "O Child," and the address to this person, "My good man."

14. At 365d–e, Adeimantus identifies precisely the three beliefs that the Athenian considers the source of impiety. Note Socrates's expression of surprise and admiration that Glaucon and Adeimantus have not been simply swept up by the cultural forces valorizing tyranny that surround them (368a–b).

15. See Laks (2006, 277–78).

16. See also 906b: human beings are to be saved by justice, temperance and wisdom, "which dwell in the animate [ἐμψύχοις] powers of the gods, and of which some small trace may be clearly seen here also residing in us." I take the manifestations of order in play and dance and the love of justice to be evidence of this "trace" of divinity.

17. The Athenian context of the cultural milieu that the stranger has been outlining is made apparent in this distinction. For a recent discussion of the significance of parrhēsia in Athens, see Monoson (2000). See also Morrow's (1993, 591–93) concluding comments on Plato and Athens in his commentary on the *Laws*.

18. The deist simply needs a vision, a scale by means of which to locate the expiation of unjust deeds. What this prelude and its charm offers him is the equivalent of a wide-angle lens, a panoptic shot.

19. As with Socrates in the *Republic*, it is the enigmatic character of the good to which the Athenian would call attention.

Chapter 10

1. My translation. Bury (1967): "it would most truly be described as a superlatively natural existence"; Saunders (1975): "it will be quite correct to say that soul is pre-eminently natural"; Pangle (1980): "it would be most correct, almost, to say that it is especially by nature." Unless otherwise

noted, the translations cited herein are those of Bury; I have made occasional revisions in consultation with the translations of Saunders and Pangle, notably replacing Bury's use of "State" to render polis with "city," and have noted these as they occur.

2. The Greek text is that of Burnet, the citations of Bury's (1926) translation are from the Loeb Classical Library; of Saunders (1975) from his Penguin edition; and of Thomas Pangle (1980) from his Basic Books edition.

3. Used by Hesiod and Homer but rare in Attic prose. The only other occurrence of this word I can find in the Platonic corpus is in the *Phaedo*'s description of the ever-flowing rivers of hot and cold water under the earth (111d).

4. While his translation takes the most liberties, Saunders (1975) is careful to note explicitly the difficulties involved in translating this line (see 528).

5. Certainly, some of the difficulty here is likely due to the decidedly unpolished character of the final two books of the dialogue; however, their connection both in form and content to the previous books of the dialogue, especially to book 10, makes textual corruption and/or hasty posthumous editing insufficient grounds for dismissing them. Sustained and careful investigation of them is both warranted and invited. I take the care needed in such an investigation to be well indicated by the cautionary issues raised by Nails and Thesleff (2003) even as I remain unconvinced of their larger claim regarding the extent of Phillip of Opus's editorship.

6. Menn's (1995) claim that nous is to be understood as the virtue that orders the cosmos, and that uses soul as its instrument in doing so, goes a long way toward clarifying the relation between psuchē and nous in several dialogues, the *Timaeus* in particular. I am indebted to his careful treatment of this issue. However, as I argue, the emphasis in the *Laws* falls less upon the work of nous than on the work of soul. This shift in emphasis troubles the relationship that Menn sees at work in the *Timaeus* and begs explanation, the preliminary formulation of which I develop in the following pages.

7. The *Laws* and the *Republic* share an inquiry into the psychological qualities with which a city must contend and an emphasis on the importance of the city's finding a way to take in hand natures possessing particular attributes.

8. The Athenian literally addresses him as "Child" (ὁ παῖ) (888a).

9. Recall the function allocated to the lie in speech in the *Republic*—as a treatment for the mad, as a cure available to the politician, and as a means of approximating the truth about matters that remain deeply obscure (382c–d).

10. As though to acknowledge that the conclusion that the Athenian is to draw from these two agreements—namely, that soul is self-motion—is in need of further argumentation, the Athenian then briefly segues into a discussion of the three things that can be attributed to any thing: substance, definition, and name. The preludes to both the deist (902b) and the one who maintains that the gods can be bribed (906b) echo the assertion that being alive entails a certain divine solicitude.

11. I take the claim that soul is πρεσβυτάτη to be strongly honorific; psuchē is oldest and first in the sense of best and greatest. At the same time, given the "definition" of soul as self-moving motion, and thus as generated but undying (904a), we must conceive of something like psychic time. Indeed, because psuchē is generated but unending, its time is a time of perpetual beginning, a time that intimates cyclical, rotational motion. As the actions of soul are the workings of love and hatred, sorrow and joy, wish, memory, opinion, etc., this would also be a time of psychic deeds and effects, a time of perpetual psychic generation. Psychic time is pathic and ergonic time, it is the working through of passion and action. While there is not space to develop this line of thought here, I submit that doing so would shed further light on Plato's use of afterlife myths in general, in which the working through or expiation of unjust deeds is a frequent topic, and in the *Laws* in particular. The fate of individual souls outlined in the charm to the deist, the time it takes a soul to migrate to the community of souls appropriate to it, offers an image of the time and space of violence and its expiation.

12. See E. N. Lee's (1976) provocative discussion of rotation and nous.

13. "the argument now in front of us is too violent [σφοδρότερος], and probably impassable, for such strength as you possess; so, lest it make you dizzy as it rushes past and poses you with questions you are unused [ἀήθεις] to answering, and thus causes an unpleasing lack of shapliness and seemliness, I think that I ought now to act in the way described—question myself first, while you remain listening in safety, and then return answer to myself, and in this way proceed through the whole argument until it has discussed in full the subject of soul and demonstrated that soul is prior to body" (892e–893a).

14. "But surely even if the soul itself moves itself, then at any rate it would be moved, so that, if every motion is a stepping outside itself of the thing moved insofar as it is moved, the soul would step outside its own thinghood, if it moves itself not incidentally, but motion belongs to its thinghood in its own right." (*De Anima*, 406b13ff.). Joseph Sachs offers a sobering warning about two possible effects of attributing to soul such a character: "To avoid this consequence, one would have to say that the soul is that which, by its very nature, moves or alters itself in ways that do not belong to its nature. Finding the nature of the soul in self-motion may sound impressive, but it seems to be either contradictory or empty" (Sachs 2001, 60). I am placing a lot of weight on Sachs's "seems" here.

15. In both references from 894c, a form of διαφέρω is used.

16. This passage and the image proposed, the motion of the sun, has powerful resonances with *Republic* 6 and with the *Phaedo*'s famous second sailing passage (99d–100a).

17. The attribution of all motion (good and bad) to soul does suggest a difference between the *Laws* and *Timaeus*; however, the weight of this difference may not be as substantial as it appears (see Parry [2002]).

18. How we are to read this division is a matter of some debate (see Mohr [2006]; Vlastos [1995]; Carone [1994 and 2005]; Clegg [1976]; Easterling [1967]; and Meldrum [1950]).

19. I take soul's reception of mind to shed some light on the characterization of soul as διαφερόντως φύσει (892c), and to suggest that the ambiguity of the phrase is fully intended. To say that soul exceeds as well as exemplifies nature is to say that soul exceeds certain boundaries and horizons, which is also to suggest that in order to operate within those boundaries and horizons, some kind of limit needs to be imposed on soul. Again, Aristotle is helpful here: "But though [fire] is in some way jointly [of nutrition and growth] it is surely not simply the cause, but rather the soul is, for the growth of fire goes on without limit, so long as there is something burnable, but all things put together by nature have a limit and a proportion of size and growth, and this belongs to soul, not to fire, and to the articulation of the meaning more than the material" (416a14ff.). Insofar as nature is the site of limit, were soul to exceed nature it would also exceed limit. Of course, for Aristotle it is the manifestation of limit as a manifestation of soul that, in part, recommends the inquiry of soul as contributing to the inquiry into nature, while it is the character of fire (for instance) to go on without limit, and I am claiming that Plato's account of viciousness suggests that body operates under certain limits which soul does not. By this reading, what Aristotle asserts about soul could only be said of soul with mind.

20. With limit understood in this sense, the presentation of soul's reception of mind in the *Laws* resonates with the *Philebus*'s presentation of the fecund and generative work accomplished by number, law, and order in bringing limit to the unlimited (*Philebus*, 23d, 25d, 26b, 27b).

21. The intimacy between mind and law is emphasized earlier on in the dialogue (see esp. 713e–714a: the ordering of mind is called law).

22. The controversy surrounding the question of whether Plato conceives of nous as separable from psuchē is long-standing; that is, while in the *Laws* the Athenian claims that soul can operate without mind, whether mind can operate without soul is less clear, and seems contraindicated by *Phil.* 30c, *Tim.* 30b, and *Soph* 248e–249d. Like Mayhew (2010) and Bobonich (2002), I remain largely neutral, noting only that Menn's (1995) argument for separability is persuasive, and adding that in

the *Laws* Plato is as concerned to indicate the intimacy of soul and mind as soul's capacity to operate without mind. Further, while Menn takes separability as evidence that Plato has a theology distinct from his metaphysics and physics, I view soul's ability to operate without mind as Plato's intimating that psychology cannot be reduced to theology, metaphysics, or even physics.

23. It should also be noted that nomos is not the only limiting or correcting entity in the dialogue. For instance, among the arsenal of techniques and instruments needed by the legislator in order to counteract the desires for food, drink, and sex that can lead to hamartia, law is listed as only one of three greatest forces (783a); the other two, fear and true account, mingle with some frequency in the preludes themselves, as well as in the Platonic corpus as a whole, and we can note throughout the *Laws* Plato's concerns about the efficacy of human legislators to properly instantiate the *Laws*. For this reason I remain, with others, unconvinced by Chris Bobonich's claims about the rationality of the procedures for legislating in the *Laws* (see Bobonich [2002]; and the comments of Kahn [2004]; Brisson [2005]; and Gerson [2003]).

24. It is also consistent with figurations of legislation in other dialogues. I have in mind here in particular the Protagoras, in which dikē is presented as a gift from Zeus meant to correct Epimethean shortsightedness in denying humans any means to defend themselves (322c).

25. It would be hasty to assume that Plato is necessarily concerned with human flourishing as such. However, the Athenian's comments in book 1 about war and peace do imply a preoccupation with human happiness in this dialogue (see also 718a).

26. "But there are certain souls that dwell on the earth and have acquired unjust gain which, being plainly bestial, beseech the souls of the guardians—whether they be watch-dogs or herdsmen or the most exalted masters—trying to convince them by fawning words and prayerful incantations that (as the tales of evil men relate) they can profiteer among men on earth without any severe penalty: but we assert that the sin now mentioned, of profiteering or 'overgaining,' is what is called in the case of fleshly bodies 'disease,' in that of seasons and years 'pestilence,' and in that of states and politics, by a verbal change, this same sin is called 'injustice'" (906b-c).

27. This charm thus reiterates the emphasis on place and the presentation of rotation as a means of attaining selfsameness which recommends it as an image of the motion of mind. Its invocation of "like to like" reminds us of the pre-Socratic context with which Plato engages throughout this dialogue.

28. I follow Bury (1967) and others here in supplying "of the truth" as that the trace of which requires knowledge of the places of the soul to see, but it is important to acknowledge that no reference to truth is made in this phrase. Literally, it simply reads, "to see a trace."

29. This connection between psychology and ontology is suggested much earlier in book 10 when an investigation into soul provokes the Athenian to investigate what it means to investigate anything; namely, to discern its substance, definition, and name (895d).

30. This point could also be stated another way: If one is to have a dialectical grasp of these activities, that is, if one is to interrogate the hypotheses that ground them, then some investigation of soul is necessary. It is difficult to see how one could attempt to reinvigorate ontology by returning to Plato without also returning to the question of the soul, no matter how much one may want to avoid this. I take the necessity of psychology for ancient ontology to be part of Jacques Derrida's concern about Heidegger's desire to set spirit aside and his inability to do so in (see Derrida 1991). But it is also the case that in order to properly understand ancient investigations of soul we would have to broaden our conception far beyond contemporary meanings of the term "psychology," a term whose inadequacy for this purpose has been well demonstrated by both Husserl and Heidegger.

31. The Athenian's assertion that the soul is affected only by itself or other souls is reminiscent of the claim in *Republic* 10 that things can only be destroyed by the form of corruption that is native to them (609a-b).

32. Here we are reminded of the myth of the *Gorgias*, wherein the soul's action have a reflexive and reverberative effect upon the soul itself, leaving scars that can be read by the discerning (that is, dead) judge (532a–524a).

33. This manner of speaking conjoins two idioms also connected in *Phaedo*, that of transmigration and that of the accounts of the soul's journey through Hades in which it is subject to landscapes that purify it of its evil deeds. And clearly, the promise of punishment resides just under the surface of this charm, in this case the punishment that the potentially impious person would like to see doled out to the unjust if he is to be convinced of the gods care for humans. I maintain, however, that the growing emphasis on the condition of human community in this passage serves to shift this desire for punishment to a fear for the condition of and care for the soul that cannot be dissociated from a care for the city.

34. See also 906b: human beings are to be saved by the justice, temperance and wisdom "which dwell in the animate [ἐμψύχοις] powers of the gods, and of which some small trace may be clearly seen here also residing in us."

35. See 897b–c: the soul with mind is wise and good, the soul or souls that rule heaven are souls with mind (and thus wise and good). I follow Mayhew (2010) in reading this discussion as suggesting that the gods are mind joined with cosmic soul, and also the possibility that there is some one god that is pure mind itself.

36. The role of the gods in this passage is further punctuated by the distinction it draws between this judgment against wrongdoing, which is a form of retribution, and legal penalty (728c). Here, as elsewhere in the dialogues, legal penalty is lesser than and receives its value from divine justice. I find Gabriela Carone's (1994 and 2005) distinction between the account of psuchē as such and the account of human psuchē in particular a compelling response to the question of how these automatic responses are also a function of divine intercession, and would add only that the question itself becomes less important if the mindful intercession of the gods in the form of the law is seen as an enhancement or augmentation (a prosthesis) that is invited by human soul.

37. Benardete's provocative claim that Hades "is nothing but another name for the city" is apropos as well (see Burger [2004, 58]).

38. I provide further development of this claim at the end of this chapter in a discussion of the image of legislation as painting at 769a–e. In brief, I would just note that the primary emphasis in this image is not on painting as a likeness or imitation (as an image of legislation as imitating or approximating), but on the need of the painter (as an image of the legislator) to acknowledge his limitations and to educate others in order to compensate for his fallibility and mortality. In short, this image includes a marked call to pluralism. See also R. F. Stalley's (1983, 184–85) brief address of the checks and balances in the *Laws* as a rebuttal to Popper (1971).

39. And indeed, one powerful such limit is found in the way in which human life confronts its own mortality, or rather in some ways of confronting this mortality; other ways fail to provide such a limit. So, one could say that the attitude toward death is a significant site for psychic limitation or the lack thereof.

40. There are a few passages in book 12 in which the Stranger speaks about laws in a manner similar to that used to speak about cosmic bodies: the archē of virtue is not to wander (πλανᾶσθαι) but to have many aims; it is not surprising that the legal customs of many cities wander (πλανᾶσθαι) (962d). This exhortation to single-mindedness and focus or singularity of aim is an equivalent to the revolution that acts as an image of the motion of mind and to the law of "like to like." It is with such a model of the city that those citizens who possess sharpness of mind, quickness of learning, power of memory, divine kinship, etc. (those citizens likely to chafe against the instantiation of unity as the highest civic value) will be reconciled to citizenship.

41. This is a way of correcting for excessive self-love, or turning such love into a love of the city (or making such a love compatible with a love for the city).

42. On this point I diverge from Carone's (2005, esp. chap. 8) claims about the *Laws*, and from Bobonich's (2002) claims about the transpolitical ends of human action.

43. There is here another point of comparison with the *Republic*. While the *Republic*'s city/soul analogy opens up parallel analyses of city and soul (and thus presents the city as a possible subject for analysis), the emphasis in the *Republic* falls upon founding a politeia in the soul. In the *Laws*, individual souls are investigated for their capacity to instantiate, through cultivation, a politeia that imitates divine nous; insofar as this politeia is that of the city itself, the city is the primary object. On the parallel analyses of city and soul in the *Republic*, see Ferrari (2005). For a general account of the priority of city in the *Laws*, see Pradeau (2002).

44. For further intimation of the necessity of incompleteness on these matters, see 769d–e and 770b.

45. The subsequent exhortation to the law wardens includes an insistence on their willingness to destroy the city or go into exile if its laws are not aimed solely toward bettering its citizens (770e). They are to be revolutionaries rather than put the city itself ahead of the betterment of its citizens. The city, it would seem to suggest, is already effectively destroyed if its laws do not aim at the betterment of its citizens.

46. Thus, neither the object nor the painting obeys that tendency toward decay that is treated in the *Republic* as a necessary feature of all composed beings (546a).

47. Ferrari 2005, 90.

48. I am thus in general agreement with Jean-Francios Pradeau's claim that, in the *Laws*, "the city philosophizes" (Pradeau 2002, 165). My estimation of the extent and significance of the failure of the *Laws*' legislative project, however, marks a divergence between our respective assessments of the dialogue.

Works Cited

Adam, James, ed. 1965. *The Republic of Plato*. Edited with critical notes, commentary and appendices. 2 vols. Cambridge: Cambridge University Press.
Agamben, Giorgio. 1998. *Homo Sacer: Sovereign Power and Bare Life*. Translated by Daniel Heller-Roazen. Stanford: Stanford University Press.
Ahrensdorf, Peter. 1995. *The Death of Socrates and the Life of Philosophy: An Interpretation of Plato's* Phaedo. Albany: State University of New York Press.
Allen, Danielle. 2000. *The World of Prometheus*. Princeton: Princeton University Press.
Annas, Julia. 1981. *An Introduction to Plato's* Republic. Oxford: Clarendon Press.
———. 1982. "Plato's Myths of Judgment." *Phronesis* 27: 119–43.
———. 1999. *Platonic Ethics Old and New*. Ithaca: Cornell University Press.
Averroes. 1966. *Commentary on Plato's Republic*. Edited and translated by E. I. J. Rosenthal. Cambridge: Cambridge University Press.
Baracchi, Claudia. 2002. *Of Myth, Life and War in Plato's "Republic."* Bloomington: Indiana University Press.
Barney, R., et al., eds. 2012. Plato and the Divided Self. Cambridge: Cambridge University Press.
Beck, Martha. 1999. *Plato's Self-Corrective Development of the Concepts of Soul, Forms, and Immortality in Three Arguments of the "Phaedo."* Lewiston: Edwin Mellen Press.
Benardete, Seth. 1992. *Socrates' Second Sailing*. Chicago: University of Chicago Press.
———. 1999. *Socrates and Plato: The Dialectics of Eros* (German and English). Munich: Carl Friedrichs von Siemens Stiftung.
Benson, H., ed. 2009. *Blackwell Companion to Plato*. New York: Wiley-Blackwell.
Bloessner, Norbert. 1997. *Dialogform und Argument*. Stuttgart: Franz Steiner Verlag.
———. 2007. "The City Soul Analogy." In *The Cambridge Companion to Plato's "Republic,"* edited by G. Ferrari, 345–85. Cambridge: Cambridge University Press.
Blondell, Ruby. 2002. *The Play of Character in Plato's Dialogues*. Cambridge: Cambridge University Press.
Bloom, A., trans. 1991. *Plato's* Republic. 2nd ed. New York: Basic Books.
Bobonich, Christopher. 2002. *Plato's Utopia Recast: His Later Ethics and Politics*. Oxford: Clarendon Press.
Bostock, David, trans. 1986. *Plato's "Phaedo."* Oxford: Clarendon Press.
Boyd, William. 1962 *An Introduction to the Republic of Plato*. London: Macmillan.
Brann, Eva, Steven Kalkavage, and Eric Salem, trans. 1998. *Plato's "Phaedo."* Newburyport: Focus Classical Library.
Bremmer, J. 1983. *The Early Greek Concept of the Soul*. Princeton: Princeton University Press.
Brisson, Luc. 2000. *Plato the Mythmaker*. Translated by Gerard Naddaf. Chicago: University of Chicago Press.
———. 2005. "Ethics and Politics in Plato's *Laws*." *Oxford Studies in Ancient Philosophy* 28: 93–121.

Brill, Sara. 2005. "Diagnosis and the Divided Line: Pharmacological Concerns in Plato's Republic." *Epoché* 9: 297–315.
———. 2006. Medical Moderation in Plato's Symposium. *Studies in the History of Ethics.* www.historyofethics.org.
———. 2007. "Alive and Sleepless: The Politics of Immortality in Republic X." *Polis* 24, no. 2: 231–61.
———. 2009. "The Geography of Finitude: Myth and Earth in Plato's *Phaedo*." *International Philosophical Quarterly* 49, no. 1: 1–23.
———. 2010. "Psychology and Legislation in Plato's *Laws*." *Proceedings of the Boston Area Collequium in Ancient Philosophy* 26: 211–42.
———. 2011. "The Prosthetic Cosmos: Elizabeth Grosz's Ecology of the Future." *Philosophy Today* 55: 245–54.
———. 2013. "Plato's Critical Theory." *Epoché* (spring 2013).
Brown, Eric. 2001. "A Defense of Plato's Argument for the Immortality of the Soul at *Republic* X 608c–611a." In *Essays on Plato's Psychology*, edited by Ellen Wagner, 297–322. Lanham: Lexington.
Brumbaugh, R. 1951. "Colors of the Hemisphere in Plato's Myth of Er (*Republic* 616e)." *Classical Philology* 46, no. 3: 173–76
———. 1954. "Plato *Republic* 616e: The Final 'Law of Nines.'" *Classical Philology* 49, no. 1: 33–34.
Burger, Ronna, trans. 1984. *The Phaedo: A Platonic Labyrinth*. New Haven: Yale University Press.
———. 2004. "The Thumotic and the Erotic Soul." *Interpretation* 32, no. 1: 57–76.
Burkert, Walter. 1972. *Lore and Science in Ancient Pythagoreanism*. Translated by Edward Minar. Cambridge: Harvard University Press.
Burnet, J. 1916. "The Socratic Doctrine of the Soul." *Proceedings of the British Academy*: 235–59.
Burnyeat, M. 1976. "Plato on the Grammar of Perceiving." *Classical Quarterly* 26, no. 1: 29–51.
Bury, R. G., trans. 1967. *Plato's "Laws."* Cambridge: Loeb Classical Library.
Carone, Gabriela. 1994. "Theology and Evil in *Laws* 10." *Review of Metaphysics* 48: 275–98.
———. 2005. *Plato's Cosmology and Its Ethical Dimensions*. Cambridge: Cambridge University Press.
Cherniss, H. 1954. "The Sources of Evil According to Plato." *Proceedings of the American Philosophical Society* 98: 23–30.
Claus, David. 1981. *Toward the Soul: An Inquiry into the Meaning of ψυχή before Plato*. New Haven: Yale University Press.
Clegg, J. 1976. "Plato's Vision of Chaos." *Classical Quarterly* 26: 52–61.
Cooper, J. M. 1984. "Plato's Theory of Human Motivation." *History of Philosophy Quarterly* 1:3–21.
Cornford, Francis M., trans. 1941. *The "Republic" of Plato*. London: Oxford University Press.
Cross, R. C., and A. D. Woozley. 1964. *Plato's "Republic": A Philosophical Commentary*. London: Macmillan.
Deleuze, Gilles, and Félix Guattari. 1983. *Anti-Oedipus: Capitalism and Schizophrenia*. Translated by Hurely, Seem, and Lane. Minneapolis: University of Minnesota Press.
Denyer, Nicolas, ed. 2001. *Plato: Alcibiades*. Cambridge: Cambridge Greek and Latin Classics.
Derrida, Jacques. 1991. *Of Spirit*. Translated by Geoffrey Bennington and Rachel Bowlby. Chicago: University of Chicago Press.
———. 1998. *Monolingualism of the Other, or, The Prosthesis of Origin*. Stanford: Stanford University Press.

Dimas, Panos. 2003. "Recollecting Forms in the *Phaedo*." *Phronesis* 48: 175–214.
Dodds, E. R. 1971. *The Greeks and the Irrational*. Berkeley: University of California Press.
Dorter, Kenneth. 1977. "The Reciprocity Argument and the Structure of Plato's *Phaedo*." *Journal of the History of Philosophy* 15: 1–11.
———. 1982. *Plato's "Phaedo": An Interpretation*. Toronto: University of Toronto Press.
———. 2006. *The Transformation of Plato's "Republic."* Lanham: Lexington.
Easterling, H. J. 1976. "Causation in the *Timaeus* and *Laws* X." *Euranos* 65: 25–38.
Edmonds, Radcliffe. 2004. *Myths of the Underworld Journey*. Cambridge: Cambridge University Press.
Everson, Stephen, ed. 1991. *Companions to Ancient Thought 2: Psychology*. Cambridge: Cambridge University Press.
Ferrari, G. F. 2005. *City and Soul in Plato's "Republic."* Chicago: University of Chicago Press.
———, ed. 2007a. *The Cambridge Companion to Plato's "Republic."* Cambridge: Cambridge University Press.
———. 2007b. "The Three-Part Soul." In *The Cambridge Companion to Plato's "Republic,"* edited by Ferrari, 165–201. Cambridge: Cambridge University Press.
———. 2011. "Glaucon's Reward, Philosophy's Debt: The Myth of Er." In *Plato's Myths*, edited by Catalin Partenie, 116–32. Cambridge: Cambridge University Press.
Fine, Gail. 1991. "Commentary on Sedley." *Proceedings of the Boston Area Colloquium in Ancient Philosophy* 5: 384–98.
Finlayson, J. 2010. "Bare Life and Politics in Agamben's Reading of Aristotle." *Review of Politics* 72: 97–126.
Foucault, Michel. 1995. *Discipline and Punish: The Birth of the Prison*. Translated by Alan Sheridan. New York: Vintage.
Frede, Dorothea. 2001. "The Final Proof of the Immortality of the Soul in Plato's *Phaedo* 102a–107a." In *Essays on Plato's Psychology*, edited by Ellen Wagner, 281–96. Lanham: Lexington.
———. 2010. "Puppets on Strings: Moral Psychology in *Laws* Books 1 and 2." In *Plato's "Laws": A Critical Guide*, edited by Christopher Bobonich, 108–16. Cambridge: Cambridge University Press.
Freud, Sigmund. 1961. *Civilization and Its Discontents*. Translated by James Strachey. New York: Norton.
Frutiger, P. 1930. *Les mythes de Platon*. Paris: Alcan.
Fussi, Alessandra. 2001. "The Myth of the Last Judgment in the *Gorgias*." *Review of Metaphysics* 54: 529–52.
Gadamer, H. G. 1980. "The Proofs of Immortality in Plato's *Phaedo*." In *Dialogue and Dialectic*, translated by P. Christopher Smith, 21–38. New Haven: Yale University Press.
Gallop, D., trans. 1975. *Phaedo*. Oxford: Clarendon.
Gerson, Lloyd. 2003a. "Akrasia and the Divided Soul in Plato's *Laws*." In *Plato's "Laws": From Theory into Practice*, edited by Scolnicov and Brisson, 149–54. Sankt Augustin: Academia Verlag.
———. 2003b. *Knowing Persons: A Study in Plato*. Oxford: Oxford University Press.
Gillespie, C. M. 1912. "The Use of Εἶδος and Ἰδέα in Hippocrates." *Classical Quarterly* 6: 179–203.
Gonzalez, Francisco. 1995. *The Third Way*. New York: Rowman and Littlefield.
———. 1998. *Dialectic and Dialogue: Plato's Practice of Philosophical Inquiry*. Evanston: Northwestern University Press.

Gordon, Jill. 1999. *Turning toward Philosophy: Literary Device and Dramatic Structure in Plato's Dialogues.* State College: Pennsylvania State University Press.
———. 2012. *Plato's Erotic World: from Cosmic Origins to Human Death.* Cambridge: Cambridge University Press.
Green, Christopher, and Philip Groff. 2003. *Early Psychological Thought: Ancient Accounts of Mind and Soul.* Westport: Praeger.
Guthrie, W. 1978. "Plato's Views on the Nature of the Soul." In *Plato II: Ethics, Politics, and Philosophy of Art and Religion*, edited by G. Vlastos, 230–43. South Bend: University of Notre Dame Press.
Hackforth, R. trans. 1972. *Plato's "Phaedo."* Cambridge: Cambridge University Press.
Halliwell, Stephen, translation and commentary. 1993. *Plato: "Republic"* 5. Warminster: Aris and Phillips.
———. 2002. *The Aesthetics of Mimesis.* Princeton: Princeton University Press.
———. 2007. "The Life-and-Death Journey of the Soul: Interpreting the Myth of Er." In *The Cambridge Companion to Plato's "Republic,"* edited by Ferrari, 445–73. Cambridge: Cambridge University Press.
Heidegger, Martin. 1996. *Being and Time.* Translated by Joan Stambaugh. Albany: State University of New York Press.
———. 1998. Letter on Humanism. In *Pathmarks*, edited by Will McNeill, translated by Frank Capuzzi, 239–76. Cambridge: Cambridge University Press.
Holmes, Brooke. 2010. *The Symptom and the Subject: the Emergence of the Physical Body in Ancient Greece.* Princeton: Princeton University Press.
Hyland, Drew. 2004. *Questioning Platonism: Continental Interpretations of Plato.* Albany: State University of New York Press.
Irwin, T. *Plato's "Ethics."* Oxford: Oxford University Press.
Jain, S. 1999. "The Prosthetic Imagination: Enabling and Disabling the Prosthesis Trope." *Science, Technology and Human Values* 24, no. 1: 31–54.
Jones, H. S., trans. 1929. Hippocrates. Vol. 1. Cambridge: Loeb Classical Library.
Kahn, Charles. 1987. "Plato's Theory of Desire." *Review of Metaphysics* 4: 77–103.
———. 2001. *Pythagoras and the Pythagoreans.* Indianapolis: Hackett.
———. 2004. "From *Republic* to *Laws.*" *Oxford Studies in Ancient Philosophy* 26: 337–62.
Kamtekar, Rachana. 2006. "Speaking with the Same Voice as Reason: Personification in Plato's Psychology." *Oxford Studies in Ancient Philosophy* 31: 167–202.
———. 2010. "Psychology and the Inculcation of Virtue in Plato's *Laws.*" In *Plato's "Laws": A Critical Guide*, edited by Christopher Bobonich, 127–48. Cambridge: Cambridge University Press.
Kerford, G. B. 1981. *The Sophistic Movement.* Cambridge: Cambridge University Press.
Konstan, David. 2003. "Aristotle on Anger and the Emotions: The Strategies of Status." In *Ancient Anger: Perspectives from Homer to Galen*, edited by Susanna Braund and Glen Most, 99–120. Cambridge: Cambridge University Press.
Laks, André. 2006. "The Laws." In the *Cambridge History of Greek and Roman Political Thought*, edited by Malcolm Schofield and Melissa Lane, 258–92. Cambridge: Cambridge University Press.
———. 2010. "Plato's 'Truest Tragedy': *Laws* Book 7, 817a–d". In *Plato's "Laws": A Critical Guide*, edited by Christopher Bobonich, 217–31. Cambridge: Cambridge University Press.
Lamb, W. R. M., trans. 1927. *Plato: Charmides, Alcibiades, Hipparchus, Lovers, Theages, Minos, Epinomis.* Cambridge: Loeb Classical Library.

Lear, Gabriel. 2011. "Mimesis and Psychological Change in *Republic* III." In *Plato and the Poets*, edited by Pierre Destrée and Fritz-Gregor Hermann. Leiden: Brill, 2011.
Lear, Jonathan. 1992. "Inside and Outside the *Republic*." *Phronesis* 37: 184–215.
Lee, E. N. 1976. "Reason and Rotation: Circular Movement as the Model of Mind (Nous) in the Later Plato." In *Facets of Plato's Philosophy*, edited by W. H. Werkmeister, 70–102. Amsterdam: Van Gorcum.
Lesser, A. H. 2003. "The Unity of Plato's *Phaedo*." *Philosophical Inquiry* 25, no. 3–4: 73–85.
Levin, Susan. 2000. *The Ancient Quarrel between Philosophy and Poetry Revisited: Plato and the Greek Literary Tradition*. Oxford: Oxford University Press.
Lloyd, G. E. R. 2003. *In the Grip of Disease*. Oxford: Oxford University Press.
Lorenz, H. 2006. *The Brute Within: Appetitive Desire in Plato and Aristotle*. Oxford: Clarendon Press.
Ludwig, Paul. 2007. "Eros in the *Republic*." In *The Cambridge Companion to Plato's "Republic,"* edited by G. R. F. Ferrari, 202–31. Cambridge: Cambridge University Press.
Mackenzie, Margaret. 1981. *Plato on Punishment*. Berkeley: University of California Press.
Mayhew, Robert. 1997. *Aristotle's Criticism of Plato's "Republic."* Oxford: Oxford University Press.
———. 2008. *Plato's "Laws" X: Translation and Commentary*. Oxford: Oxford University Press.
———. 2010. "The Theology of the *Laws*." In *Plato's "Laws": A Critical Guide*, edited by Christopher Bobonich, 197–216. Cambridge: Cambridge University Press.
McCoy, Marina. 2007. *Plato on the Rhetoric of Philosophers and Sophists*. Cambridge: Cambridge University Press.
McLuhan, Marshall. 1964. *Understanding Media: The Extensions of Man*. Cambridge: MIT Press.
McNeill, D. 2010. *An Image of the Soul in Speech: Plato and the Problem of Socrates*. University Park: Pennsylvania State University Press.
Meldrum, M. 1950. "Plato and the ARKH KAKVH." *Journal of Hellenic Studies* 70: 65–74.
Menn, Stephen. 1995. *Plato on God as Nous*. Carbondale: Southern Illinios University Press.
———. 2005. "On Plato's Politeia." *Proceedings of the Boston Area Colloquium in Ancient Philosophy* 21: 1–53.
Miles, Murray. 2001. "Plato on Suicide (*Phaedo* 60c–63c)." *Phoenix* 55, no. 3–4: 244–58.
Mohr, R. 2006. *God and Forms in Plato*. Las Vegas: Parmenides Press. Revised and expanded edition of *The Platonic Cosmology*. Leiden: Brill 1985.
Moline, Jan. 1978. "Plato on the Complexity of the Psyche." *Archiv für Geschichte der Philosophie* 60: 1–26
Monoson, S. 2000. *Plato's Democratic Entanglements*. Princeton: Princeton University Press.
Morgan, Kathryn. 2000. *Myth and Philosophy from the Pre-socratics to Plato*. Cambridge: Cambridge University Press.
Morrow, Glenn. 1993. *Plato's Cretan City: A Historical Interpretation of the "Laws."* Princeton: Princeton University Press.
Moss, Jessica. 2008. "Appearances and Calculations: Plato's Division of the Soul." *Oxford Studies of Ancient Philosophy* 34: 35–36.
Nails, Debra, and Holger Thesleff. "Early Academic Editing: Plato's *Laws*." In *Plato's "Laws": From Theory to Practice*, edited by Scolnocov and Brisson. Sankt Augustin: Academia Verlag.
Nettleship, R. L. 1901. *Lectures on the Republic of Plato*, 2nd ed. London: Macmillan.
Nichols, James, trans. 1998. *Plato: "Gorgias."* Ithaca, N.Y.: Cornell University Press.

Nietzsche, F. 1989. *On the Genealogy of Morals*. Translated by Walter Kaufmann. New York: Vintage.
Nightingale, Andrea. 1993. "Writing/Reading a Sacred Text: A Literary Interpretation of Plato's *Laws*." *Classical Philology* 88, no. 4: 279–303.
———. 1996. *Genres in Dialogue: Plato and the Construct of Philosophy*. Cambridge: Cambridge University Press.
———. 2002. "Toward an Ecological Eschatology." In *Bakhtin and the Classics (Rethinking Theory)*, edited by R. Bracht Branham. Chicago: Northwestern University Press.
———. 2009. *Spectacles of Truth in Classical Greek Philosophy: Theoria in Its Cultural Context*. Cambridge: Cambridge University Press.
O'Brien, Michael. 1984. "Becoming Immortal." In *Greek Poetry and Philosophy: Studies in Honour of Leonard Woodbury*, edited by Douglas Gerber, 185–205. Atlanta: Scholars Press.
Ophir, Adi. 1991. *Plato's Invisible Cities: Discourse and Power in the* Republic. New York: Savage Press.
Pakulak, Michael. 2003. "Degrees of Separation in the *Phaedo*." *Phronesis* 48, no. 2: 89–114.
Pangle, Thomas, trans. 1980. *The Laws of Plato*. New York: Basic.
Pappas, Nickolas. 1995. *Routledge Philosophical Guide to Plato and the* Republic. London: Routledge.
Parker, Robert. 1996. *Miasma: Pollution and Purification in Early Greek Religion*. Oxford: Oxford University Press.
Parry, Richard. 2002. "The Soul in *Laws* X and Disorderly Motion in *Timaeus*." *Ancient Philosophy* 22, no. 2: 289–302.
———. 2007. "The Unhappy Tyrant and the Craft of Inner Rule." In *The Cambridge Companion to Plato's "Republic,"* edited by G. Ferrari, 386–414. Cambridge: Cambridge University Press.
Partenie, Catalin, ed. 2009. *Plato's Myths*. Cambridge: Cambridge University Press.
Pender, Elizabeth. 2000. *Images of Persons Unseen*. Sankt Augustine: Academia Verlag.
Plato. 1900–1907. *Opera*. Edited by J. Burnet 5 vols. OCT. Oxford: Oxford University Press.
J. J. Pollitt. 2009. *The Ancient View of Greek Art: Criticism, History and Terminology*. New Haven: Yale University Press.
Popper, K. 1971. *The Spell of Plato*. Vol. 1 of *The Open Society and Its Enemies*. Princeton: Princeton University Press.
Pradeau, Jean-Francois. 2002. *Plato and the City*. Translated by Janet Lloyd. Exeter: University of Exeter Press.
Press, Gerald. 1996. "Continuities and Discontinuities in the History of *Republic* Interpretation." *International Studies in Philosophy* 28, no. 4: 61–78.
Proclus. 1970. *Commentaire sur la "Republique,"* V. III. Translated by A. J. Festugiere. Paris: VRIN.
Reeve, C. D. C. 1988. *Philosopher Kings: The Argument of Plato's "Republic."* Princeton: Princeton University Press.
Robinson, R. 1971. "Plato's Separation of Reason from Desire." *Phronesis* 16: 38–48.
Robinson, T. M. 1995. *Plato's Psychology*. 2nd ed. Toronto: University of Toronto Press.
Rohde, Erwin. 1950. *Psyche: The Cult of Souls and Belief in Immortality among the Ancient Greeks*. Translated by W. B. Hillis. New York: Routledge and Kegan Paul.
Roochnik, David. 2003. *Beautiful City: The Dialectical Character of Plato's* Republic. Ithaca, N.Y.: Cornell University Press.

Rosen, Stanley. 1961. "Thought and Touch: A Note on Aristotle's *De Anima*." *Phronesis* 6, no. 2: 127–37.
———. 1965. "The Role of Eros in Plato's *Republic*." *Review of Metaphysics* 18: 452–75.
———. 2005. *Plato's "Republic": A Study*. New Haven: Yale University Press.
Russon, John, and John Sallis, eds. 2000. *Retracing the Platonic Text*. Evanston: Northwestern University Press.
Sachs, Joseph, trans. 2001. *Aristotle's "On the Soul."* Santa Fe: Green Lion Press.
Sallis, John. 1996. *Being and Logos*. Bloomington: Indiana University Press.
———. 2002. "Phronesis in Hades and Beyond." *Epoché* 7, no. 1: 121–31.
Saunders, Trevor. 1975. *Plato's "Laws."* New York: Penguin.
———. 1991. *Plato's Penal Code*. Oxford: Clarendon Press.
Sayers, Sean. 1999. *Plato's "Republic": An Introduction*. Edinburgh: Edinburgh University Press.
Sedley, David. 1991. "Theology and Myth in the *Phaedo*." *Proceedings of the Boston Area Colloquium in Ancient Philosophy* 5: 359–83.
———. 2006. "Form-Particular Resemblance in Plato's *Phaedo*." *Proceedings of the Aristotelian Society for the Systematic Study of Philosophy* 106: 311–27.
———. 2009. "Myth, Punishment and Politics in the *Gorgias*." In *Plato's Myths*, edited by Catalin Partenie. Cambridge: Cambridge University Press.
Shields, Christopher, ed. 2003. *The Blackwell Guide to Ancient Philosophy*. New York: Wiley-Blackwell.
———. 2010. "Plato's Divided Soul." In *Plato's "Republic": A Critical Guide*, edited by Mark McPherran. Cambridge: Cambridge University Press.
Shorey, Paul. 1933. *What Plato Said*. Chicago: University of Chicago Press.
Silverman, A. 2003. "Plato: Psychology." In *The Blackwell Guide to Ancient Philosophy*. New York: Wiley-Blackwell, 130–44.
Singpurwalla, Rachel. 2010. "The Tripartite Theory of Motivation in Plato's Republic." *Philosophy Compass* 5, no. 11: 880–92.
———. 2011. "Soul Division and Mimesis in *Republic* X." In *Plato and the Poets*, edited by Pierre Destrée and Fritz-Georg Hermann. Leiden: Brill.
Smith, M., and J. Mona, eds. 2006. *The Prosthetic Impulse: From a Posthuman Present to a Biocultural Future*. Cambridge: MIT Press.
Snell, Bruno. 1982. *The Discovery of the Mind in Greek Philosophy and Literature*. New York: Dover.
Solmsen, Freidrich. 1942. *Plato's Theology*. Ithaca, N.Y.: Cornell University Press.
———. 1983. "Plato and the Concept of the Soul (Psyche): Some Historical Perspectives." *Journal of the History of Ideas* 44, no. 3: 355–67.
Stalley, R. F. 1983. *An Introduction to Plato's "Laws."* New York: Hackett.
Stern, Paul. 1993. *Socratic Rationalism and Political Philosophy: An Interpretation of Plato's "Phaedo."* Albany: State University of New York Press.
Stewart, J. A. 1905. *The Myths of Plato*. New York: Macmillan.
Stiegler, B. 2001. "Derrida and Technology: Fidelity at the Limits of Deconstructions and the Prosthesis of Faith." In *Jacques Derrida and the Humanities: A Critical Reader*, edited by Tom Cohen, 238–70. Cambridge: Cambridge University Press.
Strauss, L. 1978. *City and Man*. Chicago: University of Chicago Press.
Szlezak, Thomas. 1976. "Unsterblichkeit und Trichotomie der Seele im zehnten Buch der Politeia." *Phronesis* 12, no. 1.

Taylor. A. E. 1939. "The Decline and Fall of the State in *Republic* VIII." *Mind* 48, no. 189: 23–38.
———. 1960. *Plato: The Man and His Work*. New York: Meridian.
Thayer, H. S. 1988. "The Myth of Er." *History of Philosophy Quarterly* 5, no. 4: 369–84.
Thucydides. 1996. *The Peloponnesian War*. Edited by Robert B. Strassler; translated by Richard Crawley. New York: Free Press.
Vasiliou, I. 2012. "From the *Phaedo* to the *Republic*: Plato's Tripartite Soul and the Possiblity of Non-Philosophical Virtue." In *Plato and the Divided Self*, edited by Barney et al., 9–32. Cambridge: Cambridge University Press.
Vernant, J-P. 1990. *Myth and Society in Ancient Greece*. Translated by Janet Lloyd. New York: Zone.
Vlastos, G. 1995. "Disorderly Motion in the *Timaeus*." In *Studies in Greek Philosophy*, vol. 2, *Socrates, Plato and Their Tradition*, edited by D. Graham, 247–64. Princeton: Princeton University Press.
Wagner, Ellen, ed. 2001. *Essays on Plato's Psychology*. Lanham: Lexington.
Waterfield, Robin, trans. 1993. *Republic*. Oxford: Oxford University Press 1993.
Weller, Cass. 2001. "Fallacies in the *Phaedo* Again." In *Essays on Plato's Psychology*, edited by Ellen Wagner, 35–49. Lanham: Lexington.
Westerink, L. G., trans. 1977. *Damascius*. Vol. 2 of *The Greek Commentaries on Plato's "Phaedo."* New York: North-Holland.
White, David. 1989. *Myth and Metaphysics in Plato's "Phaedo."* Selinsgrove: Susquehanna University Press.
White, Nicholas. 1979. *A Companion to Plato's "Republic."* Indianapolis: Hackett.
Whiting, J. 2012. "Psychic Contingency in the *Republic*." In *Plato and the Divided Self*, edited by Rachel Barney et al., 174–208. Cambridge: Cambridge University Press.
Wigley, M. 1991. "Prosthetic Theory: The Disciplining of Architecture." *Assemblage* 15:7–29.
Wills, D. 1995. *Prosthesis*. Stanford: Stanford University Press.
Winspear, Alban. 1956. *The Genius of Plato's Thought*. New York: S. A. Russell.
Woolf, R. 2012. "How to See an Uncrusted Soul." In *Plato and the Divided Self*, edited by Barney et al., 150–73. Cambridge: Cambridge University Press.

Index

Adam, 226n5, 228n32, 229n13, 230n17, 230n19, 232n3, 233n19, 234n33
Alcibiades, 1, 209n2, 209n3
Alcibiades I, 1, 209n2, 209n3
anger, 118, 168, 175–76, 180–81, 182, 215n14, 221n24, 221n25, 240n15
Annas, 210n11, 211n26, 211n27, 213n2, 220n8, 221n26, 227n4, 227n16, 232n4, 232n9
Apollo, 19, 21
appearance, 70, 94, 214n2, 228n31
appetite, 45, 108, 226n3, 226n4, 227n8
Ardiaeus, 156
aristocracy, 131,
Aristotle, 9, 45, 52, 78, 132, 197, 232n3, 244n19
Atalanta, 159
atheism, 187, 189, 196
atheist, 168, 185, 185–190, 192, 195–98, 253n6, 242n10, 242n13
Atropos, 156, 160
automatic, 181, 201–3, 246n36

becoming, 3, 13, 27, 38–41, 49, 86–91, 96, 105–6, 108, 110, 113, 115, 116, 120–21, 158, 186, 193
being, 3, 8, 10, 13, 22, 23, 28–35, 42, 45–48, 54–55, 58, 69, 73, 80–82, 91, 107, 120–24, 125, 127–28, 130–31, 137, 158–59, 192–94, 212n40, 217n11, 221n22, 229n9
biological, 4, 8, 85–86, 174, 210n19, 238n6, 238n7
Bobonich, 211n25, 226n4, 229n7, 242n10, 244n22, 245n23, 247n42
body/bodily/body-like/body-loving, 2, 3, 7, 9, 10, 13, 18, 22–36, 37, 38, 40, 41, 48–63, 65, 66, 68, 69, 71, 75, 79, 80, 81, 82, 86, 100, 101, 103, 104, 110–15, 117, 118, 122, 124, 128, 141–150, 152, 153, 155, 157, 166, 167, 173, 186, 187, 197, 200, 201, 203, 204, 207, 212n37, 215n14, 215n16, 215n20, 215n21, 216n26, 217n15, 217n16, 217n17, 217n22, 217n23, 218n26, 218n27, 218n30, 219n38, 219n2, 220n12, 221n18, 224n15, 224n17, 225n21, 225n25, 227n16, 228n23, 228n24, 228n25, 228n27, 231n30, 233n23, 234n25, 234n26, 234n30, 234n31, 234n33, 236n57, 236n15, 240n11, 241n2, 244n13, 244n19
Brown, 139, 232n8, 233n16, 233n18, 233n19, 233n21, 234n33

calculation, 12, 110, 129–30, 133, 136, 147, 166, 168, 171–73, 177, 199, 204, 227n9, 230n23, 239n3

Cephalus, 83, 212n37, 214n3, 222n1
character, 6–7, 12, 25, 27, 35, 53, 83, 87–88, 92, 96, 101, 107–8, 118, 124, 131, 171, 175, 183, 189, 191, 200, 201, 202, 203, 207, 222n9, 224n11
Charmides, 9
Claus, 210n16, 225n21, 228n23, 233n23
Clōthō, 156
Cornford, 13, 209n8, 213n46
cosmology, 20, 39, 65, 184, 185–87, 190, 193–94, 196, 199, 203–4, 214n6, 242n9,
cosmos, 3, 4, 5, 12, 15, 36, 48, 79, 80, 163, 170, 186–90, 193, 194, 197, 198, 200, 204, 217n11
counting, 128–131
Crito, 9

death, 7, 10, 15, 16–18, 19–22, 23, 25, 26–27, 29, 31–33, 35, 36, 37–38, 40–41, 48–50. 53, 56, 58, 59–61, 63–65, 68–69, 80, 96, 125, 134, 143, 145–148, 151, 160, 165, 176, 180–82, 191, 201, 212n37, 215n18, 215n19, 215n21, 218n24, 218n37, 219n38, 220n11, 222n1, 228n22, 231n29, 231n30, 234n29, 235n33, 235n38, 237n3, 240n12, 241n1, 241n2, 246n39
deathlessness, 3, 13, 15, 16, 50, 51, 57, 58, 63, 68, 140, 141, 145, 149, 208, 210n11, 217n18
democracy, 131, 132,
desire, 11, 16, 21, 27, 31, 32, 33, 34, 45, 47, 49, 51, 53, 69, 75, 82, 86, 88, 92, 93, 94, 95, 98, 100, 101, 102, 105, 106–10, 114–15, 117, 119–21, 123, 124, 127, 133–34, 138, 147, 159, 169, 171, 175–77, 179, 181, 183, 185, 190, 199, 200, 210n13, 217n15, 223n16, 224n5, 224n16, 226n3, 226n4, 226n6, 226n7, 227n9, 228n29, 228n32, 229n6, 230n23, 235n34, 239n15, 239n18, 240n12, 245n23, 245n30, 246n33
disease, 11, 31, 39, 71, 73, 82, 90, 92, 103, 104, 106, 107, 111–14, 122, 132–35, 136, 140,142, 144–50, 151, 173, 189, 199, 213n45, 216n4, 217n15, 222n32, 225n21, 225n22, 226n1, 227n9, 227n11, 227n15, 227n16, 227n20, 227n21, 228n25, 230n23, 231n29, 234n25, 234n29, 234n32, 240n7, 245n26
divine, 12, 20, 22, 50, 51, 54, 55, 65, 126, 127, 137, 149, 152, 166, 167, 168, 173, 174, 180, 183, 186, 187, 189, 193, 194, 195, 200, 201–7, 210n11, 234n24, 238n10, 240n9, 243n10, 246n36, 246n40, 247n43

eagerness/zeal, 22–23, 34, 45, 60, 80, 188

257

258 | Index

education, 5, 8, 23, 65, 68, 69, 99, 100, 102, 107, 113, 116, 122, 125, 126–28, 131, 136, 137, 169, 171, 173, 183, 194, 195, 204–7, 215n12, 222n6, 229n6, 229n10, 231n35, 238n8, 239n3

embodiment, 55, 58, 113, 217n15, 220n8

Er, 7, 12, 83, 85, 89, 113, 138, 140, 153–61, 174, 180, 181, 211n27, 211n28, 212n31, 220n8, 223n9, 223n18, 232n3, 235n38, 235n47, 236n50, 236n50, 237n64

eros/Eros, 42, 46–49, 109, 120, 133, 134, 137, 225n21, 226n3, 231n34

erotic, 31, 38, 41–48, 52, 80, 107, 120, 124, 125, 171, 216n6, 216n7, 216n8, 217n12, 228n32

eschatology, 6

ethics, 2, 79, 183, 200, 204, 214n7, 215n22, 233n18

Evenus, 19, 20, 21, 24, 214n2

expiation, 7, 11, 66–69, 77–78, 180, 182, 188, 202, 242n18, 243n11

Ferrari, 207, 210n17, 223n13, 223n15, 227n10, 228n28, 229n7, 235n43, 236n50, 236n55, 247n43, 247n47

finitude, 65, 147, 149

founder, 90, 92, 98, 99, 112, 207

gaze, 3, 84, 91, 127, 129, 135, 139, 154, 222n4

generation, 40–42, 62, 124, 132, 186, 187, 192, 193, 196, 198, 200, 227n15, 243n11

Glaucus, 84, 85, 152, 235n41,

Gorgias, 2, 9, 212n31, 212n43, 220n8, 220n12, 231n33, 236n59, 240n17, 241n4, 246n32

Hades, 17, 32, 33, 38, 41, 51, 52, 54, 55, 56, 57, 64, 66, 68–69, 75–78, 128, 165, 168, 181, 183, 201, 202, 212n38, 218n24, 218n30, 219n5, 222n1, 237n2, 246n33, 246n37

health/healthy, 11, 31, 60, 82, 90, 92, 95, 98, 101, 102–4, 105–7, 111–14, 122, 123, 128, 130, 134, 135, 160, 176, 196, 199, 203, 208, 225n20, 225n22, 225n23, 226n1, 227n16, 227n18, 227n20, 227n21, 228n25, 229n6, 234n25, 235n35, 237n62, 242n10,

Hippocratic, 213n45, 216n4, 222n32, 227n11, 230n23, 231n26

Homer, 17, 57, 74, 127, 215n14, 216n24, 218n30, 243n3

hope, 32–33, 166, 168, 171, 172, 174, 175, 224n6, 239n18

iconography, 4, 94, 208, 223n4

image/imagery, 1, 3, 4, 6, 8, 9, 11, 12, 17, 43, 44, 46, 47, 51, 52, 53, 55, 56, 57, 60, 64, 65, 66, 67, 70, 71, 72, 73, 75, 79, 84, 85, 87, 88, 89, 92, 93, 101, 102, 104, 113, 115, 120, 121, 123, 127, 131, 134, 136, 146, 149, 152, 154, 166, 167, 170, 171, 172, 181, 185, 197, 198, 200, 203, 205, 206, 208, 209n9, 214n1, 214n4, 219n2, 221n20, 221n22, 222n3, 223n4, 224n14, 228n27, 229n6, 231n34, 235n41, 235n42, 235n46, 238n6, 238n8, 239n1, 240n4, 243n11, 244n16, 245n27, 246n38, 246n40

impiety, 12, 20, 170, 174, 179, 181, 182, 183–93, 194–96, 202, 241n6, 241n7, 242n9, 242n14

injustice, 20, 40, 58, 76, 77, 81, 83, 87, 90, 93, 94, 95, 96, 97, 98, 104, 111, 112, 114, 121, 127, 135, 141, 142, 146, 147–51, 154, 155, 173, 175–78, 179, 186, 188, 189, 199, 211n20, 224n6, 228n25, 231n30, 232n14, 234n32, 235n34, 235n43, 236n50, 236n60, 239n1, 240n7, 242n16, 245n26

intelligible, 3, 50, 51, 52, 62, 65, 85, 129, 130

justice, 7, 64, 65, 66, 68, 75, 81, 83, 86, 87, 90, 93, 94, 95, 96, 97, 98, 107, 111, 112, 114, 115, 140, 141, 146, 154, 158, 161, 170, 182, 184, 187, 189, 190, 195, 202, 204, 211n20, 224n6, 228n25, 235n43, 236n50, 236n60, 238n11, 239n13, 239n1, 246n34, 246n36

Kamtekar, 218n29, 227n17, 239n3

Lachesis, 156, 157

law, 5, 8, 12, 20, 21, 32, 47, 52, 59, 88, 95, 111, 116, 126, 143, 148, 149, 150, 161, 162, 163, 165, 166, 167, 168–70, 174–78, 211n22, 212n38, 221n24, 224n5, 225n25, 230n13, 237n2, 237n3, 237n4, 238n8, 238n9, 238n10, 239n12, 239n15, 239n2, 240n8, 250n15, 241n18, 241n19, 244n20, 244n21, 245n23; against homicide, 180–83; against impiety, 183–91, 193–207; against temple robbing, 179–80

lawless, 108, 133, 184

Lear, J., 89, 223n12, 235n39,

legislation, 12, 88, 165, 166, 168, 170, 172, 173, 176, 179, 180, 181, 183, 185, 186, 191, 194, 198, 202, 204, 205, 206, 207, 211n23, 238n11, 240n9, 242n8, 245n24246n38

limit, 2, 4, 5, 7, 11, 15, 23, 28, 56, 59, 60, 71, 79, 84, 85, 91, 92, 97, 98, 103, 104, 114, 118, 124, 134, 146, 149, 150, 151, 154, 158, 160, 161, 162, 167, 176, 177, 188, 194, 198, 199, 203, 204, 205, 206, 207, 208, 214n1, 217n19, 226n1, 234n30, 244n19, 244n20, 246n39

limitlessness, 5, 11, 15, 53, 59, 92, 150, 161, 162, 197, 203, 204, 207, 208

Lloyd, 225n21, 227n21

material, 3, 61, 68, 95, 207, 219n2, 244n19

mathematics, 136, 213n7, 214n7

measure, 3, 125, 155, 162, 172, 187, 202

medical, 4, 12, 39, 52, 67, 82, 90, 91, 103, 104, 105, 112, 114, 119, 124, 130, 132, 133, 136, 162, 166, 173, 174, 210n16, 213n45, 225n21, 225n22, 227n14

Index | 259

medicine, 11, 82, 90, 91, 103, 105, 162, 168, 173, 225n22, 225n23, 225n25, 227n15, 231n29, 237n62,
Menn, 229n7, 243n6, 244n22,
mind, 12, 21, 167, 184, 187, 194, 196–99, 203, 204, 206, 209n5, 238n6, 244n19, 244n20, 244n21, 244n22, 245n27, 246n35, 246n40
mimēsis, 11, 82, 86, 89, 90, 92, 95, 97, 99–103, 105, 137, 138, 139, 140, 224n10, 224n13
motion, 3, 4, 12, 13, 39, 40, 41, 49, 67, 73, 74, 75, 84, 90, 130, 149, 156, 168, 187, 192, 193–98, 201, 203, 204, 221n22, 222n6, 236n53, 239n13, 243n10, 243n11, 244n14, 244n16, 244n17, 245n27, 246n40
Muses, 131, 136
myth, 4–12, 15–18, 32, 34, 35, 38, 39, 40, 56, 57, 59, 64–81, 63, 84, 85, 88, 89, 100, 113, 138, 140, 153–62, 174, 180–82, 200, 201, 208, 209n9, 211n27, 211n28, 212n31, 212n34, 212n35, 212n36, 212n38, 212n43, 213n2, 213n5, 214n7, 217n20, 218n30, 218n32, 219n2, 219n5, 219n6, 220n8, 220n9, 220n10, 221n25, 223n9, 223n18, 229n3, 231n33, 232n3, 235n38, 235n44, 235n45, 235n47, 236n49, 236n50, 237n62, 237n64, 241n3, 241n4, 243n11, 246n32

nature, 10, 12, 16, 20, 22, 23, 24, 31, 33, 36, 41, 56, 57, 58, 59, 71, 73, 79, 83, 87, 89, 91, 92, 95, 97, 99, 101–3, 108, 110, 111, 114, 115–116, 118, 119, 121–23, 124–28, 129, 130, 131, 134, 137, 139, 140, 141, 143, 145, 148, 149, 150, 152, 153, 154, 158, 160, 161, 162, 166, 168, 169, 170, 172, 175, 177, 179, 182, 185, 186–189, 192, 195, 196, 198, 199, 200, 205, 209n10, 210n12, 211n20, 212n41, 220n9, 223n18, 224n5, 224n8, 225n25, 226n1, 226n3, 226n6, 227n19, 228n29, 229n10, 230n14, 230n14, 231n34, 231n35, 232n11, 233n21, 236n54, 240n4, 242n9, 242n1, 243n7, 244n14, 244n19
necessity/Necessity, 68, 70, 75, 76, 98, 155, 156, 157, 160, 182, 202, 221n14, 230n13, 235n46, 236n49
Nightingale, 7, 212n36, 212n42, 222n4, 239n20

Odysseus, 159
oligarchy, 131, 132
ontology, 30, 34, 35, 48, 107, 121, 130, 200, 245n29, 245n30
onto-theology, 13
opinion, 16, 22, 26, 31, 35, 37, 48, 49, 54, 55, 66, 87, 90, 93, 94, 95, 96, 99, 100, 120, 122, 123, 125, 134, 153, 166168, 170, 171, 172, 175, 187, 188, 194, 200, 210n12, 211n20, 243n11
Orpheus, 159
ownership, 166, 167, 174, 188, 199, 201, 214n10

Parker, 29, 32, 176, 215n12, 215n23, 216n24, 216n28, 222n29, 241n19,

pathology, 133, 174, 177, 231n24
perception, 68, 72, 73, 117, 121, 128–31, 168, 187, 206, 232n14
Phaedrus, 7, 9, 209n7, 209n9, 210n12, 210n14, 212n43, 213n3, 221n28
phenomenology, 7, 66, 177, 239n19
Philebus, 7, 9, 244n20
Philolaus, 10, 20, 214n6
philosopher, 6, 8, 10, 11, 19–34, 49, 51, 55, 58, 65, 76, 81, 87, 89, 90–92, 109, 110, 119–22, 124–31, 137, 140, 184, 207, 211n23, 212n40, 215n11, 215n15, 215n16, 215n17, 218n33, 224n14, 225n22, 226n6, 228n29, 228n32, 229n1, 229n2, 229n5, 229n8, 230n14, 230n24, 241n6
philosophy, 3, 8, 10, 11, 12, 16, 20, 22, 23, 25, 30, 32, 33, 34, 51, 53, 54, 55, 61, 81, 87, 89, 91, 104, 105, 123–26, 132, 133, 158, 159, 160, 162, 163, 165, 184, 207, 211n20, 212n37, 212n39, 215n11, 215n15, 218n27, 222n8, 224n8, 224n15, 229n7, 230n13, 230n24, 232n14, 237n2, 240n12, 241n6
pleonexia, 86, 110, 173, 177, 187, 190, 199, 208, 235n35
poetry, 15, 89, 96, 99, 101, 102, 103, 105, 112, 136, 137, 138, 139, 151, 168, 173, 187, 221n18, 224n14, 225n21, 225n23
poiēsis, 11, 86, 89, 90, 92, 95, 99–103, 105, 112, 142
Polemarchus, 114
politics, 4, 5, 12, 48, 81, 85, 86, 89, 97, 101, 132, 137, 163, 167, 168, 170, 173, 184, 186, 200, 202, 203, 204, 206, 207, 212n37, 213n44, 225n23, 230n15, 232n3, 233n18, 245n26
pollution, 10, 11, 19, 28, 29, 30, 32, 34, 52, 80, 82, 176, 179, 180, 182, 183, 213n45, 215n23, 216n24, 225n18, 237n63
prosthesis/prosthetic, 5, 7, 11, 12, 149, 150, 151, 154, 161, 162, 169, 170, 198, 199, 200, 201, 202, 203, 204, 206, 211n23, 246n36
psychoanalysis, 208
purification, 10, 11, 28, 29, 30, 32, 33, 34, 51, 56, 58, 67, 75, 80, 82, 176, 177, 180, 182, 183, 213n45, 215n23, 241n18, 241n19
Pythagoras/Pythagoreanism, 15, 17, 20, 23, 24, 39, 57, 67, 214n4, 214n6, 214n8, 215n12, 218n30

recollection, 42–48, 49, 56, 68, 216n8, 217n8
rhetoric, 9, 16, 24, 54, 58, 77, 78, 96, 133, 185, 213n3, 213n7, 221n28, 232n3
Robinson, T. M., 85, 209n8, 210n18, 210n19, 222n7, 226n4

Saunders, 176, 193, 221n24, 237n1, 237n3, 240n14, 240n15, 241n18, 214n19, 242n1, 243n2, 243n4,
Sedley, 6, 211n26, 212n32, 213n2, 216n8, 217n11,

Solmsen, 13, 210n18, 213n48, 225n21, 228n23,
sophist/sophistry, 4, 19, 24, 125, 184, 186, 187, 189, 210n16, 213n7, 241n6, 242n9
soul: and body, 22–32, 37–63, 68–82; and city, 4–6, 9–13, 93–105, 203–8; cause of motion, 192–204; conditions of, 1–13, 17–18, 19–36, 37–63, 68–82, 64–81, 123–37, 171–91; corruption of, 30, 52, 106–22, 131–35, 171–91; excesses of, 197–204; fragmentation and unity of, 5, 106–22, 124–31, 131–35; health and diseases of, 9–13, 82, 111–14, 131–35, 139–52, 199; images, of 1–13, 19, 56–58, 65–82, 84, 85, 152–63, 200–203; immortality of, 5, 6–8, 10, 13, 15, 16, 17, 18, 20, 24, 36, 37–63, 64–82, 83, 139–52, 153–63, 192–208; and mind, 12, 192–204; parts of, 9–13, 108–11; plasticity of, 3–5, 13, 17, 30, 34, 48, 50, 53, 58, 67, 80, 81, 89, 90, 92, 100, 101, 107, 121, 137, 139, 146, 157, 161, 171; self-motion of, 192–204
Statesman, 7, 219n 2, 230n13
Symposium, 210n11, 211n22, 216n3, 234n26

Taylor, 133, 229n13, 230n13, 230n16, 230n17, 230n19, 230n24
Theaetetus, 9, 210n12, 229n9, 229n11, 232n14
theology, 12, 13, 19, 32, 81, 174, 185, 214n1, 241n6, 245n22
therapy, 207, 210n16
Thersites, 159
thought/thoughtful/thoughtfulness, 1, 2, 3, 7, 10, 13, 21, 22, 23, 27, 31–34, 41, 42, 48, 49, 51, 57, 58, 61, 68, 69, 73, 80, 81, 89, 91, 101, 115, 128, 130, 135, 137, 138, 158, 206, 210n12, 215n15, 232n14
Thucydides, 177, 178, 216n27, 241n21

timocracy, 131, 132
tragedy/tragic, 69, 100, 101, 131, 135, 138, 151, 221n18, 224n13, 225n21, 227n14, 231n33
tyranny, 84, 90, 92, 94, 131, 132, 134, 135, 136, 151, 159, 162, 168, 175, 177, 230n24, 231n34, 242n14
tyrant, 11, 53, 84, 87, 89, 91, 92, 97, 109, 110, 114, 121, 123, 125, 128, 131–35, 136, 137, 140, 142, 148, 149, 150, 151, 156, 162, 173, 184, 189, 210n13, 228n32, 229n5, 230n14, 231n27, 231n28, 231n30, 231n33, 231n34, 235n39, 235n46

Vernant, 177, 215n23, 216n24, 216n25, 222n29, 241n20
vice/viciousness, 3, 7, 11, 56, 57, 59, 61, 66, 67, 76, 77, 78, 79, 80, 84, 89, 90, 92, 94, 96, 101, 104, 105, 106, 107, 108, 111, 112, 114, 121, 125, 133, 134, 135, 140, 141, 142, 143, 144, 146, 147–51, 158, 161, 162, 166, 167, 169, 174, 189, 195, 206, 207, 208, 209n10, 210n13, 219n37, 220n8, 225n22, 225n23, 227n16, 228n25, 231n31, 234n32, 235n35, 235n38, 244n19
violence, 7, 11, 13, 66, 139, 165, 173, 177, 180, 182, 221n24, 237n2, 237n4, 241n19, 243n11
virtue, 1, 11, 33, 34, 57, 60, 61, 78, 92, 94, 96, 107, 108, 111, 112, 114, 156, 159, 161, 167, 225n22, 227n16, 228n25, 231n31, 238n8, 238n11, 243n6, 246n40
visible, 49, 50, 51, 52, 56, 70, 72, 78, 129, 217n19, 218n34

wisdom, 1, 7, 8, 10, 11, 22, 24, 33, 55, 87, 92, 107, 109, 110, 115, 119, 123, 124, 152, 153, 160, 185, 228n31, 242n16, 246n34

zoology, 57, 220n10

SARA BRILL is an associate professor of philosophy and the director of the Classical Studies Program at Fairfield University.

www.ingramcontent.com/pod-product-compliance
Lightning Source LLC
Chambersburg PA
CBHW030533230426
43665CB00010B/878